W9-ARG-094

HISTORY
OF RUSSIA

Sergei Mikhailovich Soloviev

The
Academic International Press
Edition
of
Sergei M. Soloviev

History of Russia From Earliest Times

G. EDWARD ORCHARD
General Editor

Contributing Editors

HUGH F. GRAHAM

JOHN D. WINDHAUSEN

ALEXANDER V. MULLER

K.A. PAPMEHL

RICHARD HANTULA

WALTER J. GLEASON, JR.

WILLIAM H. HILL

G. EDWARD ORCHARD

LINDSEY A.J. HUGHES

NICKOLAS LUPININ

GEORGE E. MUNRO

DANIEL L. SCHLAFLY, JR.

ANTHONY L.H. RHINELANDER

PATRICK J. O'MEARA

PETER C. STUPPLES

T. ALLAN SMITH

MARTHA L. LAHANA

ANTHONY V. KNOWLES

HELEN Y. PROCHAZKA

GEORGE S. PAHOMOV

SERGEI M. SOLOVIEV

History of Russia

Volume 6

Russian Society
1389-1425

Edited, Translated and
With an Introduction by
George S. Pahomov

2001
Academic International Press

The Academic International Press Edition of S.M. Soloviev's
History of Russia From Earliest Times in fifty volumes.

Volume 6. *Russian Society, 1389-1425*
Unabridged translation of the text of Volume 4, Chapters 2-3 as
contained in Volume II of S.M. Soloviev's *Istoria Rossii s
drevneishikh vremen* published in Moscow in 1959-1966, with
added annotation by George S. Pahomov.

ISBN: 0-87569-228-1

Composition by Llano F. McCowen

Printed in the United States of America

A list of Academic International Press publications is found at
the end of this volume.

ACADEMIC INTERNATIONAL PRESS
Box 1111 • Gulf Breeze FL 32562-1111 • USA

www.ai-press.com

CONTENTS

Law in Lithuania—The Brutality of Warfare—Litigation—
Princely Pacts—Moral Climate

WEIGHTS AND MEASURES

Linear and Surface Measure

Arshin: 16 vershoks, 28 in. (diuims) 72.12 cm
Chetvert (quarter): 1/4 arshin, 1/2 desiatina, 1.35 acres (sometimes 1.5 desiatinas or c. 4.1 acres)
Desiatina: 2,400 square sazhens, 2.7 acres, 1.025 hectares
Diuim: 1 inch, 2.54 cm
Fut: 12 diuims, 1 foot, 30.48 cm

Obza (areal): c. 10 chetverts, 13–15 acres
Osmina: 1/4 desiatina, 600 sq. sazhens, .256 hectare
Sazhen: 3 arshins, 7 feet, 2.133 m
Vershok: 1.75 in., 4.445 cm, 1/16 arshin
Verst: 500 sazhens, 1,166 yards and 2 feet, .663 miles, 1.0668 km
Voloka (plowland): 19 desiatinas, 20 hectares, 49 acres

Liquid Measure

Bochka (barrel): 40 vedros, 121 gallons, 492 liters
Chetvert (quarter): 1.4 bochkas, 32.5 gallons
Korchago (wine): Rus, unknown

Kufa: 30 stofy
Stof: Kruzhka (cup), 1/10 vedro, c. 1.3 quarts, 1.23 liters
Vedro (pail): 3.25 gallons, 12.3 liters, 10 stofy

Weights

Berkovets: 361 lbs., 10 puds
Bezmen: c. 1 kg, 2.2 lbs.
Chetverik (grain measure dating from 16th century): 1/8 chetvert, 15.8 lbs.
Chetvert (grain measure): 1/4 rad, 3.5 puds, 126.39 lbs., c. 8 bushels
Funt: 96 zolotniks, .903 lbs., 14.4 oz., 408.24 kg
Grivenka: 205 grams
Kad: 4 chetverts, 14 puds, 505.56 lbs.
Kadka malenkaia: 12th-century, small measure

Kamen (stone): 32 funt
Korob (basket): 7 puds, 252 lbs.
Osmina (eighth): 2 osmina to a chetvert (dry measure)
Polbezmen: c. 500 g, 1 lb.
Polosmina (sixteenth): 1/2 osmina
Pud: 40 funts, 36.113 lbs. (US), 40 lbs. (Russian), 16.38 kg
Rad: 14 puds, 505.58 lbs.
Zolotnik: 1/96 lbs., 4.26 grams

Money

Altyn: 6 Muscovite dengas, 3 copecks
Bel: Rus, pure silver coin
Chervonets (chervonnyi): gold coin of first half of 18th century worth c. 3 rubles
Chetvertak: silver coin equal to 25 copecks or 1/4 ruble (18–19th centuries)
Copeck: two Muscovite dengas
Denga: 1/2 copeck
Grivna: 20 Muscovite dengas, 100 grivnas equals 1 ruble, 10 copecks
Grosh: 10 peniaz
Grosh litovsky (Lithuanian grosh): 5 silver copecks
Kopa grosh: 60 groshas, one Muscovite poltina, 1/2 ruble
Kuna: 12th-century Rus coin comparable to Westerns denarii or Eastern dirhems. Varied in value by region. Replaced late 14th century by the denga or serebro (silver). Also a marten skin.
Moskovka: 1/2 copeck
Muscovite denga: 200 equals 1 ruble
Novgorod denga: 100 equals 1 ruble
Novgorodka: 1 copeck

Peniaz: 10 equals one grosh (Lithuania)
Poltina (poltinnik): 50 copecks, 100 dengas, 1 ruble
Poltora: 1 1/2 rubles
Polupoltina (-nik): 25 copecks, 50 dengas
Rezan: 12th century Rus coin. 50 rezan equals one grivna kuna
Ruble: 100 copecks, 200 dengas
Shiroky grosh (large silver coin): 20 Muscovite copecks
Veksa: 12th-century Rus small coin equal to one squirrel pelt (belka)

Foreign Denominations
Chervonnyi: c. 3 rubles
Ducat: c. 3 rubles
Dutch efimok: "lion dollar" or levok, 1 thaler, 2.5 guilders
Efimok: foreign currency, 1 thaler, .75-1 ruble, 1 chervonets or chervonnyi
Levok: Dutch silver lion dollar
Thaler (Joachimsthaler): c. 1 ruble, 1/3 chervonets or chervonnyi

---

Note: Weights and measures often changed values over time and sometimes held more than one value at the same time. For details consult Sergei G. Pushkarev, *Dictionary of Russian Historical Terms from the Eleventh Century to 1917* (Yale, 1970).

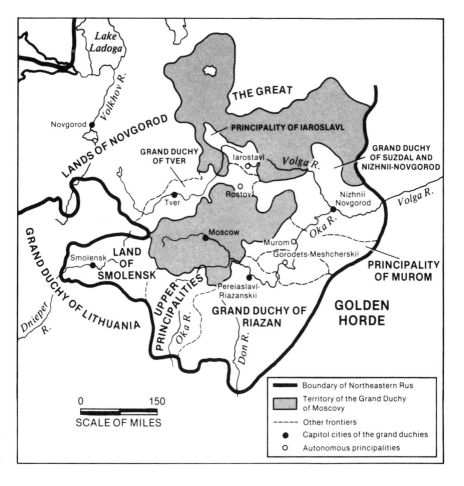

Northeastern Rus, Late Fourteenth Century

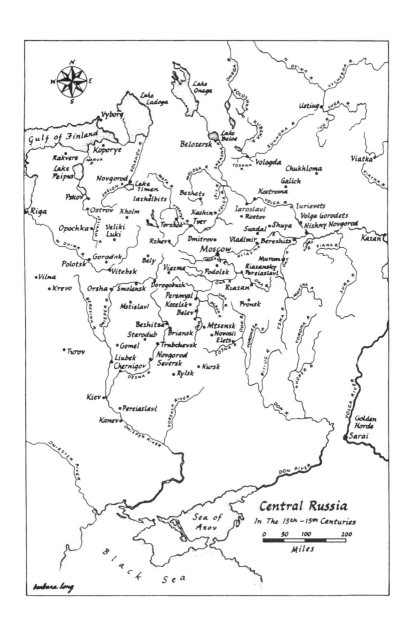

Central Russia

In The 13th – 15th Centuries

0   50   100   200

Miles

barbara Long

Heartland of Muscovy

0 25 50 75 100 Miles

barbara long

Citizens of Rus

PREFACE

This book is an unabridged translation of Volume IV, Chapter 3, which appears on pp. 449-659 in Book II of the multi-volume edition of Soloviev's *Istoriia Rossii s drevneishikh vremen* (History of Russia from Earliest Times, 29 vols., St. Petersburg, 1851-1879) published from 1959 through 1966 in Moscow.

While Soloviev's historiography and intellectual integrity are beyond reproach, the same cannot be said of his Russian prose style. Monotonous and repetitive with the use of stultifying set phrases it was intended purely as a medium of neutral exposition. This translator's task was to make it palatable to the educated reader of English while rendering Soloviev's thought and data as accurately as possible. An equally important task was the preservation of the archaic flavor of the ancient Russian chronicles which Soloviev often quotes at length. Such passages in Old Church Slavonic already were perceived as quaint by the nineteenth-century Russian reader whom Soloviev addressed.

Another refashioning is the introduction of subdivisions to compartmentalize Soloviev's continuous flow. The subdivisions are marked by subject headings throughout the text as a matter of logical convenience. Absolutely no changes in Soloviev's arrangement of material or sequence of presentation were made.

Since the era described is distant and probably unfamiliar to most readers, explanatory and interpretative remarks are provided, either directly in the text in brackets or, more commonly, as notes to each chapter at the end of the book. Soloviev's own notes which are almost exclusively bibliographic and documentary are of use only to the specialist and are not included. Whenever Soloviev's notes are included they are indicated as his.

The transliteration from Russian to English follows a modified Library of Congress system without ligatures and diacritical marks. Further, the letter "i" in initial "ia-" and "iu-" position has been replaced with a "y-." Thus, "Yatviag" instead of "Iatviag" and "Yury" instead of "Iurii."

A suffix such as "-ii," in "-skii," also was replaced by "-y." Place names, given names and family names that are known widely in English were retained in their standard English transcription ("Dnieper" rather than "Dnepr"). The combination "-iia" in feminine given names was shortened to "-ia" ("Evpraksia" instead of "Evpraksiia"). The hard and soft signs are not indicated at all except for an "i" in otherwise infelicitous combinations ("Soloviev" rather than "Solov'ev").

The system of chronological dating is not an issue for this time period because it is well before the advent of the Gregorian calendar and the resultant separation into Old and New styles.

Words of non-Russian origin which were usually rendered in Russian by Soloviev are given in their current standard English forms ("Genghis Khan" rather than "Chingiz Khan," "Wilno" rather than "Vilna" or "Vilnius"). Archaic and non-extant Russian or East Slavic forms (the names of vanished tribes, for example) were normalized when rendered into English.

One is forever being shaped and aided by people and institutions. The process continues even as one's gratitude does not reach all the agents. But in this particular work I am very grateful to Danielle Shepherd, Nickolas Lupinin, G. Edward Orchard, Karin Hoerrner and the late Serge Zenkovsky for their help, support, guidance and advice. I am equally grateful to Bryn Mawr College for its financial support and release of time.

George S. Pahomov

INTRODUCTION

At the beginning of the fourteenth century the unified Kievan state was largely a memory. The principalities of Rus to the southwest of Kiev were fragmented and under foreign domination. In the Northeast the scattered Russian lands stood before three possible eventualities: to remain under the dominance of a Mongol empire, to be engulfed by a rising Lithuania, or to forge an independent state. To contemporaneous observers the last eventuality doubtless must have seemed the least likely. Yet within two hundred years this came to be. The causes and workings of this unexpected development are the focus of Soloviev's historical investigation.

For the sake of efficiency let us recapitulate the milestone events of this period. Peter, the displaced metropolitan of Kiev, spent much time in Moscow and died there in 1326. In 1328 the grand prince of Moscow Ivan Kalita persuaded Metropolitan Theognostos to reside permanently in Moscow. The metropolitan assumed the new title "metropolitan of Kiev and all Rus," adding prestige to the new capital. In 1341 the son of Kalita, Simeon the Proud, was confirmed by the khan as grand prince. To his title of prince of Moscow Simeon added "and of all Russia." He died in 1353 leaving a weak successor, but Metropolitan Alexis worked to enhance Moscow's power and prestige. After 1357 internal strife weakened the Horde. Dmitry Donskoy reigned from 1359 to 1389. In 1378 he tested Mongol resolve and won the battle on the Vozha river. Two years later the victory at Snipe Field made the Moscow prince the champion of all those opposed to the Mongols. Dmitry's son Vasily I reigned from 1389 to 1425. Cautious and steady in his statecraft he subsumed neighboring principalities, making inroads into western Rus lands held by Lithuania.

His son Vasily II ruled from 1425 to 1462. During his reign there was civil strife and an attempt to reinstitute feudal, "lateral" rights of succession. Vasily II proved victorious and firmly cemented the lineal right of succession. An unprecedented event occurred in 1452. Mongol princes sought and were accepted into Moscow service. The Horde itself splintered into three khanates. This may be considered the climactic year in Moscow's independence from the Mongols, although formal independence did not come until 1480. In a parallel sequence of events the Byzantine Greek ecclesiastical hierarchy recognized the supremacy of the Pope at the Council of Florence in 1439. In 1443 the Russian bishops, having rejected the church union, elected their own metropolitan, Jonas, thus becoming independent of Byzantium. In 1453 the Ottoman Turks conquered Constantinople and consolidated their control over the Balkans. Moscow became the sole independent Orthodox Christian state of any consequence.

In 1462 Ivan III began a long reign that lasted until 1505. He conclusively subjugated the neighboring rivals, Novgorod and Tver, established single autocratic rule in the Northeast and definitively brought about the end of the "feudal" appanage period. In 1480 Ivan III formally renounced allegiance to the Horde and repelled all Mongol punitive attempts. In 1503 Lithuania recognized expanded Russian borders in a treaty.

These are the readily apparent events of the rise of Muscovy. Soloviev sought to understand the forces which brought them about. He sought and found similarities and differences between Eastern and Western history. Both were instrumental in furthering his understanding. He saw that in both East and West an indigenous agrarian population had been conquered. In the West the conquerors quickly became landholders and thereby inaugurated a lengthy period of stability. They came to define themselves as a class with shared values and interests, thus evolving into a significant historical entity.

While similar conquest took place in the East, the Varangian princes and their descendants did not coalesce into a stable landholding class. Rather, a lengthy unsettled and chaotic period ensued, arresting historical development. In Soloviev's view it was not until the sixteenth century that a centralized state was formed in Russia with its own nobility, which nevertheless lacked the cohesive interests of its Western counterpart.

Another impediment to an integrated state was the tradition of inheritance of the right to rule by seniority and lateral succession. It was an unpredictable system in which the country was ruled not by an individual but by an extended family of not just brothers but second cousins and great uncles and grand nephews thrice removed. This led to the fracturing of large into increasingly smaller holdings and a concomitant profusion of appanages. A world in which all children of a prince were in their

• own right a princess or a prince derivatively could be reduced to unviable parcels of land.

Along with small patrimonies in the first half of the fourteenth century there were four major principalities in Northeastern Russia: Vladimir, Rostov, Tver and Moscow. The lands stretching to the North and East were vast, with no drawn borders, underpopulated and open to expansion. The prince who could master these lands would gain great power.

Another seeming impediment, the Mongol invasion, ultimately proved to be something of an advantage. In shattering established structures it enhanced the role of the prince in creating a new order. Another apparent impediment opportunistically utilized by the Moscow princes was the rise of Lithuania which, as a threat to the Mongols, also promoted the stability of Northeastern Russia. The Mongols permitted the growth of Moscow as a buffer state, of necessity validating the central rule of its princes and abandoning the policy of encouraging inter-princely strife as a means of dividing and conquering.

In this context Soloviev viewed the princes as agents of historical integration. He placed great emphasis on the rule of Dmitry Donskoy and that juncture in 1371 when Dmitry overstepped succession by seniority and was recognized by all his relatives and the Mongols as grand prince of Vladimir and Moscow. Both principalities became his inalienable patrimony which he passed on to his son at his death in 1389. The right of primogeniture whereby the eldest son inherited all finally was established in Russia. In such a leading and autocratic role of the prince Soloviev sees the legitimate continuation of Kievan and Russian history.

Yet he overly linearizes the process. Modern historians see the Kievan state as a heterogeneous and complex system, bearing the seeds of the Southwestern model of rule by aristocracy, of the Novgorod model of direct democracy as well as the seed of centralized autocracy of the Northeast. Of the three modes of rule, Soloviev gives pre-eminence to autocracy.

There are substantive reasons. In the mid-nineteenth century, when Soloviev wrote, he lived in a Russia which was a direct successor of Muscovy. Novgorod and the Southwestern principalities of Galich and Volhynia had vanished as political entities and alternatives. It was the age of the nation-state turned empire. Even just by being, in his very ontological presence, Soloviev benefited from the triumph of the victorious entity. He felt the need to explain and in some sense justify that which was.

Such attempts were made previously. N.M. Karamzin's *History of the Russian State* written from 1803 to 1826, and N.A. Polevoy's *History of the Russian People* (1829-1833) by their very titles suggest differing views of what was meaningful in Russian history. Both served as models for Soloviev's work. In addition, Soloviev was well versed in Western historiography. According to the noted historian Kliuchevsky who was his student, Soloviev was particularly influenced by the French historian F.P.G. Guizot and his *Histoire générale de la civilisation en Europe* (General History of Civilization in Europe) as well as his *Histoire générale de la civilisation en France* (General History of Civilization in France).

Unlike Karamzin whose work had a strong literary aspect and tended to see history as the shaping of great events by great men, Polevoy and especially Guizot attempted global histories, embracing politics as well as society in all its institutions, economy, law, religion and culture. Following his two predecessors Soloviev tried to remove all that was personal and episodic and went beyond mere chronology to development and complex causality. More specifically, he implicitly criticized Karamzin's conception of the Russian state as a constant and almost primeval entity, seeing in the lands of Rus-Russia the simultaneous existence of several states up to the sixteenth century.

Soloviev worked at a time when relatively few narrative histories as of his country had been written. The overwhelming majority of his notes refer either to chronicles or official acts and other government documents. Of these specifically mentioned are the *Collection of State Documents and Treaties* (St. Petersburg, 1819), *Acts Collected in the Libraries and Archives of the Russian Empire by the Archeographical Commission of the Academy of Science* (St. Petersburg, 1836) and *Historical Acts Collected and Edited by the Archeographical Commission* (St. Petersburg, 1841). Of chronicles, Soloviev frequently refers to the recension of the New Chronicler compiled at the court of Patriarch Nikon in the mid-seventeenth century and published by N.I. Novikov in 1771. He also drew heavily on the Pskov Chronicles and the Novgorod Chronicle which was reprinted in the *Complete Collection of Russian Chronicles* (St. Petersburg, 1841). Of narrative sources besides Polevoy and Karamzin, Soloviev cites V.N. Tatishchev's *History of Russia from Earliest Times* (St. Petersburg, 1768-1784), N.S. Artsybashev's *Narrative of Russia* (Moscow, 1838), and a number of non-Russian authors among whom are Sigismund von Herberstein, *Rerum Moscoviticarum Commentarii* (Frankfurt, 1600), T. Narbutt, *Acts of the Lithuanian Nation* (Volume 6, Wilno, 1839) and J. Długosz. *History of Poland* (Volume 4, Cracow, 1877).

The contemporary English-speaking reader may be interested in some recent highly acclaimed works which, of course, were unavailable to Soloviev. These are George Vernadsky, *The Mongols and Russia. A History of Russia,* Volume 3 (Yale, 1953); Arthur Voyce, *The Art and Architecture of Medieval Russia* (Norman, Oklahoma, 1967); Daniel H. Kaiser, *The Growth of the Law in Medieval Russia* (Princeton, 1980); Henrik Birnbaum, *Lord Novgorod the Great* (Columbus, 1981); John L.I. Fennell, *The Crisis of Medieval Russia, 1200-1304* (London, 1983), also *A History of the Russian Church to 1448* (London, 1995); Henrik Birnbaum and Michael S. Flier, *Medieval Russian Culture* (Berkeley, 1984); Charles J. Halperin, *Russia and the Golden Horde* (Bloomington, Indiana, 1985); Robert O. Crummey, *The Formation of Muscovy, 1304-1613* (London, 1987); Janet Martin, *Medieval Russia, 980-1584,* (Cambridge, 1995).

In his work of synthesis Soloviev justly may be called a historian of the *national* state. In this he was grounded in the mainstream traditions of nineteenth-century European thought. He also shared the consensus of his contemporaries in the belief that geography shaped the destiny of nations and that a country's size determined its political and economic existence. In utterances such as the "organic" formation of a nation-state "may be called the highest" he openly expressed a value judgement that embraced the biological model of development indigenous to contemporary science. The nineteenth-century concept of evolution especially provided a ready matrix for applying the biological paradigm to the "organic" state.

In his integrating historiography Soloviev manifests the search for the unifying grand scheme which stimulated European thought of his time. It was a search in which Hegel's legacy reigned supreme. His philosophy of history embraced a number of central concepts. It is a given in Hegel that reality is the unfolding of what he calls "Reason" and that therefore Reason must function in human history. Yet its functioning cannot be discerned in advance through a purely mental act. We must study the course of history, all its particulars, trying to discern the overarching rational process, to see how Reason operates. In this process the particulars are manifestations of the universal infinite. The role of the historian then is ultimately to see the general by examining many particulars. It seems that Soloviev took this role seriously.

Another central concept in Hegel links "spirit" and state. It is the spirit of a people, the national spirit that is significant. This spirit is evidenced not only in the politics of a people but in its art, morals, religion, philosophy and entire culture. Such an organic, living totality of a people is synonymous for Hegel with the "state." Such a state is far greater than the legally defined state which at its worst can be nothing more than an arbitrary construct. The historical process concerns itself with national-spirit states. It is the interaction of such states that drives world history. Each legitimate state is the embodiment of the spirit of national totality. In such a state self-consciousness has risen to the level of universal consciousness. The individual is aware of being a member of a greater whole which does not suppress his self but rather fulfills it. This makes the state an organic unity in which all the individual components function in harmony. In practice Hegel can be read as favoring constitutional monarchy composed of corporate bodies or estates, not directly of individuals. One can then anticipate Soloviev's negative response to the vainglory of particular princes and the excesses of Novgorod's direct democracy.

An echo of Hegel's concept of the "world-historical individual" may be sensed in Soloviev's appreciation of the princes who acted in concert with national good and consciousness. Dmitry Donskoy would head such a grouping. Soloviev also seems to share Hegel's rather optimistic view that the moral is expressed in the rational and constitutes the dominant factor in history. Such a high-minded position may have aided him in dismissing Moscow's despotic excesses as temporary aberrations.

Also evident in Soloviev is the adoption of Hegel's periodization of history. Hegel saw four great epochs with the most recent belonging to the Germanic world. The third had belonged to the Roman world. In speaking of the Slavic nation as young and robust in contrast to the older Germanic nation Soloviev seems to suggest a fifth epoch, at once accepting Hegel and polemicizing with him.

This is historiography on the grand scale and to the modern historian it seems archaic and somewhat naïve. Modern historiography is not as sanguine of its powers. To complicate the issue there has been a proliferation of schools and disciplines. No single historian can embrace anthropology, archaeology, ethnography, sociology, political science, economics, intellectual history, art and religion as Soloviev did. The profusion and availability of data in all fields staggers the individual mind. The prevalent sensibility of relativism sees all historical investigation as inherently imperfect, tentative and incomplete. The work of such people as Spengler and Toynbee is relegated to the history of historiography.

Even a cautious attempt by any current neo-Hegelian to write history would not gain many followers. Yet it is not a totally extinct tradition. Fernand Braudel's monumental opus *The Mediterranean and the Mediterranean World in the Age of Philip II* (2 vols., Paris, 1949, revised edition 1966, English translation by Siân Reynolds, New York, 1972-1973) shares certain premises with Soloviev and even elucidates them. The structuring of his work around "the dialectic of space and time [geography and history]" could be applied readily to Soloviev. Braudel's division of historical time into the triad of geographical time, social time and individual time makes for a more intelligible comprehension of Soloviev's accomplishment.

Soloviev's contemporaries and immediate successors had high praise for the *History*. Kliuchevsky wrote of Soloviev's ability to indicate the "natural continuity of events," his striving to explain "each phenomenon through internal causes" and his "penetration into the innermost currents of national life." Russian historians of the Soviet period uniformly praised the work while admitting that Soloviev's stance does not match the contours of the requisite ideology. He was called a "bourgeois" historian for his ameliorism, gradualism and disapproval of radical (revolutionary) change, though all critics agreed that it was a foundation of Russian historiography, a classic work.

Having acquainted oneself with an author's method and the value of his work and having examined some of his prepossessions it is admittedly faithless to criticize an author for not writing a book he did not intend to write.

It may be argued that the Moscow princes had supremacy thrust on them as much as they achieved it. Two external factors fostered this. The first were the internecine wars among the Mongols beginning with Tokhtamysh against Mamay and Tamerlane against Tokhtamysh, the near anarchy after the decline of Tokhtamysh, and the splintering of the Horde into a number of warring khanates. The second factor was the decline and fall of Byzantium and the captivity of the Orthodox church. The Greek church's accommodations with Rome and its later subjugation by the Ottomans, symbolized by Mehmet II handing the crozier to Gennadios upon his installation as patriarch in Constantinople in 1453, caused Orthodox eyes to look increasingly to the Northeast. With Serbia and Bulgaria under Ottoman vassalage, the Moscow princes were virtually the only significant independent rulers in the Orthodox world.

Soloviev's anti-Mongol stance leads him to underestimate the impact of the Mongols on history, especially the resultant accelerated consolidation of the Russian state. He does not acknowledge it even as a negative stimulus toward consolidation and the furthering of administrative controls. Nor does he suggest that the interests of the khans and princes coincided under certain conditions, such as when princes sought to acquire territory at the expense of neighboring princes, when princes acted as the khans' agents in gathering tribute, when suppressing popular tendencies which from time to time erupted violently in cities such as Rostov. For instance, the murder of the chiliarch Khvost in Moscow and the subsequent riots are not mentioned by Soloviev. He merely writes that the boyars left the city.

In his assessment of the role of the church Soloviev can be somewhat idealistic. The church seems to function only to determine mores. He overlooks internal church affairs, regarding the church itself as an independent body having its own interests and seeking wealth and power. The tension and rivalry between church and state also goes unattended. The role of the crafts and trades in engendering new and entrenching established cities is not considered, nor is the linguistic and cultural separation of the Eastern Slavs (Rus) and the appearance of the future Belorussian and Ukrainian peoples.

There is also much to be praised. Soloviev moves away from the traditional historical narrative of great individuals shaping events largely within the context of clan and family. In a very significant way he sees history as the development of mutually interrelated phenomena and consubstantial causes and effects. Soloviev sees politics in the broadest sense as the force which drives history. Economic development, national growth and cultural change are largely addressed as the result of political dynamics. Though he may largely be a political historian, he was among the first to observe systematically economic, societal, and cultural questions. Thus the work is not just the history of state but also a history of the economy, society and culture which examines crafts, commerce, finance, customs and traditions, even mentioning superstitions, as well as literature. It also is among the first to make systematic and analytic use of the chronicles. Also to his credit Soloviev traces and maintains the significance of the interrelationships between Northeastern and Southwestern Rus and does not focus on Muscovy prematurely or exclusively.

In an attempt to expand the scope of historical inquiry he includes the previously excluded and is driven to look at particulars. Bee-keeping, haymaking, pasturing livestock, beaver-trapping, the fishing, hunting, the salt-making, the trade in grain, and flax and pitch, and cloth, in lumber and beeswax, the circulation of animal skins as money, the fees paid at portages and toll houses, all are activities gaining Soloviev's attention. If Karamzin can be said to have taken the royal road of historiography, Soloviev took both the high and low road. On that latter road, whenever he bends for a closer look, he prefigures Braudel. It is then that he has a purely observing, fresh sensibility. It is exemplified in the narrative of the bear and Luka and its use to illustrate everyday reality, what folks did for entertainment. Even as Soloviev seeks a unifying vision, he is charmed by the particulars of history.

HISTORY OF RUSSIA

Volume 6

Russian Society

1389-1425

I

RISE OF THE PRINCIPALITY OF MOSCOW

GENERAL COURSE OF EVENTS
The events of some two hundred years, from the death of Mstislav of Toropets [the Daring, 1228][1] to the death of Vasily the Dark [1462],[2] were investigated. We paused at the death of Mstislav the Daring because he was the last prince who united the destinies of both Northern and Southern Rus. Though a representative of the southern half, Mstislav exerted great influence on the North, while in the time of Andrei Bogoliubsky[3] and Vsevolod III[4] it was Southern Rus that was under the influence of the North. Its ruler was considered the elder without whom, according to their own admission, the Southern princes could not manage. In tracing the play of events from the old order to the new, from princely familial relations to monarchy, it was noticed that the domestic conditions of Northern Rus favored this shift while those of the South did not. It was also observed that even before Mstislav, during the reign of Roman the Great,[5] Southern Rus was ready to quit the Dnieper basin and the glorious hills of Kiev and transpose itself to the rich province of Galich which long served as an intermediary between Rus and the West.

Mstislav himself died in the city of Galich and was succeeded there by Daniel, the son of Roman.[6] Though no less valorous than Mstislav, Daniel was not a wayfaring hero. He was tied by tradition to a definite patrimony. From early youth he knew no rest in striving to gain his paternal inheritance. Having done so, he was solicitous of it, restored domestic order and strove to defend it against the Tatars, Yatviags[7] and Lithuanians, spreading his influence to the North and West. The future of Southern Rus was in the hands of Daniel and his progeny, but in vain does the historian seek in them the consolidators of Russian lands. Southern Rus was not consolidated into an independent whole. Its larger part submitted to the rule of the Lithuanian princes, while the smaller went to Poland. Lithuania and Rus were united with Poland under one dynasty.[8]

This union nevertheless was superficial and unstable. No internal fusion of state and peoples took place, for the larger part of Lithuanian holdings consisted of Rus regions in which the majority of the inhabitants were of the Russian Orthodox faith. This population, finding a matter of the utmost importance to them threatened, from the very start had to enter into a struggle with the Catholic aspirations of the Jagiellonians and their successors. The historian must observe carefully this important struggle and the significance of its outcome to the fate of Russia and Eastern Europe. He cannot, however, give the history of Southwestern Rus equal significance with that of the Northeast, where an independent Russian state was formed. For even the very importance of Southwestern Rus and the effect of its struggle with Poland on the fate of Eastern Europe was conditioned by the independent existence of Muscovy in the North. The very history of Southwestern Rus after Gediminas[9] and Casimir the Great[10] is meaningful only in the context of the history of Lithuania and Poland. It may be unfair, and in a scholarly context false and one-sided, to lose sight of Southwestern Rus after its separation from the Northeast, to treat its history, its life and relations with Lithuania and Poland only tangentially. It may be all the more unfair since its existence incorporated Russian national values, and the most apparent aspect of its relations with Lithuania and Poland was the struggle in support of these values. On the other hand, it would be equally unfair and incorrect to place the history of Southwestern Rus on a par with the history of the Northeast. The import of Southwestern Rus always remains significant, but always secondary. The attention of the historian must be turned constantly to the North.

It was here that thanks to Mstislav of Toropets and the victory at the Lipitsa river[11] that Konstantin,[12] eldest son of Vsevolod III, gained power unlike his brothers who, as the defeated, had to be content with the meager territories granted them through Konstantin's charity. Konstantin's premature death kept him from utilizing his advantage to buttress the power of his sons, who were to be content with merely the territory of Rostov. It would have been Yury's turn to strengthen his position had not this descendant of Vsevolod perished at the hands of the Tatars along with his family and two nephews, sons of Konstantin. There were yet three descendants of Vsevolod remaining with Yaroslav,[13] the eldest among them. This prince was long renowned for his spirit of enterprise and passion for acquisition. While still merely the ruler of Pereiaslavl he did not leave Novgorod alone, constantly trying to bring it under his rule, despite the lesson taught him by Mstislav on the Lipitsa river. Yaroslav began a dispute with Chernigov on the question of Novgorod. Having little hope of gaining supremacy in the North, he turned to the South and seized Kiev. By exterminating the family of Yury the Tatars provided Yaroslav with a grand principality and large territories for distribution to his sons. He gave Suzdal to his brother Sviatoslav, Starodub to his brother Ivan and his patrimony, Pereiaslavl, undivided to his eldest son Alexander.[14] The other five sons received territories from the grand principality, while the progeny of Konstantin received nothing.

It is unknown what he specifically gave his second son Andrei, but most likely it was Yuriev,[15] ceded to him by Sviatoslav in exchange for Suzdal. The third son, Konstantin, received Galich; the fourth, Yaroslav, Tver; the fifth, Mikhail, Moscow; to the sixth, Vasily, was given Kostroma. In this manner almost the whole Vladimir region came into the hands of the Yaroslav's sons. What could their uncles, the princes of Suzdal and Starodub, do against these six princes? It was clear that with the weakening of clan notions, upon the death of Yaroslav his brother Sviatoslav could not long hold the senior throne. Soon he was deposed by Mikhail Yaroslavich of Moscow and later lost even Suzdal. Sviatoslav had to be content again with only Yuriev.

It should be noted that these men were in character equal to their position. They were able to strengthen and expand their inheritance rather than squander it. Alexander received the epithet of Nevsky. Andrei's valor became indubitable when he chose to take up arms against the Tatars. Mikhail came to be called Chorobrite.[16] Yaroslav followed his father's footsteps in constantly building power, trying to bring Novgorod under his mastery. He could not do this because Vasily of Kostroma was not indifferent to the activities of his elder brothers. The short-lived enmity between Alexander Nevsky and his brother Andrei[17] did not bring harm to the family of Yaroslav.

The significance of Nevsky is not limited to his feats against the Swedes, Germans and Lithuanians, nor to his prudent behavior towards the Tatars. Immediately apparent in him is the grandson of Vsevolod III and the grandfather of Ivan Kalita.[18] He was no less fearsome to Novgorod than his father or grandfather. He also emulated his father in ruling the grand principality, giving Pereiaslavl undivided to his oldest son Dmitry. He gave patrimonies of grand princes to his other sons, Gorodets and Nizhny Novgorod to Andrei, and Moscow, the escheated appanage of Mikhail Chorobrite, to Daniel.[19] Upon Nevsky's death Vasily of Kostroma prevented Yaroslav of Tver from consolidating his position, but Vasily himself soon died heirless, thus vacating a senior throne for the sons of Nevsky. At this point the pattern was repeated. Andrei of Gorodets prevented Dmitry of Pereiaslavl from consolidating his position. A long internecine struggle began during which the elder sons of Nevsky exhausted their energies without accomplishing anything for their progeny. Moreover the son of Dmitry died childless during this period. Unnoticed during the struggle between Pereiaslavl and Gorodets two other principalities gained strength, Tver under Mikhail the son of Yaroslav Yaroslavich,[20] and Moscow under Daniel, the youngest son of Nevsky. Rivalry between them was unavoidable. Was it to be the last such conflict?

CAUSES OF THE RISE OF THE PRINCIPALITY OF MOSCOW

Up to now in their striving for territorial and material gain the Northern princes usually attempted to master Great Novgorod and affirm their position there more than previous princes. None of their struggles were crowned with total success. The means of the princes were meager, those of Novgorod great. Furthermore such attempts were too consequential not to draw the attention and apprehension of other princes, who then attempted to impede them. The Moscow princes acted more judiciously in their early consolidations. They armed themselves against their immediate neighbors who were weak and easily handled. Their designs upon them did not intrude on the main theater of action, thus not arousing suspicion or strong counteraction. Daniel, son of Alexander, invaded Riazan, took its prince captive, and also affirmed his control over Kolomna, an important point at the confluence of the Moscow and Oka rivers. His son Yury turned to the principality of Smolensk, taking from it Mozhaisk, an important point in the upper reaches of the Moscow river.

Even more significant in the context of that time was Daniel's acquisition of Pereiaslavl-Zalessk which was willed to him by his childless nephew Ivan Dmitrievich, though Andrei of Gorodets would not cede Pereiaslavl to Moscow. Mikhail of Tver took the same position upon becoming grand prince of Vladimir. Moscow kept a firm grasp on its gain, even though its princes, up to Vasily the Dark, recognized Pereiaslavl as a dependency of the grand principality. The possession of Yaroslavl itself was cause enough for internecine strife between Moscow and Tver, not to mention Yury's obvious designs on the city of Vladimir at the expense of Mikhail. At first the conflict was decided in favor of Tver. It has been seen that all the grand princes constantly strove to add

Novgorod to their patrimony. Mikhail of Tver, Novgorod's closest neighbor, could not but follow the example of his father, even though any venture against wealthy Novgorod was quite difficult. So it was now. Pressed by Mikhail, Novgorod turned to Yury of Moscow.[21] There is no doubt that it was Novgorod's money that aided Yury in allying himself with the Horde and coming to close terms with the khan's family. This became the cause of Mikhail's fall.

Tver did not fall with him. Yury, so concerned with gain by any means, having spent his life in turmoil and peregrination, did not taste the fruit of his cheerless labors. He perished heirless at the Horde by the hand of Mikhail's son. He was succeeded by his brother Ivan Kalita. Even though Mikhail's son, Alexander of Tver,[22] received from the khan the grand principality of Vladimir, it was Kalita who lured the metropolitan to Moscow, an event more significant than any entitlement granted by a khan. The struggle consequently did not cease. Kalita waited for an opportune moment. It came when an uprising and slaughter of Tatars occurred in Tver.[23] Kalita and a force of Tatars devastated and broke Tver once and for all. Later he was instrumental in sealing Alexander's fate at the Horde. Moscow triumphed. Having no other rivals, it began to consolidate the Russian land.

Though the events leading to the rise of Moscow and the consolidation of Northern Russia have been presented, there still have to be mentioned several conditions facilitating this process. First is Moscow's geographical location. The importance of Moscow's intermediary position bordering on the old, Southern, and the new, Northern Rus was noted.[24] When Southern Rus lost its significance and grew weak because of domestic strife, the subdivision of territories, and especially the Tatar devastations, conditions ceased to be safe. This inevitably brought about increased migration to the North. Moscow was the first bordering principality.

The boyar Rodion Nestorovich came from Kiev into Moscow's service with a force of seventeen hundred men. As a result of Tatar devastation, the Chernigov boyar Pleshcheev also came to Moscow. If these princes' men came, there is no reason to believe that other classes did not migrate as well. Furthermore there was a flow of people from nearby regions more endangered than Moscow, namely Riazan, Tver and Rostov. Bordering the steppes, Riazan frequently suffered from Tatar attacks, while Moscow from 1293 until the invasion of Tokhtamysh

[1382][25] suffered none. The principality of Tver, frightfully devastated by the Tatars and Kalita, subsequently suffered from strife among the princes. This caused the inhabitants, according to a direct reference in the chronicles, to move to other regions. In the principality of Rostov the violence of Kalita's Muscovites caused many residents of towns and villages to move to Moscow lands. The increase in population and the long period of safety increased the princes' income. This explains why already Kalita was rich enough to buy whole principalities such as those of Beloozero, Uglich and Galich. What forced those princes to sell? Most likely it was their inability to pay the levies of the Horde. Abundance of money enabled the Moscow princes to increase their domains and maintain their grand-princely dignity by showering the khan and his nobles with gifts. It also gave them a novel means of increasing the population of their territories by buying captives from the Horde and settling them on their lands. Thus arose a special category of population, those ransomed from the Horde.[26] They are mentioned frequently in the testaments and agreements of princes.

Abundance of money also enabled the princes to offer the new settlers terms more favorable than those of other regions with poorer princes. It is curious that ancient travellers, while praising the fertility of the land of Vladimir and Nizhny Novgorod, describe the land of Moscow proper as being of low fertility. We know that in terms of fertility the land of Vladimir has no advantage over Moscow. The comments of the travellers can be explained only by the exhaustion of Moscow soil as a result of an earlier and denser population.

Besides the income resulting from expanding population the treasury of the Moscow princes was enriched further by the advantageous commercial location of their region. Not only was it an intermediary between North and South but because of its river it was an intermediary in commerce between the Northeast and Southwest. Subsequently a major trade route between Asia and Europe grew along the Volga, Oka and Moscow rivers. Future travellers pointed to the commercial importance of the Moscow region by reason of the convenience of its river network. There is no doubt that this trade route existed in the time we are describing and even before that. This explains why the mercantile citizens of Novgorod established themselves at Volok on the Lama, an important commercial point between the Moscow, Oka, Lama and Volga rivers and their own lake region. Besides being important to the Volga trade route the Moscow river was significant to Novgorod as a route to the Riazan region which, according to travellers, was the richest in natural products of all Northeastern Rus. Especially abundant were honey and beeswax, products which Russia, by way of Novgorod and Pskov, supplied to all Europe. Thus Moscow's position in the center, on the borders of Northern and Southern Rus, was of political importance. Its intermediary river region was of importance to trade between the Northeast and Southwest. Its intermediacy between North and South held considerable significance for church affairs as well. The metropolitans of All Rus were located in the South at Kiev. After that city lost its supremacy to the North as a result of Tatar devastations, they had to turn their attention to Northeastern Rus. It was here that the Orthodox world transferred its main activities. The metropolitans began to travel frequently from South to North, finally establishing their residence in Vladimir-on-the-Kliazma. Maintaining the unity of the Russian church and retaining the title of metropolitans of Kiev and all Rus, they could not dismiss Southwestern Rus. For this purpose Vladimir was situated too far in the Northeast, not the most convenient location. Moscow, on the other hand, bordering on the old and new Rus, fully filled the needs of the metropolitans in their task of ministering to the North as well as the South.

Such were the conditions furthering the growth of the Moscow principality. Let us now examine the individual territories of that principality, and their gradual growth.

MOSCOW TERRITORIES

The Moscow territories were first listed systematically in the testament of Ivan Kalita.[27] "I bequeath to my sons," wrote Kalita, "my patrimony of Moscow. Here is how I have divided the territories among them." From these words we know that the city of Moscow was to be held jointly by the sons of the testator, a practice which continued among all the progeny of Kalita. In contrast was a prince's exclusive possession of particular territories, his appanage.[28] The appanage of Kalita's eldest son, Simeon, was Mozhaisk, Kolomna with all its territories, Gorodenka, Mezynia, Pesochna, Seredokorytna, Pokhriane, Ustmerska, Broshevaia, Gvozdna, the Ivany villages, Makovets, Levichin, Skulnev, Kanev, Gzhel, Goretova, Gorki; the villages of Astafievskoe, Konstantinovskoe, Orininskoe, Ostrovskoe, Kopotenskoe, Mikulskoe, Malakhovskoe, Naprudskoe by the town and the village on the Severets in the Pokhriansk district.

The second son, Ivan, received Zvenigorod, Kremichna, Ruza, Fomin-
skoe, Sukhodol, the Velikaia and Zamoshkaia free settlements, Ugozh,
Rostovtsy, Okateva settlement, Skirminovskoe, Trostna, Negucha; the
villages of Riukhovskoe, Kamenichskoe, Ruzskoe, Belzhinskoe,
Maksimovskoe, Andreevskoe, Viazemskoe, Domontovskoe, Semnitskoe
and a village in the Zamozhskaia district.

The appanage of Andrei was Lopastna, Severska, Narunizhskoe,
Serpukhov, Nivna, Teman, Golichichi, Shchitov, Peremyshl, Rastovets,
Tukhachev; the villages were Talezhskoe, Serpukhovskoe, Kolbasinskoe,
Narskoe, Peremyshlskoe, Bitiagovskoe, Trufonovskoe, Yasinovskoe,
Kolomenskoe and Nogatinskoe.

The princess and the younger children were willed Surozhik,
Mushkina Gora, Radonezhskoe, Beli, Voria and Chernogolovl. On the
Voria they received the small settlement of Sofronievskaia, Vokhna, Dei-
kova, Ramenie, Danilischeva settlement, Mishev, Selna, Guslitsy; also
the villages of Mikhailovskoe, Lutsinskoe, a village by the lake, Radonezhskoe, Deiguninskoe, Tylovskoe, Rotozh, Protasievskoe, Aristovskoe,
Lopastenskoe, Mikhailovskoe on the Yauza, two villages of Kolomenskoe. In his testament Kalita also lists his purchases, the village of
Avakovskoe in Novgorod, on the Ulal, Borisovskoe in Vladimir (both of
which were given to Prince Simeon); four villages on the Mas river: Peterovskoe, Oleksinskoe, Vsedobrych, and Pavlovskoe. Half of them were
bought and half acquired from the metropolitan in trade. All were given
to Prince Ivan. Two villages near Yuriev, Varvarskoe and Melovskoe,
were given to Prince Andrei. A new village bought on the Kostroma
together with Pavlovskoe, the acquisition of Kalita's grandmother, wife
of Alexander Nevsky, was bequeathed to his wife.

The village of Bogoroditskoe, bought in Rostov, was given to Boriska
Vorkov as his service tenure. Three villages, Leontievskoe, Sharapovskoe, and one on the Kerzhach were devoted to St. Alexander to pay for
the celebration of requiem services.[29] Kalita is silent on the subject of
some major acquisitions mentioned in the testament of Donskoy. These,
Galich, Beloozero and Uglich, most likely still remained under specified
conditions in the hands of their former princes. Kalita is also silent on
Kistma in Bezhetsky Verkh that appears for the first time in the testament
of Vasily Dmitrievich.

In the agreement of Grand Prince Simeon with his brothers new villages
are encountered. Novoe, on the Kupavna, and Vishnevskoe are marked as
belonging to the grand prince; Mikhalevskoe, Mikulskoe on the Pruzhenka,

Mikiforovskoe and Parfenevskoe are in the possession of the two younger brothers, Ivan and Andrei.

All six sons of Simeon the Proud[30] having died during his lifetime, he willed his whole appanage, all his movable and immovable property to his wife Maria without indicating who the inheritor was to be upon her death. Maria, while still living, whether voluntarily or not, transferred her territories to Grand Prince Ivan, keeping for herself only the two new territories acquired by her husband. Even these she promised to bequeath to Grand Princess Alexandra, wife of Ivan. Ivan himself did not divide his gains with his nephew Vladimir Andreevich.

Thus in the reign of Ivan II the two parts of the Moscow principality (those of Kolomna-Mozhaisk and Zvenigorod) became one as they were under Kalita.[31] In the testament of Simeon the Proud new territories that belonged to him are mentioned. They are Zaiachkov, given him by his aunt Princess Anna, and Gordoshevichi along with the villages of Ivanovskoe, Khvostovskoe on the Kliazma, Deiguninskoe, a church and village on its lands at Suleshna, a purchase in Pereiaslavl, the village of Samarovskoe, Romanovskoe on the Kerzhach, Ortakovskoe in Yuriev, Semenovskoe in Vladimir, Aleksandrovskoe on the Kostroma and Zabereg, a village in Dmitrovo.

At his death Ivan II divided his lands among his two sons, Dmitry and Ivan.[32] Thus the Moscow principality was again split as upon the death of Kalita, this time into three parts. The appanage of Kolomna-Mozhaisk went to the eldest son, Dmitry. Here, in the listing of the Kolomna districts, among Kanevo and Gzhel, Kashira is encountered. Simeon's acquisitions, Zaiachkov and Zabereg, are absent because they remained the property of his widow Maria. It is unknown why Simeon's other acquisitions, such as the village of Astafievskoe, are not listed. On the other hand, the names of new districts are encountered, the village of Malino, Kholmy and Meshcherka near Kolomna.

The younger son Ivan received his father's one-time appanage of Zvenigorod. There were changes here as well. Instead of Velikaia district there is the name of Isterva settlement. Ugozh, Skirminovskoe and Akatieva settlement are missing. Instead of the villages of Ruzskoe, Belzhinskoe, Viazemskoe, Semtsinskoe are encountered Mikhalevskoe, a village on the Repna in Borovets, Miltsinskoe, Vyslavskoe, Kuzminskoe, Karinskoe and Kozlovskoe. Of Riazan territories on this side of the Oka, the town of Novy Gorodok at the mouth of the Porotlia was given to Vladimir Andreevich. The rest went to Dmitry and Ivan.

Dmitry received the village of Romanovskoe on the Roksha and Ivan received Afineevskoe and a settlement near Pavlovskoe. The village of Pavlovskoe itself was devoted to St. Alexander.[33] To his wife Alexandra, Ivan willed the village of Semtsinskoe which is why it does not appear among the territories of his son Ivan. Alexandra for the remainder of her life also received, drawn from the appanages of both sons, holdings which were to revert to them upon her death. From the districts of Kolomenskoe she was given the village of Listsevskoe along with Pokhriany, Pesochnoe and Seredokorytnoe. From Zvenigorod she received Ugozh, the Velikaia free settlement of Yuriev and the villages of Kliapovskoe and Beltsinskoe with the settlement of Novoe.

In the testament of Ivan II there are also instructions dealing with the disposition of the territories of his stepmother, Princess Uliana, the wife of Kalita, upon whose death Surozhik and Luchinskoe were to go to her daughter. All other property and the customs duty from Moscow, the so-called *one-eighth duty* were to go to princes Dmitry, Ivan and their cousin Vladimir Andreevich.[34]

Prince Ivan soon died and once again two parts of the Moscow principality came into the hands of a single prince, Dmitry, as in the time of his father Ivan. Dmitry also succeeded in adding to his territory. These additions made the division of his lands into five or six parts according to the number of his sons a far less sensitive matter.

The most important result of these gains was that Dmitry's eldest son Vasily indisputably received the grand principality of Vladimir. This placated him for his loss of Mozhaisk which, together with Kolomna, until now was always the portion of the eldest son. The Moscow principality (of which Dmitry ruled only two parts, the third belonging to his cousin Vladimir Andreevich) was divided in two, half going to the eldest son and the rest divided among the others. It is in this context that we first encounter the expression *path of the eldest*.[35] "My son, Prince Vasily," wrote Dmitry, "I bless with the path of the eldest in the city and the villages of my appanage—half of the principality and half of the customs duty and the remaining share to my other sons." In addition, Vasiltsevo and Dobriatinskaia apiaries with the village of Dobriatinskoe were bequeathed to Vasily.

Among the Kolomna districts Meshcherka, first encountered in the testament of Dmitry's father, was the most important. Then came Ramenka, although not encountered previously, at least not in this form. From the previously established districts, missing are Mezinia,

Seredokorytnoe, Goretovoe and Gorki. On the other hand, new districts appear. Kochema and Komarev with its lands along the river. Of the villages previously included in the appanage of the eldest son, the following are missing: Astafievskoe, a village on the Severets, Mikulskoe and Naprudskoe. Instead are encountered the settlements of Mitin, Zhiroshkiny, and Khvostovskoe on the Kliazma, which appears for the first time in Simeon's testament. It should be noted that the Kolomna districts of Livichin, Skulnev and others following them in the testament of Dmitry are called villages. Near Moscow Grand Prince Vasily received a great meadow beyond the river.

The second son Yury received Zvenigorod as his appanage. Here among the older, new districts are encountered: Surozhik and Beli that once belonged to Princess Uliana, then Vyshegorod, Plesn and the Dmitriev settlement. Of the Moscow villages Yury received only Mikhalevskoe and Domantovskoe with the Khodyn meadow.

For the third son, Andrei, it became necessary to separate Mozhaisk and its territory from the old appanage of Kolomna-Mozhaisk. For the first time these districts were listed: Ismeia, Chislov, Boian, Berestov, Porotva, Kolocha, Tushkov, Glinskoe, Pnevichi with Zagorie, and Bolonesk. To the above Mozhaisk districts were added Korzhan and Moishin Kholm; the distant districts of Vereia, Rud, Dordoshevichi, Gremichi, Zaberega (the acquisition of Simeon the Proud), Sushov and the village of Repninskoe which previously was part of the Zvenigorod appanage. Of the Moscow villages Andrei received Naprudskoe (previously part of the territories of the eldest brother), Lutsinskoe with its mill on the Yauza and Deuninskoe (both from the territories of Uliana), Khvostovskoe in Peremyshl, Borovsky meadow and another opposite Voskresenie. Of the Yuriev villages he received Aleksinskoe on the Peshka.

Thus were divided into three appanages the two parts of the Moscow principality, literally Dmitry's inheritance from his father and grandfather, but Dmitry had yet other sons in need of appanages. Here he utilized his acquisitions. The chronicles do not tell us how Dmitrov was acquired. We only know that, along with Galich, it was in the possession of the progeny of Konstantin Yaroslavich. Galich was purchased by Kalita, but its prince finally was expelled only by Dmitry. Quite likely Dmitrov was acquired at the same time. At his death Dmitry Donskoy gave these acquisitions to his fourth son Peter. They consisted of the territories of Vyshegorod, Berendeev settlement, Lutosna with a geographically removed parcel, and Inobash. To the above were added some old Moscow regions, primarily the districts of Princess Uliana: Mushkova Gora, Izhva, Ramenka, the settlement of Ivanov, Vori, Korzeneva, Rogozh (or Rotosh), Zagarie, Vokha, Selna, Guslitsa, and Sherna-Gorodok. From the Moscow villages were added Novoe and Sulishin districts (acquisitions of Simeon the Proud). The fifth son, Ivan, was given a small territory, Raimenitse with environs, the village of Zverkovskoe with the clearing of Sokhonsk which had passed from Prince Vladimir Andreevich, and Sokhna.

FATE OF TERRITORIES IN PRINCES' TESTAMENTS

Besides Dmitrov, Galich, Beloozero and Uglich were definitively acquired during the reign of Dmitry Donskoy. Galich was given to Prince Yury with all its districts and those villages which stretched towards Kostroma, namely Nikolskoe and Borisovskoe. Prince Andrei received Beloozero and all its districts, both Volskoe and Shagotia, the fisheries of Miloliubskoe and all the settlements. Uglich was given to Prince Peter along with Toshna and Siama. The villages of Krasnoe, Elizarovskoe and Provatovo in Yuriev and Vasilievskoe in Rostov, purchased later, were all given to the eldest son Vasily. The village of Kozmodemianskoe in Yuriev with the village of Krasnoe, a new settlement beyond the Veznia, together with the village of Bogoroditskoe in Rostov, were given to Yury. One of the districts taken from the traitor Ivan Veliaminov,[36] a village in Gremichi, was given to Prince Andrei. It is likely that, during the reign of Dmitry Donskoy, Kaluga and Roshcha were added to the principality of Moscow and that Tov (?)[37] and Medyn were appropriated from Smolensk. These lands also went to Andrei. Prince Peter received the acquired village of Bogoroditskoe on the Bogona in Yuriev.

Grand Princess Evdokia was bequeathed the settlement of Shirmenevskaia with Shepnov; the village of Smoliane with the new settlement of Mitiaevskoe and its apiaries with the Vyshegorod beekeepers; Kropivna with its beekeepers and those of Ismensk, Gordoshevsk and Rudsk; the settlement of Zheleznov with its apiaries and village of Ivan Khorobrov and the settlements of Iskonskaia and Kuzovskaia. In Kolomna she received the new settlement of Samoiletsov with villages, the clearing of Savelievsk, the village of Mikulskoe, Babyshevo, and Oslebiatevskoe. Of the purchases in Yuriev, she received the village of Peterovskoe, Frolovskoe and Elokh.

Princess Feodosia (apparently Kalita's daughter by his second wife) gave to the grand prince Suda in Beloozero, as well as Kalashka and

Slobodka. She bequeathed to the grand princess Gorodok and Volochok. Feodosia had the use of these districts during her lifetime, and upon her death they reverted to the grand princess, who herself bought Lokhno. She was also assigned for the duration of her life several districts from the appanage of each of her sons. From the grand principality of Vladimir she received Yulka in the district of Pereiaslavl, Iledam and Komela in the district of Kostroma, Sol in Galich, Volskoe with Shagotia and Miloliubskoe fisheries in Beloozero. Of villages she received Andreevskoe in Vladimir and Dobroe in Pereiaslavl. In Kolomna she received Kanev and Pesochna and the villages of Malinskoe and Lystsevo. In Zvenigorod she was given the settlement of Yuriev, Sukhodol with Isteia Isterva, and the villages of Andreevskoe and Kamenskoe. In Mozhaisk she was given Vereia, Chislov and the village of Luchinskoe. In Dmitrov it was Izhvo and Siama. In her own right she owned the village of Repenskoe and the Moscow villages Semtsinskoe with the Khodyn mill, Ostafievskoe, Ilmovskoe and, finally Kholkhol and Zaiachkov.

Vasily Dmitrievich added the rich territories of Nizhny Novgorod, Murom and Torussa to his holdings. He was in a position to leave these new acquisitions together with his patrimony to his only son Vasily, who was destined to consolidate the whole Moscow principality as it was under Kalita, together with the acquisitions of Kalita's successors. The testament of Vasily Dmitrievich in favor of his son Ivan, who died before the birth of Vasily is also extant. In it, among the Kolomna districts, new place names are to be found: Radokin with its meadowlands and Krutinki. Among the districts bequeathed to Grand Princess Sophia Vitovtovna new names also are encountered: Ogloblino with all its villages and Olkha, Kolychevskoe with Zmeevskoe, a village in Levichin that belonged to Ivan Veliaminov along with the land of Chukhistov and all his purchases. Of the Moscow villages passed on to Grand Prince Vasily Vasilievich, there is Faustov's village of Grigorievskoe. Vasily Dmitrievich's richest acquisitions were those that belonged to the famous boyar Fedor Sviblo.[38] These villages were located on the Ustiug, in Otvodnoe, on the Siama, in Rostov, in Bezhetsky Verkh (Maksimovskoe with its lesser villages), in Pereiaslavl (Vesskoe and Radionovskoe), and Builovskoe with the lesser village of Alekseevskoe on the Moscow river. There were also the villages of Timofeevskoe on the Yauza, Chagino, Savelevskoe, Ivorovo and Karabuzino in Yuriev, and Nepeitsino in Novgorod. Besides which, the Grand Prince had purchased Ukhtiushka and acquired the Fomensky villages of Diakonov.

All these acquisitions passed to the grand princess for the duration of her life along with the Yuriev villages of Frolovskoe (with Olkha), Petrovskoe, Bogoroditskoe and Aleksinskoe. Vasily Dmitrievich received the latter villages in trade from his mother. From the newly acquired principality of Nizhny Novgorod the grand princess received the Alachinsky villages, Mongach, Algash, and Kurmysh with all its villages and tax income. As her dower she received two villages in Yuriev—Bogoroditskoe and Aleksinskoe.[39] Vasily Dmitrievich also must allot something to his younger brother Konstantin. The latter received Toshna and Ustiuzhna.

In the second testament, written in favor of Vasily's son, there are certain changes and innovations. In the city of Moscow itself he received the homestead of Foma Ivanovich by the Borovitsky gates and another homestead located past the church of St. Michael-beyond-the-Viazh and a new homestead beyond the city near the church of St. Vladimir. Of acquisitions in Yuriev he received the villages of Peterovskoe and Aleksinskoe. It was noted above that, according to the first testament, these villages were given to the grand princess. Now in their place from Kolomna she received Pesochna, Brasheva with a small village and with Gvozdneia and Ivan, Ustmerska and Gzhelia with its tracts and villages. In contrast to previous procedure the Kolomna villages of Ogloblina, Kolychevskoe and Zmeevskoe are not encountered here. She further received Vasilievskoe in Rostov (an acquisition of Dmitry Donskoy) and, as before, all the villages of Fedor Sviblo, the new settlement of Mitin and Semtsinskoe with Samsonov meadow in the environs of Moscow; a settlement on the Gus acquired by Donskoy (though the placename appears here for the first time); other acquisitions of Donskoy consisting of the villages of Krasnoe, Pravatovoe and Yelizarovskoe in Yuriev, and the previous acquisitions of Donskoy, Frolovskoe, Yelokh, Bogoroditskoe and Ustiushka on the Vologda. From the territories of the grand princes her allotment was, from Kostroma, Iledam, Obnora, Komela, Volochok, Kniagininskoe and Nerekhta with its saltworks, beekeepers and beaver trappers, from Pereiaslavl Yulka in the village of Dobor, from Vladimir the village of Andreevskoe and Toshna (provided the grand prince obtained it in trade from the sons of Vladimir Andreevich), from Nizhny Novgorod the village of Sokolskoe and Kirzhanets, from Murom a small village and Shatur. Of all these districts Gzhelia and Semtsinskoe were given as her dower.

Of the new acquisitions which did not appear in the first testament, among the Kolomna villages are mentioned Okulovskoe and Zakharovskoe, among those of Bezhetsky Verkh, Kistma and the Antonovsky villages (encountered here for the first time, even though they are designated as the purchases of Kalita), the settlement of Troitskaia on the Volga, the Beleutovsky villages (those of Boyar Beleut) in Volok and in the settlement of Yuriev, the village of Krilatskoe near Moscow, a small settlement on Beloozero (the lake), the villages of Ivan Golovin and Tutolmin on the Ustiug river. All these acquisitions were passed to the grand princess.

Just as the two "lots" or parts of the Moscow principality consolidated under Dmitry Donskoy were divided upon his death into five parts, so was the third part, that of Prince Vladimir Andreevich, divided into five according to the number of his sons. Vladimir Andreevich passed his Moscow patrimony, his one-third, to his sons Ivan, Simeon, Yaroslav, Andrei and Vasily according to their years. In similarity to Donskoy he blessed his first son upon the path of the eldest in Moscow and its lands, giving him the stud farms, beekeepers, gardeners, huntsmen, beaver trappers, upholsterers and men of various other functions. He also gave him Serpukhov with its districts of Gorodets, Narskoe, Nivna, Temna, Sinilishcha, Gomonin, the settlements of Yaroslavl, Mokraia, Diagileva, Lvova, Verkh-Moskvits, Kruglaia and Ostapkhova. Of the Moscow villages he gave Mikulinskoe, Gubkino, Nemtsovo, Popovskoe, Sesepeterovo, Strupikovo, Kolomenka with its mill, and Tulovskoe with all its lesser villages. Ivan also received Kozelsk, Gogol, Aleksin and the purchase of Lisin.

Prince Simeon received Borovsk with its districts, namely Golchitsy, the settlement of Khopylev, Istia with a settlement, one third of Mushkova and half of Shchitov. Of the Moscow villages he received Vypriazhkovo on Studenets river with its lesser villages, Kolychevskoe, and a mill on the Neglinnaia. In Yuriev-Polsky he received four villages: Varvarskoe, Bogoiavlenskoe, Poplovskoe, and Fedorovskoe.

Prince Yaroslav received Yaroslavl with Khotun, Vikhorna, Polianka and the small settlements of Rostunov and Moshchenskaia. Of the Moscow villages he received Saryevskoe and Kiriasovo with its meadows, and a mill at the mouth of the Mstits. Yaroslav and Simeon jointly received Gorodets on the Volga except for the internal and general customs duties which were given to their mother the princess. The two sons were to divide the town, its lands and taxes equally. Simeon received land on the near side of the river, below Gorodets, and Belogorod. Yaroslav received land on the far side of the Volga, above Gorodets, and Yurievets. If Belogorod yielded more than Yurievets and Cherniakova, Simeon was to give Koriakova to Yaroslav. Otherwise Koriakova was to be equally divided among the two brothers. The fisheries below Gorodets were to be operated jointly and the catch divided evenly. Besides all the divided endowments, Prince Simeon received Porozdna in Gorodets for himself.

Prince Andrei was given Radonezh, Beli and Chernogolovl, with those of its residents who were on the Kerzhach, Tukhachev and the small settlements of Yakovlia and Kishkina. Of the Moscow villages he received Mikhailovskoe with its mill, Kalitkinovo, Popovskoe and Ilia Sviaty on the Uch, the village of Dmitry Voronin Chetrekovskoe and Moseikovo on the Liubosivlia, and the lesser village of Sakova.

Prince Vasily received Peremyshl, Rostovets, half of Shchitov, and one-third of Dobriatinskaia. Of the Moscow villages he acquired Yasinovskoe with its lesser villages and the Panshina clearing. The town of Uglich was divided equally between Vasily and Andrei.

Princess Elena received Luzha, Kozlov Brod, and the small settlement of Badeev. Of the Luzha districts and settlements she received Lovyshina, the settlement of Yartsev, Sosnovets, Turi Gory, Bubol, Vepreika, the settlement of Yakimov, Makovets, Setunka, Terekhova, Spirkova, the settlement of Artemov, Skomantova, Gridi of Yartsev, Mikhalkova of Stepan Osipov, Dynka of Mosolov, and Gridi of Fedot Lukin. Of the Moscow villages she received Kolomenskoe with all its lesser villages and meadows, Nogatinskoe, Taininskoe with Koreevoe, Kosino with three lakes, Obukhovo, and a mill at the mouth of the Yauza. Kosino, Obukhovo and the mill were given as her dower. She further received, for the duration of her life, lands from the appanages of her sons. These were Vskhodnoe with its lesser villages and Tetkovo Lake from Ivan; Omutskoe with lesser villages and meadows from Simeon; Bovykino and the lake of Dolgoe at the mouth of the Lopastna from Yaroslav; Voronovskoe, Kovezinskoe and the beekeepers of Radonezh with their lesser villages and apiaries from Andrei, Bitiagovo and Domodedovo from Vasily and the village of Bogoroditskoe in Uglich. Upon the death of the princess, the village of Kolomenskoe was to pass on to her eldest son, Prince Ivan, Nogatinskoe to Simeon, Taininskoe with Koreevo to Vasily, Kozlov Brod and the small settlement of Badeev was to be divided between Ivan and Yaroslav. Simeon, Andrei and Vasily were to divide equally Luzha and its districts except for the villages of Bubol, Benitskoe, Medkino and Diakovskoe, which were to be disposed of by the princess as she chose. The eldest son, Prince Ivan, was bequeathed the Moscow residences of Zvorykin, Ignatiev and Butov's homestead. Simeon and Yaroslav were to share the residence of Grand Princess Maria (widow of Simeon the Proud). Simeon was also to have Terekhov's homestead lying beyond the Neglinnaia. The princess was to have half of the great Moscow residence with the other half going to Andrei and Vasily. Chichakov's residence was to be divided equally among Yaroslav, Andrei and Vasily. Sol in the district of Gorodets, except for the Fedorovskaia saltworks, was to be held jointly by Simeon and Yaroslav with the proceeds (from the sale of salt) to be shared equally.

In comparing the territories listed in the testament of Vladimir Andreevich with those bequeathed to his father in the testament of Ivan Kalita it is noticeable that Prince Vladimir was successful in increasing the appanage significantly. Though Lopastna was lost to Riazan from this appanage as early as the reign of Grand Prince Ivan II, its loss was replaced by Novy Gorodok at the mouth of the Porotlia. Prince Vladimir also acquired, as a result of Kalita's testament, a third of the territories of Princess Uliana. Grand Prince Dmitry Donskoy gave him Luzha and Borovsk. His nephew Vasily Dmitrievich gave him Volok and Rzheva with all its districts.

Later an exchange took place between the two men. Perhaps Vasily did not care for the fact that the territories of the prince of Serpukhov stretched far to the west along the borders of Novgorod and Tver. He took Volok and Rzheva back from his uncle. Instead of Volok he then gave him part of his acquisitions in the east, namely Gorodets with its districts of Belgorod and Yurievets, the settlements of Koriakovaia and Cherniakovaia, and the Unzhinskaia general customs duty. In exchange for Rzheva, Vasily gave Vladimir Uglich with the village Zolotorusskoe. Finally in the south he gave Vladimir even his patrimony of Kozelsk, Gogol and Aleksin with the purchased Peresvetovaia. The increase of villages in the environs of Moscow, of settlements in various parts, and of villages in Yuriev cannot be ascribed to anything other than Vladimir's purchases. In his testament he mentions a purchase made by one of his sons, Prince Ivan. This is evidence that princes had the means to buy districts for themselves even while their fathers were alive.

Yet another factor commands attention in the testament of Vladimir and in his agreements with Grand Prince Vasily Dmitrievich. Vladimir received Uglich from the grand prince, yet we know that this town was willed by Dmitry Donskoy not to Vasily, but to Peter Dmitrievich, prince of Dmitrov. The exchange occurred as a result of the creation of an appanage for the youngest brother Konstantin. It was noted that in his first testament Vasily Dmitrievich bequeathed Toshnia and Ustiuzhna to Konstantin, which proved insufficient. Since all princes must participate in creating an appanage, it was the childless Prince Peter who ceded Uglich to his youngest brother. For it he received Shachebal and Likurgi from Yury. These districts Peter also ceded to Konstantin. Moreover, Yury himself gave several of his Zvenigorod districts to Konstantin. For this, and perhaps for other reasons as well, Yury received Viatka from the grand prince, a territory previously part of the Suzdal-Nizhny Novgorod principality.

The grand prince subsequently took Uglich from Konstantin and exchanged it for Rzheva with Prince Vladimir Andreevich. He added some of his own holdings in Bezhetsky Verkh and gave the whole parcel to Konstantin. Volok, which the grand prince had exchanged for Gorodets, he kept for himself. This distribution of territories existed only briefly after the death of Prince Vladimir, for the grand prince soon reversed the grants he had made to Vladimir's sons, namely Uglich, Gorodets, Kozelsk, Gogol, Aleksin, the purchase of Peresvetov, and Lisin. Of these he returned Uglich to his brother Konstantin probably to make him surrender his claims to seniority. The sons of Vladimir, not having the means to resist the grand prince, had to relinquish their patrimony. One of them, Yaroslav, was forced to depart for Lithuania. The grand prince gave them some compensation. In granting Uglich to Konstantin he took Toshnia which he now gave to the sons of Vladimir while stipulating in his testament that his son re-acquire it through exchange.

Thus were divided the territories in Northeastern Rus when Prince Vasily Vasilievich, not yet of age, first sat on his father's throne. Thus began the infamous internecine strife leading to the consolidation of almost all the Moscow territories into a single whole. First there arose the problem of Dmitrov, the escheated appanage of Prince Peter Dmitrievich. Initially it apparently was added to the territories of Prince Vasily Vasilievich. Later, after a trial at the Horde, Dmitrov was given to Vasily's uncle Yury as compensation for his loss of seniority. In concluding an agreement with his nephew Vasily after the death of Morozov,[40] and his own flight from Moscow, Yury returned Dmitrov to his nephew but took instead Zurozhik, the village of Shepkova, Shachebal, Likurgi and the

Kostroma districts of Andoma, Korega, Borka, Berezovets with Zalesie, and Shylenga. He also took the remaining grand-princely holdings in Bezhetsky Verkh except for those previously granted to Konstantin and the villages of the boyar Ivan Dmitrievich which were retained by Vasily and, as the chronicles say, "taken in guilty shame."

Both brothers, Yury and Konstantin, despite their differences in age, died at nearly the same time. The escheated appanage of the childless Konstantin was taken by Grand Prince Vasily. Yury, on the other hand, left three sons. His testament is extant, but it was written well before his death, while he still held Dmitrov, that is, before it was first taken by Moscow. The testament is remarkable in that it makes no distinction between the eldest and the younger brothers. The Moscow lands are distributed evenly among the three sons with no preference given to the eldest. Perhaps it was the father's coldness to Vasily Kosoy,[41] the eldest, that was the reason. Vasily Kosoy received Zvenigorod with its districts of Ugozh, Plesn, the small settlement of Dimitrievo, Trostna, Negucha, and Andreevskoe. In Moscow he received the village of Domantovskoe and the Tumashinsky meadows in Pererva. Dmitry Shemiaka,[42] the second son, was given the town of Ruza with its district: the settlement of Yuriev, Zamoshie, Kremichna, Skirmanovoe, Belmi, Rostovtsy, Fomenskoe and the villages of Mikhailovskoe and Nikiforovskoe with all the lesser villages. In Moscow he received apiaries on the far side of the Moscow river and a meadow opposite the town itself. Dmitry the Fair[43] received Vyshgorod and the village of Kositskoe, Sukhodol with Istia and Isterva, and the small settlements of Uborichnaia, Borovkova and Smolianaia. In Moscow his portion was the village of Mikhailevskoe and the small village of Sushchevskoe, that lay close to Moscow, along with falconers, beekeepers, huntsmen and the Khodyn meadow.

The town of Dmitrov was apportioned to the three sons together. Its districts, however, were divided with Vasily Kosoy receiving Selna, Guslitsa, Vokhna, Zagarie, Rogozh and Kuney. Dmitry Shemiaka received Shorna, Korzenevo, Voria, Vyshgorod and Inobazh. Dmitry the Fair was given Izhvo, Mushkova, Ramenka, Berendeevo with the small settlement of Kuzmodemianskaia, Lutosna and Kulikova. Viatka was divided equally among the sons, but Galich, with all its districts and income, was given to Dmitry the Fair. The three sons together were given Yury's residence, a residence outside Moscow and another smaller residence. On the basis of this testament we see that, except for Viatka and Dmitrov yielded by his brother and nephew, Yury was not successful in purchasing anything for his appanage, even losing Surozhik, which apparently was given to his brother Konstantin. Nor are the villages of Yurievskoe and Rostovskoe or their disposition mentioned in the testament. It is clear that at his death Yury gave different instructions. Vyshgorod and Galich, assigned to Dmitry the Fair in the first testament now went to Shemiaka. Dmitry received the districts of Bezhetsk and Kostroma, acquired by Yury in the interim, except for Shachebal, Likurga and Andoma. Yury's death and the strife with Kosoy gave Vasily Vasilievich a pretext for aggrandizement at the expense of the other princes. He took Zvenigorod from Kosoy. Shemiaka, in concluding an agreement with the grand prince, surrendered all claims to Zvenigorod, Dmitrov and Viatka, accepting the appanage of his uncle Konstantin, namely Rzheva, Uglich and the Moscow districts of Zaridalie, Sokhna, Rameneitso, the Ostashevsky villages, Shchukinskoe, Surozhik, Shopkova and Luchinskoe. After a council near Kostroma Kosoy was given Dmitrov in place of Zvenigorod, though not for very long, as we have seen.

Thus the appanage of Peter Dmitrievich and half the appanage of Yury Dmitrievich were added to the grand-princely appanage of Kolomna, but the appanages of Serpukhov and Mozhaisk remained untouched. Serpukhov, because of the heirless death of the four sons of Vladimir Andreevich, came into the hands of Vladimir's sole grandson Vasily Yaroslavich. Mozhaisk after the death of Andrei Dmitrievich was divided into two appanages, those of Mozhaisk and Vereia. The first went to Andrei's eldest son Ivan, the second to the younger, Mikhail. Vasily Yaroslavich, the grand prince's brother-in-law, declined all bequests received by his grandfather from the grand prince's father. A part of these bequests, specifically Kozelsk, with its districts of Serensk, Liudimsk, Koropki, Vyrna, the purchase of Peresvetov, Aleksin, Lisin and Svibloe, went to Ivan Andreevich of Mozhaisk as a result of a decision in Moscow.

The alliance of Ivan Andreevich and Shemiaka which led to the seizure and blinding of the grand prince had as another of its consequences the annexation of the Mozhaisk appanage to the territories of Vasily. At that time Shemiaka was forced to cede Uglich, Rzheva and Bezhetsk, while Ivan Andreevich had to surrender Kozelsk, Aleksin and Lisin. Later, as a consequence of renouncing his alliance with Shemiaka, Ivan Andreevich temporarily was given Lisin and lands in Bezhetsky Verkh since they belonged to Dmitry the Fair, who died in 1440 and bequeathed his holdings to Shemiaka. He also received half of Zaozerie, territories belonging to the Kubena princes. Soon thereafter, as a result of certain circumstances, Ivan Andreevich lost not only his recent acquisitions but also his appanage of Mozhaisk. All the territories of Shemiaka previously were added to the possessions of the grand principality. This left the appanages of Serpukhov and Vereia. After the services rendered by Vasily Yaroslavich the grand prince recalled that Vasily, in receiving his appanage, was deprived of Uglich, Gorodets and Kozelsk. In compensation the grand prince granted Dmitrov and Sukhodol with the village of Krasnoe, recently seized from Shemiaka, to Vasily. After the exile of Ivan Andreevich[44] the two brothers-in-law engaged in an exchange. Vasily Yaroslavich returned Dmitrov to the grand prince and received Zvenigorod with those districts which formerly belonged to Kosoy, except for Plesnia and the Yershovsk villages. He also received all of Bezhetsky Verkh including the villages of the boyars and junior boyars who followed Prince Ivan Andreevich into exile, except for the villages of Tolstikov and Basharov and the patrimony of the Soprichin family, which already had been sold to Moscow boyars. Vasily Yaroslavich did not hold these regions for very long. First he was forced to return Zvenigorod and Bezhetsky Verkh, finally he lost all of his territories.

Only the appanage of Vereia remained intact. Prince Mikhail Andreevich not only maintained his patrimony, he even made several acquisitions. He received from Vasily Vasilievich half of Zaozerie, the patrimony of the local princes. To this was added one hundred lesser villages from the half of Zaozerie belonging to the grand prince himself. In exchange for half of Kubena, Mikhail Andreevich received lands from the grand prince's districts in Zaozerie suitably adjacent to his own patrimony of Beloozero. From Shemiaka's former holdings Mikhail Andreevich was given Vyshgorod with its districts, various commercial enterprises and villages. He also received districts in Zvenigorod, namely Plesn, except for the village of Plesenskoe, Smolianye, Sokhna, Zarydalie, Zerem and the beekeepers of Tarusa. The value of the grant was increased by the fact that Vyshgorod was relieved of the general tribute[45] for five years and the whole territory of Vereia for three years was to pay only half the general tribute.

Additional light is thrown on the distribution of lands during the reign of Vasily Vasilievich by the testaments of two princesses, Elena, wife of Vladimir Andreevich, and Sophia Vitovtovna,[46] mother of Vasily the Dark. Elena deemed it necessary to bequeath her lord, Grand Prince Vasily Vasilievich, the village of Kolomenskoe. She bequeathed her grandson Vasily Yaroslavich the villages of Omutskoe, Vskhodskoe, the

Luzha villages of Yurievskoe, Degotskoe, Osenevskoe, Avramovskoe, Mikhalkovo, Misedskoe and Sosnovskoe. In the environs of Moscow she gave him Tulovskoe. To her daughter-in-law Vasilisa, wife of Prince Simeon, she gave the village Nogatinskoe with its meadows and town dwellers. In Luzha she gave her Bubol and Benitskoe. She gave her other daughter-in-law Uliana, the wife of Prince Vasily, the villages of Bitiagovoe and Domodedovo and the villages of Taininskoe and Bogorodskoe in the environs of Moscow. She also passed to her grandson Vasily Yaroslavich the village of Kovezinskoe in Radonezh. Her granddaughter Princess Maria Ivanovna received the village of Voronovskoe in Dmitrov, and in the city of Moscow itself property near the old residence in the Podol area where Princess Elena herself lived. Upon Maria's death the village and the Moscow property was to go to Prince Vasily Yaroslavich.

This testament does not mention all the territories Elena inherited from her husband, nor the districts such as Obukhovo and Kosino given as her dower. On the other hand, it is known that princesses were limited to dispose of only their own districts or those of the dower. How is it then possible that Elena disposed of all of her lands? This occurrence can only be explained by the fact that Elena outlived all of her sons who were to have regained the districts taken from their appanages for her support. There is the additional fact that there was no law according to which a sole grandson, in this case Vasily Yaroslavich, was to inherit the property of all his childless uncles.

The testament of Grand Princess Sophia Vitovtovna is significant in two respects. First, in the great number of purchases which indicate the substantial means of the princess and second, in that a major part of these purchases was bequeathed to a single beneficiary, her favorite grandson Prince Yury Vasilievich. In general, princesses inherited large and rich districts from their husbands, some as a dower, the majority only for their lifetime. The income left them by their husbands nonetheless gave them the means to purchase holdings of which they could dispose at will, and thus enrich the patrimony of whichever grandson they favored. Of the fifty-two districts mentioned in Sophia's testament, only six were not purchased by her. Three of them, Babyshevskoe, Lystsevo, and Osleviatevskoe were the purchases of Dmitry Donskoy and were willed by him to his wife Evdokia. It is unclear how they came into Sophia's absolute possession. The other three were Sophia's dower, the village of Semchinskoe with Samsonov meadow, and Gzhelia. She bequeathed the first three holdings to her daughter-in-law Grand Princess Maria Yaroslavna, and the latter three to her favorite grandson Yury. Her purchases were the villages of Kolychevskoe, Nikoltsevo, Lipiatinskoe, Chukhistovo, Okulovskoe and Repinskoe in Kolomna; Kurchevskoe, Eletskoe and Varvarskoe in Yuriev, beyond the Volga on the Sheksna river the district of Ustiugla and Vereteika with all its villages. These properties were bequeathed to her son Grand Prince Vasily.

Other purchases in Kolomna were the village of Grigory Naumov on the Severets and the village of Ivan Bunkov near Malino, bequeathed to Grand Princess Maria. In Vladimir there were the villages of Tolba, Vizheksha and Golovina, given to her grandson Ivan. In Moscow she purchased Popov's village of Vorobievo, and Semenovskoe with lesser villages, on the Pochra river the villages of Miachkovo, Faustovskoe, Ladyginskoe, Levontievskoe, Tiazhino and several fishing villages. Again in the Kolomna region, there were the villages Vilino, Krivtsoso, Bronniche, Chevyrevo, Marchukovo, Rozhok, and a new settlement near Shchelin lake.

Other Yuriev purchases were the Turabievsk villages, later Kuchka, Derevenka and Shadrino. The purchases in Kostroma were Kachalovskoe, Ushakovskoe and Sviatoe, in Vologda the Maslensk, Yangasarsk and Govorovsk villages. All of the above holdings went to her grandson Yury except for the villages of Berezniki, Ratkovo and Aleksino. Princess Evfrosinia received Aleksino, while Berezniki and Ratkovo went to Grand Princess Maria and were to pass to Yury upon Maria's death. Her grandson Andrei received the village of Vysheles, and the purchased villages in Volok, those of Beleutovsky and Okorakovsky, went to her grandson Boris.

Finally all the appanages of the Moscow principality, except for Vereia, with all the acquisitions in other provinces, were consolidated by Vasily the Dark. He combined them with the grand principality of Vladimir and proceeded to distribute them among his five sons. His eldest son, the future Grand Prince Ivan Vasilievich, received a third of the Moscow principality, Kolomna, Vladimir, Pereiaslavl, Kostroma, Galich, Ustiug, Viatka, Suzdal, Nizhny Novgorod, Murom, Yuriev with Velikaia Sol, Borovsk, Sukhodol, Kaluga and Aleksin. Of the Moscow villages he received Ostrovskoe, Oriminskoe, Konstantinovskoe, Malakhovskoe, Krasnoe above Veliky Prud, and a great meadow near Moscow itself along the river.

The second son, Yury, received the third of Moscow which previously belonged to Prince Vladimir Andreevich, but Yury had to share this third with his brother Andrei the Elder according to seniority. Besides one-half of a third, Yury also received in Moscow the holdings of Prince Konstantin Dmitrievich, as well as the territories of Dmitrov, Yulka, Serebozh, Buskutovo, Rozhestvenoe, Mozhaisk, Medyn, Serpukhov, Khotun, all the districts willed him by his grandmother Sophia Vitovtovna with the addition of Shipilovsky village to those of Turabievsk.

A general desire is noticeable on the part of the princes to round out their appanages and rid them of lands belonging to others. Thus, for example, Prince Vladimir Andreevich once demanded that his son Ivan surrender a purchase that lay within the appanage of another son, Yaroslav. Then it was discovered that the testament of Sophia Vitovtovna gave Yury villages located in the Kolomna appanage of Grand Prince Ivan. As a result Vasily the Dark gave Ivan authority for an equitable transaction of holdings with Yury.

The third son Andrei the Elder received Uglich, Ustiuzhna, Rozhalovo, Kistma, Bezhetsky Verkh, Zvenigorod and the village of Sushchevskoe near Moscow. The fourth son Boris received the Moscow holdings of Prince Ivan Andreevich of Mozhaisk, as well as Rzheva, Volok and Ruza. As Prince Yury Vasilievich, by being a favorite of his paternal grandmother, received the greater part of her numerous purchases, so did Prince Boris, the favorite of his maternal grandmother Princess Maria Fedorovna Goltiaeva, acquire many districts.

The princess inherited them from her father, Boyar Fedor Goltiaev-Koshkin,[47] and from her childless brothers. These were the Proskurnikovsk and Vvedensk villages in Kolomna; a hamlet in Gorodna; the Rassudovsky villages, Zverevskoe and Biranovskoe, beyond the Pochra in Moscow; the Simizinsky villages, Lazarskoe, Kotiazino, and Yevnutievskoe on the Kostroma in Vladimir; the settlement of Nizhniaia, Bazeevskoe and Manuilovskoe on the Volga; Turandaevskoe, Ponizovnoe, Gorka, and the Kovylinsky villages on the Vologda; several hamlets on the Shoma; the villages of Sharapovo and Loshakovo near Moscow and a meadow on the Moscow river near Krutitsy; Rostovtsovskoe village in Berendeevo; Surovtsovo, Timofeevskoe and Mikulskoe in Kinel; a residence in the town of Moscow and residences in the environs.

The fifth son, Andrei the Younger, received in Moscow the holdings of Prince Peter Dmitrievich and the villages of Taninskoe, Yasenevskoe and Rameneitse outside the city. He also received Vologda with Kubena and Zaozerie, Iledam with Obnora, Komela and Volochok as well as Avnega, Shelenga, Pelshma, Bokhtiuga, Ukhtiushka, Siama, Otvodnoe with the Perkhushkovsky villages, Toshna, and Yangosar. Grand Princess Maria received for the duration of her life that part of Rostov that had belonged to Vasily the Dark. The princes of Rostov still held the rest. Maria's holdings were to go to Yury upon her death. Her purchase of Romanov and the mouth of the Sheksna were affirmed. She also received districts along the Volga and Sheksna which belonged to Prince Ivan of Mozhaisk, along with villages confiscated from the traitorous boyar Peter Konstantinovich. These were Ust-Ugly, Nerekhta, Naprudskoe near Moscow, Khodyn mill and meadow, Nogatinskoe, Novinki, the Ozeretsky villages, Mikhalevskoe, Oleshnia, villages in Luzha, Pavshinskoe, and the boyar's villages on the Istra. She received holdings from the appanages of her brothers as well.

In Kolomna passed to her the town of Brashova with a small village, Gvozdnia and Ivan, as well as Ustmerska, Pesochna, the Malinsky villages, the villages of Serkizovskoe, Mezynka, Vysokoe, Shkin, Sverbeevskoe, Lystsevskoe, Babyshevo near the town of Kolomna, Chukhistovo, and the village of Fedor Stepanov. In Pereiaslavl it was Riuminskoe, Dobroe and the settlement of Marinino; in Yuriev, the village of Frolovskoe with Yelokh, Krasnoe, Kurchevo, Yeltsy, Varvarino, Kuzmodemianskoe, Golenishchevo, Dobrynskoe, Volstinovo, Sorogoshino and the villages of Peter Konstantinovich, Matveishchovo and Vorogovo; in Suzdal, Shokshov and Davydovskoe; on the Kostroma, the villages of Mikhail Danilov and the Koldomsky villages given her by Mikhail Baburov; in Ustiug, in addition to her purchases of Leontievskoe, Piatnitskoe and Vondokurie, she received the village of Moshemskoe and Dymkova Storona.

From the appanage of Andrei the Elder she received Yelda, Kadka and Vasilkovo; from the appanage of Boris she received Izdetemlia, the settlement of Yudino, Yadrovo, and Andreevskoe in Rzheva; from Andrei the Younger,[48] Iledam with Komela and Obnora. In Nizhny Novgorod she received the villages that had belonged to Grand Princess Sophia Vitovtovna, along with Sokolskoe and Kerzhenets; in Murom, it was the small village of Muromskoe and Shatur. Later there was an additional testament written in which Maria was bequeathed the villages of Kolomenskoe, Diakovskoe, Khvostovskoe, the meadow of Prince Yury Dmitrievich that lay opposite the residence of the grand prince, Yury's meadow Kaznacheev and two districts adjacent to Marinino settlement;

in Pereiaslavl she received Gorodishche with the Volninsk villages and Barmazovo with villages; in Murom she received Pochap, Zakolpie and Chersovo; in Kolomna, the village of Oksinskoe with its lesser villages, also Miachkovo, bought from Nastasia the wife of Fedor Andreevich, and villages on the Moscow river bought from the Fedor's daughter. In Mozhaisk she received the villages of Chertakovskoe, Belevitsky, Ismeiskoe and a mill near the town. A number of villages in Murom and in Votsky Starodub were given her by Anna, the wife of Vasily Ivanovich. She received the villages of Dolmat Yuriev in Khotunskoe, Rastunov and Peremyshl as a dower. The Moscow residence of Prince Ivan of Mozhaisk was given to the eldest son Ivan. The residence of the Serpukhov princes located beyond the Archangel cathedral was granted to Yury while the residence located near the church of St. John the Baptist given him by his grandmother went to the grand princess. The residence of Shemiaka went to Andrei the Elder. The residences of the disgraced Konstantinovich boyars[49] Peter, Ivan and Nikita, as well as their property in the suburbs, passed to the grand princess to bequeath to whichever son she pleased. The villages of Okulovskoe and Repinskoe, which the grand princess gave to Fedor Basenok[50] then in her testament willed to the grand prince, were to remain in Basenok's possession and be given to Maria upon his death.

MEANS OF EXPANSION

From the above examination of the gradual expansion, division and consolidation of the Moscow territories it can be concluded that military conquest played a rather small role in the growth of the principality of Moscow. The initial expansion at the expense of the neighboring principalities, Smolensk and Riazan, and the acquisition of Mozhaisk, Kolomna, Vereia, Borovsk and Luzha did occur through force of arms. Thereafter, since the time of Kalita, expansion took place primarily through purchases and acquisitions of a kind in which force did not take part. The Moscow princes bought up (it is from here that the epithet of "buyer" stems)[51] distant principalities in the Northwest and Northeast, unpopulated and impoverished regions whose princes could neither meet the demands of the Horde nor resist their more immediate stronger neighbors.

Thus the Moscow princes expanded their lands at the expense of the weak and fragmented progeny of Konstantin, Ivan Vsevolodovich and Konstantin Yaroslavich. Kalita purchased Beloozero, Galich and Uglich. The chronicles do not relate how Dmitrov was acquired yet speak of the expulsion of the princes of Galich and Starodub during the reign of Donskoy, although the lands of these princes are not mentioned among the holdings of Donskoy or his heirs. Therefore they must have remained, under prescribed conditions, in the possession of their princes who entered Moscow's service. Nor were the principalities of Nizhny Novgorod-Suzdal and Murom taken by force of arms. Only later did it become necessary to defend them against the claims of their former princes. Moscow's expansion in the South occurred at the expense of the weak and fragmented provinces of Chernigov-Seversk. In the Southeast it was at the expense of the Meshchera princes.

While certain territories were acquired in a peaceful fashion through purchases and others forcefully yet not through military expeditions and conquests, Moscow's lengthy wars with its neighboring principalities, if often ending in Moscow's favor, did not bring new lands. Nothing was acquired from Tver upon the successful completion of a war with it during the reign of Donskoy. Nothing was gained from Riazan after the drawing of borders in the reign of Ivan II. Unsuccessful also was the attempt to acquire Novgorod lands beyond the Dvina[52] during the reign of Vasily Dmitrievich.

Along with the acquisition of whole principalities the Moscow princes also enriched themselves by acquiring numerous villages and other property. In their agreements with each other princes usually included a condition which forbade them to acquire districts in each other's holdings. As a result the Moscow princes, despite their financial means, could not make purchases in Tver or Riazan although the grand principality of Vladimir, which they constantly controlled, was open for purchases. It has been seen in the testaments how they made use of this opportunity, especially how heavily they bought up the district of Yuriev-Polsky.

Here then was another reason for the rise of the Moscow princes. Villages were acquired in one of two ways, through purchase, or through confiscation from disgraced boyars. The villages belonging to the Veliaminov, Sviblo and Vsevolozhsky families were obtained by such means from the progeny of Konstantin. The borders of the Moscow principality at the death of Ivan Kalita did not even coincide with the borders of the present Moscow province. Lacking were Dmitrov, Klin and Volokolamsk. Somewhat later the borders included parts of what are now the provinces of Tula and Kaluga, then at the death of Vasily the Dark, great-great-grandson of Kalita, the principality included not only all of the present Moscow province (except for Klin), it stretched across the provinces of

Kaluga, Tula, Vladimir, Nizhny Novgorod, Viatka, Kostroma, Vologda, Yaroslavl and Tver.

TERRITORIAL BOUNDARIES

The borders of the Moscow principality proper with that of Riazan to the southeast were set in an agreement between the respective princes. The line ran along the Oka and Ttsna rivers. Lands upstream from Kolomna along the Oka previously held by Riazan but on the Moscow side, Novy Gorodok, Luzha, Vereia, Borovsk and all other lands on the left bank went to Moscow. Downstream from Kolomna to the Ttsna and up along that river all lands on the Riazan side went to Riazan, on the Moscow side to Moscow. As a result of this division along the Oka old Riazan lands on the right bank which had belonged to Moscow even before Ivan II reverted to Riazan. They were Lopastna, the district of Mstislavl, the town of Zhadene, Zhademl, Dubok, and Brodnich with its environs. Moscow received Talitsa, Vypolzov, Takasov, and Meshchera, the purchase of Donskoy.

The above is the only meaning that can be drawn from the following quotation "We have divided lands between us along the Oka river, from Kolomna up along the Oka, on the Moscow side Novy Gorodok, Luzha, Vereia, Borovsk and any other Riazan lands that may be on that side, these to Moscow. Down the Oka, to the river Ttsna and from the mouth of the Ttsna up along the Ttsna, whatever is on the Moscow side of the Ttsna, that belongs to Moscow. What is on the Riazan side beyond the Oka, what heretofore pertained to Moscow, starting with Lopastna, and others, these lands belong to Riazan." The question arises, how could Lopastna have been on the Riazan side beyond the Oka? There is also a difficulty concerning Tula. "As to the property of Grand Prince Dmitry Ivanovich on the Riazan side, Tula, it must be as it was under Tsaritsa Taidula[53] and the rule of her baskaks.[54] Grand Prince Oleg[55] is not to interfere in this, nor Dmitry."

Tula is called the property of Grand Prince Dmitry on the Riazan side. His surrender of it is understandable, but it is not clear why Grand Prince Oleg surrendered it, and for whose benefit. Perhaps there was a mistake in Donskoy's agreement. Basing ourselves on the later agreements of the Riazan princes with Vasily and Yury, we may suppose that the Moscow princes surrendered Tula to the princes of Riazan, for in these later pacts the Moscow princes agree not to interfere in Tula. If so, the agreement of the Riazan prince Ivan Fedorovich with Vytautas[56] creates difficulties.

In it is encountered the following condition. "Grand Prince Vytautas is not to enter my patrimony, that of Ivan Fedorovich, neither its lands nor its waters within the Riazan borders nor my patrimony of Pereiaslavl except for Tula, Berestey, Retan with Pasha, and Zakoloten Gordeevsky."

It is intriguing that in the agreements of the Moscow princes with those of Riazan not only Lopastna, but also Vereia and Borovsk are called old Riazan places, while according to the entry in the chronicles under 1176 Lopastna was a dependency of Chernigov. In this same document it can be seen that the Riazan princes this early began to seize nearby Chernigov districts such as Svirelsk. Most likely Riazan also seized Lopastna, Vereia, Borovsk and Luzha shortly after the invasion of Batu Khan[57] when the Chernigov-Seversk principality[58] was depopulated, fragmented and weakened.

It can be established from contemporaneous Novgorod pacts that Volok, Vologda and Bezhetsky Verkh were considered possessions of Novgorod, yet in the agreements and testaments of the grand princes it is evident that they disposed of Volok and Bezhetsky Verkh and Vologda, an indication that these lands were controlled jointly by both parties. In fact Grand Prince Vasily Vasilievich, in affirming the control of Shemiaka and his brother Dmitry the Fair over Bezhetsky Verkh, set as a condition in the pact that they hold this territory according to the old traditions with Novgorod. It has been noted that at this juncture Novgorod wished to draw a line of demarcation between itself and the grand prince. For some reason Vasily the Dark did not wish such demarcation.

On the basis of an entry under the year 1220 stating that Grand Prince Yury Vsevolodovich ordered his nephew Vasilko Konstantinovich of Rostov to send troops against the Bulgars from Rostov and Ustiug, it may be concluded that Ustiug was dependent on the Rostov princes. It is unknown whether they managed to hold Ustiug in their own period of weakness and dependence on the grand princes, or whether Ustiug was lost to Vladimir. Known only is that Ustiug is mentioned as belonging to the Moscow princes initially in the testament of Vasily the Dark, when the towns of the Vladimir principality were combined indiscriminately with those of Moscow, and for the first time Rostov was bequeathed by the grand prince to his wife.

As for the Southeastern Russian borders in general, it can be assumed with great validity that they coincided with the borders of the dioceses of Riazan and Saray, which was within the Tatar lands proper. According to metropolitans' documents, the diocesan border was the Great

Vorona river. According to these same documents there were Christians in the lands along the Cherleny Yar river and in outposts near Khoper on the Don. On the eastern bank of the Don, where that river is as broad as the Seine at Paris, Rubruck[59] found a Russian settlement built by Batu and Sartak. Its residents ferried merchants and emissaries across the river. The journey of Metropolitan Pimen[60] to Constantinople provides additional information about the borders. The metropolitan set out overland from Riazan, taking with him three boats and a barge set on wheels. Upon reaching the Don the party lowered its vessels and sailed downstream. Here is how they describe the voyage along the Don. "This journey was sad and bleak, for there was wasteland on both sides of the river. Neither town nor village was to be seen. Only the ruins of towns once beautiful and extensive could be discerned. Nowhere was a man to be seen, but there was a multitude of beasts, goats, elk, wolves, foxes, otters, bears, beavers, and a multitude of birds, eagles, geese, swans, cranes and various others." Having passed the Medveditsa river, Vysokie Gory and Bely Yar, the one-time location of the ancient Khazar city of Sarkel, the travellers began to encounter Tatar encampments. It is apparent that on the Don system of rivers in the fourteenth century Yeletsk was the furthermost Russian principality. The Tatar encampments began in what are now Don Cossack lands near that area where the Don is closest to the Volga.

Concerning the southwestern borders with Lithuania, it is known that during the time of Vasily Vladimirovich of Moscow[61] and Vytautas of Lithuania the Ugra river was designated as the border line, though this designation was one-sided. It also has been observed how Riazan determined its borders with Lithuania, but the process is totally incomprehensible. From the pacts and testaments of the princes it is known that Peremyshl, Likhvin (Lisin), Kozelsk and Trosna were considered to be Moscow dependencies. As for the lands of the princes in the service of others, such as Odoevsky, Belevsky and Vorotynsky, the borders are impossible to determine.

In the words of Ivan III himself these princes concurrently served his progenitors as well as those of Casimir of Lithuania. It is also known that the town of Odoev, for example, was divided into two halves, one belonging to the princes dependent on Moscow, the other to those dependent on Lithuania. From the negotiations between Moscow boyars and Lithuanian emissaries during the time of Ivan III, it is evident that the agreements made with Lithuania under Vasily Dmitrievich and his son Vasily the

Dark were disadvantageous to Moscow, for it had to cede territories which belonged to it according to previous agreements concluded during the time of Simeon the Proud and his brother Ivan II. During the time of Algirdas[62] half of Serensk belonged to Moscow and half to Lithuania. In the pact made between Vasily the Dark and Casimir it was agreed that the town of Kozelsk was to be "searched," that is, it was to be determined who possessed the town originally, but no search took place, and Kozelsk remained in the hands of Moscow. On the Smolensk side, that of the Upper Dnieper province, the Ugra river was the border between Moscow and Lithuania. Further north the border followed the watershed between the Dnieper and Volga basins.

The borders between Lithuania and Novgorod (including Pskov) were those that existed between the Smolensk and Polotsk principalities and Novgorod. As in the East there were territories here, such as Torzhok, Volok and Bezhichi, which were in joint possession by Novgorod and the princes of Vladimir. This was true in the South as well. Novgorod and the grand princes of Lithuania jointly held Velikie Luki, Rzheva (the Novgorod one) and some ten lesser territories. The actual lands belonged to Novgorod, but tribute and certain other income flowed to the Lithuanian grand prince. Just as there were two prince's agents[63] in Torzhok, one from Novgorod and one from Moscow, so were there two in Velikie Luki, one from Novgorod and one from Lithuania, each ruling his own half.

Clearly such conditions in Velikie Luki, Rzheva and other places were inherited by the Lithuanian princes from Smolensk, a principality which fell into their hands. The system of joint possession, in which a district belonged to one state but its tribute went to another, existed not only in the Novgorod provinces. The following is found in the pacts between Tver and Lithuania. "The borderlands which pertain to Lithuania or Smolensk but gave tribute to Tver shall be as they were in the past, just as those lands which pertain to Tver but gave tribute to Lithuania or Smolensk shall now pertain as before, and give tribute also as before."

The western borders, those of Pskov with the Livonian Order, coincided with the present borders of Pskov province with the Baltic region. As for Novgorod borders with Swedish holdings in Finland, we cannot determine them before 1323, from which time there stems a pact between Grand Prince Yury Danilovich and the Swedish king Magnus.[64] The pact states that Yury, along with Novgorod, ceded three Karelian districts, Savolaks, Eskis and Egrepia.[65] The borders could thus be determined.

There is also extant a listing of Novgorod districts in the Dvina region. They are Orlets, Matigory, Kholmogory, Kur island, Chiukhchelema, Ukht island, Kurgia, Kniazh island, Lisich island, Konechnye Dvory, Nenoksa, Una, Krivoy, Rakula, Navolok, Chelmakhta, Emets, Kaleia, Kiriia Gory, and Nizhniaia Toima. Of the Northern areas there is mentioned Velsk, Kubena, Sukhona, Kem, Andoma, Chukhloma, Kargopol, Kokshenga and Vaga. Of the Viatka towns, Orlov and Kotelnich are mentioned. The borders in the east are difficult to ascertain. We only know that there was a Russian town of Kurmysh, belonging to Nizhny Novgorod, on the Sura river.

II

CHANGES IN RELATIONS BETWEEN ELDER AND YOUNGER PRINCES

The historical expansion of Moscow and its growth at the expense of neighboring principalities now has been examined. And, along with the growth in strength there must have been a change in the relationship between the eldest prince and the younger. This change also will be examined historically by first looking at the relationship of the grand princes of Moscow and Vladimir with their closest relatives, the appanage princes,[1] then at their relationship with more distant relatives. These, as a result of the slackening of family ties, also called themselves grand princes within their districts and claimed rights equal to those of the grand princes of Vladimir, who nevertheless tried to bring them down to the level of their appanage princes whenever the opportunity arose. Such were the princes of Tver, Riazan and Nizhny Novgorod.

In their testaments the grand princes determined the relationships between the eldest and the younger sons in accordance with the old traditions. "I charge to you, my son Simeon," says Kalita, "your younger brothers and my princess with the small children. You will look after them before God."[2] "My children, younger brothers of Prince Vasily," wrote Donskoy, "honor and heed your brother Prince Vasily as you would me, your father. My son Prince Vasily is to keep his brother Yury and his younger brothers in brotherhood without harm."[3] In contrast to the testament of Kalita, we find an innovation in that of Donskoy. He gave his eldest son additional districts, singling him out for a senior role, the "path of the eldest."[4] Vasily Vasilievich in his testament gave a similar exhortation to his children on the relationship of the younger to the eldest.[5] Yet this period was one of transition from a system of family to that of rulership relations. The first was weakening but the second was not yet in full force. Therefore it is not surprising to find princes' testaments in which the relationship of the eldest and the younger princes is not mentioned at all. Such were the testaments of Prince Vladimir Andreevich[6] and Yury Dmitrievich.[7] It might be thought that since these testaments were written by younger, appanage princes, the relationships between the sons were not mentioned because they were all in the position of younger brothers in respect to the grand prince. In that case the duties of the sons to the grand prince would have been mentioned, instead no such reference is found. Thus Prince Vladimir Andreevich did make a distinction between his eldest and younger sons. To the eldest he assigned special districts, giving him the senior role. He also determined the duties of the sons to their mother, his wife, saying that they are to honor and heed her, that they are to live in accord and unison. Yet he did not add the old customary formula that they honor and heed the eldest brother as a father.

Now let us examine how the duties of the appanage princes with respect to the grand prince were defined in the pacts between them. In the pact of Kalita's sons the younger brothers call the eldest grand prince and lord, swear to live in unison until death and to hold and honor the eldest brother as they would their father. Whoever is an enemy to our eldest brother, they said, shall also be our enemy. Whoever is his friend shall be our friend. Neither the eldest without the younger, nor the younger without the eldest were to make pacts with anyone. If anyone sought to embroil them in quarrels they were to look into the matter, punish the guilty and not have enmity toward each other. The eldest was not to seize districts received by the younger from the father. "He must watch over their interests and not harm them." Whenever one of the younger died the eldest was to take care of the family of the deceased, not harm its members and not take districts received as inheritance from the father, nor was he to take away acquisitions and purchases. If the eldest mounted his steed (set off on a military campaign), the younger too must mount theirs. If the eldest did not go on a campaign himself but sent his younger brothers, they must go without disobedience. Should some misdeed occur, either on the part of the grand prince, or the younger princes, or a chiliarch or vicegerent of theirs, the princes must investigate the matter and not harbor anger toward each other.

In the pact of Dmitry Donskoy with his cousin Vladimir Andreevich important additions are encountered. The younger "brother" takes upon himself the obligation to regard the elder's position "respectfully" and "in dread," wishing him favor in all things. The grand prince obligated himself not to harm the appanage prince and to maintain brotherly relations. "You mind your patrimony and I will mind mine." Upon hearing either good or evil about the grand prince, his patrimony or all Christians, whether from a Christian or an infidel the younger, kissing the cross, must relate everything truthfully to the grand prince. These conditions were to be reciprocal. Both princes obligated themselves not to purchase villages in the other's appanage, to forbid the same to their boyars, and not to hold each other's indentured servants or quitrent farmers.[8] Nor were they to grant letters of privilege or patents. Should one prince have a claim against the subjects of another, the second prince was to rectify the matter. The younger was obligated to send his military commanders with those of the grand prince. Should a commander disobey, the grand prince might punish him along with his prince. If during a campaign an appanage prince chose to leave one of his boyars behind, he must report this to the grand prince. The two must come to a mutual decision as to who was to stay and who went on campaign. The younger must "serve" the eldest obediently according to the agreement, as is fitting and proper for the two of them. The grand prince in turn is obligated to be the benefactor of the appanage prince in accordance with his service. When both went to war the boyars and servants of the appanage prince must be under his banner, no matter where they might live. Should some difficulty arise between the two princes, they were to delegate their boyars to seek a solution. If the boyars could not settle the matter, they must seek out the metropolitan. Should no metropolitan reside in the Russian land they must seek a third party of their own choosing to decide the matter. When a prince lost a decision, his boyars were not responsible for that loss.

Vladimir Andreevich declined the senior position in favor of his nephew whom he agreed to acknowledge as his "eldest brother." Of course Vladimir remained Vasily Dmitrievich's uncle, therefore the agreement they concluded was rather favorable to Vladimir. He promised to regard his nephew, the "eldest brother, respectfully." The words "in fear" were omitted. The grand prince in turn took it upon himself to regard his uncle as he would a younger brother, to uphold brotherly relations and do him no harm. In a second agreement the aging uncle obtained the right not to go to war if his nephew the grand prince himself did not go. This second agreement is remarkable in the fact that both parties sought to affirm and extend their relations. Here for the first time princes, in pledging to fulfill the conditions of an agreement, swore an oath in their name and in the name of their children. In his testament Vladimir Andreevich entrusted his wife, children and boyars to his "elder brother" the grand prince. Should there be dissent among his sons they were to send their boyars to negotiate a solution. Should the boyars come to no agreement, they must seek the old widowed princess. Whichever son she finds in the wrong, from him the grand prince was to take indemnity in rectifying the matter. In doing so the grand prince must see that no loss occur to either the patrimony or the appanage of that prince. On the question of the use of the appanages Vladimir Andreevich specified that his sons must not enter each other's lands nor that of their mother for their "amusement," that is, hunting. Nor might they send constables into each other's appanages or conduct court proceedings therein.

Dmitry Donskoy readily could bend to his will his cousin, who had not the means to resist the master of two-thirds of the Moscow and all of the Vladimir principality. Besides, neither in Moscow nor Vladimir did the prince of Serpukhov have a right to seniority. In contrast, Vasily Dmitrievich was on totally different terms with his brothers, who had to be pleased and soothed in order for them to renounce seniority in favor of their nephew. Hereby it becomes clear why in the agreements between Vasily and his brothers the harsh expressions and outright stipulations of service of the appanage prince to the grand prince are missing, those that marked the agreements between Donskoy and Vladimir Andreevich. The younger brothers took upon themselves only the obligation of regarding Vasily as they would their father. In a separate agreement with his eldest brother Prince Yury Dmitrievich promised to hold Vasily merely as his senior. Neither the expression "respectfully and in fear" nor the obligation "to serve" occur.

Vasily Dmitrievich was unsuccessful in convincing his brother Yury to surrender seniority in favor of his nephew. This caused internecine strife during the reign of Vasily Vasilievich.[9] That strife ended with the triumph of the new order, the consolidation of appanages, yet while this strife endured the grand prince occasionally found himself in difficult straits and could not deal very harshly with the appanage princes. Thus Yury Dmitrievich, the uncle, under pressure to renounce seniority, called his nephew "elder brother," yet nevertheless concluded pacts with him as an equal without a definition of how he must regard the "elder brother." Yury also freed himself of the obligation of going to war even when the grand prince himself set off on campaign.

Concerning this circumstance, several conditions occur in the first pact. If Vasily Vasilievich went to war Yury must send his sons, boyars and servitors. If the grand prince sent his younger uncles or Yury's sons, Yury must send his sons with boyars and servitors. If the grand prince sent his commanders, Yury had to send only his commander and men. The second pact had several changes. When Vasily himself went to war or sent his uncle Konstantin, Yury was to send a son. If the grand prince sent his cousins or military commanders, Yury was to send only his military commanders. If the grand prince sent only Yury's son, he was to go without disobeying. The expression "respectfully and in fear" is not encountered in the pacts made during the early reign of Prince Vasily Vasilievich. It is absent even in the pacts with his cousins, the progeny of Andrei. It is encountered only in the pact with Prince Vasily Yaroslavich, the grandson of Vladimir Andreevich, but not found in the pact of the progeny of Andrei with Yury. After the death of Yury, it appears constantly in the pacts of Vasily Vasilievich and the appanage princes.

The pacts of the grand princes of Moscow with the grand princes of Tver and Riazan are similar to the pact of Grand Prince Vasily Vasilievich with his uncle Yury. The difference was that Yury, as an appanage prince, was not allowed direct contact with the Horde and must send his tribute through the grand prince. The princes of Tver and Riazan maintained relations with the Tatars totally independent of Moscow. As in the ancient expression, they personally "knew" the Horde. Even if a prince of Tver occasionally obligated himself to regard a prince of Moscow as "elder brother" such relations were not defined in further detail. In the event of war the pacts usually stipulated the following. When the grand prince of Moscow set off, the respective princes must also take part. If the Moscow prince sent his commanders, the respective princes must do the same. It is only in the pacts of Donskoy and his son Vasily with Mikhail of Tver that variations occurred. In the first pact the grand prince of Tver is required to go to war only if Vladimir Andreevich, the cousin of the Moscow prince, himself set off. "Should the khan or Tatar warriors come in war against us," the pact of Vasily Dmitrievich reads, "I myself will mount a steed along with my brothers, and you, brother, will in my aid send two of your sons and two nephews, leaving one son by your side.

Should the Lithuanians, Poles or Germans march against us, you are to send your sons and nephews in aid. Forage will be provided them, but they must not expect any other gain. Should the Tatars, Lithuanians or Germans march against you, I myself will come to your aid with my brothers. Should it be necessary for me to leave a brother behind for defense, I will leave one. As for communications with the Horde and the khan, the road is clear for you, your sons, grandsons and men." This pact was concluded on the basis of total equality. The prince of Tver had even more privileges than his Moscow counterpart. This is doubtless the result of the greater age of Mikhail Andreevich, who never was obliged to go to war in person.

The form of the pacts up to the time of Prince Vasily Dmitrievich did not vary and usually began with the words "Through the blessing of our father the metropolitan...." The first pact that began otherwise, "'Through the grace of God and the blessed Mother of God...," was that of Vasily Dmitrievich and Prince Mikhail of Tver. This formula began to appear continuously only from the time of Vasily the Dark, specifically in his pact with Prince Vasily Yaroslavich of Serpukhov. The above words are followed with "In all this (name and subject omitted) you are to kiss the cross to me (name omitted)." The pacts end with similar words. "In all this you are to kiss the cross to me as a sign of your love for the truth, without guile." When as a result of aforementioned ambitions the enmity between relatives, between the grand and appanage princes, reached an extreme, when peace was made only through necessity, with hatred in the heart and the intention to shatter peace at the first opportunity, stronger means of moral persuasion evolved in order to impel the maintenance of agreements. There appeared the so-called "pacts of sacred oath," which pacts and the strengthening of moral constraints did not achieve their goal. They merely are evidence of the intensification of the struggle which the participants pursued without discriminating among means or morals in their instinct for self-preservation. The princes' testaments usually began with a formula "In the name of the Father, the Son and the Holy Spirit. Here I, the sinful, unrighteous servant of God (name omitted) write my testament without duress, sound in mind and body."

STATE OF WOMEN IN THE PRINCELY FAMILY

It was noted when examining the distribution of princely lands that a significant part usually was left by the princes to their wives. Such rich bequests were commensurate with the strong moral and political influence bestowed upon wives in their husbands' testaments. Kalita in his testament places his wife and small children in the charge of his eldest son Simeon, who must be her caretaker in God. The testator asks nothing of his sons except that they take care of his wife because she, Princess Uliana, was only a stepmother to them. The degree to which a stepmother was alien to the sons of the first wife is evident in the fact that Ivan II, son of Kalita, never called his stepmother anything other than Princess Uliana, nor did he ever call her daughter his sister. This further explains the age-old attitude of the sons and grandsons of Mstislav the Great[10] to the son of his other wife, Vladimir, "the stepmother's son."[11] Totally different were the relations of sons to their true mothers as determined in the princes' testaments. "You, my children," Donskoy charged his sons, "live in unison, obey your mother in all things. Should one of my sons die, the princess will divide his appanage among the rest. Whatever she gives to each, that is what he shall have. My children shall remain under her will. Should God grant me another son, the princess will provide for him, taking a share from each of his elder brothers. Should one of my sons lose part of his patrimony, that which I gave him, the princess will recompense him with shares from the others. You, my children, obey your mother. Should God take my son Prince Vasily, his appanage shall go to my second son. The princess then will divide the appanage of the second son among my other sons. You, my children, obey your mother. Whatever she gives to each, that is what is his. I have charged my sons to my princess. You, my children, obey your mother in all things, do not overstep her will in anything. Whichever son does not obey his mother, my blessing will not be on him."

The agreement between Grand Prince Vasily Dmitrievich and his brothers began "In the word and blessing of our mother Avdotia." Into his agreement with his brother Yury, Vasily entered this condition. "Our mother we must hold in filial respect and honor." Vasily Dmitrievich charged his son to hold his mother in filial respect and honor, as God commanded. In another testament he obliged his son to honor his mother just as he had honored his father. Prince Vladimir Andreevich of Serpukhov gave his wife the right of final arbitration in disagreements among his sons, whom he ordered to revere and obey their mother. Vasily the Dark ordered his sons to do likewise. Concerning widowed princesses and their daughters these instructions are encountered in the testament of Vladimir Andreevich. "Should God take any one of my sons, leaving a wife who does not marry, let her and her children remain in her husband's appanage. When she dies, the appanage is to go to her son, my grandson. If a daughter is left, all my sons will marry off the daughter of their brother and equally share his appanage. Should she not have any children at all, let my daughter-in-law remain in her husband's appanage praying for my soul until her death. Until her death my sons are not to enter the appanage of their brother in any way."

It has been noted that the districts left to princesses were divided into those of which they could not dispose freely in their testaments, and those which they could, the so-called "widow's portion." There was another category of districts in the Moscow principality, those assigned for the maintenance of princesses and always remaining in their possession. They were called the princesses' "old holdings." In his testament Grand Prince Vasily Dmitrievich mentions them in these instructions. "As for the princess's old holdings, they belong to her, and she is to have them until my son marries. After that she must give to the princess of my son, her daughter-in-law, those villages which have been the princess's since times of yore."

A princess was the absolute proprietress of such districts. Dmitry Donskoy left instructions concerning the matter. "To the extent that the free district officials functioned as judges under me, so shall they do under my princess. If in those districts, settlements and villages which I took from the appanages of my sons and gave my princess, a peasant has a grievance against the district official, my princess will look into and remedy the matter, and my sons are not to interfere." Vladimir Andreevich left these instructions. "My sons are not to send their constables to, or judge the town collectors of excise, sales tax or general customs. Her own customs collectors and general customs collectors shall be judged by my princess."

The clergy, in the name of religion, supported the relations between sons and mothers as determined in the prince's testaments. Metropolitan Jonas[12] wrote the following to princes who seized lands from their mothers that were bequeathed to them. "Children! Your mother, and my daughter, has grieved to me against you, she complains about you that you have seized districts from her which your father gave her as a widow's portion[13] to live on. You he gave separate appanages. In this, children, you perform an act that is against God, to the perdition of your souls both here and in the afterlife... I bless you that you may petition your mother and ask forgiveness of her, and that you may accord her customary honor. Obey her in everything and do not offend her. Let her rule over what is hers, and you over what is yours, as your father willed. Make written response to us how you have settled with your mother. We will pray to God for you in our holy duty and in your pure repentance. Should you again offend and insult your mother I can do nothing other than myself, in fear of God and in my holy duty, send for my son, your bishop and for other many priests and, upon consulting together with them concerning God's laws, having conversed and deliberated, we will impose upon you a spiritual burden of the church, an opprobrium that will be mine and that of the other priests."

SERVICE PRINCES

Such were the relations among princes in Northeastern Rus. It can be seen that the transformation of relations from those of family to those of a realm, the transformation of appanage princes from relatives into service princes as reflected in pacts and agreements, occurred very slowly. This was due to the long tenure of familial relations and the fact that in this transformation the grand princes had to increase their power at the expense of very close relatives who insisted on maintenance of old familial forms in the determination of relations through agreements. Of course these relations changed with changing reality. Through new needs and new concepts the familial forms themselves were altered, clearly showing the atrophy of old relations. In this way, for example, the expressions encountered in the pacts of the period "to regard as an uncle, regard as a nephew, to regard as an equal brother" held no meaning in a framework of older true family relations of fathers and sons, uncles and nephews, elder and younger brothers. The obligation of the appanage prince—service to the grand prince—and the obligation of the grand prince to support the appanage prince in accordance with his services is mentioned once in the agreement of Dmitry Donskoy with his cousin Vladimir Andreevich and then disappears because Donskoy's son, Vasily Dmitrievich, and his grandson, Vasily Vasilievich, found themselves in a less advantageous position with respect to their relatives. Even the rather indefinite expression "to hold the grand principality respectfully and in fear" is insisted upon infrequently in the pacts.

The agreements of service princes with those into whose service they entered have not come down to us from Northeastern Rus, though there are ample numbers of such pacts from the Southwest. In 1448 Prince Fedor Lvovich Vorotynsky, receiving the town of Kozelsk as vicegerent of Casimir, king of Poland and grand prince of Lithuania,[14] entered his

master's service without "servility" or "guile." In 1455 Casimir wrote that
he gave a patrimony to Vorotynsky, having observed his faithful service.
The pact of the princes of Novosil and Odoev with Casimir began with
the princes' supplication to the grand prince that he admit them into his
service. He accepted them and they swore to serve Casimir faithfully,
without guile, to obey his will in all respects, to pay him an annual tribute and to hold the same friends and enemies. In turn Casimir promised
to respect them, keep them in good will and defend them from all enemies. He further obligated himself and his heirs not to break the pact or
intrude into the princes' patrimony. Should such infraction occur princes
would be released from their oath and become free. He promised them
fair trial and justice. His arbiters were to meet with those of the princes
and, upon kissing the cross, were to settle matters honestly. If the arbiters could not agree the matter was to be taken to the grand prince for resolution. Conflicts between the princes also were to be resolved by Casimir.

It is illuminating to compare the testament of Algirdas's grandson
Prince Andrei Vladimirovich with the testaments of the Moscow princes.
These written documents, as all others, are marked by distinctions peculiar to the character of the nations in which they were written. Both the
Moscow and the Southern Rus testaments begin with the words "In the
name of the Father, the Son and the Holy Spirit." The Moscow testaments, as we have seen, continue with a statement that the testator is of
sound mind and body, a comment necessary to give the testament full
force. Then without further circumlocution the provisions of the will are
laid out. The testament of Andrei Vladimirovich does not mention mental or physical well-being. Instead he speaks at some length of how he,
his wife and children came to Kiev to pray to God, how he devotedly
visited all the holy places, was blessed by Archimandrite Nikolay, prayed
at the graves of his kinsfolk and at those of the holy fathers and pondered
in his heart how many graves there were, and yet all these deceased once
lived on this earth and were now gone to God. Having reflected that he
too is bound to join his forefathers, the prince thought it appropriate to
write his testament.

PRINCELY TITLES

It has been remarked that previously "prince" was the general, inalienable title of all the progeny of Riurik, the eldest having the title of "grand
prince." It was also noted that the title "grand" occasionally was given
to a younger prince in respect and overabundant zeal on the part of a

given correspondent. In the period under consideration, with its weakening of familial ties and the striving of princes for autonomy, there are encountered, as expected, many princes who simultaneously dignified themselves with the epithet "grand." Such expectations proved to be true. The Moscow princes bore this title legitimately, having the throne of Vladimir as their constant heritage. Still, the princes of Tver and Riazan also referred to themselves as "grand." The princes of Pronsk, of the Riazan family, did the same in their continuous striving for independence. Even the lesser appanage princes who never dared call themselves "grand" in official documents, are so termed in unofficial writings. Thus St. Cyril of Beloozero[15] in his testament gives the title of "grand prince" to Andrei Dmitrievich, the appanage prince of Mozhaisk!

Previously, when familial relations rather than holdings were of foremost importance, the eldest prince naturally was counterbalanced by his younger brothers. Later, with the disintegration of familial ties and the ascendancy of status and holdings as the basis for relations, titles came to be a counterbalancing factor for the younger, appanage princes. It is known that even in early times certain princes, such as Monomakh and Yury Dolgoruky, held the title of grand prince of All Rus. In the period under consideration official documents relate that Ivan Kalita and his successors had that title. Among the early encountered princely titles there is "lord" and the somewhat later "sovereign."[16] The derivation of the first title suggests that it had the same meaning as the word "prince." The word "sovereign" signified the head or father of a family.[17] It should be noted that the first title was used more in the South and the second prevailed in the North. "Lord" and "sovereign" can be found in conjunction, as in the following example. "For we, lord grand prince, your impoverished subjects have no means of resisting those who do us harm, except for God, O Lord, and the Blessed Mother of God and your kindness and graciousness, our lord and sovereign."

The fact that the meaning of "sovereign" was much more important than the meaning of the earlier "lord" is borne out by the tenacious resistance of the men of Novgorod to its introduction in place of "lord." "Sovereign" was set off in opposition to the service princes. "Whomever one serves, he goes with his sovereign." Other titles used to designate the grand princes were "grand sovereign of the land," "great Russian sovereign" and "grand sovereign autocrat." The most complete title of the Moscow princes, used in foreign relations, is encountered in a pact with

Casimir of Poland. "Through the will of God, our love and God's mercy I, Grand Prince Vasily Vasilievich of Moscow and Novgorod and Rostov and Perm and other lands...." As before, all subjects and the whole population are set off from the princes by the term "black people,"[18] free peasants who lived on lands not belonging to manors or the church.

PRINCELY SEALS

The authentic princes' documents that have reached us have seals affixed, bearing various representations and inscriptions. Ivan Kalita's seal has a representation of Jesus Christ on one side and that of St. John on the other. It is bordered with the inscription "Seal of Grand Prince Ivan." The seal of Simeon the Proud has St. Simeon on one side and the inscription "Seal of Grand Prince Simeon of *All Rus*" on the other. The seal of his brother Ivan II has a representation of St. John with the inscription "Hagios Ioann"[19] on one side and the inscription, "Seal of Grand Prince Ivan Ivanovich," on the other. That of Dmitry Donskoy has the representation of St. Demetrius[20] on one side and "Seal of Grand Prince Dmitry," on the other, but another seal of Dmitry's bears the additional words *of All Rus*. Vasily Dmitrievich had several seals. One bore the image of St. Basil of Caesarea[21] and the inscription "Seal of Grand Prince Vasily Dmitrievich of All Rus." Another seal had the representation of a horseman with lance reversed, a third that of a horseman with a raised sword. There were other seals as well. A horseman at rest with the lance held vertically appeared on the seal of Vasily the Dark, while the seal of Prince Boris Alexandrovich also bore an image of a horseman with a raised sword.

ENTHRONEMENT

The accession of a prince in these times was accompanied by a particular ritual of enthronement. Here is a description of the enthronement of Alexander Nevsky in Vladimir. "His Eminence Metropolitan Cyril met him with crosses, with the consecrated assembly[22] and a multitude of others, and enthroned him in his grand princely rule in Vladimir, on the throne of his father, with the *sanction of the tsar* (meaning khan)." Grand Prince Vasily Dmitrievich was enthroned by an envoy of Tokhtamysh. Vasily Vasilievich was enthroned, in turn, by another envoy of the khan at the church of the Mother of God before the Golden gates. This ritual clearly indicated the dependence of the Russian princes on the Tatar khans.

RELATIONS WITH TATARS

In order adequately to determine the significance and status of the grand prince in Rus the degree of his dependence on the khan must be ascertained. Was this dependence limited to asking for the khan's sanction, his entitlement, to the obligation of paying tribute, or did it influence, and thus restrict, the prince's domestic actions? Here it must first be determined how the khan kept the activities of the prince under surveillance, whether he had a representative of his constantly with the prince. In the well known account in the chronicles concerning Akhmat, the Tatar baskak in Kursk, it also is stated that there were baskaks in other towns throughout the Russian land and that their power was great.[23] In the narrative of the martyrdom of St. Michael of Chernigov[24] it is said that Batu placed his deputies and lords in all the Russian towns. In a census report it is written that Tatar officials placed ruling officials of appropriate ranks in various locales and, having set everything in order, returned to the Horde. An entry in the chronicles for 1262 states that there were gatherings in protest against the Tatars whom Batu and later his son Sartak placed as lords in all the Russian towns. The princes, having come to an agreement among themselves, expelled the Tatars on account of their great abuses. The rich in their avarice bought from the Tatars the rights to collect tribute, while the poor had to labor under usurious rates.[25] It was during the expulsion and killing of the Tatars that the apostate Zosima (or Izosima), who with the permission of the khan did great evil to Christians, was killed.[26] In 1269 Grand Prince Yaroslav, in preparing a campaign against the Germans, came to Novgorod with Amragan, the grand baskak of Vladimir. Later Grand Prince Vasily Yaroslavich campaigned against Novgorod with that same Amragan. An entry for 1275 mentions the second census-taking and one for 1290 describes an uprising against the Tatars in the town of Rostov.

After the entry about Amragan no further mention is made of baskaks in the North. One is encountered in the southern province of Kursk, but only once, in an entry for the year 1284. This is a clear sign that there were no more baskaks in the North, otherwise the chroniclers would not have remained silent about them when they described events in which the Tatars took an important part, such as the struggle among the sons of Nevsky. In that description only Tatar envoys, temporarily appearing in Russian towns, are mentioned. No census-taking is ever described after 1275, a clear indication that the Tatars, for various reasons, began fully to trust the Russian princes, who assumed responsibility for the delivery of tribute to the Horde. Nevertheless in an entry for 1266 the chronicles still speak of devastation as a result of Tatar abuses upon the death of Khan Berke.[27] At the same time we find that Prince Andrei Alexandrovich of Gorodets accused his older brother, Dmitry of Pereiaslavl, of not paying tribute to the Horde. Had there been at this time a baskak, or a chief collector of tribute[28] in Russia, it would not have been his own brother who informed on Dmitry, nor would the khan have based himself solely on these denunciations. If Tatar officials were involved in this matter, why where they left unmentioned by the chronicles when the Tatar envoy Kavgady[29] was mentioned? Thus through the removal of baskaks, census-takers and collectors of tribute, the princes were totally freed from Tatar influence in their domestic affairs. Even during the presence of baskaks there is no basis for assuming they had any great sway on domestic affairs, for there is not the slightest evidence of such influence.

In the Southwest the most detailed description of an enthronement is provided by a Volhynian chronicle that relates the enthronement of Mstislav Danilovich in Vladimir, the principality left him by his cousin Vladimir Vasilkovich. Mstislav arrived at the cathedral, gathered the boyars and citizens, Rus and others, and had Vladimir's testament read to them. All heard it, from the greatest to the least. After this the bishop with a holy cross blessed Mstislav to rule. Here, in the South, the inhabitants of Brest refused to obey Vladimir's will and acknowledge Mstislav as their prince. Nothing of the kind is ever encountered in the North, nor is there any documentation of bargaining or compacts of citizens with princes, nor is there documentation of princes calling a popular assembly and announcing a military campaign. As before, the princes most often led their troops themselves, without delegating military commanders, but in none of them is evident the belligerence noted among the princes of ancient Southern Rus.

LEGISLATIVE POWER OF PRINCES

The lawmaking activity of the Northern princes is reflected in the statute charter written by Grand Prince Vasily Dmitrievich for the province of Dvina, the judicial charter given to Pskov by Grand Prince Alexander Mikhailovich and the statutes of Konstantin Dmitrievich for the same city. In 1395 Metropolitan Cyprian[30] wrote to the residents of Pskov "I have heard that the bishop of Suzdal, Dionisy, during his visit to Pskov, wrote a charter and appended to the charter of Grand Prince Alexander the laws that are to be followed, how laws are to be executed, and how men should be punished, adding a damnation upon anyone who acted otherwise. Bishop Dionisy exceeded his authority in this, overstepping law and regulations. If Grand Prince Alexander set forth laws to be followed, *it was his right, as it is the right of each tsar in his tsardom and each prince in his principality, to decide all manner of affairs and write charters.* Thus Grand Prince Alexander held the right to issue a charter of laws to follow for the good of Christendom, but *Bishop Dionisy has meddled in matters which do not concern him.* He wrote an unlawful charter which I strike out. You, my children, residents of Pskov, follow the charter of Grand Prince Alexander as you did before. As for Dionisy's charter, send it to me. I will tear it up myself. That charter is invalid. As for the damning and denial of the patriarch's blessing that he wrote there, I remove it and bless you. Follow the laws, children, that you did before, and execute them in the old way. Should you pardon a guilty man, you are free to do so. Should you punish him for his guilt, you are free to do so. Do things as you did them before, with pure heart and without sin, as all Christians do."

Concerning the princes' right to hold trials and mete out punishment, the following appears in a pact between Dmitry Donskoy and his cousin Vladimir Andreevich of Serpukhov. "You are not to hold trials in Moscow without my vicegerents," writes Donskoy. "Should I hold trials in Moscow, we will do so together. If by chance I am out of Moscow and one Muscovite grieves against another, I will send a constable to your vicegerents so that they can settle the matter together. Should someone of the grand principality grieve against a Muscovite, against one of your boyars, I will send a constable for him, and you are to send one of your boyars. If one of my people grieves against one of yours, who lives in your appanage, I will send someone to you and you will decide the matter. Should one of your men grieve against one of mine, who lives in my appanage and in the grand principality, you will send someone to me, and I will decide the matter. The men to be sent are to be our boyars."

FINANCES

It has been noted that within a certain span of time Russia freed itself of Tatar census-takers, the princes themselves collecting tribute and delivering it to the Horde. The pact between Dmitry Donskoy and Vladimir Andreevich of Serpukhov provides information on how the tribute was actually collected in the holdings of the progeny of Kalita. "If I have to send my collectors into the town, or to ferrying places, or the districts of

Princess Uliana," wrote the Grand Prince, "you are to send your collectors along with mine, but I am not to send my collectors into your appanage." Consequently it is evident that each prince collected tribute independently in his own appanage and then turned it over to the grand prince for delivery to the Horde. In another pact between the same two princes it is written "Whatever our tribute collectors gather in town (Moscow), in the environs and the saltworks, shall go into my treasury (that of the grand prince), and then I will pay tribute."

After the cessation of census-taking the amount of tribute obviously depended on an agreement between the grand princes and the Tatars. Doubtless the grand princes from the very first offered the Tatars a greater sum of money than that gathered by the Tatar collectors and their tax-farmers. Later this sum changed as a result of various conditions. Thus it has been remarked that occasionally princes, in vying for entitlement from the Horde, increased the amount of tribute. Mamay demanded of Dmitry Donskoy the tribute his ancestors paid to Khans Uzbek and Janibek,[31] but Dmitry would agree only to the sum on which he and Mamay most recently settled. The invasion of Tokhtamysh and the captivity at the Horde of the prince's son Vasily later forced Donskoy to pay an enormous tribute.[32] A great tribute was paid by the whole principality of Moscow, wrote the chronicler. A half-ruble was taken from the lesser villages, and even gold was sent to the Horde.

In his testament Dmitry mentions a tribute of a thousand rubles from all the districts belonging to his sons. The share of each of the five appanages was Kolomna 342 rubles, Zvenigorod 272, Mozhaisk 235, Dmitrov 111, the appanage of Prince Ivan 10. The share that fell upon Serpukhov, the appanage of Vladimir Andreevich, of course was not in the testament. The historian is thus deprived of the opportunity to compare the Serpukhov appanage with others of the Moscow principality in terms of tribute, and consequently of material means. Serpukhov's share was determined later in a pact between Grand Prince Vasily Dmitrievich and his uncle[33] Vladimir Andreevich, and is also mentioned in Vladimir's testament. It consisted of 320 rubles, but the total amount of tribute paid the Tatars, as listed in the two documents, was five thousand rubles. In yet a second pact between them, the total tribute is listed as seven thousand rubles.

From these same sources it is known that the principality of Nizhny Novgorod paid fifteen hundred rubles in tribute. The individual shares of the five appanages into which Serpukhov was divided upon the death of

Vladimir Andreevich are also known. The princess paid 88 rubles from her holdings, the prince of Serpukhov 48.5, the prince of Borovsk 33, the prince of Yaroslavl 76, the prince of Radonezh 42, and the prince of Peremyshl 41. From Gorodets Princes Semeon and Yaroslav paid 160 rubles of the total of 1,500 that was the Nizhny Novgorod tribute, with Uglich contributing 105 rubles. The relatively small share of Prince Semeon of Borovsk, 33 rubles, gives us pause. It is also intriguing that the means of Gorodets alone exceeded that of both Borovsk and Yaroslavl, the appanages of Princes Semeon and Yaroslav.

The prescribed levy which each appanage contributed to the total tribute did not include the extraordinary tribute which the princes took from their greater and richer boyars according to their holdings and the grants given them by the princes. The expression "according to grants and holdings," the fact that tribute taken from the city of Moscow and its environs was distinct from a census-oriented poll tax, the expression "imposing tribute on districts according to the people's ability to pay," and the expression "to draw tribute according to the lands and waters" all show that tribute was not based on a poll. "As my children take up life in their appanages," wrote Grand Prince Vasily Vasilievich in his testament, "my princess and children shall send scribes who will detail their appanages upon kissing the cross and impose a tribute according to plows and population. According to this levy the princess and children will make payment to my son Ivan for tribute." Edigey,[34] in a letter to Grand Prince Vasily Dmitrievich,[35] accused him of taking tribute of one ruble from every two plows throughout his holdings, sending none of this silver to the Horde. Variations in the total amount of tribute were anticipated by standard provisions in the princes' pacts such as "Should more or less tribute come, it shall be taken commensurately." From the time of Donskoy a standard item appears in the agreements and testaments of princes, the provision that should God deliver them from the Horde the princes were to keep the tribute collected from their appanages for themselves, sending none of it to the grand prince. Thus they maintained the equality of kinship as opposed to the subservient state of subjects, most sharply marked by the tribute which the princes of Western Rus already were paying to the grand prince of Lithuania.

Besides the general tribute there were costs and burdens of another nature imposed by the Tatars, such as the obligation to provide transportation for Tatar officials,[36] to maintain the Tatar envoys and their enormous predatory suites. Finally, there were the princes' visits to the Horde, where gifts must be made to the khan, his wives, grandees and anyone of the slightest significance. It is not surprising that the princes were occasionally short of funds and had to borrow from the Horde's Muslim[37] merchants. Later, to repay them, they were forced to borrow from their own Russian merchants. It is from here that stems the division of princes' debts into the categories of Muslim and Russian. Yury Dmitrievich, prince of Zvenigorod,[38] wrote the following in a pact with his nephew Vasily Vasilievich. "I have borrowed six hundred rubles from leading merchants and cloth dealers[39] and have paid your Horde debt to Rezep-Khozia and Abip, signing for it in good faith. You may strike this six-hundred-ruble debt to me, but deal with the merchants on your own. I will only give you the names of those men from whom I borrowed the money." It is evident that when the means of the grand prince exceeded those of the appanage princes he not infrequently dealt kindly with them, temporarily permitting them to intermit tribute from a whole appanage or some part of it.

WEALTH OF PRINCES

Tribute went into the princes' coffers only when there were no demands from the Horde, or rather when the princes felt it possible not to meet the demands. The constant source of the princes' income continued to be trade duties and court taxes as well as profits coming from private domains. Trade duties usually were specified in the princes' pacts. The princes customarily requested of each other that no new trade duties be considered. The old, usual trade duties were collected on the basis of a denga from a cart and a fraction of a denga from a man. When someone passed without a cart but on horseback for purposes of trade, he also paid a denga. If someone evaded the trade duty collector he was to pay six altyns per cart and again as much as indemnity, no matter how many carts there might be. Deliberate driving around the duty collection station constituted evasion of payment. When someone drove past the station and no duty collector was there, this was not illegal. Should a duty collector catch up to the merchant, he was to pay the standard duty but no fine or indemnity. The duty on vessels was one altyn from a boat and two from a raft. A customs tax was imposed at the rate of one altyn per ruble but only when someone was engaged in vending. If someone merely drove by, he was to pay only the appropriate trade duty. If someone drove past without merchandise, he was to pay neither trade duty nor taxes of any kind.

Besides these taxes sources mention quite a few others. These included a tax on merchants for use of warehouses, a tax on the weight of goods normally handled in bulk, a fee for weighing goods, a tax on cast silver objects, a tax on fur, a fine for evading sales tax, a fee for mooring vessels at shore, a fee for branding horses, a tax on produced salt, usually paid in kind, a charge for safekeeping of goods, a tax on honey, a tax on fisheries, a tax on mowed hay, a tax on the proceeds of commercial associations such as those of hunters, a tax on the manufacture of clothing.[40] The following court taxes are mentioned. Various fines paid by the guilty, a fine for the possession of stolen property,[41] escheat, the reversion of property to the prince for lack of heirs,[42] a fine for thievery, a fee for an appeal to a higher court. Finally a marriage fee is mentioned, the so-called newlyweds' marten skin.

In the time period described there is no mention of two other sources of princes' income which appear in the well-known charter of Prince Rostislav of Smolensk.[43] This practice of princes traversing their holdings, holding legal procedures and accepting gifts is mentioned as early as the writings of Constantine Porphyrogennetos.[44] It is also encountered in the chronicles of the end of the twelfth century. Then the terms disappear, but it is unclear when or whether the tradition disappeared. The problem remains impossible to resolve.

It has been noted how rich the princes were in land. The produce of these lands served not only to supply the court but was sold as well, as indicated by a provision in a pact with a Riazan prince freeing the grand princes' tradesmen from paying trade duty. There are also contemporary sources describing a kind of quitrent which men settled on the princes' lands paid twice a year, in spring and on St. George's day in the autumn [November 26].[45]

One of the most important sources of income was beekeeping and processing of honey. Princes constantly mention this in their pacts and testaments. The princes' saltworks are mentioned as next in importance, the so-called Sol [saltworks] in the province of Galich, Velikaia Sol in Nerekhta, near the town of Yuriev, and Rostovskaia Sol in Rostov. The princes had saltworks in Gorodets on the Volga as well. The importance of commercial fishing is suggested in the testament of Prince Vladimir Andreevich of Serpukhov. He tells two of his sons to construct a fishery below Gorodets and share equally in the catch. Beaver trapping was a most important activity. The princes even had a special name for the men engaged in it.[46] The fact that beavers at that time were found even near

Moscow is attested in the will of Prince Vladimir Andreevich which bequeathed some beaver trappers in the Moscow environs to the eldest son.

The income from trapping and passion for hunting led the princes to place great value on hunting and fowling rights. Simeon the Proud, in respect to his seniority, demanded that his brothers cede both these rights to him in the environs of Moscow. Originally they were granted to all the princes. In his testament Vladimir Andreevich forbade each of his sons to hunt in the appanage of another without permission. That dogs were used in hunting is attested by the name given the hunters, "houndsmen."[47] In fowling, special nets were used as well. The princes sent their men in teams[48] to the White Sea and the Arctic Ocean, into the Terek and Pechora regions, for fish, game and fowl. It is known from a charter of Grand Prince Andrei Alexandrovich that already at that time three such groups had reached the sea, each under the leadership of its chief.[49] In his time Ivan Kalita gave a charter of privileges to the Pechora falconers.

The princes' testaments and agreements also speak of "horse rights," the right to keep and pasture horses. Ivan Kalita bequeathed one herd of horses to Simeon and another to Ivan. The rest were to be divided equally among his wife and remaining sons. Simeon the Proud left his wife fifty riding horses and two herds. Ivan II bequeathed to each of his sons a half of his herds, stallions, colts and mares. Dmitry Donskoy divided his herds among his wife and sons. Vladimir Andreevich of Serpukhov bequeathed his whole riding herd—stallions, hinnies and colts—and his brood mares to his wife. Finally gardens with a given number of gardeners attached were another source of income for princes.

It has been observed that princes used the remnants of their income to acquire immovable property. A rather complete picture of what their movable property consisted can be drawn from their testaments. Ivan Kalita left behind him twelve golden chainlets, three golden waistbands, a large waistband with pearls and precious stones, a gold waistband with fasteners, a carnelian waistband edged in gold, a foreign-made gold waistband with pearls and precious stones, a waistband of gold hooked on silk, and a specially magnificent gold waistband. He also left two gold chalices with pearls, two gold drinking vessels, two round gold cups, two golden goblets, a small gold dish with pearls and precious stones, ten silver dishes, two large and two somewhat smaller gold ladles and a golden box. His first wife left fourteen bracelets, a necklace, a worked necklet, a headpiece and a breastpiece. Kalita also mentions silver vessels and gold items he acquired. The fine garments left to the children by Kalita were a leather coat with gold and pearls, a leather coat strung with pearls, two leather coats with precious stones and pearls, a grand robe with a stole, a mantle of sable with shoulder coverlets decorated with pearls and precious stones, a robe of expensive scarlet fabric decorated with pearls, with a broad stole-collar of black silk overlaid with jewels and a coronet of gold. All this movable property was divided among Kalita's three sons and wife. The effects of the first wife went to her daughter. The share of Prince Andrei Ivanovich of Serpukhov went to his son Vladimir. Simeon the Proud willed everything to his wife. She passed only a few items on to Grand Prince Ivan II, who left three icons, five golden chainlets, three of which had crosses, one golden coronet, one stole, four waistbands, two of which had pearls and precious stones, two golden sabres, two gold sashes, two pearl earrings, two maces of gold with precious stones and pearls, three gold drinking vessels, two large golden dippers, a box made of carnelian edged with gold, a silver pail decorated with silver castings, a light caftan of scarlet fabric decorated with pearls, a pectoral with pearls, a round golden shoulder and breast piece made of rings and decorated with precious stones and pearls, a small pectoral with pearls, a gold cup and a Byzantine glass encased in worked gold. To each of his future sons-in-law the grand prince left a gold chainlet and a waistband of gold.

Dmitry Donskoy left one icon, one chain, eight waistbands, a stole, a golden coronet, a cloak with pearls and stones, gold adornments, a shoulder coverlet, a pectoral and two golden dippers.

Vasily Dmitrievich left his son large crucifixes,[50] the cross of Patriarch Philotheos, an icon executed by the master Paramsha, a cross chain, a gold coronet, a stole-collar, three waistbands, a box of carnelian, a golden dipper of Simeon the Proud, a vessel edged in gold, a stone vessel that was a gift of Vytautas, and a crystal goblet gift of the king of Poland. Yury Dmitrievich, the appanage prince of Zvenigorod, left three icons framed in gold, three waistbands and a large platter.

Grand Princess Sophia Vitovtovna left a chest of relics, an icon in a frame of mosaic, an icon of the blessed Mother of God with a shroud and headcloth, an icon of St. Cosmas and St. Damian, and an icon of St. Theodore Stratilatus worked in sheet silver. She also left two chests of oak, large and small, as well as a coffer and a box with crosses, icons and relics.

Grand Prince Vasily the Dark left five golden crosses among which was one of Peter the Miracle Worker,[51] one done by Paramsha, another formerly belonging to Patriarch Philotheus. He also left an icon of gold and one of emeralds, a coronet, a stole-collar, a carnelian box and two waistbands.

It is evident from this listing that the movable property of the Moscow princes did not increase since Kalita. On the contrary, it diminished. The meagerness of the bequeathed items is especially striking in the testaments of Donskoy, his son and grandson. This impoverishment can be ascribed, first of all, to the division of property among sons and its passing to daughters. A second reason was the desire of the princes to increase their immovable rather than movable property. There were other reasons such as the invasion of Tokhtamysh and the subsequent demands of the Horde, the great cost of acquiring the rights to Nizhny Novgorod and Murom from the Horde during the reign of Vasily Dmitrievich, the internecine strife during the reign of Vasily Vasilievich and, finally, the fact that both Vasily Kosoy and Shemiaka robbed the Moscow treasury.

Beginning with the testament of Kalita the golden coronet is constantly willed to the eldest son, though Kalita left the stole-collar and prince's garments to sons other than the elder. Only with the testament of Ivan II does the stole-collar always appear in the lists of garments willed to the eldest son as does the edged-in-gold carnelian box. Kalita does mention a gold box which he left to his princess and daughters. The bequeathing of icons first appears in the testament of Ivan II. It is unusual that weapons—the two gold sabres—as well as the two earrings are found among the possessions of only this prince. The testament of Dmitry Donskoy lists very few garments. Those of Vasily Dmitrievich and Vasily the Dark list none at all.

The movable property of the Southwestern princes apparently consisted of much the same items. It is known, for instance, that Prince Vladimir Vasilievich of Volhynia distributed all his possessions among the poor before his death, gold, silver, precious stones, gold and silver waistbands, both his and those of his father. He melted down the large silver platters and gold and silver goblets into grivnas, and did the same with the gold necklaces of his mother and grandmother.

III

SOCIAL RELATIONS

LIFE OF A RUSSIAN PRINCE IN THE NORTH AND SOUTH
During this time the life of a Russian prince in the North or South differed little from that of previous Russian princes. It is noticeable that the old "princely" names disappear from use and are replaced by names taken from the Greek calendar of saints. The old Slavic names remaining are those of Orthodox Slavic princes who became saints, such as Vladimir, Boris, Gleb and Vsevolod.[1] Among the progeny of Konstantin Vsevolodovich only one Mstislav is encountered. Only one Yaroslav and one Sviatoslav are found among the progeny of Yaroslav Vsevolodovich.[2] The old "princely" names are encountered more in the provinces that were once part of old Rus, namely Smolensk, Riazan or Chernigov.

If the tradition of giving princes the old Slavic pagan names died, nevertheless the tradition of giving them two names, though both were not taken from the calendar of saints, remained. Thus it is known that the son of Vasily the Dark had two names, Ivan and Timofey, though only the first was used. Frequently members of the clergy were godfathers to the princes. Bishop Vasily [Kalika][3] of Novgorod travelled to Pskov for the christening of Mikhail, son of Alexander Mikhailovich of Tver,[4] while Metropolitan Alexis[5] christened Prince Ivan Borisovich of Nizhny Novgorod.[6] St. Sergius of Radonezh[7] christened Dmitry Donskoy's son Yury.[8] Nikon, abbot of the Holy Trinity monastery and successor to St. Sergius,[9] christened Dmitry, son of Prince Vasily Mikhailovich of Kashin.[10] The boy's grandmother, Grand Princess Evdokia,[11] was godmother. Zinovy, another abbot of the same monastery,[12] christened Ivan, the son of Vasily the Dark.

A great multitude came to a prince's christening, including kinsmen-princes, their wives, brothers, children and boyars. The ritual of hair-cutting[13] was maintained. Concerning the upbringing of princes, it is known that Prince Mikhail Alexandrovich of Tver travelled to his god-father Bishop Vasily of Novgorod[14] to learn letters. The young prince was then seven years of age. Governors or tutors often are listed among a prince's boyars. The princes married between the ages of fourteen and twenty. As in times of old, the weddings were marked by great feasts. The marriage ceremony was performed in the town where the bride's father ruled. The first feast was there, then all the guests and relatives went to another feast hosted by the bridegroom's father.

Gleb Vasilievich, prince of Rostov, married his son Mikhail to the daughter of Prince Fedor Rostislavich of Yaroslavl in this way. The wedding took place in Yaroslavl, where the groom's father and many other princes and boyars gathered. Subsequently, the groom's father threw a huge feast also in Yaroslavl, at which he received his daughter-in-law's father Prince Fedor Rostislavich and all the guests, princes, boyars and servants. Such feasts were called *kasha*.[15] The tradition of marrying in the town of the bride's father led to the expression that such and such a prince was married at such and such a prince's. This tradition was practiced only if the groom was young, lower or equal in prestige to the bride's father, and if the bride's father was living. When a prince who was no longer young married, or even if he was young but exceeded the bride's father in importance, or he married an orphan, the groom did not himself go to the bride's town, instead sending his boyars to fetch her.

Thus Simeon the Proud, grand prince of Moscow,[16] sent two boyars to Tver for his bride, the orphaned daughter of Prince Alexander Mikhailovich.[17] Dmitry Donskoy married [Evdokia] the daughter of the Nizhny Novgorod prince, Dmitry Konstantinovich.[18] In this case the wedding was held neither in Moscow nor in Nizhny Novgorod, rather in Kolomna, a point midway between the two towns, for the road from Moscow to Nizhny Novgorod followed the Moscow river and the Oka right past Kolomna. The choice of Kolomna also is explained by the fact that neither of the two grand princes wished to lower his prestige. The Moscow prince refused to go to Nizhny Novgorod, and its prince did not wish to travel to Moscow for the wedding of his daughter to a sixteen-year-old son-in-law.

Alexander Nevsky married the daughter of the prince of Polotsk in similar fashion. The wedding and first feast took place in Toropets with a second feast held in Novgorod. Bishops performed the wedding ceremony. If the town in which the prince married had no bishop, the prelate in whose bishopric the town was located was invited for the ceremony. Thus the bishop of Rostov travelled to Kostroma to marry Prince Vasily Yaroslavich.

The testament of Ivan II[19] tells us that it was traditional for the bride's father to make gifts to his son-in-law. Ivan II bequeathed a gold chainlet and gold waistband to each of his future sons-in-law. The tradition of dowry existed even before that time but the word itself is not encountered until documents of this period. Thus Dmitry Shemiaka,[20] in a pact with Grand Prince Vasily Vasilievich, speaks of his dowry mentioned in the testament of his father-in-law, which was seized by his brother Vasily Kosoy.[21]

In the times described princes also married their own kin. They also frequently married Lithuanian princesses and sent their daughters to marry in Lithuania. Occasionally they married Tatar princesses at the Horde. Grand Prince Vasily Dmitrievich gave his daughter in marriage to the Byzantine crown prince John, son of Manuel.[22] Last, princes married the daughters of boyars and gave their own daughters in marriage to them. The daughter of Dmitry Konstantinovich, grand prince of Nizhny Novgorod, was married to the Moscow boyar Nikolay Vasilievich, son of the chiliarch Veliaminov. Two daughters of the Moscow boyar Ivan Dmitrievich[23] were married, respectively, to Andrei, a son of Vladimir Andreevich of Serpukhov,[24] and to a prince of Tver. Prince Peter of Dmitrov, son of Donskoy, married the daughter of the Moscow boyar Polievkt Vasilievich. One of the sons of Mikhail Alexandrovich, grand prince of Tver,[25] was married to a daughter of the Moscow boyar Fedor Andreevich Koshka.[26] A granddaughter of the same boyar was married to Yaroslav, son of Vladimir Andreevich of Serpukhov. Occasionally princes married as many as three times, as in the case of Simeon the Proud. That prince divorced his second wife, Evpraksia, sending her back to her father, a Smolensk prince. Prince Vsevolod Alexandrovich of Kholm also sent his princess back to her family in Riazan.

Because of the nature of the sources there is less information about the activities and functions of the princes in this period than in previous times. As opposed to the past, the princes now had a new, grave and burdensome duty in the form of visits to the Horde. Ivan Kalita went there nine times. His son Simeon the Proud in his short reign [1340-1353] went five times. Sometimes the princes set off for the Horde with their wives and children. Other times several princes would meet and go there together. It is said of Prince Gleb Vasilievich of Rostov that he served the Tatars from his early youth and thus saved many Christians from harm. Occasionally princes were required to set off on military campaigns with the Tatars.

AMUSEMENTS AND TRADITIONS

As to the princes' other activities, the Volhynian chronicler writes that Prince Daniel of Galich,[27] while accompanying his troops, single-handedly killed three wild boars with a boar-spear and his squire killed as many. It is written of Daniel's nephew Prince Vladimir Vasilievich of Volhynia that he was an excellent and fearless hunter. Whenever he spotted a boar or bear he would not wait for his servants but immediately slew the beast himself. It is not known whether the Northern princes shared a passion for hunting to the degree of their Southern brethren although we have observed that Vladimir Andreevich of Serpukhov in his testament forbade his sons to hunt in the appanages of others without permission, and that the princes had hunters, dog-handlers and falconers whom they prized.

On the other hand, it is known that hunting was a commercial enterprise for the princes as well, and that they sent their hunters for game by themselves. Thus in the Tale of Luka Kolotsky[28] it is written that whenever the falconers of the appanage prince of Mozhaisk, Andrei Dmitrievich,[29] went forth on the prince's orders to hunt with hawks and falcons, Luka attacked and robbed the falconers, took the hawks and falcons for himself, and that this occurred many times. Prince Andrei Dmitrievich endured this and occasionally sent emissaries to Luka, who bade them answer the prince harshly and unyieldingly, all the while persisting in attacking and robbing the falconers and the prince's hunters as well, taking their bears.

Once one of the hunters decided to take revenge on Luka and found an opportune circumstance. Having caught a particularly fierce bear, he had the beast led past Luka's homestead. Spying the bear, Luka came out with a young servant and ordered the prince's hunter to release the bear in his yard. The hunter did so before Luka could enter the house. The beast charged and mauled Luka so severely that the servants rescued him barely breathing. This story suggests that mature bears often were taken alive and used for entertainment.

How a prince spent his day is partially described in a report of the battle at Suzdal. It is written that Grand Prince Vasily Vasilievich had supper in his rooms with all the princes and boyars, and that the feast lasted deep into the night. On the next day (July 7) at sunrise he ordered that matins be celebrated. After the service he went back to bed. Later in the morning the prince's sons, boyars and other men came to him on matters of management and administration. A prince's imminent death was usually preceded by tonsuring, donning a habit, and taking monastic vows. It is told of the demise of Prince Dmitry Sviatoslavich of Yuriev that when the bishop of Rostov administered the vows to him the prince suddenly lost the power of speech. Subsequently he again began to speak and, glancing at the bishop with joyous eyes, said "Master father, Archbishop Ignaty! May God fulfill your labors, that you have prepared me for a long journey, for eternity, having equipped me as soldier for the true tsar, Christ our God."

There is a detailed description of the demise of Prince Mikhail Alexandrovich of Tver. Two years passed since Mikhail, as was his custom, sent emissaries to Constantinople with a donation to the Holy Wisdom cathedral and the patriarch. The emperor and patriarch received and dismissed the emissaries of Tver with great honors. The patriarch sent his own emissary to Mikhail with an icon of the Last Judgement, relics of the saints and blessings of peace. When the grand prince heard that the emissaries were approaching Tver he bade them enter the town towards evening. A thought had come to him never to return home after accepting the icon from the holy place and receiving the patriarch's blessing. On the morning of the next day, when his sons, other princes, boyars and men awaited him with the usual matters of municipal administration, he bade that no one enter his quarters and called only Bishop Arseny. He told the bishop of his intention of taking vows and asked him not to reveal this to anyone.

Despite this, the rumor that Mikhail wished to abdicate and be tonsured a monk swept the city. The populace was thunderstruck, some disbelieved, but everyone gathered as if at a wondrous miracle. Boyars and the prince's adolescent sons shed tears, cleaving to each other. The princess, his wife, and the young princes wept, but in the presence of Mikhail none dared say a word, for everyone feared him. He was an awesome man and his heart verily a lion's.

Meanwhile the emissaries from Constantinople entered the town bearing the sacred gifts. The bishop, all the clergy, and a great multitude came forth to meet them with candles and censers. The grand prince himself came out, having risen from bed with difficulty. He met the emissaries at his own residence by the church of St. Michael. Upon bowing to the icon, Mikhail bade that it be taken to the cathedral of Christ the Savior. He himself accompanied the icon there. After it was set in its prepared place he came out of the church to the people, stopped on a high step and bowing to all sides said "Forgive me, brothers and my retinue, noble sons of Tver. I leave you my beloved and eldest son Ivan. Let him be prince to you in my stead. Cherish him as you cherished me, for he is to care for you as I did."

The multitude responded with bitter tears and praise for their old prince, who humbly again bowed to everyone and departed for the St. Athanasius monastery to be tonsured. There, for a certain fee, he was graced by a monk named Grigory to live with him. On the fourth day he took the vows and the name of Matthew. Eight days after this ritual he died. The narrative goes on to say that the prince's funeral was postponed for seven days until the arrival of his cousin Dmitry Shemiaka. After the requiem the body was placed into a coffin of hollowed-out wood[30] which then was sealed with pitch and taken to Moscow for burial in the church of Archangel Michael, the burial abode of all the progeny of Kalita, both grand and appanage princes.[31]

Grand Prince Vasily Vasilievich the Dark, according to the chronicler, also wanted to take monastic vows before his death, yet was prevented from doing so.[32] He died on a Saturday at approximately three in the morning and was buried the next day, Sunday. Thus unless there were extraordinary circumstances, funerals took place on the day after death.

In the Southwest, the funeral of the Volhynian prince Vladimir is described. The princess and the court servants washed the body, wound it with patterned velvet and lace, and took it on a sledge to Vladimir, where it was placed in the antechamber of the church of the Mother of God because of the late hour. A funeral with the traditional lamentations was held on the next day. The praise that the chronicler accords the good prince is little different from previous formulas except that the customary passage on the prince's relationship to his retinue is omitted.[33]

Of Grand Prince Vasily Yaroslavich of Kostroma[34] it is written that he was a man of many good deeds, loved God with the purity of his whole heart, was merciful, dutifully fulfilled his religious obligations, honored many bishops as superiors and pastors, cherished and honored the clergy and monastic orders, was kind and readily forgave those who sinned against him. Of Prince Gleb Vasilievich of Rostov it is said that he spared neither food nor drink and served it to those who asked, built and embellished many churches with icons and books, revered the clergy and monastic orders, was charitable and merciful to all. He despised vainglory, turning from it as from a serpent. His death aroused much pity and lamentation among all those who knew him.

An idea of the princes' dress may be found on the basis of the listing of items left by the Moscow princes. The chronicles, in describing the flight of Prince Vasily Mikhailovich of Kashin,[35] say that he escaped dressed only in a high hat and without a shako. In a description of the appearance of Prince Vladimir Vasilkovich of Volhynia, it is said that he shaved his beard.

PRINCES' RETINUE AND COURT

The changes occurring in the relations among the princes inevitably were reflected in the status of the princes' retinues. The permanent settling of princes in fixed principalities led to a similar settling on the part of the retinue, whose members now could acquire land and gain importance as established, rich landholders, privileged with inherited positions and serving the prince. The progeny of Daniel Alexandrovich never moved from Moscow. Beginning with Ivan Kalita all Moscow princes constantly kept the grand principality of Vladimir for themselves, nor did they permit the boyars of others to purchase villages in their territories. Only Moscow boyars had the right to purchase villages in Vladimir since it permanently belonged to their princes, and they made use of that right. Therefore it was to these boyars' advantage to keep to the province of Vladimir, simultaneously maintaining the primacy of their princes, so they zealously strove to do both.

That the significance of the Moscow boyars rose commensurately with the increase in power of their princes is evident in the fact that both the Nizhny Novgorod and Tver princes sought familial ties with them. Despite the paucity of sources from that period there are fairly clear indications of the increased significance of the boyars. It has been mentioned that the migration of boyars from the South into the Moscow principality helped strengthen their position. This increase in strength in turn served further to attract rich, well-known and capable boyars from all regions.

The great service performed for Moscow by the Volhynian boyar Dmitry Aliburtovich Bobrok, an arrival from the South, has been observed. He did not just come suddenly to Moscow. Before that he served as chiliarch to the Nizhny Novgorod prince Dmitry Konstantinovich.[36] Here it is evident how the particular status of the retinue in Rus facilitated the strengthening of one principality at the expense of others. Since all the princes in

Ancient Rus were of one family, the land maintained its unity. A retinue member in going from one prince to another did not in any sense betray his allegiance to the Land of Rus or the line of princes which ruled the land conjointly. Later, in the North, the retinue members retained this right of free transfer.[37] Thus, as soon as they observed the disadvantage of serving a weak prince and the advantage of serving a strong one, they freely went over. There was no betrayal of the previous prince here, merely the exercise of a right acknowledged by all princes. It was thus that Grand Prince Vasily Dmitrievich, having swayed the retinue of the Nizhny Novgorod prince, came to possess that principality without hindrance.[38]

In genealogical registers it is mentioned that together with Daniel Alexandrovich there came to Moscow a member of his court, Protasy, the progenitor of the famous Veliaminov family.[39] More properly, it is stated that Protasy was a chiliarch during the rule of Kalita. Subsequently this title was inherited by the progeny of Protasy. With a similar permanent settling of princes and boyars in principalities other than Moscow a similar development occurred. Boris Fedorovich, nicknamed Polovoy, left Chernigov and became a boyar in Tver. His son was also a boyar there, the grandson, great-grandson and great-great-grandson became chiliarchs. Besides the Veliaminovs, there is a whole series of notable surnames stretching from Kalita to the time of his great-great-grandson.

Next to these so-called indigenous Moscow boyars there was a constant flow of new arrivals. There came to serve the Moscow princes not only notable men from Southwestern Rus or from foreign lands, but also princes from the South and North who were the progeny of Riurik, and from Lithuania the progeny of Gediminas.[40] The entry of a renowned newcomer into a prince's service on condition of receiving a high position has been noted. To grant the newcomer such a position, it first had to be taken from some other long-standing boyar, thereby lowering him and a whole series of boyars who were his subordinates.

In the language of the time this was called an "overriding."[41] A newcomer "overrode" the old boyars, who were forced to move down in order to give the higher post to him. In Kalita's reign Rodion Nestorovich, a newcomer from the South, overrode the boyar Akinf[42] and his friends. At that time Moscow had not yet achieved clear supremacy over other principalities, so Akinf could afford to slight it. Vexed by being overridden, he left for Tver. Later, when Moscow's power was established firmly and the boyar families lived there for some time, it was disadvantageous for them to leave. Then in the case of overriding they tended to submit and surrender the higher position to the newcomer.

In the reign of Donskoy, Bobrok, a newcomer from Volhynia, "overrode" Timofey Vasilievich Veliaminov and his followers, who yielded the primary position. In the reign of Vasily Dmitrievich, Prince Yury Patrikeevich, a newcomer from Lithuania,[43] "overrode" several boyars, specifically Konstantin Sheia, Ivan Dmitrievich, Volodimer Danilovich, Dmitry Vasilievich and Fedor Koshkin. A curious piece of information has come down concerning this event. The grand prince granted the position to Prince Yury Patrikeevich when he gave his sister Grand Princess Anna in marriage to Prince Yury (according to the chronicles, it was his daughter, Maria).[44]

Yury had an older brother named Khovansky. At Yury's wedding feast the boyar Fedor Sabur took a seat which outranked the place of Khovansky. Somewhat piqued, Khovansky said to Sabur "Why don't you take my brother Prince Yury's place?" "Because he's got God under that tiara, and you don't," replied Sabur, taking the place of higher honor. "He's got God under a tiara" meant that the man to whom it was applied was lucky. The luck was Yury's wife, through whom he received his position.

There is also a curious charter of the Nizhny Novgorod grand prince Dmitry Konstantinovich dealing with the protocol of seating. "Grand Prince Dmitry Konstantinovich of Nizhny Novgorod, Gorodets and Kurmysh has hearkened to his boyars and princes and granted them a charter on seating according to their petition, to the solicitude of Archimandrite Jonas of Nizhny Novgorod and the Caves monastery, his own spiritual father and also to the blessing of Bishop Serapion of Nizhny Novgorod, Gorodets and Kurmysh as to who shall sit with whom and who shall sit below whom. The prince wishes that next to his own place there be seated his chiliarch Prince Dmitry Aliburtovich of Volhynia. Prince Ivan Vasilievich of Gorodets is to sit next to Dmitry.

"Opposite him is to sit Dmitry Ivanovich Lobanov. Next to Prince Ivan is to sit the Polish prince Fedor Andreevich with his Boyar Vasily Petrovich Novosiltsev next to him. Opposite is to sit the treasurer, Boyar Tarasy Petrovich Novosiltsev, made a boyar because twice he ransomed from captivity his sovereign Grand Prince Dmitry Konstantinovich, and on a third occasion Grand Princess Martha. Then is to be seated Prince Peter Ivanovich Berezopolsky, followed by Prince Dmitry Fedorovich of Kurmysh. The grand prince wishes that his boyars and secretary affix their signatures to this rule of seating. The charter was penned by the grand prince's secretary Peter Davydov Rusin." It is evident on the basis of this charter that the more powerful princes acquired territories for themselves while making the indigenous princes their servitors. Here these princes had to sit below plain boyars. In the heading of the charter the boyars were mentioned first.

It is known from the testament of Dmitry Donskoy,[45] and from other sources, that boyars continued to be counsellors to princes, who deliberated with and consulted them on various matters. Beginning with Simeon the Proud boyars became witnesses to princes' testaments. Grand Prince Oleg Ivanovich of Riazan began his testament, "Having consulted with my [spiritual] father Bishop Vasily and with my boyars (here their names are listed), I have...," and so forth. It must be noted that no such expressions are found in the charters of Moscow princes.

There were those occasional boyars who, having the special trust of particular princes, might exercise great influence. Such were Simeon Tonilievich during the reign of Andrei Alexandrovich,[46] the boyar Fedor Andreevich Koshka and his son Ivan Fedorovich during the reign of Vasily Dmitrievich, and [Semeon] Morozov during the reign of Yury Dmitrievich.[47] It is reflected in the chronicles that the influence which passed from the older Koshka to his relatively young son aroused the indignation of the elder boyars.

The division of the retinue into elder and junior elements was maintained as in earlier times except for some changes in terminology. The senior retinue continued to carry the name of boyars, or "boliars." The right of the boyars to go from one prince into another's service, either from a grand to an appanage prince or the other way around, or from a grand prince to another grand prince—for example, from a Moscow prince to one of Tver or Riazan, or conversely—was upheld in the charters of all princes. The princes obligated themselves not to bear enmity against boyars who left them, nor to confiscate their villages and houses left in the lands of the previous prince. As a result of the boyars' right to retain property after their departure princes' appanages constantly contained districts of unallied boyars despite the fact that such boyars were forbidden to buy property in appanages not of their allegiance.

Another reason for the existence of the property of unallied boyars was that principalities passed from the hands of one prince into those of another. For example, the principality of Serpukhov first belonged to Vladimir Andreevich. His boyars at that time freely could purchase villages within its boundaries, then upon his death the principality was divided among his sons, the boyars also distributing themselves among them. Thus it readily could occur that a boyar stayed to serve the eldest brother yet his village was in the appanage of the prince of Borovsk.

These conditions forced the princes to include a provision in their pacts which specified that, for legal purposes and for tribute, boyars fell under the jurisdiction of the prince in whose lands they resided and where they had immovable property. The princes were obliged to consider these boyars as theirs, but in case of war such boyars were to march with the prince they served. Yet if the town in which, or near which, they resided was besieged, they were to remain and defend that town. In the event of a dispute between a prince and the boyar of another, both princes were each to send a boyar for resolution of the matter. If the two boyars could not come to an agreement they were to choose a third party as judge, whilst any matter between a boyar and his prince was decided by the prince. For their service boyars received from their princes districts and villages for their maintenance.

Ivan Kalita in his testament mentions the village of Bogoroditskoe which he had bought and given to the boyar Boris Vorkov. "Should this Vorkov," writes Kalita, "serve one of my sons, the village remains his. If he does not serve my sons, the village is to be taken away."[48] Concerning the income from such holdings, Simeon the Proud ordered the following in his testament. "If any of my boyars is to serve my princess and keep his districts, he must turn over to the princess my half of the income." Dmitry Donskoy and his cousin Vladimir Andreevich came to this agreement regarding the boyars' maintenance. "If a boyar leaves your service for mine, or my service for yours, without completing his service, he will be given maintenance according to what is due him, that is, only for the time that he served. Otherwise he is obliged to fulfill his service."

There exist the so-called charters of obedience[49] issued at the granting of maintenance holdings. They ordered the residents of the district in question to honor and obey whoever was sent to them for maintenance. He was to be their master and judge, and was to send his officials among them. He was to take income according to a fixed assessment. Maintenance districts were granted with trade duty stations, ferries and the rights to all the income and taxes normally collected.

There were distinctions among the senior members of the retinue. Among boyars, the term "great" boyar[50] is found. The chronicles state that after the murder of the chiliarch Alexis Petrovich Khvost the Moscow "great" boyars departed for Riazan. Dmitry Donskoy requested of his cousin Vladimir Andreevich that should he, the grand prince, take tribute from his great and "administrative" boyars,[51] the appanage prince should take tribute from his boyars as well and turn it over to Donskoy. The tribute was to be commensurate with the maintenance allotments and administrative posts.

Grand Prince Vasily Vasilievich and Shemiaka agreed that, should their mutual judges come to no settlement, they were to designate a third judge from a list comprising two of the grand prince's boyars and one of Shemiaka's "great" boyars. Except for the agreement between Donskoy and Vladimir Andreevich, the term "great boyar" is not encountered in the same context with "administrative boyar." Elsewhere the former term is replaced by "privy boyar."[52] Concerning the privy and administrative boyars, the provision continuously is encountered that both types of boyars were exempt from the obligation, common to other boyars, of joining the garrison of a town or defending the town in which they lived when besieged.

In addition, concerning the administrative boyars the agreement between Vasily Dmitrievich and Vladimir Andreevich states "If we are to take tribute from our administrative boyars, you are to take tribute from ten of yours." In the charter granted by Grand Prince Vasily Vasilievich to the Trinity monastery in 1453 the following is found. "If anyone brings a charge against the steward of the abbot, then I, the grand prince, or one of my privy boyars shall judge him." In the genealogical table of the Kikins it is said that Loggin Mikhailovich Kikin was a privy boyar in the service of Grand Prince Dmitry Ivanovich and that he was a "townholder," holding the towns of Volok and Torzhok in perpetuity. Loggin's son Timofey also was called a privy boyar.

The terms "privy" and "administrative" can be explained only in the context of other similar titles. It has been noticed that one charter uses the term "great" where others have "privy." It therefore may be concluded that the terms had equal meaning. Later the term "privy secretary"[53] also is encountered. The difference between "privy," "great," and "administrative" can be discerned further in the passage from the agreement between Dmitry Donskoy and Vladimir Andreevich referred to above. "If the grand prince is to take tribute from his boyars, the great and the administrative, the appanage prince must also take tribute from his boyars according to their maintenance and responsibility."

On this basis it may be concluded that a great or privy boyar was one who was a town-holder, receiving towns and districts for his maintenance.

An administrative boyar received his maintenance from the income of the various departments of the princes' domains, the so-called "amenities."[54] An administrative boyar therefore had to have a function at court. For example, the master of the horse was a boyar whose income came from the districts designated for horse raising. Thus the ancient word "way" or "road,"[55] and the contemporary word "income,"[56] from the very meaning "to reach, to arrive," express the same concept.

Another term encountered in this period is lord-in-waiting.[57] It is found in a 1284 charter of the Smolensk prince Fedor Rostislavich as well as in the pact between Simeon the Proud and his brothers. Prince Vladimir Andreevich of Serpukhov made a lord-in-waiting of Yakov Yurievich Novosilets, his vicegerent in the town of Serpukhov. In the tale of the battle with the Tatar Begich a Moscow lord-in-waiting Timofey Veliaminov is mentioned. In the charter granted by the Riazan prince Oleg Ivanovich[58] to the St. Olga monastery there is a lord-in-waiting named Yury who is mentioned among the boyars whom Oleg consulted in granting the charter. This Yury is listed sixth among the boyars, which suggests that the lords-in-waiting at that time and later, though they were members of the senior retinue and with the great boyars made up the prince's council,[59] nevertheless occupied a secondary position.

The same charter also lists Manasy, the prince's mentor, in a position above that of a lord-in-waiting and a cupbearer, Yury, in a position immediately below. In another Riazan charter the title "table attendant" appears above that of cupbearer[60] as it does in Moscow charters. The nature of these titles readily may be determined from the words themselves which point to the function.

What could have been the function of the lord-in-waiting? Later sources tell us that a lord-in-waiting acted in marches during military campaigns, that he preceded the tsar in his travels through his domains, and that in the latter case "courtiers" [see below] occasionally were appointed lords-in-waiting, a clear sign that "lord-in-waiting" was not only a title but a function as well. If this information about the term "lord-in-waiting" is compared to what is known of the administrative boyars there is reason to assume that they were identical, especially since the administrative boyars stood in the same relationship to the great or privy boyars as the lords-in-waiting did later.

The junior retinue, as opposed to the senior, boyar retinue, bore the general name of "servitors" or "courtiers," but most documents speak of the composite parts of the junior retinue. The first place here, second only to the boyars is given to the "junior boyars," a term clearly showing the origin of the men who made up this highest level of the junior retinue. Like the boyars, the junior boyars enjoyed the right to leave a prince's service while retaining their districts. Unlike the boyars, they could not be members of the prince's council.

The second level of the junior retinue consisted of the so-called "servitors," "free servitors" and "courtiers."[61] These frequently were granted holdings for their maintenance and had the same privileges of service and property as the junior boyars, differing from them only in their origins.

There was yet another class of servitors different from the above. These were tradesmen and craftsmen such as beekeepers, gardeners, hunters, beaver trappers, upholsterers and men who performed various services.[62] The Moscow princes undertook not to demand military service from this class of men, to regard them as a distinct group, and did not buy their lands. Should one of these men choose to leave he might do so, but he forfeited his land to the prince. In the charters these servitors usually were called "servitors under the majordomo," since they were under his control. This term further differentiated them from the free servitors of the first rank who had maintenance grants and access to the court.

Finally there was the category of unfree servants, slaves,[63] who performed the same functions as the servitors under the majordomo as well as in higher functions in the administration of the princes' private domains or crown territories. Some of these functions were that of local judges,[64] estate managers, stewards, elders, treasurers and secretaries. Men holding such positions were called "great men" as opposed to plain slaves or "lesser men." The ancient terms for low-ranking servitors and the bodyguard they constituted[65] now disappeared, whereas those for upper-class freemen[66] still were encountered occasionally at this time.

SOUTHWESTERN AND LITHUANIAN PRACTICE

In the Southwest boyars, servitors and court servitors also are encountered. Among the servitors there is the category of court junior boyars. From the period of Lithuanian rule the title of boyar as applied to the senior members of the retinue, while remaining in the Rus provinces, disappeared at the grand prince's court, where it was replaced by "lord" and "lord of the council."[67] There exist charters granted by Lithuanian grand princes to the Rus who joined their retinue. When a Lithuanian grandee attested before the grand prince to the nobility of the newcomer he was received at the Lithuanian court with the honors due his previous position, as a man well-born and a knight. He was given the privileges of either a prince, lord or a court member of high rank.[68] The new servitor swore allegiance to the grand prince. He was to be on peaceful terms with all those with whom the grand prince was at peace, and conversely. He also fulfilled his military obligations along with the gentry, princes, lords or landed proprietors.[69]

Such was the differentiation in titles of the servitors at the court of the Lithuanian grand princes. There also exist charters of allegiance pertaining to grandees to whom the Lithuanian princes granted towns. The new "town-holders" swore to hold the town faithfully and not to cede it to any realm save the grand principality of Lithuania. In the event of the grand prince's death the town was to be ceded to his successor. The narrative of the seizure of the domain of the boyar Sudislav provides a picture of the wealth of the South Russian, specifically Galich, boyars. Listed among the items seized is a great quantity of wine, vegetables, provender, lances and arrows.

Sources of the period also clearly testify to the fact that Southern boyars were granted districts by princes. Daniel Romanovich ordered that no Chernigov boyars be accepted into his service, but that districts be given to Galich boyars only. This is followed by a notation that the income from the Kolomyia saltworks was distributed among the armorers. A report was made to the sick prince Vladimir of Volhynia that his brother Mstislav, not yet having succeeded to rule, already was distributing towns and villages among the boyars.

There is information from the Lithuanian period that servitors were granted lands in perpetuity. The recipients were obliged to perform military service, bringing a specified number of armed servitors with them. Land grants made in perpetuity included the right to will the property to children or relatives, the right to sell, give as gifts, or to dispose of them in the most advantageous manner. Algirdas's grandson Prince Andrei Vladimirovich specified in his testament that the boyars to whom he gave lands must serve his wife on the basis of those grants. Boyar patrimonies in Southwestern Rus since ancient times never were subject to tribute. In Smolensk tribute, or "plowland tax,"[70] was taken only from those boyar holdings granted by Grand Prince Vytautas and his successors.

According to the charter[71] granted by Grand Prince Casimir IV[72] in 1457 princes, lords and boyars could go to foreign lands, except to those of an enemy, to increase their wealth and perform military service with the condition that, in their absence, their service obligations to the prince not suffer. They held the same rights in dealing with their patrimonies or grants made by Vytautas as did the Polish princes, lords and boyars, namely the right to sell, exchange, divide, give as gifts or use in any way to their advantage. Their subjects were exempt from all tribute, payments, requisitions, tribute collected in silver, and from other levies as well as from the obligation to supply wagons, from carting stone, logs and wood for firing brick and lime, from mowing, and so forth. They did have to perform work necessary for the building of new and the repair of old fortifications. Certain other traditional obligations also remained in force, among them the obligation of quartering soldiers, certain extraordinary levies, the construction of new and repair of old bridges, and road repair. Their men, enslaved and dependent, could not be taken by the grand prince or his officials. Should there be litigation against one of these men the grand prince was not to send his court agent, the slave's master was to resolve the matter. Only if the matter was not resolved by a specified date was a court agent to be sent. In either case, the guilty paid a fine only to his master and to no one else.

ADMINISTRATIVE PROCEDURES AND TITLES

Among the household boyars in the North we have encountered the titles of table attendant and cupbearer. In addition there were titles such as master of the horse[73] and majordomo.[74] Contemporary sources indicate one function of the majordomo, namely oversight of a prince's servitors, both craftsmen and tradesmen. Of course this hardly could have been his sole function. Terms such as treasurer, steward, and agent[75] are also encountered. All these positions were filled by either freemen or slaves.

Concerning stewards who were freemen an order is found in the testament of Prince Vladimir Andreevich of Serpukhov. "My stewards are not bought men, but while acting as my stewards they have bought villages. The stewards themselves are not needed by my children, but their villages shall go to my children." In the tale of the rout of Mamay a bodyguard[76] is encountered who had the duty of bearing the grand prince's standard. Among administrative ranks there was the title of "chiliarch" [77]which was abolished in Moscow during the reign of Dmitry Donskoy. The term "burgrave"[78] no longer is encountered. It was replaced by "vicegerent," "district official," "regional official" and "local official."

These positions differed from each other according to the extent and importance of the administered areas. It was customarily stated in charters that the prince's vicegerents and officials were forbidden to enter the districts in question and had no jurisdiction over them. Grand Prince Vasily Dmitrievich demanded that his uncle Vladimir Andreevich hold no courts in Moscow without the grand prince's vicegerents. When in the absence of the grand prince from Moscow a Muscovite registered a complaint with him against another Muscovite, he was to designate a constable and send him to his vicegerents. Together they were to resolve the matter with the vicegerents of the appanage prince. Reeves are mentioned as performing their functions as previously. The officials engaged in the juridical process were constables and informers. Villages were managed by chiefs who, as mentioned, could come from the ranks of the prince's unfree servitors. Secretaries [scribes] and assistant secretaries acted in all written matters. Secretaries also served as emissaries. Thus Shemiaka sent Fedor Dubensky, a secretary of his, to Kazan in an effort to ensure that Grand Prince Vasily Vasilievich not be released from captivity. Inventory and registration of lands was performed by clerks. Tax agents bore titles associated with the type of function they performed. Thus there were tax collectors for beaver trapping, apiaries, mown hay, the courier service, squirrel skins and forage.

In the Southwest, before Lithuanian domination, the term "majordomo" is encountered, a position of great significance in times of both peace and war. In Galich the majordomo Grigory and Bishop Artemy were of foremost importance. Both men headed political resistance to Prince Daniel Romanovich, and both later appeared before him with the proposal that he take charge of the city. Daniel's famous majordomo Andrei was a prominent figure in military campaigns. It is apparent that as a result of the influence of neighboring states, Poland and Hungary, the position of majordomo in Galich assumed the important meaning of "palatine."[79]

Another title of importance in the South was "keeper of the seal,"[80] as exemplified by Kirill who was sent to Bakota to register the excesses of the boyars and pacify the land. The title of keeper of the seal also is encountered in Smolensk at the end of the thirteenth century. There was a keeper of the seal under Dmitry Donskoy in Moscow, the famous priest Mitiay.[81] "Table attendants" are encountered in the South as well. The title "master of the saddle" took on a new, higher meaning than it had in Kievan Rus. The new title "horseman" appears among the boyar ranks.[82] "Clerk" was used in the South with the meaning of "secretary" in the North.[83]

Such was the composition of the retinue and, in effect, the princely court both in the North and South. Besides the above titles and divisions there were occasionally among a prince's servitors other princes who were descendants of Riurik or Gediminas who lost their patrimony or the right of independent rule. At the beginning of the period under consideration these princes were not included in the hierarchy of servitors and made up a separate division of the retinue. Usually, though not everywhere, they held a rank higher than that of boyar. There was an agreement among the princes that should these servitor princes leave their service they were to forfeit their patrimony. The origins of the rest of the members of a retinue were varied. In the North they were arrivals from Southern Rus, Lithuania, the Horde and even Germany.

In the Southern town of Vladimir-in-Volhynia there was a German expatriate named Markolt who held high rank. In the same town, in the service of Prince Vladimir Vasilkovich there was an expatriate from Silesia named Kafilat as well as a man from Prussia. A priest's grandson, the boyar Grigory reached high rank in Galich during the time of troubles[84] there. Together with him are mentioned two men of low class (peasant) origins, Lazar Domozhirich and Ivor Molibozhich. Whether this was the result of the time of troubles or of a natural order of events cannot be established. Men of noble origin not yet members of the senior retinue formed a special division of the junior retinue under the name of junior boyars.[85]

ARMY AND ARMS

Apart from the retinue the army was, as before, composed of townsmen. Regiments made up of Moscow residents are mentioned in princely pacts under the name of Muscovite soldiery.[86] It is known that Vasily the Dark led Moscow merchants and other residents against his uncle Yury. The charter of Vasily the Dark to the Trinity monastery speaks of rural residents obliged to serve as border guards. In the South, Rostislav Mikhailovich of Chernigov gathered many lower class men[87] for war against Daniel of Galich. The chronicler notes that these commoners made up the infantry that gave the victory to Rostislav, though at the famous battle at Yaroslavl the same Rostislav entered combat with only his cavalry, leaving the infantry at the town, and was defeated by Daniel who had both cavalry and infantry.

In the North, upon hearing of the approach of an enemy, the princes sent notices of mobilization to all the districts. As has been seen, such mobilization proceeded at too slow a pace when it came to confronting an enemy such as Algirdas or Tokhtamysh. When the enemy was quite close the first soldiery to gather were formed into a vanguard regiment and sent to fight a holding action for as long as possible. When setting out on a campaign scouts went ahead to reconnoiter the movement of the enemy and obtain prisoners for interrogation. Taking a prisoner for such purposes was, in the expression of that time, called "getting a tongue."[88] On a march the army fed itself at the expense of the districts it traversed. It is said that Grand Prince Vasily Vasilievich, having concluded an armistice with Vasily Kosoy, dismissed his troops, who subsequently dispersed to forage for provisions.

Before entering battle the army was deployed as in earlier times. A major element took the center with two elements on its left and right, the so-called left and right "arms." A vanguard preceded it and a rearguard, widely used as a reserve element, followed. It was such a reserve that decided the battle of Snipe Field in favor of the Russians. It was also the use of a reserve that enabled Prokopy and his two thousand Novgorod "raiders"[89] to defeat a five-thousand-man army of Kostroma. As before, princes made speeches before the start of a battle. As before, at the flight of the enemy the soldiery dashed to strip the dead, sometimes before the enemy was in flight, as at the battle of Suzdal. Both in the South and North the old tradition of exchanging insults with the enemy persisted.

In the Southern chronicles the Rus style of fighting is mentioned as having its particular traits. A Northern chronicler says of the battle between Vasily the Dark and Kosoy that the Lithuanian expatriate Prince Baba Drutskoy equipped his troops with spears in the Lithuanian manner, which differed from that of the Rus, though the use of spears cannot possibly mark a Lithuanian style of combat, for the Rus used this weapon as well. The description of the Snipe Field battle, for example, states that a rear rank of troops placed their spears on the shoulders of a front rank, with the spears of the first rank being shorter than those of the second.

A Hungarian general is said to have expressed the opinion that Southern Rus soldiery had great zeal for battle and for the first strike, yet lacked persistence. The Southern Rus preferred to fight in open fields and clear spaces. Daniel of Galich during a campaign against the Yatviags[90] said to his troops "Do you not know that open space is a fortress to Christians and a pen to heathens." The Northern chronicles state that when Grand Prince Vasily Vasilievich sent his troops to the Oka river against the Tatars under the command of a Zvenigorod prince, the Tatars took fright and turned back.

Other commanders[91] behaved differently. Prince Ivan Vasilievich Obolensky-Striga[92] and Fedor Basenok[93] during the war with Novgorod once encountered five thousand of the enemy while themselves having only two hundred men. "If we do not enter battle," they said, "we will perish at the hand of our sovereign, the grand prince." They fought and won the day. The South preserved the tradition according to which a prince must ride at the head of his troops because he was most skilled at warfare and most obeyed. Thus Rus and Polish princes once said to Daniel Romanovich[94] "You, king, are the head of all the troops. If you send one of us to the front, the men will not obey us. You know military honor, warfare is a tradition with you. Each man will fear you and feel the urge to fight. You ought to go to the front." Daniel, upon forming his troops, himself rode in the front along with a majordomo and a small number of retainers. In the North, according to tales of the rout of Mamay, Grand Prince Dmitry, after riding in the vanguard for a while, returned to the main corps.[95]

In the North armament consisted of shields, helmets, pikes, spears, lances, sabers, war clubs and battle-axes.[96] A Southern chronicler, describing the armament of the troops of Daniel of Galich, writes "Their shields were like the dawn, helmets like the rising sun. Lances trembled in their hands like so many reeds. Archers marched on both sides holding their bows in their hands with arrows set in them." At another time, having set out to the aid of the Hungarian king, Daniel armed his troops in the Tatar manner. The horses had head-plates and armor of leather, the men also wore leather armor. Daniel himself was dressed in the Rus manner. The saddle on his horse was of annealed gold, the arrows and saber were decorated with gold and intricate designs, his coat[97] was of Greek [Byzantine] fabric decorated with lace of gold thread. His boots were of green Morocco embroidered with gold. When the Hungarian king asked to come to his camp, Daniel led him into his tent.

Among the names of weapons encountered in the South there are "bear spears"[98] as well as swords and spears. The testament of the Volhynian prince Vladimir mentions armor of wooden slats. The horses and arms seized from an enemy was the so-called war booty.[99] In the South the term banners[100] still was used, while the word "standard"[101] came into use in the North. The tale of the rout of Mamay mentions a black standard that was carried above the grand prince. The army was called to arms by trumpets. Vasily the Dark himself began to sound a trumpet at the approach of Kosoy.

NATURE OF WAR

Concerning the nature and intensity of wars in the North [including the provinces of Severia, Riazan and Smolensk], of ninety reports of domestic or internecine struggles there are only twenty reports of actual combat. Thus seventy campaigns led to no fighting at all. If the period of 234 years under consideration is divided into equal halves, it is seen that the first period, ending in 1345 during the early reign of Simeon the Proud, witnessed only five battles. The other fifteen fall into the second period. Of these fifteen, seven, or almost half, occurred in the internecine conflict during the reign of Vasily the Dark, the result of that prince's struggles with his uncle and cousins and evidence of the increased bitterness toward the end of the conflict.

During a seventeen-year span in the South, from 1228 to the battle of Yaroslavl, there are twelve reports of campaigns, and four of battles, two of which, at Zvenigorod and Yaroslavl, were extremely fierce. There are 160 reports of foreign wars in the period, yet only fifty reports of battles, more than thirteen of these being won by the Russians. Of these wars 45 were against the Tatars, 41 with Lithuanians, 30 with the Livonian Order, and the rest with Swedes, Bulgars and others. In the South, before Lithuanian rule, there are some forty reports of foreign wars, and eleven battles, eight of which were won by the Rus. During the internecine wars in the North there are some 35 reports of the taking of towns and some five reports of unsuccessful sieges. In foreign wars there are some fifteen citings of towns taken and seven of unsuccessful sieges. The Rus successfully defended their towns seventeen times but lost their towns some seventy times, primarily to the Tatars during the invasions of Batu, Tokhtamysh and Edigey. In foreign wars in the South the Rus took seven towns, were unsuccessful once, lost eleven and successfully defended three.

In descriptions of sieges during the very beginning of our period various siege engines, trebuchets,[102] battering rams and siege towers are already encountered. During the siege of Chernigov by Daniel Romanovich of Galich and Vladimir Riurikovich of Kiev the attackers set up a trebuchet which cast stones half again the distance of a bow shot.[103] It took four strong men to lift a stone. Rostislav Mikhailovich of Chernigov used trebuchets at the siege of Yaroslavl.

Here is how the storming of the town of Gostiny in Volhynia by troops sent to the aid of the Polish prince Conrad [of Mazovia][104] is described. "When the troops reached the town and halted, they began to prepare for its storming. Prince Conrad rode about and spoke to the Rus. 'My brothers,'

he said, 'dear Rus, let us all pull together.' The soldiery charged the fortifications, while other troops stood by to guard against a surprise
sortie by the Poles [the garrison was Polish]. When the soldiery reached
the fortifications the Poles began sending stones down upon them like a
hailstorm, but the arrows of the attackers prevented the besieged from
leaning out over the fortifications. Then they began to go at each other
with spears. Many were wounded in the town by spears and arrows and
the dead began to fall from the fortifications like sheaves. Thus was the
town taken and burned, the inhabitants slaughtered and led into captivity."

In the North the citizens of Novgorod, preparing for a campaign
against Rakovor [1267],[105] found craftsmen who built trebuchets for them
at the prince's court. During the siege of Tver by Dmitry Donskoy the
besiegers surrounded it with a palisade, put up towers and piled up
earthworks around the whole town. The siege continued for four weeks,
but the town was not taken because the Tver prince hastened to conclude
peace. The first task of all besiegers was to burn the suburbs and all structures around the besieged fortress or town. Sometimes this was done by
the besieged themselves as they prepared for the defense.

In the tale of the siege of Moscow by Tokhtamysh cannons and fire-
arms, used by the defenders, are mentioned for the first time. Crossbows
also are mentioned. Besides loosing stones and arrows the besieged also
poured boiling water on the attackers. The Moscow Kremlin was never
taken by force, for Tokhtamysh took it by a ruse. Smolensk was taken twice
by Vytautas, also by ruse. Tver was never taken after the Tatar invasion with
Kalita. Novgorod was never taken at all, and Pskov successfully defended
itself six times against the Germans.

As to the size of armies, there is even less information than for the
preceding period. Though there is information about the size of the Russian army which fought at Snipe Field, it is drawn from exaggerated
narratives. There are also other reasons for doubting its veracity. When
Dmitry Donskoy counted his soldiery after crossing the Oka river he
found that there were two hundred thousand of them. Even so, he lamented the shortage of infantry and left one of his commanders, Timofey
Vasilievich, at Lopasna to hasten the movement through the Riazan lands
of those infantry and cavalry units that were to arrive later. In fact, later
it is stated that much infantry, plain folk and merchants, did join him from
numerous regions and towns, so that after their arrival the army numbered
some four hundred thousand. Yet considering that Dmitry could draw
only on the resources of the grand principality of Vladimir and Moscow,

his servitor princes and the forces of the two descendants of Algirdas, that the information of the arrival of Novgorod troops is more than doubtful, that help from Tver was unlikely, and that there is no mention at all of troops from Nizhny Novgorod or Suzdal, the figure of four hundred thousand cannot appear other than exaggerated.[106]

In the battle at Suzdal [1445] Vasily the Dark had only fifteen hundred men, including the retinues of the princes of Mozhaisk, Vereia and Serpukhov. This figure represented the entire strength of Moscow, except for the force of Shemiaka. Novgorod fielded five thousand men against Vasily the Dark. The chronicler called this a great host. Of course the campaign of Vasily the Dark against the Kazan khanate cannot be compared with the campaign of his grandfather Dmitry against Mamay. The very complaint of the chronicler at the extreme exhaustion of the Moscow regions after the Snipe Field battle indicates an effort that was extraordinary. Such was the state, according to sources, of the retinue and the army in general.

IV

CITIES

POLITICAL DECLINE

Let us now turn our attention to the rest of the population, both urban and rural. At this time the towns of Northeastern Rus take on a significance different from those in ancient Southwestern Rus. Whereas internecine strife among princes continued as before, the towns no longer took part in it. Their voice was not heard. Not a single prince called a popular assembly to announce a military campaign or some other important matter to the townsmen or coordinated his doings with them. A number of princes struggled for Vladimir and its lands, the princes of Pereiaslavl, Gorodets, Moscow and Tver. Yet the preference of the residents of Vladimir for a given contender is never weighed as a factor in deciding the struggle as it was previously concerning the leanings of the Kievans.

Though highly valuing the importance of Vladimir and its province, the princes nevertheless no longer made the capital city of their fathers their residence, preferring to live on their private lands. Surely this situation should have given the residents of Vladimir great independence in choosing one of the rival princes, but nothing of the sort occurred. Internecine strife began in the principality of Moscow between an uncle and his nephew. One expelled the other from the city, as once in Kiev, yet there is not a single mention of the voice of the Muscovites, no indication that the rival princes hearkened to or even solicited this voice. Mention is made of a plot of numerous Muscovites, boyars, merchants and clergy in support of Shemiaka and against Vasily the Dark. But there is not a word about the vocal expression of the people's opinion, or of factions among the citizens, as there was in earlier times in the South.

Deprived of its princes, Moscow twice was left on its own, during the invasion of Tokhtamysh and after the battle of Suzdal. In neither case is a town assembly mentioned. The chronicler speaks only of unrest which, in the first case, was quelled by the arrival of Prince Ostey. In all, popular assemblies or uprisings are mentioned three times: two assemblies of citizens against boyars in Kostroma, Nizhny Novgorod and Torzhok; one assembly in Rostov against the Tatars. Town risings against the Tatars with the participation of princes, incidentally, are mentioned as occurring earlier, though only in the old towns of Smolensk, Murom, and Briansk does the citizenry take part in the struggles among princes. The citizens of Smolensk rejected as their prince Sviatoslav Mstislavich, who had to take the throne by force. The citizens of Briansk gathered in an assembly against their prince Gleb Sviatoslavich. The men of Murom formed two factions, one for Prince Fedor Glebovich, the other for Yury Yaroslavich.

NOVGOROD THE GREAT

There was a city in the North which preserved the prominence of the old cities, their power, their tradition of gathering in a popular assembly. It did so despite the efforts of Andrei Bogoliubsky, Vsevolod III, his son Yaroslav, his grandson Yaroslav and great-grandson Mikhail. This city was Novgorod the Great. It has been remarked that, as a result of the peculiarities of princely familial relations and internecine strife, accommodations between princes and townsmen occurred at times.

Thus in Kiev, after Vsevolod Olgovich [died 1146], the position of steward became elective. It also has been noted that as a result of similar but more acute conditions accommodations were instituted in Novgorod, the offices of mayor and chiliarch becoming elective. The beginning of such accommodation must be ascribed to the period of Vsevolod Mstislavich [died 1195], although the oldest existing pact between

Novgorod and princes is from the period of Yaroslav Yaroslavich [1263-1272].¹ After this prince there is a whole series of similar pacts with very few changes from one to another, for the citizens of Novgorod held to the old ways. The new conditions which arose in the North offered no new advantages to the citizens of Novgorod, all of whose efforts of necessity were directed toward retaining the past.

Thus at the beginning of the pacts the citizens of Novgorod usually asked that the prince "kiss the cross" to what his predecessors, his "fathers and grandfathers" swore, to rule Novgorod in the traditional, ancient way without injustice. After enumeration of all the provisions it was stated that this was the way it had been since the time of their fathers and grandfathers. The pacts of Yaroslav Yaroslavich only mentioned the prince kissing the cross, but in the agreements of his son Mikhail the oath also was sworn by the citizens of Novgorod to uphold the prince's reign respectfully, as in ancient times, without injustice. At the time that the lesser Moscow appanage princes began to swear their allegiance, and to hold the reign of the grand prince "in respect" and "in fear," the citizens of Novgorod also had to add the words "in fear" to their pacts. The agreements were concluded in the name of the archbishop, the mayor, chiliarch, all the hundredmen, and all the greater and lesser citizens—in short, all of Novgorod. The archbishop sent the prince his blessing, the rest of the clergy and the citizens their greetings.

According to the conditions determining the rights of a prince as ruler, he administered the Novgorod districts not through his own men, rather through the men of Novgorod. It must be remembered that the term "district" in olden times included not only the geographical concept that it does currently. It also included the functions and incomes associated with it. The prince did not distribute lands or grant patents without the mayor. The prince actually had to be in Novgorod to fulfill his functions and distribute lands. He could not do so from Suzdal, for example, nor could he deprive someone of his land without cause. The prince could trade in the German market only through the intermediacy of Novgorod merchants. He had no right to close the public market or send his constables to it. He could not break agreements concluded with German cities. In the expression of the time used in the pacts he was to guard the soul of Novgorod, that is, not make the citizens of Novgorod oath-breakers to the Germans.

From these conditions it may be seen that grants of patents [of rights] and the concurrent reinforcement of existing privileges through them belonged to the prince only with the participation of the mayor. In this sense Novgorod later forgot the past, and patents came to be granted directly at a town assembly without the prince's participation. An example is the charter granted to the Trinity monastery which begins "Through the blessing of the master, his grace Archbishop Evfimy of God-saved Novgorod the Great, and according to an ancient patent, the grant is made by the mayor of Novgorod the Great, Dmitry Vasilievich, and all the old mayors, by chiliarch Mikhaila Andreevich and all the old chiliarchs,[2] and boyars, and citizens, and merchants and lord Novgorod the Great itself at a town assembly in the Court of Yaroslav."[3]

Grand Prince Vasily Vasilievich annulled this innovation.[4] A provision in his pact with the citizens of Novgorod reads "There are to be no town assembly patents," and another provision states "The seal is to be that of the grand princes." In assuming the right of granting patents in the name of the town assembly the citizens of Novgorod fixed their city seal to these documents.

LEGAL SYSTEM

According to the provisions determining his judicial rights a prince could not hold a trial without the mayor. The citizens of Novgorod undertook not to deny a prince's vicegerent the right to hold trials except in two cases, namely during enemy attack, or when all the citizens were engaged in fortifying the city, and neither plaintiff nor defendant would have time to appear in court. At no time might a hundredman or a labor contractor hold trials without a prince's vicegerent and the mayor. A trial was announced throughout the district by special town criers[5] designated for the task by the prince and by Novgorod. Within the city announcing was done by a Novgorod official and the prince's master of the horse.[6]

When the prince received a denunciation against someone he was to give it no heed until the matter was investigated. The prince was not to annul charters granted by earlier princes. He was not to interfere in an out-of-court settlement amicably reached by the parties involved. He was not to initiate a trial himself. He was not to heed the false accusations of a serf or a slave against a master, nor was he to try a serf or slave without their master. The prince's servitors were not to move a trial beyond the borders of Novgorod nor demand fees for arresting and shackling the suspect.[7] When a prince's man litigated against a citizen of Novgorod, a prince's boyar and a Novgorod boyar were to be the judges. They were to judge justly, with kissing the cross. Should the two men come to argument and be unable to decide the matter, it was to be decided when the grand prince, his brother or his son came to Novgorod. The prince was to send his justices throughout the districts on St. Peter's Day [June 29]. Provisions relating to the prince's income stipulated that it be collected from all the Novgorod districts. In Torzhok and Volok the prince maintained an agent in the part of town that belonged to him. No agent was maintained in Vologda. In two taxation districts, Imovolozhskoe and Vazhanskoe, the prince took marten skins. The direct taxes were collected by the prince at stations on his way to Novgorod rather than when setting out from the city. The citizens of Novgorod undertook not to conceal court fees and fines or other income and payment due the prince. Trade duties and taxes were paid to the prince and to the metropolitan by the bishop as in the past. The *kriuk* tax[8] was paid to the grand prince every third year also as in the past.

The prince was assigned certain areas for hay mowing, hunting, fishing, and making honey. The prince collected tribute in the Novgorod possessions beyond the portages[9] either by farming this tribute out to Novgorod or dispatching one of his retainers. In the latter case the prince's man must set out specifically from Novgorod and not from the Lower Towns.[10] He was restricted to two barges and had to return directly to Novgorod without going to the prince. The tribute was to be allocated in the Lower Towns by the prince.

TAXATION AND FINANCE

Annual collectors of tribute were sent by the prince to the Vod [Northern] district.[11] The prince's servitors and agents enjoyed the right to collect road tolls but might not seize carts from merchants in the villages except perhaps in extreme cases, such as when it became necessary to give warning of the approach of an enemy. Neither the prince, princess, boyars, nor courtiers were permitted to own villages, buy them, or accept them as gifts in the Novgorod territory. Neither might they found new settlements or put up customs posts.

All these provisions point to the fact that Novgorod did not pay tribute to the grand prince except in the trans-portage areas which are mentioned as paying as early as 1133. In 1259 the Tatars took a census and exacted a tribute from Novgorod. The chronicler states that the Tatars registered each Christian house. The rich had it easy while the poor suffered. This suggests that the sum levied was uniform for all residents—the tribute assessments were made regardless of an individual's ability to pay.

The Tatars soon ceased gathering tribute themselves, turning the collection over to the princes, who thus began to gather as it suited their needs. The citizens of Novgorod acted in a similar fashion. They paid the grand prince the so-called "black collection"[12] for the khan and entered the provision into their pacts. "Should the grand princes have to gather a black collection, we will pay the black collection as before." Thus when Dmitry Donskoy had to pay a great tribute after the invasion of Tokhtamysh he sent to Novgorod for the black collection.

How the collection was made is evident from a patent granted by Novgorod to Grand Prince Vasily Vasilievich for the black collection in the Novy Torg districts. "The grand prince is to take the black collection from everyone in the Novy Torg districts as it was done in the past, a new grivna[13] per wooden plow, and twenty squirrel skins from each wooden plow for the prince's scribe. A wooden plow is one that has three horses harnessed to it. A cauldron for tanning leather is the equivalent of a wooden plow, so is a fishing seine and a shop. An iron plow is equivalent to two wooden plows, a smith to one wooden plow, four "pedestrians"[14] equal one plow, a boat is two plows as is a large saltpan. A sharecropper must pay half a plow. A citizen of Novgorod who works a boat or is a vendor in a shop is to pay nothing, neither is an elder.[15] Whoever is impoverished and receives a monthly allotment[16] also pays nothing. Whoever leaves his residence and flees to a boyar's manor, or does not make his plow payment and is discovered, pays a fine that is twice a plow." It is evident that tribute was paid from commercial ventures and determined by the wealth of the owner and that all income was gauged by a "plow," the definite unit of wealth based on agriculture.

Relations of a solely financial nature between the grand princes and Novgorod were determined as far back as the time of Yaroslav I [reigned 1036-1054]. The determination of relations in other spheres, as encountered in the pacts, began in later times and no earlier than the reign of Yaropolk Vladimirovich in Kiev [reigned 1132-1139]. The internecine strife that began in this period between the descendants of Monomakh and those of Oleg [of Chernigov] as well as strife among the many lines of descendants of Monomakh themselves led to a rapid succession of grand princes with repercussions in Novgorod, for that city always recognized its dependence on the grand princes and indeed accepted its own princes from them.

POLITICAL PRACTICE

Disturbance, strife, rapid turnover in positions, the expulsion of princes, partisan politics and the ready shifting of allegiances now occurred in Novgorod as well. If at first the princes were replaced because of a change of ruler in Kiev, later they came to be replaced as the result of the victory of one or another faction in Novgorod itself. Princes' officials, mayors and chiliarchs began to be elected and replaced after the triumph of the faction which successfully made an agreement and accommodation with a given prince. The Southern princes, preoccupied with their own feuds and strife, looked with indifference upon the new order of events in Novgorod. If the descendants of Oleg conceded to the residents of Kiev the election of a previously appointed high official, there is nothing surprising in the fact that other Southern princes readily agreed to the conditions set by Novgorod. Iziaslav Mstislavich [reigned 1146-1154] behaved in like manner at both the Kiev and Novgorod popular assemblies.

When the position of supremacy was won by the Northern princes there was a continual collision of interests between them and the traditions of Novgorod. This developed further and was defined more keenly than the collisions with the other old, established cities. Vsevolod III almost brought Novgorod under his power. His son, Yaroslav, strove to do the same, to rule Novgorod from the bytown of Torzhok. But both men were kept from their goal by the Southern prince Mstislav.

Alexander Nevsky followed in the steps of his forebears. His brother Yaroslav wanted to subjugate Novgorod with the help of the Tatars, then was stopped by a third brother, Vasily. Alexander's son Dmitry was stopped in his similar designs on Novgorod by his brother Andrei. Mikhail of Tver similarly was halted by Yury [Vsevolodovich] of Moscow. The Moscow princes upon achieving supremacy then changed the policy of their predecessors toward Novgorod. They left Novgorod alone with its traditions to itself meanwhile checking the further expansion of Novgorod rights, such as exemption from the metropolitan's jurisdiction. They turned their attention to obtaining as much money from Novgorod as possible, to possess its primary income derived from areas beyond the portages.

Ivan Kalita had conflicts with Novgorod, always on the basis of money. He wanted more than his due and was the first to attempt conquest of the trans-portage [Novgorod] lands. His son Simeon the Proud began his reign with a campaign against Novgorod on monetary grounds, the citizens of Novgorod having refused him the collection of tribute in the Torzhok districts. Dmitry Donskoy marched on Novgorod when he was sorely pressed for money as a result of Tokhtamysh's invasion. Vasily Dmitrievich renewed Kalita's attempt to conquer Novgorod lands. Vasily the Dark took great indemnity payments from Novgorod, but Vasily was much more powerful than all his predecessors. He had rid himself of his kinsmen, acquiring their appanages. He found no rivals in Tver or Nizhny Novgorod, nor did he fear Lithuania or the Horde. Therefore he could contemplate the final blow against Novgorod and destruction of its ancient ways. Contemplate it he did, but death prevented the realization.

Long before this, most likely in the second quarter of the twelfth century, the mayor of Novgorod became an elected official and took a position next to that of the prince in the judicial system and in the distribution of districts. The prince did not lose influence in the selection of the mayor, retaining the right to demand his removal upon disclosure of wrongdoing. Thus in 1171 Prince Riurik Rostislavich took the mayoralty away from Zhiroslav and expelled him from the city. Prince Sviatoslav Mstislavich was unable to do the same to the mayor Tverdislav because, contrary to the agreement, he wanted to remove him without cause.

During this era, Alexander Nevsky was successful in his insistence that Anania be removed from the office of mayor. Nevsky's brother, Yaroslav, demanded that three boyars be removed from their positions. The citizens of Novgorod begged him to forgive these men and be content with giving the position of chiliarch to someone devoted to him. A foreign source from the beginning of the fifteenth century, [Ghillebert de] Lannoy, confirms the fact that mayors and chiliarchs were replaced annually.[17]

Yet the grand princes continuously sent their vicegerents to Novgorod. What was the significance of these officials? Under the year 1342 the chronicler mentions a grand prince's vicegerent named Boris who, along with Archbishop Vasily, pacified quarreling factions. For the year 1375 there is another entry concerning a vicegerent. The citizens of Novgorod, in their desire to entreat Archbishop Alexis not to leave his archbishopric, gathered in a popular assembly at the Court of Yaroslav and sent a petition to the archbishop. The petition bearers were the grand prince's vicegerent Ivan Prokshinich, the mayor, chiliarch, many other boyars and men of standing. Here, as might be expected, the vicegerent took precedence over the town elders. Also during this period whenever there is mention of the rather significant wars of Novgorod with Sweden, the Livonian Germans, and Lithuania, which were declared formally and ended with peace treaties, the degree of the prince's or his vicegerent's participation in external affairs, in decisions concerning war and peace, can be discerned.

FOREIGN RELATIONS

For 1242 an entry states that after the battle of Lake Peipus[18] the Germans sent a mission to Novgorod with reverence, and that peace was concluded without the presence of Prince Alexander. Under 1256 there is a curious entry stating that Alexander Nevsky set out on campaign with his troops and those of Novgorod, who did not know where and against whom they were marching, a sign that Alexander did not announce the campaign at a popular assembly, nor did he ask the citizens' consent.

The peace treaty with the Swedes concluded at Orekhov island in 1323[19] begins "I, Grand Prince Yury with Mayor Varfolomey, Chiliarch Avram and all Novgorod have come to terms with my brother the Swedish king." During the time when the Moscow princes left Novgorod to itself and permitted the Lithuanian princes to punish citizens of Novgorod for their offenses against them, the popular assembly attained great freedom in determining its foreign relations. When the Swedish king Magnus sent a demand that Novgorod convert to Roman Catholicism or face the threat of war the council which met on that occasion included the archbishop, mayor, chiliarch and all the citizens of Novgorod, with no mention at all of the grand prince's vicegerent.

In the agreement with Prince Mikhail Aleksandrovich of Tver[20] the citizens of Novgorod included a provision which forbade the prince to plan war without their consent. The prince nevertheless did not lose his role in foreign affairs. In 1420 the Teutonic Order sent emissaries to Novgorod with a proposal to meet for peace negotiations. At that time Prince Konstantin Dmitrievich,[21] having quarreled with his brother Grand Prince Vasily, was living in Novgorod. The citizens of Novgorod received him with great honor, gave him bytowns in the environs that previously belonged to Lithuanian princes, as well as the proceeds of a tax collection[22] throughout the Novgorod territory.

At the same time there was present in Novgorod the vicegerent of Grand Prince Vasily, Prince Fedor Patrikeevich.[23] Then, according to the chronicler, the German emissaries agreed with Prince Konstantin and with all of Novgorod the Great that the master of the Order was to come personally to the negotiations, and that Prince Konstantin and the citizens of Novgorod were to send their boyars. The city sent the grand prince's vicegerent, Prince Fedor Patrikeevich, Prince Konstantin's boyar Andrei Konstantinovich, two mayors[24] and three Novgorod boyars. Finally, among the extant treaties of Novgorod with Lübeck and Gotland, there is one from the end of the thirteenth or beginning of the fourteenth century written in the name of Grand Prince Andrei, the mayor, chiliarch and all of Novgorod. It states that foreign merchants shall be in the hands of God, of the prince and of all Novgorod. Another charter, pertaining to the second half of the fourteenth century, the period of Muscovite supremacy, was written in the name of the archbishop, mayor, chiliarch and all of Novgorod.

POLITICAL UNREST

Of the twelve periods of unrest in Novgorod which the chronicler mentions between 1054 and 1228, only two were not linked to the replacement of princes. These were the uprising following the escape of Matvey Dushilchevich in 1218, and the uprising against Archbishop Arseny in 1228. From 1228 to 1462 the chronicler mentions twenty-one instances of unrest, only four of which were connected with princely relations. For the most part citizens of Novgorod rose up against their elders, and clearly discernible is the struggle of two factions here—the more and less privileged.[25] It has been observed that from 1054 to 1228 the mayors usually were chosen from a particular group of prominent families.

If selection to other offices went along these same lines it is easy to understand the important position these prominent families achieved, the common goals they pursued and the unrest created in the city by the mutual hostility of some of these families. The effects of the clash between Stepan Tverdislavich and Vodovik in 1230 have been described elsewhere.[26] At a council in 1255 the privileged decided to crush the opposition of the "have-nots" and install a prince according to their will. The divided interests of the two factions further are indicated by the chronicler in his description of the Tatar tribute assessment. The same division is apparent in the unrest of 1418.

A question arises here of the origins of the Novgorod boyars, namely, whether the title was hereditary in certain families. It is well established in Russia's ancient history that in no place and at no time was the title of boyar ever hereditary. The term was applied to senior members of the retinue, advisors and counsellors to the prince. It was he who raised men

to this title. The prince passed it to the sons of his old boyars and retinue members generally according to their merit. He gave it to incoming
members of the retinue also according to their merit, as well as other
conditions. Understandably, if someone was the son of a famous or favorite boyar, he enjoyed more right and greater ease in attaining the same
rank. Yet in times of necessity even a minor servitor[27] might be made a
boyar, something Prince Vladimir Mstislavich once promised on a particular occasion.[28]

Nevertheless we must differentiate rigorously in the sources between
the term "boyar" as applied to a senior member of a retinue, where it was
used in contrast to the junior members, and the same term used in a general sense. Here it was used to designate distinguished, powerful men as
well as members of the retinue in general, in contrast to the populace at
large, the plain folk. In the Novgorod chronicle the term is used in the
general sense of distinguished men as opposed to the populace at large,
the plain folk. The term "boyar" or "great, powerful men" in Novgorod
included men executing government functions as well as those no longer
in office who were all members of the distinguished families, which successfully concentrated the reins of government in their circle.

The son of a mayor enjoyed importance in his own right as well as
being the son of a well-known, powerful and influential man. Consequently he belonged to the number of great, distinguished men—boyars.
He thus was called a boyar in contrast to common men, not because he
had the special title of boyar or belonged to the boyar class. At one point
the Tatars, fearing popular unrest in Novgorod, asked Prince Alexander
to provide them with guards. In response the prince ordered the mayor's
son and all the junior boyars to serve as guards. At the death of Alexander
Nevsky the citizens of Novgorod sent for his brother Yaroslav. The mission consisted of the mayor's son and the senior boyars.

SOCIAL DISTINCTIONS

The term "boyars" in its meaning of "best, distinguished men" as opposed
to commoners is used in the Novgorod and also in all the other chronicles.
Understandably in the other principalities the term usually was used to
designate the members of the retinue in contrast to the rest of the population. In an entry for 1315 the chronicler states that Prince Afanasy Danilovich went from Novgorod to Torzhok with the Novgorod boyars, but
without the commoners. In a description of internecine strife in Tver it
is stated that circumstances were hard for the boyars and servitors as well

as for the commoners. It is said of Dmitry Donskoy that in his efforts to forestall Mikhail of Tver he required all the boyars and commoners of all the cities to swear allegiance. The Novgorod chronicler states that many noble boyars and commoners without number fell at the battle of Rakovor [1268].[29]

"People," the ancient term for commoners used in contrast to boyars and retinue in general, also is encountered. Thus it is stated that the prince of Tver, Mikhail Alexandrovich, having burned the suburbs, districts and villages of Dmitrov brought boyars and "people" back to Tver as captives. In the Volhynian chronicle we encounter the term "simple people" in contradistinction to boyars. Finally, in contrast to the retinue the remainder of the population also bore the name "people of the land."[30] In this fashion all who were not specifically princes were called commoners. In contrast to boyars and retinue members, the general population also bore the name of commoners. From this general population there were to rise new upper classes and in contrast to them the remaining lower classes also were termed commoners.

In Novgorod a detailed accounting of the resident classes shows, after boyars, the "well-off people" who were marked by their wealth. These did not belong to the urban aristocracy, to the ruling individuals and families, or to the merchant class, for they did not engage in trade. The well-off people, sometimes also called "men,"[31] were followed by the merchants and finally the commoners. In an entry for 1398 the chronicler states that the archbishop of Novgorod was visited by a group of petitioners composed of the mayors, boyars, junior boyars, well-off people and lesser merchants. Occasionally the well-off people were listed after the merchants.

These same urban classes, except for the well-off people, may be observed in all the other cities of Northeastern Rus. When Prince Yury Yaroslavich restored the abandoned city of Murom and located his court there he was followed by boyars, grandees, merchants and commoners. In Moscow during this period merchants already were divided into "leading merchants" and "cloth merchants."[32] In their pacts the Moscow princes agree to protect and regard all the merchants and city dwellers as one, and not accept them into their service. The last condition is explained by the fact that the merchants and city dwellers were subject to various kinds of taxation. Permission for them to join the retinue would have removed a major source of the princes' income and means of paying tribute to the Horde.

Later, in the seventeenth century, it will be seen what a loss for Moscow finances was created by the striving of city dwellers to rid themselves of tax obligations through entering the service of, or by becoming dependent on, the clergy, boyars and government officials, and what strong measures the government took to inhibit such movement.[33] The same motivation made princes agree not to take men subject to taxes, merchants, commoners and those registered for tribute into their service nor to buy their lands. When someone bought such lands the previous owners were to repurchase them if they could. If they could not, the new owners descended to become members of the commoner class. If they resisted this change in status they forfeited their lands, which then were distributed at no cost among the commoners. This is identical to later regulations forbidding individuals not subject to taxes[34] to buy land from the taxed.

Similar motivation caused the Moscow princes to agree not to keep indentured servants in Moscow, nor to buy men with their homesteads. The princes further agreed not to buy the lands of men of various trades, crafts and occupations settled on the princes' lands[35] or of captives redeemed by the princes from the Horde and also settled on the princes' lands.[36]

The city population subject to taxes was divided into hundreds as before. The citizens of Novgorod wrote in their charters that a merchant must belong to his hundred and a commoner[37] to his tax collection district. The word "commoner" here is used to mean a rural dweller. In their agreements the Moscow princes also speak of commoners who are under the jurisdiction of a hundredman, but sometimes they speak of commoners as being under a district official. Perhaps in the first case the commoners referred to were city dwellers, and rural dwellers in the second case. The hundredman retained his old prominent role in Novgorod.

The agreements between the city and princes usually began with the archbishop sending his blessing to the prince with the mayor, chiliarch, and hundredmen adding their salutation. If the merchants and urban dwellers in general were under the jurisdiction of their hundredmen, these hundredmen must have been subordinate to the chiliarch.[38] A grand prince in his pacts with appanage princes specified that the Moscow soldiery march under his military commander as earlier, and that the princes were not to accept any of that soldiery into their service. The last stipulation suggests that this soldiery consisted of urban dwellers. It is also known that the title of military commander was given primarily to chiliarchs.

Besides urban dwellers proper subordinate to urban hundreds, the princes' slaves and rural dwellers also could live in city residences. Dmitry Donskoy, in an agreement with Vladimir Andreevich of Serpukhov,[39] promised to send his vicegerents to Moscow and clear it of slaves and rural dwellers. This established the fact that there were residences in Moscow under the jurisdiction of rural regions.

As to the conditions in Viatka province, there is only the evidence found in the first lines of a missive of Metropolitan Jonas, who addressed himself to three regional military commanders, to all *vatamans*,[40] constables, boyars, merchants, the well-to-do and to all Christians.

SOUTHWESTERN CITIES

A most remarkable occurrence in the life of cities of Southwestern Rus before Lithuanian domination was the influx of an alien population of Germans, Jews, and Armenians. In an entry for 1259 the Volhynian chronicler provides curious information about the founding and population of the town of Kholm. Once while hunting Prince Daniel Romanovich noticed a beautiful forested place on a mountain, surrounded by a plain. He was enamored of the place and first built a small fort on it, then a larger one, summoning Germans and Rus, foreigners and Poles from every direction. Many craftsmen and artisans of all kinds fled here from the Tatars: saddle-makers, bowyers, hatters, smiths, coppersmiths and silversmiths. Life began to bubble in the town surrounded by the plain, and its environs and villages came to be filled with homesteads.

Prince Mstislav Danilovich summoned the residents of Vladimir-in-Volhynia—Russians and Germans—to the funeral of his cousin Vladimir Vasilievich. Germans, Jews and Surozhanians[41] wept at Vladimir's funeral. During the period of Lithuanian domination the Jews received great privileges. According to a charter issued by Vytautas in 1388, murder, injury and assault suffered by a Jew was to be punished just as if suffered by a member of the gentry. If a Christian dispersed a Jewish assembly [presumably a religious service] he was to be punished according to the traditions of the land and all his property confiscated into the crown treasury. For an insult to a synagogue the guilty party had to pay a fine of two pounds of pepper to the prince's elder.

A Jew could be asked to swear on the Ten Commandments only in a major suit, involving no fewer than fifty grivnas of cast silver. In other cases he was to swear outside the synagogue doors. A Jew who was a pawnbroker could not be forced to redeem a pawned article on the Sabbath.

Should a Christian accuse a Jew of the murder of a Christian child, the crime must be attested by three Christians and three upstanding Jews. If the witnesses proclaimed the accused guiltless, the accuser suffered the punishment in store for the accused. During Lithuanian rule Rus cities received the German, Magdeburg law.[42] Upon becoming king of Poland in 1387 Jogaila immediately gave Magdeburg law to Wilno. In 1432 Grand Prince Sigismund, son of Kestutis,[43] reaffirmed this charter with a charter in Russian. As a result the residents of Wilno, whether of Roman or Rus faith, were freed of the authority of military commanders, justices and all the grand prince's officials, answering in their affairs only to their own mayor. Sigismund also granted the residents of Wilno, both Poles and Rus, the right to conduct trade without the payment of trade duties throughout the Lithuanian principality and without payment of weight and other fees in their own city. Grand Prince Casimir, son of Jogaila, released them from the obligation of supplying wagons. In the charter of King Casimir granted to Lithuania in 1457 urban dwellers were given the same rights as princes, gentry and boyars, except to go abroad or deal arbitrarily with those subservient to them.

Old Polotsk, which held to the same traditions as Novgorod the Great, retained those traditions, or at least significant traces of them, under the Lithuanian princes as well. It concluded pacts with Riga and with the master of the Livonian Order, affixing its seal to these treaties. "We order," stated King Casimir in his statute charter to Polotsk, "that the boyars, burghers, the city nobles, and all citizens live in harmony and tend to our city affairs in unison as in olden times. They are to gather in that same place where they have long gathered. The burghers, nobles and commoners are not to hold assemblies without the boyars." For collecting royal taxation in Polotsk there was a strongbox with four keys: a boyar key, a burgher key, a nobles' key and a key of the citizenry. For the safekeeping of these keys two upstanding, fit and faithful men were elected from each class, none of whom could open the strongbox without the presence of the others. Who were the nobles? Without doubt, the servitors of the former princes of Polotsk.

ARCHITECTURE

The external appearance of Russian cities did not differ from that of the previous period. Stone fortifications (the Kremlin) appeared in Moscow only during the reign of Dmitry Donskoy. It has been observed how the

Muscovites boasted during Tokhtamysh's invasion that their city (fortress) was of stone and strong, their gates of iron. In 1394 appeared the idea in Moscow of digging a moat from Kuchkov field to the Moscow river. People suffered greatly, states the chronicler. Many houses were demolished, much effort was expended, but nothing was accomplished. Five years after the laying of the Moscow Kremlin, a stone kremlin was laid in Nizhny Novgorod as well. The chronicler ascribes the laying of an extensive fortress in Tver as early as the reign of Mikhail Yaroslavich [the saint].[44] Yet in an entry for 1368 we encounter the remark that a fort of logs chinked with clay was erected in Tver. Later Prince Mikhail Alexandrovich ordered a moat dug along the fort embankment, and the embankment extended from the Volga to the Tmaka. In 1394 the same prince ordered that the old wall be torn down and immediately replaced with one of finished logs.[45]

It is apparent that Donskoy's Kremlin was the sole stone fortification in the whole principality of Moscow. In Serpukhov, Prince Vladimir Andreevich had fortifications of oak built. There is much more information on city structures in the chronicles of Novgorod and Pskov. A stone fortress was founded in Novgorod in 1302. In 1331 Bishop Vasily had a stone wall erected from the church of St. Vladimir to the church of Our Lady and from there to the church of St. Boris and St. Gleb, which construction was completed in two years. Lavrenty, archimandrite of the St. George monastery, had a wall with a parapet forty sazhens[46] long built near the monastery. In 1334 the archbishop ordered the stone walls covered with a roof and the following year built a stone fort from the church of the Prophet Elijah to the church of St. Paul.

In 1372 a moat was dug near the Liudin quarter, Zagorodie and the Nerev quarter. In 1383 a moat was dug along the Holy Wisdom quarter toward the old ramparts. In 1387 ramparts were thrown up near the Market. In the year 1400 Archbishop John[47] began the construction of a central, inner citadel. To the foreign traveller Lannoy[48] Novgorod seemed remarkably large but poorly fortified. Pskov, in his estimation, was far better fortified. In fact we frequently encounter mention of fortifications in Pskov. In 1309 a wall of limestone was built from the church of St. Peter and St. Paul to the Velikaia river. In 1374 the residents of Pskov built a fourth sandstone wall along the old wall from the Pskov river to the Velikaia which, with its oak superstructure, was a little higher than a man. A year later two stone beacons were built in the marketplace. In 1387 three stone towers were put up on the new wall at the entrance. A number of redoubts were built in 1394, and four stone towers were added in 1397. In 1399 a new wall with three towers was laid. Two towers were added that same year, and in 1401 a wall was added to the old one near the Velikaia river. In 1404 a new covered stone wall was laid at the Pskov river and along the old wall which was thicker and higher. In 1407 a higher and thicker wall was built opposite the breastworks from the embankment at the guard house. In 1417 master craftsmen were hired and a wall with a tower was completed before St. Peter's Day [June 29] which collapsed by the Feast of the Dormition [August 15]. In 1420 a new tower and breastworks were erected. Two hundred men did the work and charged Pskov one thousand rubles. Another two hundred rubles were paid the craftsmen who fired the limestone blocks, but the structure fell apart in three years.

In 1452 a new wall with five underground vaults was erected by the breastworks. In 1458 a new wall was built up on the old one at a cost of 150 rubles. Besides Novgorod and Pskov there were several other stone-walled cities in their territories, namely Koporie, Oreshek, Yamsky Gorod, Porkhov, Izborsk and Gdov. The ease and speed with which timber forts were built is evident in an entry for 1414 which states that the citizens of Pskov erected the fort (town) of Kolozhe in two weeks. During Kalita's time the timber fort walls of Moscow were begun in November and finished early in the spring of 1338.

Between 1228 and 1462 no less than one hundred and fifty churches were built in Novgorod, including those in monasteries but excluding the replacements of old churches. At least a hundred were of stone. In the preceding period some seventy were built. Since the number built during the time of Vladimir and Yaroslav I could not have been more than twenty, the total number of churches in Novgorod in the mid-fifteenth century must have been approximately two hundred and thirty. It is curious that in a forty-two-year period, from 1228 to 1270, the chronicler mentions the erection of only two churches in Novgorod. In Pskov there were thirty-five churches built during the period under consideration—twenty-three of stone, two of wood, and ten of unspecified material. In Moscow the chronicler mentions the erection of just fifteen stone churches. Thus evidently the major city of Northeastern Rus lagged behind Novgorod and even Pskov. The total number of churches in Moscow in the mid-fourteenth century may be established from the account of the fire of 1342, which states that all of Moscow burned, including eighteen churches.

At the end of the fourteenth century there were thirty-two churches in Nizhny Novgorod. Pavements are mentioned in Pskov. For example, in 1308 the mayor Boris decided to have the marketplace paved. This was done, and everyone was pleased, concludes the chronicler. In 1397 the marketplace again was paved. No conclusions concerning other Russian cities may be made on the basis of Pskov and Novgorod. Even in Pskov only the marketplace was paved, where there was a constant traffic of people who, of course, must have been pleased when they did not have to stand in mud up to their knees.[49] The pavement, naturally, must have been of wood, for there was no stone pavement here even in the seventeenth century. The Novgorod and Pskov chronicles give accounts of bridge-building in some detail. In 1435, forty hired craftsmen were employed to build a bridge on the Pskov river. The beams were supplied by the hired men, and the other structural components were provided by Pskov. The craftsmen were paid seventy rubles. In 1456 a large bridge was erected across the Pskov river, for which the craftsmen were given sixty rubles and later an additional twenty. Of the constituent parts of the city, districts, avenues, streets and alleys are mentioned.

Concerning the outward appearance of Southwestern Rus cities, a king of Hungary is known to have said of Vladimir-in-Volhynia that never had he encountered such a city in the German lands. In the South, as in the North, city walls were reinforced with trebuchets and arbalests. In Kholm, during the time of Daniel Romanovich, a high tower was built in the center of the town from which all the environs could be observed. It had a stone base of fifteen cubits, and the rest was made of hewn timber which was whitewashed to the appearance of cottage cheese and shone all around. There was a thirty-five-sazhen well next to it. In the town square there was a stone column on which stood a carved stone eagle. The stone was ten cubits high, twelve with the base and capstone. The chronicler says that Prince Vladimir Vasilkovich built many towns and, incidentally, put up a stone column in Kamenets that was seventeen sazhens high, marvellous to behold. In the fifteenth-century Wilno, the capital of the grand principality of Lithuania, consisted of shoddy wooden buildings, a wooden fort and several brick churches.[50]

CONFLAGRATIONS

Since during this period, except for walls and churches, all structures in Russian cities were of wood, fire must have wreaked havoc among them as it did earlier. The chronicles mention a fire in Moscow for the first time

in 1330. In 1335 Moscow burned, as did several other cities. There was
another great fire in 1337, in which eighteen churches burned. This was
followed by a strong rain so that everything carried into vaults and
squares was inundated. The year 1342 saw a similar fire. In 1357 everything in Moscow burned, including thirteen churches. In 1364 Moscow
began to burn during a time of drought and high heat. A windstorm came
up and spread the flames throughout the city. This fire, which started at
All Saints church, was reputedly immense.

Nearly all of Moscow burned in 1388. Several thousand houses burned
in 1389 and again in 1395. Fires in Moscow are mentioned in 1413, 1414,
1415, 1422 and 1441. In 1445 there was the notorious fire after the battle
of Suzdal. The entire citadel was destroyed in 1453 and nearly a third of
the city burned in 1458. Thus in 130 years there were seventeen major
fires, one for every seven years. In Novgorod the entire Slavno quarter[51]
burned in 1231. The fire was so fierce, states the chronicler, that flames
"walked" the water across the Volkhov river. In 1255 the Slavno quarter burned again. Eighty houses burned in 1261. The Nerev quarter
burned in 1267 with a great loss of goods in boats on the Volkhov river.
Everything burned within an hour. Many grew rich from profiteering as
a result, though many others were impoverished. In 1275 the market area
and seven wooden churches burned. Five stone churches were damaged,
one being the German [Roman Catholic]. In 1299 a fire started at night
on Varangian street. A windstorm swept in and the flames spread from
the German market to the Nerev quarter. The large bridge burned and
there was large general loss. Twelve churches burned on the Market side,
and ten in the Nerev quarter. There were three major fires in 1311. Nine
wooden churches burned and forty-six were damaged.

There were other major fires in 1326, 1329, and 1339. A most fierce fire
is mentioned in 1340. The archbishop's residence burned as did the church
of the Holy Wisdom, from which all icons were not carried out in time. The
large bridge burned to the water line. In all, forty-three churches burned
(fifty according to some sources) and seventy people perished. Still other
sources cite forty-eight wooden churches burned, and three stone churches
that collapsed. Three churches burned during a great fire in 1342, and much
hardship was created. The citizens were afraid to live in the city. Some
moved into the fields while others found shelter in boats along the banks.
The whole city was in motion and the hubbub continued for more than a
week. Finally the archbishop and clergy decided on a fast and visited all
monasteries and churches in a religious procession.

In 1347 six streets burned out. There were two fires in 1348. Five streets burned in the second of these, and four wooden churches were destroyed. In 1360 the Podol area and Potters' quarter burned, including seven wooden churches. In the words of the chronicler there was a particularly "malevolent" fire in 1368. The entire inner citadel and the archbishop's residence were desolated and the church of the Holy Wisdom was damaged. Part of the Nerev and all of the Carpenters' quarters were destroyed. The Slavno quarter burned the following year. A year later there was another fire in which the whole Podol and other parts of the city were consumed. In 1377 seven wooden churches were destroyed and three stone churches were damaged. In 1379 eight streets and twelve churches burned. In 1384 a fire in the Nerev quarter incinerated two churches. The following year two quarters burned, the Carpenters' and the Slavno, as well as the market. Twenty-five stone and six wooden churches were obliterated. The fire began Wednesday morning, burned all day, all night, and all morning Thursday. Seventy people perished.

In 1386 a part of Nikita street burned. The Market side[52] was consumed in 1388. Twenty-four churches were destroyed and seventy-five people perished. In 1391 eight wooden churches burned (fifteen in other sources), three of stone were damaged (seven in other sources) and fourteen people perished. That same month the whole Liudin area was consumed, including seven wooden and fourteen stone churches. In 1394 the archbishop's residence and the adjacent area burned, including two wooden churches, with eight stone churches damaged. A conflagration destroyed the river front in 1397. In 1399 there was a fire in the Carpenters' quarter. The Slavno quarter burned completely with twenty-two stone and one wooden church. In 1403 part of Carpenters' and all of the Slavno quarters burned. Fifteen stone churches (seven stone and two wooden in other sources) burned. There were two fires in 1405, one on Yanevaia street which swept fifteen houses, and a second which destroyed the Liudin area, part of Prus street and part of the citadel. Five wooden churches and one of stone were leveled, twelve stone churches were damaged and thirty people perished.

The prince's residence burned in 1406. The next year a fire ravaged the Nerev quarter and damaged twelve churches including the Holy Wisdom. Six wooden churches burned. The Nerev quarter was consumed again in 1414. Five wooden churches were destroyed and eight stone churches damaged. Two quarters burned in 1419, the Slavno and Carpenters', with twenty-four churches. In 1424 the Market side and all of the

Liudin area burned. Two city quarters burned in 1434. There were three fierce fires within one month in 1442. Thus on the average, in the time period considered, Novgorod experienced one major fire every five years. A chronicle entry for 1391 describes a method which the citizens of Novgorod devised for forestalling fires. After a major fire occurring that year they took ten thousand rubles in silver from the vault of the church of the Holy Wisdom saved by Archbishop Alexis, distributing one thousand to each quarter.[53] The money was used to put up stone fire walls on both sides of stockade walls separating the streets of the city.

Ten major fires are mentioned in Pskov, seven in Tver, two in Smolensk, two in Torzhok and one each in Nizhny Novgorod, Staritsa, Rostov, Kolomna, Murom, Korelsky Gorodok, Oreshek and Molvotichi. As for the population figures of cities, an entry for 1230 states that 32,000 people died of the plague in Smolensk. According to a foreign source (Krantz),[54] eighty thousand died of the plague in Novgorod in 1390. According to one source, 24,000 perished in Moscow when it was sacked by Tokhtamysh, though other sources quote half that number.

V

PEASANTRY

RURAL POPULATION

Tracts of land belonging to a city were called its "region,"[1] which term was used not only to mean lands belonging to a city. The same term could be given to the totality of lands belonging to a particular village. A village with a "district" in fact is encountered. For administrative purposes a region was divided into districts which in turn were divided into sub-districts,[2] further divided into "'neighborhoods."[3] Populated points in a region variously were bytowns, large settlements, small settlements, villages, small villages, hamlets, and even smaller units such as new clearings and clusters of homesteads. Villages are encountered belonging to settlements, villages within settlements, and hamlets belonging to villages. It is well known how extensive the land holdings of Novgorod the Great were. According to long-established opinion in scholarship the Novgorod territories were divided since ancient times into five large areas, or "fifths," corresponding to the division of the city of Novgorod itself into five quarters. Thus a resident of a fifth was under the administration of the elder of the quarter to which the fifth belonged. Herberstein[4] speaks of this clearly and simply. Of Russian sources, the Life of St. Savva Vishersky[5] states that the saint, in need of land for building a monastery, sent to the Slavno quarter for aid. Still extant are the copies of land-grant charters given by the administration of the quarter to the Vishersk monastery. The objection may be raised here that these charters do not necessarily deal with the relationship of fifths to the quarters but merely speak of lands that were not far from Novgorod (seven versts) and happened to belong to the Slavno quarter. Yet it is known that fifth lands, such as those of Obonezh in which the Vishersk monastery was located, were contiguous to Novgorod itself and that there were other church lands in the Obonezh fifth, such as Derevianitsk and Volotovsk, that were closer to Novgorod than the Vishersk monastery.

SETTLERS

During the period under consideration princes and landholders in general strove to increase the population on their lands by granting privileges to new arrivals. During the reign of Dmitry Donskoy a man named Evseika decided to move from Torzhok to Kostroma in the prince's patrimony. The grand prince freed him of all taxes except for a quitrent of five marten skins[6] per year. Besides that, he assigned him to the care of his uncle Vasily the chiliarch. When granting land to a monastery or a private individual the princes usually included a provision in their patents stating that if the landholder populated the given tract the population was freed of all taxes or compulsory labor for a number of years. Furthermore the provision covered two separate situations, the case of the landholder populating his land with settlers who lived there before,[7] or the population of the lands with settlers from other principalities. The latter received greater privileges such as exemption from all taxes for a period twice that of the first category, usually ten instead of five years.

In case of the successful settlement of a given tract, a landholder received new privileges and rewards. For example, the monks of the St. Cyril monastery[8] for transforming the virgin tract granted them into farmland, for settling it with people, and establishing a small village and hamlets, received the privileges from Prince Vasily Vasilievich that no officials visit the village and hamlets, stay there or requisition provender, guides or wagons. The conditions under which new arrivals settled uninhabited tracts depended, of course, on a mutual agreement between them and the landholder. They could be hired to work the land for wages and thus be called "hired men." They could cultivate the land and give the landholder half of what was produced; such were called half- or third-sharecroppers.[8] A peasant who borrowed money from the landholder upon arrival was called a "silver man."[10] Finally there was the term "contract men" stemming from some particular agreement or arrangement.[11] Princely charters show that such men moved from one area and from one principality to another. Clearly the privileges offered for settling unpopulated districts motivated them to move. In the opposite case, if they lived in one locale beyond the expiration of a given period, ten years for example, they lost their privileges. It was not advantageous for them to resettle elsewhere just in order to receive privileges again. Limitations on free movement already appear for men of two classes, the "orphans"[12] and "Christians"[13] (as the rural population was called at that time). The orphans could leave the land only in autumn upon the cessation of field work, specifically during a period of two weeks before St. George's Day [November 26] and the week after it. If the man was a "silver man"[14] he had to repay his loan at that time.

There was injunction against the free movement of peasants as a benefit to certain landholders. Grand Prince Vasily Vasilievich bestowed a privilege upon the abbot and brethren of the Trinity monastery by forbidding the old-resident peasants[15] from leaving the monastery-owned village of Prisek and its lesser villages. A further limitation forbade landholders whose lands were exempt from the prince's taxes and outside his legal jurisdiction to accept tribute-paying men of the district who were legally and for tax purposes in the prince's jurisdiction. The landholders had to be content with recruiting men from other principalities. Thus Ivan Kalita forbade the archimandrite of St. George's monastery to take onto his lands district men who were subject to taxation or settlers from the Moscow principality.

Grand Prince Vasily Dmitrievich set the same conditions in permitting Metropolitan Photius[16] to buy a lesser village in the district of Talsha. Occasionally a prince gave a landholder the right to keep his peasants from leaving, as well as the right to return those who left previously. Grand Prince Vasily Vasilievich granted such rights to the abbot of the Trinity monastery concerning men who left the monastery villages in the region of Uglich. As for relations between the itinerant rural population and the landholders, it is known that princes granted to some landowners the right to try men settled on their lands except in the case of murder, and in other instances of joint trial, in which case the landholders held trial together with the prince's vicegerent, district agent or justice. Occasionally landholders received the right to hold trial in all cases except for murder, banditry and robbery.[17]

SERFS AND OTHERS

Coexisting with the itinerant rural population were men who were not free but belonged to the landholder. In patents granted landholders distinction is made between men bought or redeemed [from captivity] and old residents or new arrivals. In their agreements princes differentiated between their slaves and villagers, spoke of men who were bought, of bought beekeepers and quit-rent men,[18] of convicted men they bought or acquired [as a result of the latter's inability to pay the fine for the committed crime], of "total slaves" [those born into slavery and totally unfree], of bound men who freely entered slavery on a contract basis. Also mentioned is a category of men who, under particular conditions, pledged or indentured themselves to someone else. Since a chief motivation for such indentured service was the desire to escape the obligations and duties placed on free and independent men, the princes agreed not to have indentured men in the city of Moscow.

In this era, then, we must differentiate between free and independent men, non-independent men (such as the indentured) and unfree men who were in that state either permanently or temporarily, depending on whether they were born into slavery, bought, taken prisoner or had consigned themselves freely into slavery for a specified number of years. The terms "full slaves" or "field slaves"[19] were used for the first category. The expression "send forth"[20] meant to free such men. It is curious that instead of the expression "free man"[21] the expression "grand prince's man" was used. Concerning the status of slaves, the citizens of Novgorod in their agreements insisted that a slave's bearing of information against his lord be given no weight, and that judges not judge a slave or sharecropper without the lord's presence.

In discussing the various social classes of Ancient Rus we cannot avoid the question of who could possess landed property. Along with servitors and clergy, merchants also appear as landholders. An entry for 1371 states that a leading merchant of Nizhny Novgorod named Taras Petrov redeemed from captivity a great number of men of various classes and bought himself a patrimony of six villages beyond the Kudma river from the grand prince. Nevertheless the specific meaning of the term "leading merchant" [22]is not defined in the chronicles. Sometimes it was used in the sense of merchant in general and sometimes in the sense of the most established, richest merchants. In Novgorod sources the term "leading merchant" did not signify a special class. Rather it was used broadly in its meaning of simply merchant,[23] though clearly only the richest of merchants, the "leading merchants," could acquire landed property. Only they with their means could be involved both in trade and agriculture, while the lesser merchants could not conduct trade in a store and simultaneously live in a village.

Also the conflict with government interests must have led already to a prohibition against merchants owning land, for a landholder was subject to the prince's service whereas a merchant was subject to taxes and made payment to the princely treasury from his enterprise. Should a merchant become a landholder he must have to meet two orders of government obligation, namely service and the payment of taxes. Clearly he could not satisfy both obligations. Furthermore it has been noted that because of financial demands he could not leave his trade and enter government service, for the princes made pacts with each other not to accept merchants into their service. All landholders entered the class of men subject to princely service, for princes refused to recognize any classes between that of men subject to service and men of commerce and industry. Thus in later times, according to the legal code,[24] sons of non-service fathers who bought patrimonies had to enter the tsar's service, otherwise the patrimonies were confiscated by the crown. A class of landholders living on their lands could not have formed during this period because, even as before, there was continuous colonization of the Northeast territory and constant movement and wandering.

It was disadvantageous for a tiller to stay long in one place by reason of the poor quality of the soil in the Northeast, which nowhere held the promise of continuous fertility. A short time after it was first occupied, burned and slashed the land began to demand great effort. It was advantageous for the tiller to move to new soil. Besides, we also observe throughout the whole span of ancient Russian history a tendency for the relatively poor and insignificant to indenture themselves to the rich who enjoyed special rights and privileges, finding safety and relief from obligations under their protection. This tendency is evident as well in other European states during the Middle Ages. It is natural in newly-born societies in which there is an absence of security, where government and laws are not yet strong enough to provide protection and security to all members of society. Thus it was advantageous for tillers to move to the lands of rich and established landholders, bishops, monasteries and grandees, for along with the privileges granted at initial settling the settlers benefitted from other privileges stemming from the diverse rights exercised by various landholders. Most of all, the settlers had the protection of powerful men.

COLONIZATION

In turning our attention to the distinguishing characteristic of Russia's ancient history, the colonization of the country, the question of the origin of landed property and its various forms easily is resolved. As soon as Northeast Rus appeared on the historical stage there appeared strong colonization under the protection of the princes. Even if there was no definitive evidence of such colonization it would have to be assumed, for history initially finds Northeastern Rus a country of Finns, and later of Slavs. Therefore, even assuming that the Finnish population did not disappear but became Slavicized, strong Slavic colonization must be admitted, though this colonization did not occur in prehistoric times when, as the expression states, "each lived with his own kin and in his own lands."[25] It occurred within historical memory, when Northeastern Rus comprised a definite region and principality in which a certain line of princes ruled.

It follows, therefore, that colonization could not have taken place without the knowledge and influence of an existing authority which ruled over an enormous, sparsely populated but well-defined region. For the progeny of the first settlers, both urban and rural, the land was under common ownership. This is indicated by the customary method of landholding by urban and rural communes. That still leaves broad, unpopulated expanses belonging to no one, or rather, belonging to Rostov. For in Rostov there was the head of the realm, the prince, who ruled the entire area through his officials and regional agents. Therefore no further change could have taken place, no new rights or relationships could have arisen, without the knowledge or will of the prince. Granted, in the early stages the prince ruled in his regions not without the knowledge and participation of the eldest city, but there is no basis for assuming that after Andrei Bogoliubsky and Vsevolod III the princes ruled with the consent of the citizens of Rostov.

First of all the princes were masters of their territorial lands. They could place them into the complete possession of the members of the retinue along with the right of populating it with all kinds of men, both

free and slave. They could give it to the clergy and, finally, they could
sell it to rich merchants such as Taras Petrov, who were capable of populating the land. Such are the various forms of the origin of private landed
property, of patrimonies. On one hand, it has been observed that for residents of cities and villages there existed the age-old tradition of considering lands which belonged to the cities and villages as common heritage.
Land belonged to the commune, not to its separate members. When commoners lost their independence in relation to the prince the land became
the property of the sovereign.

On the other hand, there was still much land left. Acting as private
individuals, landholders strove to populate their holdings by recruiting
men from wherever they could. The prince did the same in relation to its
unpopulated lands. Farming settlers arrived and were received with joy,
but exactly how did they settle? They did not buy land from the prince,
for there was no advantage in buying since they could use the land for
free and, upon finding it unproductive, move elsewhere. When settlers
remained for long on their plots the land passed to their children, without new forms or agreements, though clearly the prince and the inhabitants fully understood that the land occupied by them was not in their full
possession. It was not their patrimony, not granted them for their services
or bought by them, rather given them only for their use even though it
benefited the prince that this use continue as long as possible and pass
from generation to generation.

Such was the origin of the so-called "black" or princely lands. What
was true of rural areas was true of cities as well, for the cities were populated in the same manner. A man of commerce or an artisan settled in a
city on a parcel of land assigned by the prince. He put up a house, left
the house and land as inheritance to his children or passed the property
on for money, selling it to someone like himself. In all these instances the
prince did not interfere as long as the "black" land did not become
"white," did not become someone's totally private property. From here
stem all the prohibitions against buying the land of "black" men, that is,
against the transfer of princely property to private ownership.

Besides the obligations placed on rural dwellers mentioned in the
passages on the princes' income, there were other duties they must fulfill. For example, they built city fortifications, erected the prince's residence and that of the district official, fed the prince's horses, mowed hay,
assisted in the hunt (for bear and elk) on orders of the prince's huntsmen
and provided provender, wagons and guides for the prince, chiliarchs,

vicegerents, district agents, justices and various officials and envoys of the prince.

Together with the social classes mentioned above, at the end of the first half of the fifteenth century there occurs for the first time mention of Riazan Cossacks who came to the aid of Riazan and Moscow against the Tatar prince Mustafa. They came armed with spears, pikes and sabers.

POLITICAL AND NATURAL DISASTERS

So far the efforts of princes to increase the population of their principalities has been described. Let us now turn our attention to the factors which hindered this increase, the political and physical catastrophes such as internecine and foreign wars, famine, plague and other disasters. In the period considered, ninety instances of internecine strife have been observed in the North, sixteen in Vladimir (including the cities of Pereiaslavl, Kostroma, and Galich), fifteen in Novgorod, fourteen in Moscow, thirteen in Tver, nine each in Smolensk, Riazan and the Dvina lands, four each in Severia and Suzdal-Nizhny Novgorod, three in Yaroslavl-Rostov, two in Viatka and one in Pskov. Thus Vladimir province, which suffered the most from internecine strife, was laid waste almost once every fifteen years, and Northern Rus in general saw internecine strife approximately every two years.

Devastation at the hands of foreign enemies occurred twenty-nine times in Novgorod, twenty-four in Pskov, seventeen in Riazan, fourteen in Moscow, eleven each in Vladimir and Nizhny Novgorod, eight in Severia, seven each in Smolensk and Tver, four in Yaroslavl-Rostov and one in Viatka. Therefore Novgorod province, apparently suffering more than the others from foreign wars, suffered invasions once every eight years. There were approximately 133 foreign incursions. Of these, forty-eight came at the hands of the Tatars, including accounts of the devastating excesses of the baskaks in various cities. If the figure for foreign invasions is added to that of internecine strife, the total comes to 232, or a devastation almost every year.

Of course, no conclusions may be drawn purely from these figures. For though Novgorod and Pskov suffered more from foreign invasions than the other provinces, they nevertheless remained the richest cities in all of Northern Rus. During this time the city of Pskov was in the hands of the enemy only once, even then apparently not suffering great harm. Novgorod was not taken even once. Many of the German, Swedish and Lithuanian invasions of Novgorod and Pskov were limited to the border districts and cannot be compared in any way with the invasion of Batu , the two Tatar devastations during the strife among the sons of Nevsky, the devastation of Tver province by the Tatars and Kalita,[26] or the invasions of Tokhtamysh and Edigey.[27]

The figures cited for the Eastern provinces are equally deceptive. They show, for example, that the principality of Moscow was more subject to devastation than the rival principality of Tver. But analysis of other factors, specifically the nature of the catastrophes and the time of their occurrence, change the picture completely. Tver suffered total devastation at the hands of the Tatars and Kalita during the reign of Prince Alexander Mikhailovich. Then, before it had a chance to recover, strife began among the princes, which caused the population to leave their native lands for other principalities. Moscow, on the other hand, suffered no destruction from foreign enemies from the time of Kalita to that of Donskoy. Internecine strife began there only during the reign of Vasily Vasilievich. By that time, utilizing its period of peace, Moscow gained final supremacy over all the other principalities.

The figures show that it was the border provinces of the Southeast and Northwest that suffered most from invasions, namely Riazan, Novgorod and Pskov. Riazan suffered from the Tatars and Novgorod and Pskov from the Swedes, Germans and Lithuanians. The numerical majority of invasions occurring in the Northwest. Yet it has been noted that Swedish and German invasions bore no comparison to those of the Tatars. On the other hand, the harm that Russia suffered from the Tatars need not be exaggerated. It should not be forgotten that the yoke was extremely burdensome only during its first twenty-five years. As early as 1266 the chronicler speaks of it as becoming lighter, that Tatar baskaks disappeared by the end of the thirteenth century, and the princes administered the tribute.

After the Tatar devastations resulting from internecine strife among the sons of Nevsky to the devastation of Tver by the Tatars and Kalita, and then right up to Tokhtamysh's invasion, that is for a period of more than fifty years, Eastern Russia did not experience Tatar invasions, save for those in the border principalities of Riazan and Nizhny Novgorod. In the subsequent period, except for the invasions of Tokhtamysh, Edigey and Ulu-Mahmet, there were raids which touched only the borderlands, with primarily the principality of Riazan suffering as it did previously. In general, figures in history must be treated with caution.

During this time natural disasters were also of consequence. Under 1230 the chronicler speaks of a famine which ravaged all of Russia except for

Kiev. In mid-September a severe frost destroyed the grain crop in Novgorod province, and thus the great sorrow began, says the chronicler. Bread began to sell at eight kunas, a tub of rye cost twenty grivnas, of wheat—forty grivnas, of millet—fifty grivnas, of oats—thirteen grivnas. The city and district of Novgorod was abandoned by its people and foreign cities and lands were filled with "our brothers and our sisters," states the chronicler. Those who stayed behind began to die. Corpses lay in the streets. Little children were eaten by dogs. People ate moss, pine, linden bark and various greenery. Some of the commoners killed the living and ate them. Others cut the flesh off corpses, still others ate horses, dogs and cats. Criminals were executed, hanged and burned, but now a new evil appeared. The houses of prosperous men were set afire in the hope of finding rye, their possessions were looted. Kinsmen had no pity for each other. A man would not break off a piece of his bread for his neighbor. Fathers and mothers sold their children as slaves to foreign merchants for bread. There was anguish in the streets at the sight of unburied corpses and grief at home at the sight of children begging for bread and dying of hunger. Prices rose so high that a quarter-tub of rye sold for a grivna of silver.

Archbishop Spiridon put up a mortuary for indigents and had a good and humble man named Stanila carry the dead on horseback there from all over the city. Stanila worked day and night unceasingly and gathered 3,030 corpses. The mortuary was filled and another was built and filled with 3,500 corpses. The Pskov chronicler describes the horror in that city in much the same terms. He was especially aghast that people ate horse meat during Lent. "I would write of worse things," he ends, "but it is bitter enough." Four mortuaries built in Smolensk were filled with 32,000 corpses. In 1251 heavy rains in Novgorod province inundated the grain and hay, and frost destroyed the grain crop that autumn. The same thing recurred in 1291. In 1303 the winter was warm with no snow cover at all. Again there was no grain crop. In 1309 a severe famine raged throughout the Russian land because mice ate much of the grain. There was a great increase in prices in 1331 and the famine was called the time of "rye grown high [in price]." Haze covered the land from midsummer of 1364, the heat was intense. Forests, swamps and the soil itself burned, the rivers ran dry. This recurred the following year and caused a great famine.

In the autumn of 1370 a great deal of snow covered the grain, thereafter the winter was warm and the snow melted by Lent, at which time the grain was reaped. That summer black spots like nails appeared on the sun. The haze was so intense that nothing was visible at a sazhen's length. Men bumped foreheads, birds plummeted onto people out of the air, beasts mingled with people, bears and wolves wandered in villages, rivers, swamps and lakes dried up, forests burned, famine was severe throughout the land. In 1373 there was great heat and not a drop of rain all summer. The summer of 1407 was murky and rainy. The "winged worm" [locust] flew from the east, ate the trees and caused them to wither. Many died of hunger in 1409. There were high prices in Nizhny Novgorod in 1412. In 1418 it began to snow on September 15 and continued for three days and nights to a height of four spans of the hand. Frosts set in, then it turned warm and the snow melted. Little grain was harvested after the snow, sending famine throughout the Russian land.

In 1421 a famine raged in Novgorod and all the Russian land. Many died of hunger, others fled to Lithuania. Some froze on the way because the winter was very cold. In Moscow a small barrel of rye sold for one and a half rubles, in Kostroma for two, in Nizhny Novgorod for six. At that time the storehouses in Pskov were full of grain from previous years. A great trek began toward the city, people of Novgorod, Karelians, Chud, Vod, people from Tver and Moscow, great numbers from all Russia, simply came to buy rye for export from Pskov, its suburbs and bytowns. Prices rose so that a standard grain measure of rye began to sell at seventy nogatas, of spring wheat at fifty, of oats at thirty. The citizens of Pskov then forbade grain exportation and expelled the newcomers from the city and all the districts. Some left, but many of those who stayed died, so that four mortuaries were filled in Pskov alone. Those who perished in the bytowns and the countryside were without number.

In the autumn of 1429 the earth and forests burned. Smoke filled the air and it was hard for people to see each other. Fish and fowl perished from the smoke. For two years fish smelled of smoke. As a result there was severe famine throughout the Russian land. In 1436 frost destroyed the grain at reaping, and there was a large rise in prices. Fierce frosts in the winter of 1442 brought great misfortune to man and beast. There was another fierce winter and hay at high prices in 1444. In an entry for 1446 the Novgorod chronicler states that grain in his region was expensive not only that year, but for the ten preceding years. Two baskets cost a half ruble. Sometimes there was more, sometimes less, sometimes none at all. There was enormous anguish. All that could be heard was crying and weeping in the streets and marketplace. Many fell dead from hunger, children before parents, fathers and mothers before children. Many fled to Lithuania, to the Germans, the heathens and the Jews. Some sold themselves to merchants as slaves for bread.

PLAGUE

Plague is not mentioned for a long period. For 1284 the Southern chronicler mentions a great plague that felled animals in Rus, Poland and among the Tatars. Horses, cattle and sheep all perished. The Northern chronicler mentions a livestock-killing plague in the year 1298 and one that killed people in 1308. In 1318 there was plague in Tver. In 1341 in Novgorod there was a plague that killed cattle. That same year there was a massive plague in Pskov. There was no place to bury the dead. Children, sometimes as many as seven or eight, were buried in one grave with their father or mother. This calamity was merely the precursor of far greater. Soon the fearsome second half of the fourteenth century set in, but even for the year 1348 the chronicler mentions plague in Polotsk.

In 1350 there was news of the plague in distant lands and in 1351 it began in Pskov exhibiting these symptoms. The victim coughed blood and died on the fourth day. Foreseeing immediate death, men and women entered monasteries and died there, having taken vows. Others prepared for death at home by tending their souls and distributing their property to churches, monasteries, spiritual fathers and beggars. Priests had not the time to go to the house of each of the dead, asking instead that the corpses be brought to the churchyard. Toward morning there were thirty or more corpses at each church. A single funeral service was held for all, save for the final prayer which was said over each of the deceased. Then from three to five were placed in each grave.

So it was at all the churches. Soon there was no more space for burial. Then burials began at a distance from the churches and finally empty areas totally removed from churches were designated as cemeteries. Many assumed that none would be left alive because, once plague entered a kin group or family, rarely did anyone live. If the dying gave their children or possessions to someone, these would also sicken and die. As a result people were afraid of accepting anything from the dying. Even relatives began to avoid each other. Some magnanimous in spirit, having repulsed all fear, buried even dead strangers for the salvation of their own souls.

The citizens of Pskov sent to Novgorod for Archbishop Vasily to come and bless them. The archbishop came and traversed all of Pskov with the clergy, bearing crosses and holy relics. All the citizenry followed the crosses, beseeching "Lord have mercy." After several days in Pskov the archbishop returned to Novgorod in a state of health, then sickened and died on the way at the Uza river. The plague followed the bishop from Pskov to Novgorod. It ravaged Pskov from spring to winter and Novgorod from the Feast of the Dormition [August 15] till spring of the following year. Along with Novgorod it simultaneously ravaged Smolensk, Kiev, Chernigov and Suzdal. In Glukhov and Belozersk it left not a single survivor. In 1353 the plague struck Moscow.[28] In 1360 there was a second plague in Pskov which exhibited a new symptom, a swelling of the glands which meant rapid death. The citizens of Pskov sent to Novgorod for Archbishop Alexis. He came and blessed everyone from the mighty to the wretched, traversed the whole city with crosses, celebrated three liturgies, and the plague began to abate.

In 1363 plague came from the Lower Volga to ravage Nizhny Novgorod, then the Riazan, Kolomna, Pereiaslavl, Moscow, Tver, Vladimir, Suzdal, Dmitrov, Mozhaisk, Volokolamsk and the Beloozero districts. As the disease set in, a victim felt as though struck by a pike in the shoulder blade, or in the chest at the heart, or between the shoulder blades. He then coughed blood, suffered high fever followed by profuse sweating and finally trembling. That would be all. The sickness lasted a day or two, rarely three. The glands did not swell in a consistent place. Sometimes it was in the neck, or below the chest, or under the cheekbone or shoulder blade. Fifty to a hundred people died a day, sometimes more. Going as it did from city to city, the calamity lasted more than one year.

For the year of 1373 the chronicler mentions severe plague and livestock murrain as a result of heat and drought. In 1375 there was plague in Kiev, in 1387 severe plague in the province of Smolensk. Only five men walked out of the city alive and closed the gates as they did so. There was severe plague in Pskov in 1389 and in Novgorod the subsequent year. Plague is mentioned in Smolensk in 1402. In 1403 plague of the gland-swelling type is mentioned in Pskov, said to have come from Dorpat. In 1406 Pskov was struck anew by the calamity. In 1409 blood-coughing plague ravaged the districts of Rzheva, Mozhaisk, Dmitrov, Zvenigorod, Pereiaslavl, Vladimir, Yuriev, Riazan and Tarussa, appearing in some districts of Moscow.

The symptoms were spasms in the arms, legs and neck, gnashing of the teeth, a crackling of the bones and joints, screams and moans. Some had their mental faculties affected and suffered loss of reason. Some died after being sick one day while others lasted thirty-six to forty-eight hours. Still others recovered after being sick for three or four days. In 1414 there was a grave disease throughout the Russian land, the so-called "bone-wracker." In 1417 a plague marked by coughing blood and swollen glands devastated Novgorod, Ladoga, Rusa, Porkhov, Pskov, Torzhok, Dmitrov and Tver. In Novgorod Archbishop Simeon, the clergy of all seven cathedrals, and all residents circled the city in a religious procession. Then the people of Novgorod, some on foot and others on horseback, set out for the forest, brought back logs and erected the church of St. Anastasia. That same day it was blessed and a liturgy celebrated. The remaining timber was used to erect the church of the Prophet Elijah.

In Torzhok a church was also built in a day, that of St. Athanasius. An entry for 1419 mentions plague in Kiev and other Southwestern lands. The year after that plague began to sweep the Northeastern zone, the districts of Kostroma, Yaroslavl, Yuriev, Vladimir, Suzdal, Pereiaslavl, Galich, Pleso and Rostov. Grain was left in the fields, for there was no one to reap it. Sometime later plague and famine devastated Novgorod and Pskov. In 1423 there was plague of the blood-coughing and gland-swelling type in Novgorod, Korela and throughout the Russian land. In 1425 there was plague in Galich. In Moscow and other regions it continued from Pentecost into the following years. A new symptom appeared, pustules. If they were blue in color, the patient died on the third day. If red, they healed and the victim recovered. Plague of the swollen gland type began in Pskov in December of 1441 and continued into the summer of 1442, until January 1443 in the outlying districts. The last account of plague appears for the year of 1448. Horses and livestock were struck by murrain, though humans did not suffer greatly.

In the period considered there are no less than twenty-three accounts of plague in various locales. Considering the fact that there are only three or four accounts of plague before the second half of the fourteenth century and that all other accounts pertain to this unhappy half-century, we conclude that there was incidence of plague every five years in that period. It must be observed further that plague struck in the very first years of the second half of the century at a time when the principalities of Moscow, Vladimir and Nizhny Novgorod during the reign of Kalita and Simeon the Proud were enjoying a peaceful period marked by the absence of domestic and foreign wars. Later these were to begin again as Moscow renewed its struggle with Tver, Riazan and Novgorod. Again there was the devastation of Tatar and Lithuanian invasions. Despite this

Dmitry Donskoy found the means to field at Snipe Field an army strong enough to defeat Mamay's hordes. It must particularly be noted here that after natural calamities ruinous to a given population, this population strives to replenish itself with greater than normal energy. Thus, a whole new generation took the field at Snipe Field, born after the fearful plague which devastated Rus at the end of Simeon the Proud's reign.

OTHER CALAMITIES

Of destructive natural phenomena the chronicles mention an earthquake in 1230, and then not again until 1446. The first is mentioned in the chronicles of Suzdal and Novgorod, the second by the chronicler of Moscow. The Suzdal chronicler was told by eyewitnesses how, during the earthquake of 1230 in Kiev, the stone church of Our Lady at the Caves monastery[29] was sundered into four parts and all food and drink was swept from the tables in the refectory.

In Pereiaslavl-Russky[30] the church of St. Michael split in half. The ground shook everywhere on the same day and hour, May 3, during liturgy. On the tenth of that same month the sun at its rising had an odd appearance, like that of a "large round loaf." In the words of the chronicler, it then became as small as a star and "perished." On the fourteenth the sun again began to vanish and for three days appeared in the shape of the moon. On that same fourteenth day when the sun was in the shape of the moon, red, green and blue pillars appeared on either side of it, and a flame descended from heaven like a huge cloud over the Lybedia brook. It seemed to all that the final hour had come. Everyone embraced and bade each other farewell, weeping bitterly. Then the fearful flames flashed through the whole city without causing harm, fell into the Dnieper and were extinguished.

The Novgorod chronicles speak of severe floods. In May 1421 the waters of the Volkhov rose and carried away the great bridge, two others, and a church. In many churches services could be held only on platforms because there was water below. Under 1399 the chronicler mentions an unusually early spring and fearful thunderstorms from which many perished. Similar thunderstorms occurred in 1406. For that same year there is the following entry in the chronicles. After St. Peter's Day [June 29] there was such a storm in the Nizhny Novgorod province that the wind swept up a man along with a horse and wagon. The next day the wagon was found up in a high tree on the other side of the Volga. The horse was on the ground dead, the man never was found. An entry for

1442 again mentions fearful thunderstorms and tempests in the summer and fierce frosts in the winter.

In Moscow in June of 1460 there appeared a fearsome dark cloud from the west and such a storm came up that nothing could be seen for dust. People were in despair, but this time the gloom and wind soon disappeared. The next day, toward evening, a cloud rose up from the south and again a fearsome storm began. Even many stone churches trembled. The parapet was torn off the Kremlin walls and demolished. The roofs and superstructures of churches were shorn off. In the villages churches were ripped from their foundations and cast far away. Old forests, groves and oaks were torn out by the roots.

Of customs which had a harmful effect on the health of the populace there was the one of burying the dead within cities, near churches. On the other hand, any precautionary measures taken during plagues are unknown. There is almost no information on medical practice. It is known only that Grand Prince Vasily Vasilievich ordered that tinder be burned frequently on many places of his body as a preventative against ataxia. The burns became infected and the sickness ended in death.[31]

VI

THE ECONOMY

TRADE

The period is marked by conditions which furthered population growth in certain regions as opposed to others, the principality of Moscow being an example of growth. Of regions which even previously had a relatively dense population as a result of a favorable trading location, only Novgorod and Pskov maintained their significance. The trade role of Novgorod for Eastern Europe at this time did not decline in the least. As before, the city served as an intermediary between Asia and Eastern and Northern Europe. The accumulation of wealth in Novgorod explains its expansion and increase of its population, as well as the beautification of the city itself. After the fall of Kiev, Novgorod was indisputably the richest and most vital city in all of Russia. Novgorod merchants are encountered in the distant Southwest, in the city of Vladimir-in-Volhynia.

Everywhere Novgorod obtained ready passage without tariffs for its merchants and those of Torzhok and its bytowns. It was for this that a khan's patent was bought in the Horde. The city prevailed upon the princes to promise not to break the treaties it had made with German cities, not to close the German market or place constables in it, and to trade there only through Novgorod merchants.

That Novgorod was highly valued by the Germans is seen from the fact that when there was a severe famine there in 1231 German merchants arrived from beyond the sea with grain and did much good, in the words of the chronicler, namely that they sold their goods at a low price. From 1383 to 1391 there was no firm peace agreement between Novgorod and the Germans, whereupon in 1391 the Novgorod and German emissaries met at Izborsk. Among the Germans there were emissaries from Riga, Yuriev, and Reval, as well as some from beyond the sea, from Lübeck and Gotland. The chronicles speak of a special class of Novgorod merchants who dealt in salt and of the market halls of Gotland and Pskov. Finally, there exist three agreements of that period between Novgorod and Lübeck, Gotland and Riga. The first pertains to 1270 and is little different from the agreement cited previously. The second is dated at the end of the thirteenth, or the beginning of the fourteenth century, the time of Andrei Alexandrovich's reign [1293-1304],[1] in which Novgorod assigned three overland and one water route through their territories to merchants of Latin [German] language. It specified that should any route become dangerous, the prince was to warn the foreign merchants and provide men for their safe passage.

In another charter, relating to the second half of the fourteenth century, Novgorod undertook not to make future claims [against Germans] for harm done Novgorod merchants by German pirates along the Neva river. This agreement establishes the fact that the merchants of Novgorod journeyed to trade in Lübeck, Gotland and Stockholm. Some details of German trade in Novgorod as expressed in statements of terms[2] are quite interesting. For example, Germans were forbidden to take goods on credit from the Russians, to enter into trade partnerships with them or transport their goods. It was forbidden to export adulterated beeswax or import fake fabric. Retail sale of goods was generally forbidden, but permitted with restrictions to the so-called *Kindern*.[3] No one was permitted to bring in goods with a value exceeding one thousand marks in silver.

The right to elect aldermen was granted only to the deputies of Lübeck and Visby, and the former must be citizens of those places. The same rules held for the selection of priests. It was forbidden to seek privileges for personal gain or make new terms without the consent of Lübeck and Visby. It was forbidden to allow entry to foreign merchants (primarily Lombards) who were not members of the Hanseatic League. The main route for foreign trade ran, as before, by way of the Neva river, Lake Ladoga and the Volkhov past Staraia Ladoga to the rapids. Here, for a fee, traders were taken through by special pilots. The route continued to the Fishers' Tavern[4] (a fishing village 33 versts from Lake Ladoga) then to Gestevelt[5] (the merchant's harbor 34 versts from Ladoga) where tariffs were paid, and finally to the port of Novgorod.

Smolensk maintained its trade ties with Riga which were so profitable that the governments of both cities agreed in 1284 not to hinder mutual trade even if the Smolensk province and the bishop or master [of the Livonian Order] fell into disagreement. Along with emissaries of the master or citizens of Riga two merchants concluded the agreement, one from Brunswick and the other from Münster. There is also an agreement between Smolensk and Riga from the mid-fourteenth century written along patriarchal formulas and old charters. The Smolensk prince called the master "brother" and promised to see to Germans in his lands just as he did his own citizens. The Riga government undertook to behave reciprocally toward Smolensk citizens in its lands.

Polotsk continued its trade with Riga even while under Lithuanian hegemony. In 1407 the citizens of Polotsk and those of Riga wrote an agreement of free trade between the two cities. It was agreed by each party not to engage in retail trade in the city of the other. Citizens of Polotsk had the right to travel by way of Riga on land or water to any country they wished. Citizens of Riga enjoyed the same right with respect to Polotsk. If a Polotsk citizen committed a crime in Riga he was to be sent to Polotsk for trial, and conversely. The same scales counterweight was to be used in Polotsk for weighing salt as was used for weighing beeswax. The Polotsk counterweight was to be half a pud heavier than that of Riga. Initially the men of Riga were to send their weights and scales to Polotsk at their own expense. Later, when the weights wore down, broke or were lost, the Polotsk citizens were to send them to Riga for repair at their expense.

A scale for weighing silver capable of half a zolotnik[6] more than a ruble was to be maintained in Riga. The scale attendants were to kiss the cross and swear that they were weighing honestly. Both men were to step back from the scales during weighing and not touch them with their hand.

The weighing fee asked of Polotsk citizens in Riga was to be the same as that paid by Riga citizens in Polotsk. Should litigation occur between men of the two cities, the litigants were to settle the matter privately. Outsiders were not to interfere in the matter or obstruct trade because of it. Merchants were allowed right of passage even during strife between the master of the Order and the resident population. Goods brought by German merchants were grain, salt, herring, smoked meat, cloth, linen, yarn, mittens, pearls, carnelian, gold, silver, copper, tin, lead, sulfur, needles, beads, parchment, wine and beer. Exported were furs, leather, hair, bristle, suet, beeswax, timber, livestock, and artifacts from the East such as pearls, silk, luxury clothing and weapons.

German products imported into Pskov included wine, grain and vegetables. Items which had the word "Russian" as part of their description were gloves, bedding and cups. There was growth in price of food. An idea of normal prices in the North is suggested in the charter given by Grand Prince Vasily Vasilievich to the Trinity monastery. "From two iron plows the district official is to receive half a carcass of cured meat, an animal-skin sack of oats, a wagon of hay and ten baked loaves. If the half-carcass is unsuitable, then two altyns.[7] If the oats are unsuitable, an altyn. If the wagon of hay is unsuitable, an altyn. If the bread is unsuitable, a denga for each loaf."

Novgorod, Smolensk, and Polotsk, these ancient Russian trade centers, continued as earlier to grow rich because of their advantageous location. But Kiev, the ancient focus of Southern, Greek trade in Rus, devastated by internecine strife and the Tatars, ceased to be the chief city. Scorned by the stronger princes, those of Suzdal, Galich and Lithuania, it presented a pitiful sight in the second half of the thirteenth century. Piano di Carpini[8] counted no more than two hundred houses there. Nevertheless its natural advantages remained. Merchants from many nations continued to visit through force of habit. Thus merchants from Breslau accompanied Piano di Carpini. Later many merchants travelled from Poland, Austria and Constantinople. Those arriving from Constantinople were Italians, of Genoese, Venetian and Pisan origin.[9] Merchants from Turin came to Volhynia and Galich. In 1320 the prince of that region, Andrei Yurievich, who called himself duke of Vladimir and lord of Russia,[10] gave the Turin merchants a patent under which none of his customs collectors or agents might demand cloth or other goods from them.

The prince also renewed all rights they held during his father's reign and promised that if any suffered an injustice he would receive two dinars for each wrongful seizure. Later the progeny of Gediminas, reigning in Volhynia, refused eastward passage "to heathen lands"[11] to merchants from Poland or Germany in order to ensure storage of goods in Vladimir-in-Volhynia, Lutsk and Lvov as in olden times. There is information of Galich and Podolian trade in Moldavia, Bessarabia and Hungary in a charter of statutes the sovereign of Moldavia accorded merchants of Lvov and Podolia in 1407. The Russian merchants bought Tatar goods in Moldavia such as silk, pepper, silk brocade, incense and Greek wine. They also bought livestock such as pigs, sheep and horses, as well as squirrel and fox skins, sheepskins, leather, fish and beeswax. They sold cloth (which was stored in Suceava), hats, leggings, belts, swords, Hungarian silver and marten skins. The Black Sea trade was routed through the city of Soldaia, or Sudak, in Tavrida [Crimea]. All merchants bound north from Turkey and those bound south from Russia to Turkey gathered here. The northbound primarily brought cotton, silk and spices, the southbound generally brought furs. That the fur traders were specifically Russian merchants is attested by Friar William of Rubruck[12] in his description of the covered wagons pulled by oxen used by Russians to transport furs. Again according to Friar William, merchants from all of Russia visited the Crimea for salt and paid the Tatars two lengths of cotton fabric as customs duty for each loaded wagon. Other sources indicate that in the fourteenth century Russian merchants could be found in Kaffa, Otsa [modern Odessa] and in Greece.

There is evidence of trade with the Tatars along the Volga. The chronicler states that the Tatar prince Arapsha killed many Russian merchants and stole their riches, and that Tokhtamysh sent his men to the Bulgar region to seize Russian merchants with their boats and goods. In this period Nizhny Novgorod, because of its location, was a trade center of significance. The chronicles state that the Nizhny Novgorod river pirates[13] robbed many merchants, Tatars and Armenians as well as those of Nizhny Novgorod itself. They seized vast goods and smashed the boats, different types of which are listed. Among them were shallops, sloops, skiffs, lighters, cutters and flatboats.

Eastern merchants traded in Russian cities under Tatar protection. The citizens of Tver, in their uprising against the Tatars, annihilated such merchants as well, both the established, and those who had arrived with Shevkal [the Tatar agent]. Under 1355 there is mention of the arrival of a Tatar envoy in Moscow and of Surozh merchants[14] who came with him.

An entry for 1389 mentions a certain Avraam, an Armenian who lived in Moscow. It is also known that merchants from the West, specifically Lithuania, came to Moscow. The efforts of the citizens of Novgorod to ensure for their merchants the right of passage through the Russian principalities have been noted. The grand princes of Northeastern Rus equally provided for such rights in their pacts among each other and with the grand prince of Lithuania. Monasteries received the right to trade without paying customs duties. In the middle of the fifteenth century the citizens of Novgorod at a popular assembly gave a patent to the Trinity monastery which included the condition that the mayors of the Dvina region, Kholmogory and Vologda, their agents and customs duty collectors were prohibited from collecting duty from or trying men of the Trinity monastery, whether monks or laymen, sent by the monastery to the Dvina region, on wagons in winter and on eleven boats in the summer. "Whoever violates this patent of Novgorod, wrongs the commercial agent of the Trinity monastery or the captains and crew members [of its fishing vessels], he shall pay the mayor and chiliarch and all of Novgorod the Great fifty rubles without fail. You, the Dvina boyars, well-to-do men and merchants, defend the agent of the Trinity monastery even when Novgorod the Great is at odds with certain lands. Protect the monastery's agent and his men as if they were yours, because all of Novgorod the Great acts kindly toward the Trinity monastery and holds it dear, and you, mayors, boyars and their bailiffs and customs duty collectors, do not disobey this charter of Novgorod."

The metropolitan sent his servants from Moscow to Kazan with trade goods. The grand princes of Lithuania in order to improve their capital, Wilno, granted its merchants duty-free and unhindered trading rights in Lithuanian and Rus provinces. There were fairs in Wilno twice a year and markets in the cities of Eastern Russia every Sunday.

MONETARY SYSTEM

In the first half of the fourteenth century grivnas were replaced by rubles with the old silver grivna and the new ruble being identical in value. The word "marten skin"[15] in the general meaning of "money" began to be replaced with the widely used Tatar word.[16] Since there is evidence of leather money in this period, the ancient, important and complicated system must be examined more closely in the historical literature. Two moments must be differentiated here, the use of intrinsically valuable fur as money, and the use of leather money, pieces of the skin of a given animal, which had no intrinsic value and was used as money through convention. Historians hold opinions of two extremes on the question of the monetary system. Some will not admit the existence of metal coins and set the limit at furs only. Others will not admit the existence of furs alongside coins.

Irrefutable evidence has been presented against the first opinion, and there is evidence against the second opinion that is equally irrefutable. For example, we find in the statutes of Prince Rostislav of Smolensk [reigned 1125-1167] "The city levy on Mstislavl is six grivnas, with a grivna to be counted as three foxes. The levy on Krupl is one grivna, with five nogatas for a fox," or "Vlasy has put up as collateral half a village for a loan of ten rubles and three forties of squirrel skins to be repaid by the feast of St. Nicholas [December 6]." It is clearly evident that along with grivnas and rubles fur was taken as payment. This shows, without doubt, that there was a time when the use of furs as money for payments of various kinds was dominant. The prince of Smolensk, or his tax collector, took three fox furs on a par with a ruble. A private individual by the name of Vlasy borrowed three "forties" of squirrel skins along with ten rubles and obligated himself to repay the same.[17]

In exactly the same fashion the first princes took tribute from subjugated tribes only in black marten and squirrel, for those tribes had no access to silver. It was in this fashion that private persons made payments purely in fur. Metal coins had appeared but had not yet replaced fur. The phrase "five nogatas for a fox" indicates a stage of transition from furs to coins. If princes and commoners accepted furs as payment instead of money, it stands to reason that the value of the furs fluctuated in relation to whoever needed or did not need them, in relation to how rich a given region was in furs and in relation to the quality and the degree of wear of the furs, which lost value in the very process of circulation. Clearly no tax collector of the prince of Smolensk would accept three shabby fox furs, nor would the above-mentioned Vlasy borrow three "forties" of shabby squirrel skins. It is also true that if a fox was worth five nogatas in Smolensk province, it could very well have been worth either more or less than that in Chernigov.

The appearance of specifically leather money having a fixed value is more difficult to explain. Yet there are many historical occurrences which cannot be explained but cannot be dismissed, because there is clear, undisputed documentation. Such is the evidence of contemporary eyewitnesses, William of Rubruck and Ghillebert de Lannoy. The names of the units of this old monetary system may have confused Herberstein,[18] who admitted that the use of heads and ears of squirrels and other animals as money fell from use a hundred years before his time. Yet can we deny the eyewitness accounts of Rubruck and Lannoy? One earlier researcher, denying the existence of leather money, laughed at an account of the circulation in Livonia of squirrel ears punctured with silver nails called *nogatas*.

Another, later researcher found the account noteworthy. In his opinion, it may point to our forebears' custom of storing small silver coins in strips of animal skin, thus giving rise to the view held by foreigners that in Russia squirrel and marten heads and ears circulated as money. These parts were unsuitable for fur, but dependable for keeping coins. Researchers may rest assured on the matter of the use of leather strips with nails, for that was the form of some of the oldest currency in Europe. In 1241 Emperor Frederick II[19] placed leather money into circulation in Italy. It consisted of a leather strip with a small silver nail on one side and an image of the sovereign on the other. Each strip had the value of a gold Augustal thaler.[20] It is also known that money of a similar nature circulated in fourteenth-century France. Can it really be assumed that Lannoy in Novgorod, Rubruck in the Volga steppes, as well as Italian and French historians in the West, all agreed to concoct the existence of leather money and give it circulation only in their accounts? Finally, it is known that the Tatars at this time had paper and leather money on the Chinese model.

The transition to coins is described in various accounts. In 1410 the chronicler states that Novgorod began using Lithuanian heads of animals[21] and groschen and German Lübeck three-pfennig pieces[22] in internal commerce instead of marten skins. An entry for 1420 states that citizens of Novgorod began using silver money, and that they sold the three-pfennig pieces, which they had been using for nine years, to the Germans. The Pskov chronicler (in correspondence with the Novgorod entry for 1410) says in an entry for 1409 that marten skins were replaced by peniaz,[23] and for 1422 that pure silver became a coin. The same Novgorod chronicler states that at this time money began to be minted in Pskov and used throughout the Russian land.

These changes could not proceed without unrest in Novgorod. In an entry for 1447 the chronicler relates that the citizens of Novgorod began to deprecate silver money and disturbances and great fights took place. The mayor, Sokira or Sekira, got the coiner Fedor Zherebets drunk, brought him to the popular assembly and began interrogating him as to who led him to cast rubles. Zherebets implicated eighteen persons, some of whom the crowd threw from the bridge,[24] and ransacked the homes of others and even took their property from churches,[25] something unheard of, notes the chronicler. Evil boyars prompted that same Fedor to accuse falsely many men by threatening him with death.

When Zherebets was sober he said "I poured for everyone, for the whole land and did the weighing with my fellow coiners." Then the whole city fell into great sorrow. Only the court agents, corrupt barristers and men who arranged bribes rejoiced. Zherebets was sentenced to death. His property was taken from a church and plundered. To alleviate the wrong the mayor, chiliarch and all Novgorod appointed five coiners, recasting the old money and minting new money to uniform specifications while paying wages of a half-denga for each grivna produced. There was great anguish among Christians, and loss in the city and the districts.

GEOGRAPHY AND COMMERCE

The chief trading cities of ancient Rus—Novgorod, Kiev, Smolensk, Polotsk—owed their commerce and their riches to their convenient location on water routes. In the period we are studying the cities of Northeastern Rus—Moscow, Nizhny Novgorod and Vologda—owed their relative prosperity to the same factor. Even much later, overland routes in Russia could be traveled only in winter. In summer only water routes could be used, which is why they hold such great significance in Russian history. Frost and snow in winter, and rivers in summer, cannot be excluded from the list of the most important factors in the history of Russian civilization. The princes traveled to the Horde by water. It is known that Vasily, son of Dmitry Donskoy, set off to see Tokhtamysh from Vladimir in boats down the Kliazma river into the Oka and thence down the Volga. Prince Yury Danilovich of Moscow visited the Horde for the last time from Zavolochie by way of the Kama and the Volga. Cities along the Oka and Volga were reached by water from Moscow. The new Metropolitan Jonas left Moscow by boat for Murom to negotiate with the princes Riapolovsky about the children of Vasily the Dark.[26] Epifany in The Life of St. Stephen of Perm[27] states "To each who wishes to journey to the land of Perm there is a convenient route from the city of Ustvyma up the Vychegda into Perm itself."

The existence of convenient water routes in the summer and sledge travel in winter allowed the favorable trade conditions for trade noted above to continue. In dealing with the factors that hindered trade, first must be mentioned the Tatar devastations from which Kiev, for example, could not recover. Here it must be stated again that Kiev fell not only as the result of being sacked by the Tatars. Its decline began well before the Tatars with the outflow of vital forces to the Northeast and the West. The other major trade centers—Novgorod, Pskov, Smolensk and Polotsk— were untouched by Tatar devastation. After the entrenchment of Tatar rule the khans and baskaks needed to treat Russian trade favorably for the sake of their own profits. Everything could be bought at the Horde, and the citizens of Novgorod had a patent from the khans securing their trade. Also, after the first twenty-five years, the Tatar yoke grew lighter and there was significant growth in eastern trade and in traffic on the Volga. In fact, it may be said positively that the consolidation of Tatar rule in Central Asia and in the lower basins of the Volga and Don, as well as inclusion of Russia into the Horde, greatly promoted the growth of eastern trade.

The period of time from Kalita to Dmitry Donskoy [1304-1389] must be considered as the most favorable for eastern trade because the immediate pressure of the yoke no longer was felt. The Tatars, calmed by the submissiveness of the princes and their tributes and gifts, did not lay waste to the Russian lands or block the trade routes. After the attempts to become independent of the Tatars, after the battle of Snipe Field or even somewhat earlier, conditions became less favorable for eastern trade. Devastating invasions began anew, the regions of Riazan and Nizhny Novgorod suffering especially, Nizhny Novgorod even more so because it was primarily dependent on the eastern, Volga trade.

Now the khans, arming themselves against Russia, immediately seized all Russian merchants within their reach. An entry for 1371 provides a revealing account which simultaneously shows the wealth of Nizhny Novgorod merchants as well as the fatal effect of Tatar devastation on Russian borderlands. There was in Nizhny Novgorod, the tale says, a merchant by the name of Taras Petrov who was the richest man in the city. With his purse he redeemed from captivity many men of various classes and bought himself a patrimony of six villages on the Kudma river from the prince. When this district was laid waste by the Tatars he moved from Nizhny Novgorod to Moscow. Yet it was not forever that Russia was hostile to the Horde after Mamay, nor could the old and tried path be abandoned all at once.

TRADE AGREEMENTS

In the treaty between Dmitry Donskoy and Algirdas there were mutual provisions for free trade. Yet this treaty did not end the struggle between Moscow and Lithuania, a struggle from which trade could only suffer. Open enmity between Moscow and Lithuania was not a constant occurrence. Even during its clashes with Moscow, Lithuania was on peaceful terms with Riazan, Tver, Novgorod and Pskov. Though Pskov frequently clashed with the Germans, its foreign trade made it one of the richest and most important Russian cities, an indication that frequent clashes with the Germans did not harm trade very much. Novgorod also was not always at peace with the Germans. It has been observed that there was no stable peace between them from 1383 to 1391. When peace was settled in the latter year German emissaries visited Novgorod, collected their goods, kissed the cross and began to erect their market anew. This means that at the beginning of the conflict the citizens of Novgorod seized the Germans' goods and destroyed their market. The charter also indicates that Novgorod merchants frequently suffered at the hands of German pirates on the very banks of the Neva river.

The Swedes looked unfavorably on the trade of Novgorod with the Germans. King Birger[28] wrote the citizens of Lübeck in 1295 that only to please the emperor would the Swedes not disturb German merchants on their way to Novgorod with goods. For himself, Birger, this trade was disadvantageous because it increased the power of his enemies [the citizens of Novgorod]. He lent the merchants the right of passage to Novgorod with the condition that they not bring arms, iron, steel and such. Trade along the Volga must have suffered greatly from the Novgorod river pirates,[29] but this trouble was not of long duration. When speaking of river piracy it must be noted that it serves to demonstrate the development of Volga trade in the fourteenth century. There must have been something to rob if such numerous pirate gangs existed.

ARTS AND CRAFTS

Trade must have promoted the spread of crafts and arts in those areas where it most blossomed. The richest trade cities, Novgorod and Pskov, are marked by the durability of their fortifications and the great number of churches. As before, even stone churches were built rapidly. The church of the Archangel Michael in Moscow[30] had its foundation laid, was built and consecrated all in one year. The same is said of the church of Archangel Michael of the Miracles monastery.[31] Some wooden churches, the so-called "commonplace" were begun, completed and consecrated in one day. On the other hand, the cathedral of the Holy Trinity in Pskov was constructed over three years. First the citizens of Pskov paid two hundred rubles to hire men to tear down the walls of the old church. The rubble was dumped into the Velikaia river, for it was considered improper to use it for anything else. The following year the foundation for the new church was laid. The craftsmen were given four hundred rubles and were much feted.

In Tver during the construction of the cathedral of Christ the Savior a small wooden church was raised inside it and used for services while craftsmen finished the large building. As before, churches occasionally were built poorly. No sooner was a stone church completed in Kolomna than it collapsed. In Novgorod the moment the craftsmen completed their work and descended from the church of St. John Chrysostom it collapsed. The chronicles use the foreign word "masters" in their accounts of church construction yet nowhere is it evident that foreigners were engaged for these structures. During the reign of Vasily Dmitrievich three craftsmen Ivan, Kliment and Alexis were known in Novgorod as skilled builders.

Besides churches and bell towers, an entry for 1409 mentions the construction in Novgorod by Archbishop John of a stone chamber in which water was consecrated monthly. Mention is made as before churches being roofed with tin. In 1420 the citizens of Pskov hired Fedor and his group of craftsmen to sheathe the Holy Trinity church with lead, but could not find either in Pskov or Novgorod a craftsman who could pour lead slabs. A request for help was sent to the Germans in Yuriev [Dorpat]. The heathens, in the expression of the chronicler, would not send a craftsman. Finally one came from Moscow from Metropolitan Photius and taught Fedor how to pour the slabs. The craftsmen received forty-four rubles. Archbishop Evfimy of Novgorod had the church of St. George in Ladoga covered with a scale-like pattern. There continued to be accounts of gilding cupolas, or poppy-head domes [resembling an unopened poppy]. The gilding of the casket of Prince Vladimir Yaroslavich and his mother Anna in the cathedral of the Holy Wisdom in Novgorod is mentioned. It is said that Bishop Fedor of Tver had doors of bronze made for the church of Christ the Savior, and that the Nizhny Novgorod church of Christ the Savior had wondrous doors of gilded bronze. Bishop Ignaty of Rostov ordered the floor of the church of the Mother of God inlaid with red marble. Bishop Fedor of Tver duplicated this in his church of Christ the Savior.

There are accounts of churches decorated with painting. In 1343 Greek artists executed frescoes in the cathedral of the Dormition in Moscow. An entry for the subsequent year speaks of frescoes in the monastery church of Christ the Savior in Moscow. In the latter instance the artists were Russians (students of the Greeks) named Goitan, Simeon and Ivan and their students and craftsmen. For 1395 there is mention of frescoes painted in the church of the Nativity of the Mother of God and in the additional altar of St. Lazarus in the Kremlin. The artists were Theophanes the Greek[32] and Simeon the Black.[33] The same Theophanes the Greek did frescoes in the church of St. Michael the Archangel in 1399. In 1405 the church of the Annunciation in the prince's residence installed frescoes by the icon painter Theophanes the Greek, the aged monk Prokhor from Gorodets,[34] and the monk Andrei Rublev.[35] An entry for 1409 mentions frescoes in the church of Our Lady of Vladimir done by Daniel [the Black], the icon painter,[36] and Andrei Rublev. The same two men decorated the church of the Holy Trinity located over the grave of St. Sergius [in the Trinity Monastery] and a church in the Andronikov monastery in Moscow.

In Novgorod church painting also was done by Greeks. An Isaiah Grechin [the Greek] is mentioned in 1338. The above-mentioned Greek artist, Theophanes, painted the church of Christ the Savior on St. Elias street in Novgorod in 1378. Under 1385 in a description of a great fire in Novgorod it is said that the church artist Ivash, apparently a Russian, perished along with others in the St. Paul monastery. An entry for 1345 says that three large and two smaller bells were cast in Moscow, and that the work was done by a craftsman named Boris Rimlianin.[37] Apparently even before that, in 1342, that same Boris was called from Moscow to Novgorod where he cast a large bell for the Holy Wisdom cathedral. In 1403 a large bell was cast in Tver for the cathedral of the Transfiguration, but the craftsman is not mentioned. Of secular structures there is mention of a stone bakery (kitchen?) built in Novgorod for Archbishop John in 1409. In 1433 the Novgorod archbishop Evfimy built a stone hall with thirty doors on the grounds of his residence. The work was done by German craftsmen from beyond the sea (in other words, not Livonian Germans) together with those of Novgorod. In 1439 the same archbishop commissioned a granary of stone. The following year he had a small stone chamber erected. In 1441 the archbishop's great hall and antechamber were done in fresco. In 1442 the archbishop built two stone kitchens and a stone chamber, and in 1444 he added a stone bakery and guardhouse.

In Moscow it was only in 1450 that Metropolitan Jonas ordered a stone foundation for a hall laid in his residence. Finally there is an account of the installation of a clock. An entry for 1404 says that a clock was installed in Moscow at the prince's residence behind the church of the Annunciation, and that the work was done by a monk named Lazar who had come from Serbia. The clock is described as follows. "This horologe is called an hour-measure. Each hour it strikes a bell with a hammer, measuring and counting both the night and day hours. It is not a man who does the striking, but it is man-like, self-ringing and self-moving. It is wonderfully strange and beyond the imagined and the conceivable that it was created by man's cleverness." In 1436 in Novgorod Archbishop Evfimy put in a clock which struck the hours above the hall, and it is said that in 1449 the same archbishop erected a clock tower.

Some information on the construction and decoration of churches in Southwestern Rus may be derived from the Volhynian chronicler's description in 1259 of building churches in Kholm by Daniel Romanovich. A beautiful and magnificent church of St. John was built. It had four columns linked by arches which stood on four human heads carved by some gifted man. Three windows were decorated with Roman glass. Two columns of continuous stone stood at the entrance to the sanctuary with an arch above. The ceiling was decorated with golden stars on azure. The floor was cast from copper and pure tin and gleamed like a mirror. Two doors decorated with stone from Galich and with white and green cut stone from Kholm were cleverly crafted by a man named Avdey. The relief work was done in gold with the Savior represented on one side of the doors and St. John on the other to the amazement of all viewers. The icons, brought from Kiev, were decorated with precious stones, pearls and gold.

Some of the bells were also brought from Kiev, while others were cast locally. Another church was built in honor of St. Cosmas and St. Damian the Forgiving. Its top was supported by four columns cut from whole stone. There was also built a church of the Mother of God that in size and beauty was the equal of the others. It was decorated with wondrous icons. Prince Daniel brought a chalice from Hungary that was of reddish-purple marble and wonderfully made with serpents' heads all around. The prince placed it before iconostasis entrance called the royal doors[38] and water was blessed in it at Epiphany.

Prince Vladimir Vasilkovich built a church of the Annunciation in Kamenets and decorated it with golden icons. He had silver vessels made for use in the services and gave a Gospel bound in silver and an icon of the Elevation of the Cross. In the city of Vladimir the prince commissoned the whole church of St. Demetrius done in frescoes, had silver vessels made, the icon of the Mother of God framed in silver and precious stones and its shroud sewn through with gold thread, and others were of patterned velvet. In the cathedral of the Mother of God he had the large icon of the Savior framed in silver and the Gospels bound in silver. The vessels used in the services were made of gold and precious stones in his memory.

To the Peremyshl cathedral the prince gave a Gospel bound in silver with pearls. To the Chernigov cathedral he sent a Gospel with a gold inscription, bound in silver with pearls and an enameled image of the Savior in the center. To the Lutsk cathedral he gave a large cross of gilded silver with sacred wood.[39] In Liubiml he built a stone church of St. George and decorated it with icons with hand-worked frames. He also provided silver vessels, patterned velvet shrouds sewn with gold and decorated with pearls and images of cherubim and seraphim, a sacramental cloth all sewn with gold and another sewn of squirrel skins, two sacramental cloths for the chapel sanctuaries also of squirrel skins. There was also a Gospel bound in gold with precious stones and pearls with a golden icon of Christ Enthroned on it and decorations of enamel, as well as a second Gospel covered with pewter, two censers, one of silver and one of copper.

There was a local icon of St. George executed in gold. The prince added a golden grivna and pearls to this icon. Another icon, of the Mother of God, was executed in gold and decorated with a chain of gold and precious stones. The church doors were of bronze. The prince began the painting of frescoes in the church. The three sanctuaries were completed and work was about to begin on the rest, then were left unfinished because of the prince's illness. The bells which were cast were so remarkable in their tone that none comparable existed in all the land.

As for the crafts in general the chronicler's narration of the settling of the city of Kholm in Galich mentions the chief and most necessary ones, arms manufacture and metallurgy. There began to gather in Kholm, he says, saddlemakers, bowyers, hatters and iron-, copper- and silversmiths. In Novgorod we encounter shield makers and silversmiths. Other crafts such as shoemaking and tailoring most likely were satisfied by households and servants. There is almost no information on furniture, the comforts of home life, or the layout and decoration of living quarters. Everyday domestic life continued in its earlier simplicity. Vladimir Vasilkovich, the wealthy Volhynian prince who built so many cities and churches and decorated them so richly, lay on a bed of straw during his illness. An idea of the wealth of the Moscow princes can be drawn from their testaments in which are mentioned icons, expensive garments, chains, occasionally weapons, and eating and drinking vessels but in such small numbers that all of it required little space, was readily hidden, gathered or taken away. If it was thus with princes, what might we expect among common men? Except for the most simple and indispensable items they had nothing. Everything a little better and a little more expensive was stored in churches as places least subject to fires and robbery. Living quarters apparently were laid out in the old way. Here is a description of a fire which occurred in the home of the grand prince of Tver, Mikhail Yaroslavich. The antechamber began to burn and the prince's entire residence was consumed. In God's charity Prince Mikhail himself woke up and leapt out the window along with the princess. The antechamber was filled with the prince's and boyar children who slept there. There were many guards as well, but no one sensed anything.

Princely garments were mentioned above. As to the dress of commoners, various garments are encountered.[40] Of decorative items there were rings, pins and chains of gold wash.[41] There are no details on food, though it is known that the poor ate oats.

VII

THE CHURCH

MISSIONARY ACTIVITY

Let us now turn to spiritual matters. In describing the state of religion and the church during the preceding period the opposition which Christianity met in the Finnish north from paganism and its priests required mention. In the period under review there are no such episodes. On the contrary, Christianity successfully spread throughout the Finnish regions. As early as 1227 the chronicler speaks of the conversion of the Karelians, whose lands soon were contested by Novgorod and Sweden. This controversy allowed the Karelians an opportunity to shift their allegiance from one nation to another, their faith changing in the process.

Orthodoxy spread uncontested in the Northeast. Here St. Stephen served as apostle to the Zyrians.[1] He was the son of a psalm reader from Ustiug and was tonsured in Rostov. Probably he was familiar with the Zyrian language even from his Ustiug days. Stephen prepared himself for his apostolic task by inventing an alphabet and translating liturgical books into Zyrian.

Despite all the obstruction on the part of the pagans Stephen's work was crowned with success. On the sites of demolished pagan temples he founded churches, with schools for children. Later he was installed as bishop of Perm. Conclusions about the nature of his services in this calling may be drawn from the Lament of the Perm Land on the Death of Stephen that is included in his hagiography. "We have lost a kind provider and protector who prayed to God for the salvation of our souls, took our grievances to the prince, saw to our privileges and our interests. He was our solicitous defender before the boyars and the mighty. Often he delivered us from hardship, labor or sale by the bailiffs and lightened the burdensome tribute. Even the men of Novgorod, river pirates and bandits, heeded him and did not attack us." The successors to St. Stephen were Bishops Isaac, and Pitirim, who was taken prisoner and killed by the Voguls.

If as a result of the Tatar yoke there was a case of apostasy by Zosima or Izosim,[2] there are also accounts of the baptizing of Tatars. Thus for example in an entry for 1390 the chronicler states that three of the khan's chamberlains petitioned Grand Prince Vasily Dmitrievich to enter his service and wished to accept Christianity. Metropolitan Cyprian[3] himself baptized them with the names of Ananias, Azarias and Misael.[4]

CHURCH HIERARCHY

The metropolitans continued to head the Russian church and during this period their activity was much more noticeable for two most important reasons. The preceding period was characterized by the dominance of princely family relations and the resultant internecine strife. The clergy might counteract such strife, pacify it, but could not act openly or successfully against the cause of the strife, against the dominant tradition. It has been noticed how the chronicler, undoubtedly a cleric, preferred the uncles against the nephews. Such were the prevailing concepts of the rights of princely seniority among all the Russian people and all the Russian clergy. Even if the metropolitans who came from Byzantium regarded such concepts unfavorably their opinion carried little authority. They were foreigners. The very fact that the metropolitans were foreign was the second main reason for their lack of influence.

The era under consideration is characterized by events of a different nature. This was a time of conflict between the old and the new order, which was to end in monarchy. The clergy could not remain indifferent or impartial in this struggle. It must favor whoever promised the land an end to internecine strife and establishment of domestic peace and order. Together with this well-known struggle the attention of the clergy and metropolitans must heed other and new relationships, specifically those with the Tatars, Lithuania and rapidly failing Byzantium. Consequently, in this later period, the importance of new developments replaced the uniformity and skew of the preceding period. The immediate connection of these events to the interests of the church spurred the clergy to great activity. There was the important fact that metropolitans began to be ethnically Russian. It cannot be overlooked that the most significant activity during this period was that of three Russian metropolitans, namely Peter, Alexis and Jonas.[5]

It was noted that Constantinople did not agree to the division of the Russian metropolitanate and installation of a special metropolitan for Northern Rus at Vladimir. The stature which Northern Rus gained under Andrei Bogoliubsky and Vsevolod III forced the Kievan metropolitans to give it special attention. They were compelled to travel to Vladimir to make peace between the indigenous princes and those of the South, as well as to maintain accord between the two halves of Rus necessary for unity in the administration of the church. After 1228 and after the Tatar destruction, when the significance of Kiev and Southern Rus around the Dnieper collapsed, the metropolitans of Kiev and all Rus were to pay even greater attention to the North. Thus in an entry for 1250 we encounter a reference to the journey of Metropolitan Cyril II[6] (ethnically Russian) from Kiev to Chernigov, Riazan, the land of Suzdal and, finally, Novgorod the Great.

Cyril again is encountered in Vladimir in 1255, and in 1263 at the funeral of Alexander Nevsky. After this he went to Kiev, then the chronicler speaks of his return to Vladimir in 1274. That same year in Vladimir, Cyril called a council on church reform. Finally, before his death Cyril again visited the land of Suzdal from Kiev. He died in 1280 in Pereiaslavl-Zalessk[7] during the reign of Dmitry Alexandrovich but was buried in Kiev. If on the basis of the above accounts it cannot yet be said that Cyril moved the metropolitanate from Kiev to Vladimir, it is at least evident that he appeared in the North a number of times. Very likely he lived there, if not longer, then at least as long a time as he lived in the South. If Cyril II did not do what is customarily ascribed to Metropolitan Maxim,[8] transfer his residence from the South to the North, at least he thoroughly laid the groundwork for the event. The account of Cyril's death in Pereiaslavl-Zalessk is also noteworthy. It was an act by the metropolitan of all Rus necessitated by circumstances, the choice of a city in which the strongest prince lived over a city that was paramount in name only.

Cyril did not live to witness an event vital for all Northern Rus, the beginning of the struggle among the sons of Nevsky, between Dmitry, the eldest, and Andrei, the youngest. He did take part in another significant event, the struggle between Grand Prince Yaroslav Yaroslavich and Novgorod. Thanks to the metropolitan's mediation Novgorod made peace with the prince. In another sphere, it was during Cyril's time that church relations with the Horde were fixed. All Russians were made subject to tribute, except for the clergy. Another result of Tatar tolerance was the establishment of an Orthodox bishopric dependent on the Russian metropolitan in Saray, the very capital of the khans. In 1261 Cyril installed Mitrofan as bishop there. For 1279 there is an entry that the bishop of Saray, Theognostos,[9] for the third time returned from Constantinople, where he was sent by Metropolitan Cyril and Khan Mangu-Temir with gifts and epistles for the patriarch and the emperor. This noteworthy information suggests the significance of the Russian bishop of Saray to the Christian East.

Cyril's successor was Maxim, a Greek by birth. There is no evidence that Cyril ever traveled to the Horde, but Maxim immediately made the journey upon his arrival in Kiev from Constantinople. At the very outset Maxim indicated that Kiev must remain the seat of the Russian metropolitanate. All Russian bishops were to gather there to present themselves to him in 1284. The next year he appeared in the North, even in Novgorod and Pskov. But during the infamous strife in the North among the sons of Alexander nothing was heard of the metropolitan, who remained in Kiev. Perhaps it was this strife that held him in the South because as soon as it died down Maxim moved permanently from Kiev to Vladimir. He was accompanied by his choir and all his worldly goods, wrote the chronicler, who also supplied a reason for the move. Maxim could not suffer the coercion of the Tatars in Kiev, though it is difficult to assume that Tatar coercion was greater in this period than previously. Thus Maxim took a decisive, final step, with which he demonstrated that the life forces had ebbed from the South towards the North. To this point, though Kiev may have lost its previous role and wealth, Galich and Volhynia still maintained themselves in the Southwest. Then, after the death of Daniel, Vasilko and Vladimir Vasilievich little hope remained even here of anything strong and lasting.

Maxim did not live long in the North. Not having exerted any moral influence or mediating power in the internecine strife among the sons of Nevsky, nonetheless he attempted to hinder the strife between the princes of Moscow and Tver. Here also his efforts were in vain. He died in 1305 and Peter of Volhynia,[10] ethnically Russian, was installed as his successor. After taking office he halted in Kiev only briefly in his haste to go north, where he did not stay long either, and again set off for the South. In Briansk he attempted to persuade Prince Sviatoslav to share his lands with his nephew, or even leave him everything and quit the city without a struggle. It is not known whether Peter went further south than Briansk or whether the cessation of the internecine strife was the reason for his going there.

Most likely he returned north, to Vladimir, for the following year there is an entry in the chronicles stating that he forbade the young prince of Tver, Dmitry Mikhailovich, to wage war against Nizhny Novgorod. The proper consecutive order of years in the chronicles cannot be proven. Perhaps the metropolitan stopped in Briansk to persuade that prince to a course of action while on his way for the first time from Kiev to Vladimir. Later there is no further mention of St. Peter's travels south. Metropolitan Cyril wavered between the North and the South. Maxim moved north with his choir and his goods, and Peter took a new step. Vladimir, where Maxim settled, was the capital of the senior prince in name only. Each prince who gained seniority and rule over the grand principality of Vladimir remained living in the city of his patrimony. Consequently there was a struggle for supremacy among these cities as to which finally would consolidate the Russian lands. Peter marked Moscow as having the final victory by staying there longer than in the other cities, choosing Moscow as the place of his final retreat in old age and the place of his burial.

It is curious to note that during all that time the metropolitans, representatives of the spiritual unity of Rus, had no constant abode but wandered from the North to the South. Even in the North they did not stay constantly in Vladimir. St. Peter, in the words of the author of his Life, traveled from place to place and town to town. Growing fond of Prince Ivan Danilovich of Moscow, he began to linger in Moscow longer than in other places. This movement by the metropolitans best expresses the ferment and transition in which Rus found itself. This period ended when the life of the land found a center at Moscow, an occurrence which, as has been noted, was aided considerably by St. Peter favoring that city and its prince. To what degree such favor was the result of the animosity of Tver and its bishop Andrei towards St. Peter cannot be determined, but it remains a factor that should not be dismissed.

RELATIONS WITH TATARS

Like Maxim, Peter also had to go to the Horde. The visit took place after the death of Khan Tokhta[11] when, upon accession to the throne of Uzbek,[12] in the words of the chronicler, everything was renewed. Princes and bishops alike beat a path to the Horde for new charters. Peter was received at the Horde with great honors, and soon was permitted to return to Rus. Even at the very beginning of relations with the Tatars everyone was made subject to tribute except the clergy, who were given a charter attesting to this exemption. The extant charter of Mangu-Temir[13] reflects in detail the charters of privilege granted the clergy by the early khans, and Mangu-Temir's desire to leave them unchanged. Therefore Mangu-Temir's charter may by all rights be considered identical to all preceding charters.

In his charter the khan addresses the baskaks, princes, tribute collectors and various other Tatar officials with the announcement that he has granted charters with privileges to the Russian metropolitans and all the clergy, both monks and parish priests, that they with clear hearts and without sorrow might pray to God for him and his whole tribe and bless them. Neither is tribute to be taken from them, nor general customs duty, nor plow tax, nor tax for post stations, nor wagons, nor military assessments, nor provender. No tariff of any kind shall be required of them, neither that of the khan, nor the khan's wife, nor the prince, nor the tax inspector, nor the envoy, no tariff by any collectors. No one shall dare occupy church lands, waters, gardens, vineyards, mills, and winter or summer quarters. No one shall dare take these church people as workers or soldiers whether craftsmen, falconers or other workers. No one shall dare steal, tear or ruin icons, books or any other liturgical items, that the clergy will not damn the khan, but pray in peace. Whoever censures their faith or blasphemes against it shall suffer swift and vicious death. The brothers and sons of priests living with them and sharing their bread are also exempt from all tribute and tariffs, but if they depart the household they are to pay tariffs and tribute. Whoever of the baskaks or other officials takes any tribute or tariff whatsoever from the clergy shall be executed swiftly. At Uzbek's accession to the throne, as mentioned, new charters were distributed, that is, bought, and Metropolitan Peter received a new charter in his name. This charter was identical to that of Mangu-Temir but wordier. It added that Metropolitan Peter was to rule his people and judge them in all matters, including criminal cases, and that all church people were to obey him.

Peter's successor, the Greek Theognostos,[14] came north when the struggle between Moscow and Tver ended. Tver province was devastated and its prince in exile, and the Moscow prince reigned supreme without a rival. There was nothing for the new metropolitan to do save follow the example of his saintly precursor so Theognostos, in the words of the chronicler, assumed the seat of St. Peter and took up residence in Moscow, which was not very pleasing to the other princes. It has been seen what an important ally Kalita had in Theognostos. Through fear of excommunication Theognostos forced the citizens of Pskov to renounce their defense of Alexander of Tver. Having settled affairs in the North Theognostos had to hurry south, where lately a great change had occurred. Instead of the separate, petty, and weak princes that were the progeny of Riurik, the South was now ruled by the strong Lithuanian prince Gediminas,[15] a pagan but not a persecutor of Christianity. Consequently, the attitude of the metropolitan of all Russia toward Southwestern Rus had to assume a different character. Previously it was possible to leave the South for the North, ignoring the dissatisfactions of the numerous weak and divided princes, even if they ventured to express their dissatisfaction at the absence of the metropolitan. Now the powerful Lithuanian princes could not be ignored, requiring Theognostos to dwell in Volhynia for a long time. There is also an account of a journey by Theognostos to that region at yet another time. This account cannot but be connected with another contemporaneous account of Polish excesses in Volhynia and the persecution of Orthodoxy. Furthermore, the earlier departure of the Kievan metropolitan for the North led the South to consider selection of its own metropolitan who, as a result of self-evident circumstances, would have had his residence in Galician Rus rather than along the Dnieper. There exist letters from the Byzantine emperor to Metropolitan Theognostos, Grand Prince Simeon of Moscow and Lubartis the Volhynian prince, relating to the elimination of the Galich metropolitanate established by the previous patriarch.

Theognostos was summoned twice to the Horde. Great trials awaited him there on his second journey. Some Russians lied to Khan Janibek[16] that the Russian metropolitan disposed of enormous income, that he held much gold, silver and other riches, and that he could well afford to pay annual tribute to the Horde. The khan demanded this tribute from Theognostos, who instead endured confinement in close quarters, made gifts of a great deal of money to the khan, the khan's wife and the princes, yet regained his previous privileges.

SELECTION OF METROPOLITANS

It has been noticed that since Cyril II and up to this era Russian and Greek metropolitans alternated. After the Russian Cyril there was the Greek Maxim, then again the Russian Peter followed by Theognostos, a Greek. Little is known of how these metropolitans, whether Russian or Greek, were selected, or whether this was done through the suggestion or consent of particular Russian princes.

The facts of the selection of the successor to Theognostos are known. During the reign of Prince Yury Danilovich [1303-1325] a boyar named Fedor Pleshcheev left Chernigov for Muscovite service. His son, Elevfery-Simeon, godson of Ivan Kalita, at the age of twelve adopted the manners of a monk and at twenty was tonsured in the Moscow monastery of the Epiphany under the name of Alexis. Having become famous for his spiritual life, Alexis was chosen by Metropolitan Theognostos as a coadjutor, whose function was to hold trial over members of the clergy. After fulfilling this function for twelve years Alexis was installed as bishop of Vladimir by Theognostos who, while still living, blessed him as his successor to the metropolitan throne. Messengers were sent from the grand prince and the metropolitan to the patriarch in Constantinople to ensure that he keep Alexis in mind and not install anyone else as Russian metropolitan. Upon the death of Theognostos, Alexis set off for Constantinople for the installation ceremony.

Even so in Constantinople, another metropolitan, Roman, was already installed without waiting for word from Moscow. Later, in fear of denying the Moscow prince, Alexis was installed as well, and both men were sent to Rus. A schism developed among the higher clergy, something previously unknown in Rus, says the chronicler. Messengers from both metropolitans visited the regional bishops, and everywhere there was great difficulty for the priestly order. Thus Constantinople now inclined towards something it rejected previously, specifically the division of the Russian metropolitanate. Room must be made for two metropolitans. When Alexis came to Moscow Roman went to the Lithuanian and Volhynian lands. Yet Alexis, consecrated as metropolitan of Kiev and all Rus, could not surrender Kiev, and visited there in 1358. A year later, when he returned to Moscow, Roman appeared in Tver. Theodore, the resident bishop, refused to see him and showed him no reverence whereas the princes, boyars and some others, according to the chronicler, gave him his due. An especially great reverence was displayed and expensive gifts were given him by Prince Vsevolod Alexandrovich of Kholm. Vsevolod's act is explained readily, for he was at loggerheads with his uncle Vasily Mikhailovich, who was supported by the Moscow prince and Metropolitan Alexis.

Vsevolod in turn found support in Lithuania from his kinsman by marriage, Algirdas,[17] whose intermediacy he doubtless owed to the fact that his uncle ceded him a third of his patrimony. Vsevolod returned from Lithuania to Tver at the same moment Metropolitan Roman arrived there. It is very likely, therefore, that Roman came with a mission from Algirdas to make peace among the princes and to obtain a territory for Vsevolod. Even if this were not the case, it is understandable that Vsevolod, as a relative and ally of Algirdas, had to demonstrate that he was thoroughly well-disposed toward the metropolitan recognized in Lithuania.

ALLIANCE WITH MOSCOW

There is no need here to speak again of the great assistance St. Alexis rendered the Moscow princes in consolidating their power over the other princes. It was no accident that Grand Prince Simeon charged his brothers not to listen to foolhardy men, instead heed the eminent Alexis and the old boyars who wished their father and themselves only good. Both Tver and Nizhny Novgorod experienced the effect of St. Alexis's active benevolence for the sons and grandsons of his godfather Ivan Kalita. Although he was not a Greek, Alexis succeeded in maintaining the constant favor of the Constantinople patriarch for himself and the Moscow court. The patriarch wrote Donskoy of his special favor towards him and his brother Vladimir, and of his anger at other princes hostile to him. In another missive the patriarch wrote that he would not remove the anathema placed by Alexis upon certain Russian princes until they fulfilled the conditions he had set, until the metropolitan wrote that they repented, for these princes had given solemn oath to the Moscow prince to march together against enemies of the faith.

Sviatoslav, prince of Smolensk, complained that he was anathematized by the metropolitan, to which the patriarch replied that the metropolitan's action was just, for Sviatoslav aided Algirdas against Moscow. The prince of Tver also complained about the metropolitan and laid charges against him. The patriarch answered that he found it improper for a prince and a metropolitan to conduct litigation before an emissary of the patriarch. The renown of the Russian metropolitan's devout life reached even the Horde. Taidula, wife of Khan Janibek, when struck with an eye disease, sent to Moscow asking for Alexis. St. Alexis went to the Horde, and the khan's wife was cured.

As his successor Alexis wished to see a man renowned for his holiness. Sergius, the abbot and founder of the Trinity monastery,[18] was such a man, yet the humble monk declined. Meanwhile the authorities in Constantinople had no wish to wait for Moscow's selection. Many complaints came to Constantinople from various quarters about the metropolitan abandoning the South for the North. The Polish king, Casimir,[19] who ruled Galician Rus, demanded his own metropolitan and threatened otherwise to convert the Rus to the Latin faith. The threat had its effect, and Constantinople installed a special metropolitan in Galich with the bishoprics of Kholm, Turov, Peremyshl and Vladimir-in-Volhynia subordinate to him. From another quarter Algirdas of Lithuania wrote complaints to the patriarch stating that Moscow injured his brother-in-law Mikhail of Tver, his son-in-law Boris of Nizhny Novgorod and another son-in-law Ivan of Novosil, taking many towns. He further complained that the metropolitan blessed the Moscow prince in these actions with the acquiescence of the patriarch. The metropolitan came neither to Lithuania, nor Kiev. He absolved men who fled from Lithuania into Moscow's service of their oath sealed by kissing the cross. Algirdas demanded another Kievan metropolitan for Smolensk, Tver, Little Russia, Novosil and Nizhny Novgorod.

TENSION WITH LITHUANIA

In answer to the requests of the southwestern Russian princes Constantinople installed Metropolitan Cyprian,[20] a Serb by birth, with the condition that upon the death of Metropolitan Alexis he become the metropolitan of all Russia. Understandably if Lithuania wanted its own metropolitan, no less did Moscow. Cyprian was recognized neither in Moscow, Novgorod nor Pskov, and was forced to live in Kiev. Consequently previous events repeated themselves, and again the schism of the Russian metropolitanate reappeared, for Moscow refused to recognize Cyprian even after Alexis's death. It had its own candidate.

There was in the town of Kolomna a priest by the name of Mikhail-Mitiay. He was an unusually prominent man, handsome, literate, with fluent and clear speech, and a strong and pleasant voice. He surpassed all others in his ability to interpret the deep contents of books. He had an unusual memory, knew all the olden tales, books and parables. In all matters and trials he deliberated eloquently and intelligently. Such merit caught the attention of Grand Prince Dmitry who took Mitiay as his spiritual father and keeper of the seal. From year to year Mitiay continued to gain renown and importance. No one, in the words of the chronicler, enjoyed such fame and honors as Mitiay. The grand prince refused him nothing. Everyone honored him as if he were a king and, more importantly, everyone loved him.

THE MITIAY INCIDENT

In the monastery of the Savior (within the Kremlin) the position of archimandrite became vacant. The grand prince and boyars without fail desired Mitiay in this position. Mitiay refused. The grand prince tried to persuade him. "You see, Alexis the metropolitan is quite old," he said, "and after him you will be metropolitan of all Rus. You have only to be tonsured as a monk and you will be archimandrite in the monastery of the Savior and my spiritual father as before." Mitiay agreed. He was tonsured before noon and was appointed archimandrite in the afternoon. Now the metropolitan had to be persuaded to bless Mitiay as his successor, but St. Alexis refused. "Mitiay only recently has become a monk," he said. "He needs yet to suffer temptation and to shroud himself with good works and spirituality." The grand prince begged him for a long time. He came in person, or sent his cousin Vladimir Andreevich or the boyars, all in vain. "Whoever is sent by the Lord God, the Mother of God, the patriarch and the ecumenical council," came back the answer, "him I will bless."

Despite this, when St. Alexis died in 1377 Mitiay moved into the metropolitan's residence, donned the metropolitan's vestments and began to treat the clergy and to rule as would a metropolitan. At first he intended to travel to Constantinople to be installed by the patriarch, then thought better of it and said to the grand prince "In the laws it is written that two or three bishops install a bishop. Let there now gather some five or six Russian bishops and install me as metropolitan." The grand prince and the boyars agreed and the bishops gathered. Now that which occurred in the twelfth century at the installation of Metropolitan Klim[21] by a council of Rus bishops now occurred again. As Nifont of Novgorod rose up then against what he considered to be the improper installation of Klim, so now Dionisy, bishop of Suzdal,[22] rose against the installation of Mitiay.

Dionisy's opposition forced Mitiay again to consider a journey to Constantinople. Dionisy also prepared to go there, desiring the metropolitanate for himself. Learning of these plans, Mitiay advised the grand prince to seize Dionisy lest he jeopardize matters in Constantinople, whereupon the grand prince ordered the Suzdal bishop held under strong guard. To escape imprisonment, Dionisy swore to the grand prince that he would not go to Constantinople without his permission, to which St. Sergius of Radonezh served as guarantor. Dionisy did not keep his word. From Suzdal he went to Nizhny Novgorod, thence by way of the Volga to Saray, and from Saray to Constantinople. Mitiay was against Dionisy's release from the very beginning. He suspected that St. Alexis did not wish to bless him, following the advice of St. Sergius, who still remained active against him in concert with Dionisy. When Mitiay found out about Dionisy's escape to Constantinople his indignation knew no bounds. "I pray the Lord God," said St. Sergius at that time, "with a grieving heart, that He not permit Mitiay to carry out his threat of destroying this holy place and expelling us who are without fault."

From other quarters there appeared a new rival to Mitiay. Cyprian was travelling to Moscow from Kiev and reached Liubutsk, whence he notified St. Sergius that he was on his way to his son the grand prince with peace and blessings. The grand prince, learning of the approach of this uninvited guest, ordered roadblocks everywhere so that he could not enter Moscow. Cyprian was seized and dishonorably sent back.

The movements of Dionisy and Cyprian spurred Mitiay's voyage to Constantinople. He finally left with full authority from the grand prince to act in any manner appropriate to the circumstances. Accordingly Mitiay took with him sheets of blank parchment with the grand-princely seal to allow him to give a note of obligation or voucher if needed. Dmitry permitted Mitiay to borrow a thousand rubles or even more in the prince's name. Mitiay set off accompanied by three archimandrites, many other clerics and the grand prince's great boyar Yury Kochevin[23] as well as the metropolitan's boyars. In the steppes Mitiay was seized by Mamay but not held very long. The Black Sea was already successfully crossed when suddenly, in view of Constantinople, Mitiay took sick and died. Among the accompanying clerics and boyars there arose great confusion. Some wanted to install John, archimandrite of St. Peter's monastery in Moscow, as metropolitan, while others wanted Pimen, archimandrite of the Goritsk monastery in Pereiaslavl. Finally the boyars who supported Pimen gained the upper hand and nearly killed John, who would not agree with them. Then on one of the blank sheets of parchment they wrote in the name of the grand prince a letter to the emperor and the patriarch with the request that Pimen be installed as metropolitan.

CYPRIAN AND PIMEN

At first, matters did not go well. The emperor and patriarch replied that a metropolitan, namely Cyprian, was long since installed and sent to Russia, and there was no need for a second. Then the Russians borrowed money at high interest rates from Italian and Eastern merchants, writing a promissory note on a second blank parchment. They proceeded to give expensive gifts in all quarters and thus achieved their purpose in Constantinople, although not so in Moscow. When news arrived that Mitiay had died at sea, that Pimen was installed, and when, as usually happens, rumors began to fly that Mitiay did not die a natural death the profoundly grieved grand prince said "I did not send Pimen to be metropolitan. I sent him as a servant to Mitiay. What occurred to Mitiay I do not know, only God knows, and only God judges, but Pimen I will not accept and do not wish to see him." Pimen was still lingering in Constantinople when the grand prince sent his spiritual father to Kiev to call Cyprian to the metropolitan's throne, and Cyprian came to Moscow. When news came of his arrival Pimen was stopped at Kolomna, his white cowl[24] was removed, and he was incarcerated.

Cyprian did not remain long in Moscow this time, neither did Pimen long await his turn. Just as previously the existence of several princes all of whom claimed seniority made for the possibility of a choice among them, so now the existence of two metropolitans, already installed in Constantinople, made possible a choice between them. It was noted that during Tokhtamysh's invasion Metropolitan Cyprian left Moscow for Tver. It is unknown whether it was Cyprian's flight itself, or the fact that he went specifically to Tver, whose prince sought to obtain the privilege of rule from the Horde immediately after Tokhtamysh's invasion, or whether it was some other disinclination of the grand prince toward Cyprian. What we do have is information that Dmitry did not want Cyprian back in Moscow. Cyprian then set off for Kiev, where he took his place as metropolitan and was received by all with honor and joy. There he proceeded to dwell, governing church affairs as usual.

Meanwhile Pimen was called to Moscow from imprisonment. He too was received with honor and took his position in governing the church. Thus there were again, for South and North, for Kiev and Moscow, two separate metropolitans, but the matter did not end here. There arrived in Kiev from Byzantium yet a third metropolitan, Bishop Dionisy of Suzdal, whom the prince of Kiev, Vladimir the son of Algirdas, ordered seized and held. It was there that Mitiay's rival died a year later. After several years Pimen died in Chalcedon, on his way to Constantinople. The death of Pimen once again united the Russian church under one metropolitan, Cyprian. He no longer found obstructions in Moscow because Donskoy had died and his son Vasily received Cyprian with honor.

RELATIVE PEACE

The accord between the grand prince and the metropolitan was not disrupted even once from that time on. It was noted above how the two men acted in concert in dealing with Novgorod. The alliance of Vasily Dmitrievich with his father-in-law Vytautas of Lithuania[25] also preserved church ties between Lithuanian Rus and Muscovy. Thus when the Moscow prince went to Smolensk for a meeting with his father-in-law, Metropolitan Cyprian went there as well, and from there to Kiev, where he

remained a year and a half. Later, in an entry for 1404, there is another
account of a journey by Cyprian to Lithuania to greet Vytautas, and a visit
to Kiev. The metropolitan received high honor and many gifts from
Vytautas and Jogaila, and was honored highly by all the princes and
gentry and the whole land. In Kiev he ordered his locum tenens Archimandrite Timofey and his servants seized and taken to Moscow. During
this same journey Cyprian removed Bishop Anthony of Turov from office, banishing him to the St. Simeon monastery in Moscow. This was
done at the insistence of Vytautas, to whom Anthony was slandered as
having dealings with the Tatars. The chief reason for Lithuanian enmity
toward Anthony was probably that bishop's zeal for Orthodoxy.

RUPTURE

Soon there followed a rupture between the princes of Moscow and
Lithuania, which necessarily led to the division of the metropolitanate as
well. Cyprian did not live to see this event. Upon Cyprian's death the
Moscow prince, having no candidate of his own, sent envoys to Constantinople to request that a metropolitan be sent for all Rus. Meanwhile
Vytautas sent Bishop Theodosius of Polotsk to Constantinople as well. "Install Theodosius as our metropolitan," he beseeched the emperor and patriarch, "that he sit on the Kiev metropolitan's throne as of old, build God's
church as before as our metropolitan, for through God's will we rule that
city, Kiev."

Vytautas's wishes were not fulfilled in Constantinople. Instead Photius, an ethnic Greek from Morea, was sent to be metropolitan for all Russia. There is no reason to assume that Vytautas, in desiring installation
of Theodosius of Polotsk as metropolitan, had in mind division of the
metropolitanate and installation of a metropolitan in Lithuania. Rather he
wanted the all-Russian metropolitan to dwell as before in Kiev, that is,
under Lithuanian sovereignty, where consequently he would be Vytautas's metropolitan. He wanted to lure the metropolitan away from
hostile Moscow, about which doubtless he came to agreement with his
candidate Theodosius. Vytautas's position was thus totally different than
that earlier of Algirdas who, complaining to the patriarch that Metropolitan Alexis was a partisan of Moscow, did not think that the patriarch
would remove Alexis from office for that reason, or that Moscow would
ever agree. Therefore he asked for a separate metropolitan for Lithuania.

Now the situation was different. A metropolitan common to the North
and South had died, and Vytautas rushed to promote his candidate to the

office, who in keeping with the old custom would remain in Kiev. It is unknown why Theodosius was not installed in Constantinople. It is likely that Constantinople did not want to favor a prince of another faith at the expense of the sovereign of Moscow, especially since shortly before that, in 1398, the Muscovite prince sent Emperor Manuel[26] a great sum of money in aid. The existence at that time of friendly relations between the courts of Moscow and Constantinople is denoted by the fact that in 1414 Manuel married off his son John to Vasily Dmitrievich's daughter Anna.

If the Moscow prince extended the courtesy to the emperor and patriarch of letting them choose the metropolitan as in ancient times, it would have been odd to answer such courtesy with installation of a man favored by a prince hostile to Moscow. Finally, it may have happened that Photius was installed before Theodosius's arrival. In any case, when Photius arrived in Kiev Vytautas at first would not receive him. He did so later upon promise that he would reside in Kiev. Nevertheless Photius, after spending some seven months in Kiev set off for Moscow, where he busied himself with the daily affairs of the metropolitanate. "After the Tatars," writes the chronicler, "and after the frequent plague epidemics, the population began to increase in the Russian land, following which Metropolitan Photius began to restore church possessions and income, to search out what was lost and what was taken by princes, boyars and others as income, tariffs, lands, waters, villages and districts." Such searches for seizures from the church made many powerful men angry with Photius. They accused him falsely before Grand Prince Vasily Dmitrievich, creating dissension between him and the metropolitan.

At first Photius wrote the grand prince asking him to confirm in a document the gifts given the church and determine its income. Then in a second missive he implored the prince not to abase the church, rather to turn to it with penitence, to re-establish its rights and to return what was granted and confirmed by his progenitors. The resolution of the difficulties between Photius and the Moscow prince is unknown. The chronicler states only that those slanderers who once were close to the metropolitan had to flee from Moscow to the bishop of Chernigov, thence to Vytautas in Lithuania. This information suggests that Vasily Dmitrievich finally took the side of the metropolitan, forcing the slanderers to flee Moscow. Vytautas, to whom they fled, was already angry with Photius for preferring Moscow to Kiev. Now Photius's enemies insisted to the Lithuanian prince that the metropolitan was transferring the church's richly decorated vestments and vessels from Kiev to Moscow, and that he was devastating Kiev and the whole South with heavy taxation and tribute.

These accusations provided Vytautas with a pretext for settling affairs with the metropolitan in Moscow by installing his own in Kiev. He gathered the Rus princes subservient to him and decided with their aid to depose Photius from the Kievan metropolitanate. A complaint against Photius was sent to Constantinople, along with the request that a special metropolitan be installed in Kiev, namely Gregory Tsamblak, a Bulgarian by birth. Yet the reasons which previously prevented Vytautas's wish from being realized were still in force in Constantinople. There still existed with the Moscow court a tight bond of common faith which was further strengthened by ties of kinship. As before, Constantinople did not favor the candidates of others and, with the empire in a disastrous state, hoped to obtain more aid from its own Photius than Vytautas's Gregory, a Bulgarian. The Lithuanian prince's request was rejected.

TWO METROPOLITANS

Vytautas ascribed the rejection to the venality of the Constantinople court and the patriarch, who named a metropolitan according to the wishes of the highest bidder. Whosoever gave them more, sent them Russian money, enjoyed their favor. He then gathered the bishops and the archimandrites and announced the necessity of installing their own metropolitan. "It saddens me to see all this," said Vytautas, "strangers will say 'See, the sovereign is of another faith, and so the church has become impoverished.' There can be no such rumors, for it is clear that the present mood of the church and its neglected state stems from the metropolitan and not from myself." "It is not for the first time," responded the bishops, "that we hear and see that the church is becoming impoverished, and that the emperor and patriarch do not provide our church with a goodly builder."

According to other sources the bishops, or at least some of them, decided to break ties with Photius only after coercion. It is evident from Vytautas's communication itself that in breaking with Photius there was no desire to break with Constantinople. Having considered, they responded to their prince "Let us make a plea once again to Constantinople, to the emperor and the patriarch." Vytautas sent emissaries to Constantinople in March 1415 with the threat that, if his wishes were not fulfilled, a metropolitan would be seated in Kiev by his own Rus bishops. The deadline was set at the Prophet Elijah's Day [July 20] and the feast of the

Dormition [August 15] as the absolute limit. Later the imperial and patriarchal ambassadors, returning from Moscow through Lithuanian lands, asked for an extension to St. Philip's Day [October 22]. When even that date passed Gregory was installed by a council of Rus bishops. Photius, having learned of Vytautas's plans, hurriedly set off for Kiev to make peace with the Lithuanian prince and, if that was impossible, to proceed to Constantinople and block Vytautas's intentions. At the Lithuanian border the metropolitan was seized, robbed and forced to return to Moscow.

SOUTH-NORTH DISCORD

To justify their deed the Southern Rus bishops sent a missive to Photius in which they generally reproached him for certain improper actions at the very beginning of his rule. They also mentioned some great transgression, the admission of which they left to Photius. They themselves did not wish to announce it, reluctant to shame him. In the council order of the election and installation of Gregory written on behalf of eight bishops it is said that the bishops, observing the Kievan church neglected by the metropolitan who, while collecting its income removed it to another place where he resided, had installed Gregory as metropolitan upon counsel of the grand prince, all other princes, boyars, nobles, archimandrites, abbots, monks and priests. In so doing they were heeded by apostolic law, the previous example of the Rus bishops who, during the reign of Prince Iziaslav, installed Metropolitan Klim,[27] and the example of their brothers the Bulgarians and Serbs. "With this act," said the bishops, "we do not secede from the Eastern church. We continue to venerate the Eastern patriarchs, metropolitans and bishops as fathers and brothers. In accordance with them we profess the same faith. We wish only to avoid the coercion and intrusion of laymen, simony, and the recent excesses when Cyprian, Pimen and Dionisy contested the metropolitanate."

The bishops wished to avoid the simony for which they reproached the court in Constantinople, yet in 1398 Bishop John of Lutsk promised King Jogaila two hundred grivnas and thirty horses should he help him obtain the metropolitanate of Galich. Vytautas, on his part, issued a general edict about Gregory's elevation in which he listed his reasons for the installation. Having minutely described the course of events, he concluded "We write [the bishops] so that you know and be cognizant of how events occurred. Whoever wishes to remain as of old under the rule of the metropolitan of Kiev, well and good! Whoever refuses does as he wishes. Be aware of one thing. We are not of your faith. If we wished your faith exterminated and your churches stand neglected in our lands, we would not strive to look after any of yours. Rather, in the absence of a metropolitan or at the death of a bishop we would install our own cleric and take the income of the church, the metropolitan and bishop for ourselves. Yet we, not wishing to extinguish your faith, and desiring that your churches have support, have installed a metropolitan, approved by a council, in the Kievan metropolitanate, that Rus honor may remain in its own land."

Photius for his part also issued a general missive to the Southern Rus Orthodox population. Without mentioning Vytautas the metropolitan in very strong language censured the action of Gregory Tsamblak and the bishops who installed him. The missive disclosed that Gregory first went to Constantinople for installation, was unfrocked there by Patriarch Euphemius and barely escaped with his life. Photius provided this incident as proof of the absence of venality at the Constantinople court inasmuch as Gregory himself, just as Theodosius of Polotsk before him, promised much gold and silver for his office yet did not receive what he desired. Photius asked of the Orthodox that they avoid the bishops whose design it was to divide the metropolitanate.

Tsamblak, who was famous among his contemporaries for his eloquence, remained true to the rule expressed in the missive of the bishops who installed him. He remained true to Orthodoxy. In the chronicles there is an account that he asked Vytautas why he was not of the Orthodox faith. Vytautas responded that if Gregory were to go to Rome and there win a debate with the Pope and all his wise men, he would convert to Orthodoxy with all his subjects. This account may indicate the motives which made Gregory accept Vytautas's mission to the Council of Constance.[28] The Lithuanian mission arrived at the conclusion of the council when it reached Constance on February 18, 1418 simultaneously with the emissaries of the Greek emperor Manuel II,[29] whose mission was to begin negotiations with the Pope on the unification of the churches.

COUNCIL OF CONSTANCE

The Greek and Lithuanian missions were received with great pomp and granted the right to perform religious services according to their own ritual. Yet they left empty-handed because the council dispersed without taking up the questions of church unification. Gregory did not live very long upon returning from Constance and died in 1419. At this time Vytautas's enmity toward Moscow subsided, all his attention now engulfed by relations with Poland. This is why he made no effort upon the death of Tsamblak toward selection of a favored metropolitan for Kiev. Photius thus once again received jurisdiction over the Southern Rus church. Notifying the Orthodox of this event, he wrote "Christ, creator of all the universe, once again has adorned His church with ancient splendor and peace and has brought my humility into His church through the counsel of the noble, good and glorious Prince Alexander (otherwise Vytautas)."[30] In 1421 Photius was in the Southwest, in Lvov, Vladimir and Wilno. In 1430 he was in Troki and was received along with the Moscow Grand Prince Vasily Vasilievich by Vytautas in Wilno, where he was shown great honors by the Lithuanian prince. The metropolitan was accorded the same honors by Vytautas's successor Svidrigailo.[31]

We have noted above the significance of the step with which Photius signalled his political activity in the North, in Moscow, by announcing himself solemnly on the side of the nephew and against the uncle. There was no open conflict in Photius's lifetime, for Yury recognized the seniority of his nephew. Immediately upon the death of the metropolitan the princes again quarreled and made preparations to go to the Horde. Internecine strife did erupt between Vasily and Yury when the metropolitan was absent from Moscow. It safely may be said that his presence would have changed the nature of events, for it has been noted how the support of Metropolitan Jonas greatly assisted Vasily the Dark. It also has been noted how defeated princes beseeched the victor that he not summon them to Moscow during a metropolitan's absence, for only he could guarantee their safety.

CONFLICT WITH ROMAN CATHOLICISM

For a long time unrest in Moscow prevented the designation of a new metropolitan. Bishop Jonas of Riazan finally was elected.[32] Not only was he the first Russian-born metropolitan, he was born and raised in Northern Rus, specifically in the Sol Galitskaia region. While Moscow delayed, Lithuania hastened, and before Jonas could depart for Constantinople Bishop Gerasim of Smolensk[33] arrived from that city as metropolitan. He halted in Smolensk to await the cessation of internecine strife in Moscow. The strife ceased, yet Moscow never saw Gerasim. After quarreling with the Lithuanian prince Svidrigailo the metropolitan was seized by him and burned at the stake. Now Jonas set off for Constantinople, and again he was preempted. Isidore already was installed. He was the last Russian metropolitan to be a Greek and be installed in Greece. The Council of Florence, periods of unrest and the fall of Byzantium inevitably led to the

Russian metropolitanate's independence from the patriarch of Constantinople.

Isidore, having arrived in Moscow, began preparing to attend the
council called in Italy for the unification of the churches. The very location of the council in a non-Orthodox country must have raised suspicions
in Moscow. The grand prince did not want Isidore to go to Italy. When
he could not dissuade the metropolitan, he said to him "Take heed, and
bring us the ancient faith which we took from our progenitor Vladimir.
Do not bring anything new or alien. If you do, we will not accept it."
Although Isidore stoutly swore to hold to Orthodoxy even on the way his
Orthodox traveling companions began to notice in him Latin inclinations.
At Yuriev-in-Livonia (Dorpat), when the city's Russian population came
out to meet him with priests and crosses and the Germans simultaneously
came out with their crosses, he approached the Germans first. At the
council Isidore accepted unification.

Among other motives Isidore may have had in mind was the promise
of large funds to support unity of the metropolitanate. Great advantages
would accrue to the Russian metropolitan were the two princes, those of
Moscow and Lithuania, no longer of different faiths. Yet Moscow wished
nothing further than maintenance of the ancient faith. When Isidore returned to Moscow, bringing with him the new and the alien, when he
began to be called a papal legate and ordered that a Latin cross and three
silver staffs be carried before him, dissatisfaction appeared. When he
ordered that the Pope receive prayers in the liturgy instead of the ecumenical patriarchs, and when after the liturgy he ordained that the writ
on unification of the churches be read from the central dais, there was
discord. When it was heard that the Holy Spirit proceeds from the Father
and the Son[34] and that both unleavened and leavened bread may equally
transubstantiate into the body of Christ, the grand prince called Isidore
a heretical Latin seducer, a wolf. He ordered him removed from the
metropolitan's residence and placed under guard in the Miracles monastery. Meanwhile he summoned bishops, archimandrites, abbots, and
monks and charged them to decide the matter. They found that it was all
a papal stratagem, not in accordance with godly laws and traditions. In
the meantime Isidore escaped. The grand prince did not order pursuit.

NORTHERN AUTONOMY

The Council of Florence finally forced a decision to do what Mitiay had
advocated in the North, and what the bishops who installed Tsamblak

later did in the South. The grand prince sent a missive to the patriarch in Constantinople. "It has been more than four hundred and fifty years," wrote Vasily, "that Russia has maintained the ancient faith accepted from Byzantium in the time of St. Vladimir. Upon the death of Metropolitan Photius we pressed Bishop Jonas of Riazan to go to you. He is a spiritual man who since childhood has lived a virtuous life. We do not know why you did not entertain our request, paid no attention to our charters and emissary, and instead of Jonas sent Isidore, for whom we did not send, whom we neither requested nor demanded. Only the entreaties of the emperor's emissary, the blessings of the patriarch, the contrition, the humility, the beseeching of Isidore himself barely led us to accept him. At that time we could not even imagine what he would become with time! He brought us the Pope's innovations, returned as a legate with a Latin-style crucifix and was evilly pluralist in calling himself a preceptor and dean of two churches, the Orthodox and the Latin. We have gathered our Orthodox clergy, to all of whom Isidore's behavior seemed alien, strange and unlawful. Because of this we all pray your most revered holiness to send us your most honored writ allowing our bishops to choose and install a metropolitan in Rus, because just as necessity has imposed in the past. Now we have an invasion of godless Turks[35] and upheavals and uprisings in neighboring lands. Besides this we must communicate with the metropolitan on important matters and when the metropolitan is a Greek we must speak to him through interpreters. In this way these insignificant men in this manner learn important secrets before all others."

This document never reached Constantinople. Information came to Moscow stating that the Greek emperor allegedly had accepted the Latin faith and moved to Rome. Then the grand prince ordered the emissaries to return. Soon after that new troubles and unrest began in Moscow. The imprisonment of Grand Prince Vasily, first by the Tatars and then by Shemiaka, left no opportunity for deliberating the installation of a metropolitan. It should be noted that the lack of a metropolitan significantly affected the course of events, for it is unlikely that Shemiaka or Prince Ivan of Mozhaisk[36] could have realized their plan had there been a metropolitan. When Vasily regained his hold on the grand-princely throne, he hastened to name a metropolitan. Installed by his own bishops was Jonas of Riazan, who much earlier was named to the metropolitanate, and who already had performed important services to the grand prince and his family.

148   RELATIONS WITH BYZANTIUM

RELATIONS WITH BYZANTIUM

The services performed by Jonas to the Moscow government after his installation as metropolitan have been described elsewhere.[37] Now attention must be turned to relations with Byzantium and Lithuanian Rus. After the installation of Jonas the grand prince sent Emperor Constantine Paleologos[38] a letter. "After the demise of Metropolitan Photius," he wrote, "we, having consulted with our mother the grand princess, and with our own brothers the Russian princes, both the greater and the lesser, as well as with the sovereign of Lithuania, with the bishops and all the clergy, with the boyars and all the Russian land, and with all Orthodox Christians, selected and sent with our emissary the Riazan bishop Jonas to you in Constantinople for installation. Before he could arrive there the emperor and patriarch installed Isidore and assigned him to Kiev as metropolitan of all Rus. To Jonas they said 'Go to your throne, the Riazan bishopric. Should Isidore die or something else befall him you must be prepared to be blessed for the metropolitan's throne of all Rus!'

"In your blessed domains there has been discord in God's church. Travelers to Constantinople suffer myriad difficulties on the way. There is much upheaval in our countries, the invasion of the godless Turks and internecine wars. We have suffered great injury not from strangers but from your brothers. Therefore in this great exigency we have gathered all the Russian bishops according to the law, installed Jonas as head of the Russian metropolitanate, for Kiev and for all Rus. We have acted thus because of the great exigency and not in pride or impertinence. Till the end of time we shall cleave to the Orthodoxy granted us. Our church always shall seek the blessings of the church of Constantinople and obey it in all things in accordance with the ancient faith. Our father Metropolitan Jonas also pleads blessings and union despite the current new discord. We beseech your majesty to be kindly disposed to our father Metropolitan Jonas. We wanted to write of all these church affairs to the holy Orthodox patriarch as well, to ask his blessings and prayers, yet we do not know whether or not there is a patriarch in your imperial city. If, God grant, yours is a patriarch in accordance with the ways of the ancient faith, we shall inform him of our concerns and ask his blessings."

FALL OF CONSTANTINOPLE

In 1453 Constantinople was taken by the Turks. In Moscow news of this came from a Greek named Demetrius who had escaped from captivity.

Through an encyclical Metropolitan Jonas informed all the Orthodox of the fall of Constantinople, of the fearful sufferings of the Greek people, and sought aid for Demetrius that he might ransom his family from Turkish captivity. Jonas wrote Patriarch Gennadios beseeching his blessing and sending whatever gifts he could find. "Do not be angry," wrote Jonas, "at our meager gifts, for our land also has become scourged by heathens and internecine wars. Please exhibit toward us, master, spiritual love and send my son, the grand prince, your honored commendation for the spiritual good of our great Orthodox faith. All missives received from the previous patriarchs we have maintained as solemn documents and for the good of our spirit, but all perished by fire during disorders in the land." Perhaps a writing from the patriarch was necessary to Moscow as proof that the independent installation of a metropolitan did not destroy unity with Constantinople, and that there was no anger there at the change in relations.

RELATIONS WITH LITHUANIA

The Moscow prince and metropolitan undertook to remain in unity with Byzantium on condition that the ancient faith be maintained there although the innovations of the Council of Florence brought by Isidore met strong resistance in Moscow, foremost from the government itself. Yet it is understandable that the innovations were received differently when their source was the Catholic rulers of Lithuanian Rus. In 1443 the Polish king Władysław, son of Jogaila,[39] granted a charter of privileges to the Rus clergy in which he announced that the Eastern church, Greek and Rus, was brought into the long-desired union with the church of Rome. As a result the Rus clergy which hitherto, in the words of the king, suffered a certain amount of oppression, was granted all rights and privileges exercised by the Catholic clergy. Isidore, forced to flee from Moscow, did not stop anywhere in Rus. The next year, 1444, King Władysław was slain at Varna.[40]

Casimir, his successor,[41] found himself in a difficult position between the demands of Poland and Lithuania, which caused him to end his enmity towards Moscow. Peace most readily might be concluded through the influence of Metropolitan Jonas, and the Lithuanian prince, wishing peace with Moscow, was pleased to win Jonas's favor by subjugating the Russo-Lithuanian church to him. Jonas for his part had to make every effort to ensure peace between Casimir and Vasily because only under conditions of such amity would church union be preserved. Should misunderstandings arise after the conclusion of peace Casimir, sending his envoy to Moscow, instructed him to seek the metropolitan's mediation to preserve the peace. Jonas, referring to himself as one who prayed for both parties, answered Casimir that he had spoken with blessings and prayer to Grand Prince Vasily about amity, and that Vasily desired brotherhood and love between himself and the king. "I thank your majesty," wrote Jonas, "for your kind disposition and bless you in the love of your brother Grand Prince Vasily Vasilievich, who wishes the same. I, who pray for both of you, rejoice in my religious duty to pray to God and strive for peace between you. I thank and bless you for your great kindness and gifts." The great kindness for which Jonas thanked Casimir was known. He promised to restore the unity of the Russian church as it was of old, and to send Jonas his decision upon his return from Poland to Lithuania. The king held to his word and subordinated the Southwestern Rus church to Jonas, who in 1451 appeared in Lithuania.

CONTINUED CONFLICT

The perilous consequences of the Council of Florence for Southwestern Rus did not end with the Isidore affair. The Popes did not cherish relinquishing what once was fallen into their hands, and the Lithuanian prince, a Catholic, could not stand against the intentions of the head of the Catholic church. In 1458 Gregory Mammas, the patriarch of Constantinople residing in Rome, installed Gregory, a disciple of Isidore, as metropolitan for Rus.[42] Notification of this was sent to Moscow immediately. Even before Gregory's arrival in Lithuania Grand Prince Vasily sent men to tell King Casimir not to receive the metropolitan from Rome, nor impose innovations upon their common father Jonas or break the traditions of old. "Our old traditions," wrote Vasily, "dating to the time of our progenitor Vladimir who baptized the Land of Rus, are that the choice of metropolitan always has belonged to our progenitors, the grand princes of Russia, and belongs to us now rather than to the grand princes of Lithuania. Whomever we favor, he shall be ours and all Russia's. A metropolitan from Rome we shall never have. I have no need of such, neither, brother, need you accept him. You, not we, will cause a schism in God's church."

Jonas, who could not visit Lithuania because of his age and infirmities, dispatched two of his archimandrites with a missive to the Orthodox bishops, princes, lords and boyars charging them to stand fast in support of Orthodoxy in accordance with the ancient laws laid down at the seven ecumenical councils.[43] A council of the bishops of Northern Rus who were consecrated by Jonas was called in Moscow. The bishops swore an oath there to be relentless supporters of the holy Muscovite church and of their lord and father Jonas, metropolitan of all Rus, and to obey him and his successor in all things. The metropolitan is selected by the Holy Spirit, the laws of the apostles and the holy fathers, and the sway of the lord Grand Prince Vasily Vasilievich, Russian autocrat. The installation takes place in the cathedral of the Mother of God in Moscow at the grave of the metropolitan St. Peter, the Russian miracle worker. They also swore to abjure the impostor Gregory, disciple of Isidore, who caused the schism between the Moscow and the Kievan churches, nor accept his edicts or hold counsel with him on any matter. This oath, made public in a writ of council, is significant because in it Moscow for the first time was described as the seat of the Russian metropolitanate. The prelates swore not to withdraw from the Moscow cathedral church of the Mother of God.

PERMANENT DIVISION

Up to this point the metropolitan's title was that of Kiev and all Rus. In this writ he is called simply the metropolitan of all Rus or the Russian metropolitan. This writ also defined the installation procedure for future Russian metropolitans. The lawful Russian metropolitan henceforth must be the candidate installed in Moscow at the behest of the prince, without any connection to Byzantium. The Northern bishops attending the council—those of Rostov, Suzdal, Kolomna, Saray and Perm—sent a missive to those in Lithuania—the bishops of Chernigov, Polotsk, Smolensk, Turov and Lutsk—with an exhortation not to accept the metropolitan from the Latins.[44] In his own name Jonas sent an encyclical to the Lithuanian bishops with the same message. He wrote separately to the bishops of Chernigov and Smolensk,[45] exhorting them not to accept Gregory. Were they coerced, he invited them to Moscow as a safe haven from Latin excesses. If they acted otherwise he threatened them with excommunication.

Finally, he wrote to the rest of the Orthodox population of the Lithuanian-Rus lands. He promised to visit his Lithuanian flock when his illness eased, and urged them not to heed Gregory or his teachings which were like those of Macedonius,[46] and to bear witness for Orthodoxy even unto death, for a martyr's crown lay ready for such sufferers. All these measures were in vain. Casimir could not refuse to accept a metropolitan from Rome. He even sent emissaries to try to convince Grand Prince

Vasily to acknowledge Gregory as the common metropolitan, because
Jonas was too old. The Moscow prince of course having refused, the
Russian metropolitanate divided once and for all. Jonas did not outlive
by much what, to him, was a sad event. He died in 1461, having appointed as his successor Archbishop Theodosius of Rostov, who was
installed according to the new tradition in Moscow by the council of the
Northern Russian bishops.

TRIUMPH OF MOSCOW

Such were the main events in the history of the Russian church hierarchy during this era. The idea which arose naturally for the first time when
Andrei Bogoliubsky contemplated giving Northern Rus a separate, independent existence, even hegemony over Southern Rus, was realized when
the two halves of Rus were separated under two equally powerful and
mutually hostile dynasties. As a result of this division the metropolitanate
too was divided. Instrumental in this was the creation, thanks to political events, of the separate metropolitanate of Galich and the transfer of
the Kiev metropolitan's throne to the North. This transfer, the misfortunes
of Byzantium, unrest, the Council of Florence and, finally, the fall of the
Byzantine empire freed the Moscow metropolitanate from immediate
dependence on the patriarch of Constantinople.

The Council of Florence and the measures of Isidore have great significance in Russian history because they forced Northeastern Rus conclusively and radically to express itself on union with Rome. It is clear
that Moscow's resolve to hold to the traditions of the forefathers, to the
ancient faith, not to permit innovations in the church, are factors which
determined the destiny of Eastern Europe. In the activity of the Russian
metropolitans during the decisive circumstances of the period the considerable influence of Byzantium and the nature of the Eastern church
readily may be determined. The Russian metropolitans made no attempt
to gain an autonomous existence independent of the secular power. Such
purpose could have been obtained most easily by choosing to reside in
Kiev among weak princes, far from the strong princes and from the main
theaters of political activity.

Kiev did not become the Russian Rome. The metropolitans abandoned
it in their northward surge for the protection of secular power. In the
North they did not long remain in Vladimir which, abandoned by the
strong princes, could have held the significance of Kiev for the metropolitans. Instead they moved to the capital city of one of the strongest princes,

and strove with all their might to aid this prince in overcoming his enemies and establishing monarchy. The metropolitans did not exploit the conflicts accompanying this development, or the influence they won, or that given them by the princes, to further their own sway and mastery over the princes. In return for their help they did not seek special rights, nor did they strive to strengthen their privileges by reducing the princes' rule through creating dissension. Unlike Western practice they did not seek to incite rivals or support them with their influence against the strongest prince most dangerous to their privileges. On the contrary, they strove as rapidly as possible to strengthen one prince at the expense of the others. Consequently church and secular power could not but assume the same traditional relationship they had in Byzantium.

CHURCH RIGHTS

Concerning the definition of relations between the metropolitans and the grand princes there is information in a document composed mutually by Grand Prince Vasily Dmitrievich and Metropolitan Cyprian. Here it is evident that everyone belonging to the church was subject to the metropolitan's ecclesiastical court. When a grand prince's man lodged a complaint with the prince against an abbot, priest or monk, a joint tribunal convened, meaning the metropolitan and prince judged together. When the metropolitan was absent the prince judged alone and shared the profit [fine] equally with the metropolitan. Should someone lodge a complaint with the prince against a metropolitan's coadjutor, tithe collector or regional administrator, the grand prince judged alone.

When the grand prince himself marched in war the metropolitan's boyars and servitors must march also under the metropolitan's military lieutenant and under the grand prince's banner. Boyars and servitors who had not attended Metropolitan Alexis and entered the metropolitan [Cyprian]'s service recently must march with the grand prince's military commander according to the area where he lived. The metropolitan was not to accept the grand prince's servitors or tribute-paying men as priests or deacons because this created a loss for the prince's service and treasury. This explains why the clergy consisted only of men from the ranks of the clergy. However, a priest's son, even when in the grand prince's service, might become a priest or a deacon as he desired. A priest's son who lived with his father and ate his bread was subject to the metropolitan's jurisdiction, whereas one who lived apart from his father and ate his own bread belonged to the grand prince.

It is evident from this document that the metropolitan convened his own judicial court, maintained his own boyars and servitors and that his residence was called a palace. There is mention of the metropolitan's boyars and retainers in the chronicles as well. It is said of Mitiay that the metropolitan's boyars served him, and the retainers ministered to him. Wherever he went both boyars and retainers preceded him. The metropolitan had his own table attendants. Thus Metropolitan Cyprian sent his table attendant Fedor Timofeev to summon the bishop of Novgorod to Moscow. He had his own keeper of the seal and his own master of the horse. From these court servitors the metropolitan sent men to govern districts (district officials), to serve in the church courts (tithe collectors) and so on.

LEGAL AND MORAL INFLUENCE

The large significance of the metropolitan in princely affairs has been noted. Therefore the metropolitan's signatures and seals are found frequently on princely edicts, pacts and testaments. Of extant documents the agreement between Dmitry Donskoy and his cousin Vladimir Andreevich is the first to begin with the words "At the blessing of our father Alexis, metropolitan of all Rus." At the close of Dmitry Donskoy's testament we read "I wrote this document as my final testament and brought it to my father Alexis, metropolitan of all Rus, who attached his seal to this document." On one side the metropolitan's seal has an image of the Mother of God and the infant Jesus. The other side bears the inscription "Through God's will the seal of (name) the metropolitan of all Rus." The testament of Vasily Dmitrievich bears the signature of Metropolitan Photius in Greek. The same signature may be found on the agreement between Vasily Vasilievich and his uncle Yury. Beginning in 1450 missives were written with the blessing of Metropolitan Jonas and confirmed by his signature "The humble Jonas, archbishop of Kiev and all Rus." Such also was the signature of Jonas's successor Theodosius.

SELECTION OF PRELATES

In the patriarchs' writs to newly installed metropolitans it was stated that the grand prince must honor the metropolitan, express Christian love with veneration, obedience and observance just as all other Russian princes, dignitaries, clergy and Christian populace. The metropolitan appointed archbishops, priests, monks, deacons, subdeacons and readers, consecrated churches and presided over all church affairs throughout the realm. The selection of bishops apparently was made as it was in the preceding period. Thus we read in the chronicles for 1289 that Grand Prince Mikhail Yaroslavich of Tver sent his mother along with an abbot named Andrei to Kiev. There Metropolitan Maxim named Andrei as bishop of Tver. This Andrei, incidentally, was the son of a Lithuanian prince. On the other hand there exists, dating from the end of the period under consideration, a statute on selection of bishops. It says that in the selection procedure the metropolitan gathered all the bishops subordinate to him. Those unable to attend were to state in writing their agreement with the decision reached by the others. The assembled bishops were to select three men whose names were to be forwarded to the metropolitan in a sealed scroll. The metropolitan was to choose one of the three as bishop.

This procedure could only have been instituted when the significance of regional princes had declined. Before his installation the chosen bishop swore to uphold Orthodoxy, obey the metropolitan, not impede gathering the metropolitan's tax in his bishopric, not practice the duties of his rank in other bishoprics, to attend unfailingly the metropolitan at first summons, not to permit the Orthodox in his bishopric to marry Armenians or Catholics or become their in-laws. The newly selected bishop further pledged that he had not bought his office and that he had not promised to pay anyone nor would he pay. He wrote this statement with his own hand over his signature. The installation documents sent by metropolitans to bishops followed those of patriarch to metropolitan. Archbishops and bishops did not call the metropolitan brother, only father. Otherwise they were subject to rebuke.

REMOVAL OF PRELATES

A metropolitan could remove bishops from office. In 1280 Metropolitan Cyril, while inspecting the bishoprics under his jurisdiction, came to Rostov and discovered that the local bishop Ignaty removed the body of Prince Gleb Vasilkovich from the cathedral at midnight and unceremoniously buried it in the monastery. For this the metropolitan immediately removed the bishop from office, forgiving him only because of the heartfelt appeals of Prince Dmitry Borisovich. He gave the following admonition to Ignaty. "Do not be overweening and do not think that you are without sin. Do more to assist and forgive than to forbid and excommunicate. Weep and repent till your very death for this brazen act, for you have judged before God's judgement a man long dead in fear of a living man, from whom you have taken gifts and with whom you have eaten, drunk and made merry. When he [Prince Gleb Vasilkovich] could have been reformed, you did not redeem him, but now you wish to redeem a dead man through such harsh expulsion. If you want to aid him in the other world, do so through good deeds and prayer."

Metropolitan Peter defrocked Izmail, bishop of Saray. Metropolitan Theognostos removed but then forgave Daniel, bishop of Suzdal. A prince who was displeased with his bishop might complain to the metropolitan. The bishop of Tver, Evfimy, aroused severe indignation in his prince, Mikhail Alexandrovich,[47] who in 1390 sent men to summon Metropolitan Cyprian to Tver. Cyprian set out with two Greek and several Russian bishops. At a distance of thirty versts from Tver the metropolitan was met by the prince's grandson, at twenty versts by the eldest son, and at five by the grand prince himself. After greetings at the city gates by the clergy bearing crosses, Cyprian celebrated a liturgy in the cathedral and then dined with the prince, where he received gifts and great honors.

For three days Prince Mikhail thus feted the metropolitan. On the fourth day the clergy and boyars gathered at the prince's residence. When Cyprian arrived, everyone complained about Bishop Evfimy. The metropolitan and the other bishops deliberated. According to some evidence, the accused could not exonerate himself, the truth did not abide on his lips, but according to other evidence the accusations were slanderous. In either case the sources agree that the displeasure with Evfimy was fearsome, and the metropolitan, without even attempting to reconcile the prince with the bishop, sent Evfimy to Moscow. In his place he installed his archdeacon Arseny, who barely agreed to become bishop amidst such enmity and unrest.

LEGAL MATTERS

At the beginning of this period, specifically in 1229, there is a curious incident concerning a court decision made by a local prince against a bishop as a property owner. "There came," says the chronicler, "an ordeal for Bishop Cyril of Rostov. In one day all his wealth was taken from him because he lost in litigation. The case was decided by Prince Yaroslav in favor of Cyril's adversaries. Cyril was very rich in money and villages, in numerous goods and books. In a word, there never yet was so rich a bishop in the land of Suzdal."

There is also mention of a complaint by a bishop against a metropolitan addressed to the patriarch in Constantinople. It was in this manner that the above-mentioned Bishop Andrei of Tver, a Lithuanian by birth, complained against Metropolitan Peter. To settle the matter the patriarch sent to Russia his own emissary, on whose arrival a council was called in Pereiaslavl. The accused was present, as was the accuser, accompanied by two princes of Tver, Dmitry and Alexander Mikhailovich, also other princes, grandees and clergy. The accuser was found in falsehood, but Peter forgave him and, upon enlightening those present, dissolved the council.

In parallel to this statute which specified that a council selected a bishop there is information that a council also met for his dismissal. Thus in 1401 Metropolitan Cyprian called a council in Moscow at which John of Novgorod and Savva of Lutsk renounced their bishoprics. In 1274 Metropolitan Cyril took advantage of a council summoned to install Serapion as bishop of Vladimir in order to propose a rule for the establishment of clerical and lay decency and decorum. "I have seen myself and heard from others about severe ecclesiastical disorder," wrote Cyril in his decision. "In one locale they hold to one tradition, in a second to another. There is much discord and coarseness.... What have we gained from having abandoned God's laws? Has not God scattered us across the face of the whole earth? Have not our cities been seized? Have not our powerful princes fallen under sharp swords? Have not our children been driven into captivity? Have not God's holy churches stood empty? Are we not daily tormented by the godless and profane pagans?" The metropolitan inveighed first of all against simony, giving laws concerning such appointments.

PUBLIC MORALS

Among the people there still existed the passion for fisticuffs and fighting with clubs so strong in the preceding period. "I have discovered," Cyril writes, "that the devil's tradition of the thrice-damned Greeks is still held. On God's holy days licentious drunkards call each other forth by whistles, cries and shouts. They fight to death with clubs and then take the clothing of the slain. This is done as an affront to God's holy days and as vexation to His church." Cyril also inveighed against drunkenness which obstructed the celebration of services from Holy Week to All Saints' Day.[48]

Other matters were decided at ecclesiastical councils as well, for example altercations over the borders of a bishopric. In a missive Metropolitan

Alexis wrote the inhabitants of Krasnoiarsk that the boundaries of the Riazan and Saray bishoprics were fixed at the council of Kostroma. At another council Archbishop Theodosius of Rostov was convinced that he was in error concerning the kind of food consumed on the eve of Epiphany should it fall on a Sunday. The wrongness of Isidore's measure was determined at a council. It was at a council that the bishops of Northeastern Rus decided to stand by the Moscow metropolitan Jonas and to abjure Gregory of Kiev. Besides general councils convened by the metropolitan of all Rus attended by the bishops under his jurisdiction, there were local ones called by a bishop of a given region, composed of the clergy under his jurisdiction. Thus in 1458 Archbishop Theodosius of Rostov called a council in Belozersk to avert certain abuses such as granting permission for fourth marriages.[49]

Apart from employing councils metropolitans strove to eradicate immorality by means of missives to clergy and laity. An example is the sermon of Metropolitan Photius to priests and monks on the importance of their orders, "how they should be intercessors for men's souls before the Ruler of all rulers." The metropolitan calls the priests to look after the sanctity of marriage among their parishioners, not to permit them to abandon their lawful wives and cohabit with concubines, as was done frequently. He called on them categorically not to permit fourth marriages. Yet another tradition was retained from the preceding period, that of the clergy turning to the metropolitan with various questions which they themselves could not resolve. There are still extant the responses of Metropolitan Cyprian to the queries of Abbot Afanasy, and responses of the same metropolitan to the questions of unknown members of the clergy.

DOMESTIC DIFFICULTIES

The unique situation in Novgorod, Pskov and Viatka demanded the special attention of the metropolitans. In the era under discussion the archbishops in Novgorod were selected in this manner. Three candidates were chosen at a popular assembly and their names or lots were placed on the altar in the church of the Holy Wisdom. Then the gathered clergy celebrated the liturgy while the people assembled before the church. At the end of the service the archpriest of the Holy Wisdom brought out the lots one by one to the people. The last name was hailed as archbishop.

Prelates played major roles everywhere, the more so in Novgorod because of the attitude of its inhabitants to princes, their frequent discord with them and the perseverance of interregnums and domestic unrest. In

Novgorod in the absence of a prince the archbishop was the leading figure of government. His name is encountered before all others in edicts. He was the city's intermediary in its strife with the grand princes and the pacifier of domestic unrest. Nothing of importance was undertaken without his blessing. Yet the archbishop of Novgorod was installed by the metropolitan and was dependent on him. Hearings judged by the archbishop could be appealed to the metropolitan's jurisdiction. When the metropolitans began to reside in Moscow and lend assistance to the grand princes in attaining power and absolute rule, Novgorod was forced to abandon its separate and unique way of life. Consequently the position of the Novgorod archbishops grew very difficult. Archbishop John blessed the citizens of Novgorod in their war against the grand prince for the return of the Dvina lands, and paid for it with a three-year imprisonment in Moscow.

Mentioned above was the difficult correspondence of Metropolitan Jonas with the archbishop of Novgorod on the subject of Shemiaka.[50] Metropolitan Jonas also felt duty-bound to admonish the archbishop of Novgorod and his flock to abstain from violence at popular assemblies. "I have heard, children," wrote the metropolitan, "that at the devil's instigation deeds odious to God take place in Novgorod the Great, *the patrimony of my son the grand prince.* Not only do these deeds occur among common folk, they happen also among those of honor and rank. Every important or trifling matter brings forth anger. Anger turns to rage, quarrel and conflict. Both hostile parties draw a great number of people. Riff-raff, drunks and men ready to spill blood are hired. Fights are plotted and Christian souls perish."

Jonas's precursor Metropolitan Photius also sent an admonition to the Novgorod archbishop and his flock. He exhorted the people of Novgorod to abstain from foul language (a habit of which the chronicler accuses the Slavic tribes of even pre-Riurik times). Photius added that nowhere among Christians did such a habit exist. He further exhorted the people of Novgorod not to listen to false tales nor receive evil crones, not to use amulets, spells, potions, sorcery or anything of that kind. He ordered that at christenings there be total immersion in the font and not pouring water as in the Latin tradition. He forbade the marriage of girls before they were thirteen. He prohibited the white and black clergy from selling goods or lending money at interest. Should a man come to a priest for Holy Communion before going to the "field" (dueling) he is to be denied. When a duelist kills another he shall be excommunicated for eighteen years, neither shall the slain be buried in consecrated ground.

RIVALRY OF PSKOV AND NOVGOROD

The close political and church relations between Novgorod and Pskov demanded the metropolitan's attention as well. It has been noted that Pskov, grown rich through trade, for a long time strove towards independence from Novgorod, which began to exhibit dislike toward Pskov occasionally expressed in open warfare. It is understandable how difficult the position of Pskov was in such a situation because in church affairs it was dependent on the archbishop of Novgorod. Thence stems the natural desire of the inhabitants of Pskov to rid themselves of this dependence and obtain their own archbishop. It has been seen that their efforts were in vain, for Metropolitan Theognostos refused to name a bishop for them. In truth the people of Pskov picked an inappropriate time. Metropolitan Theognostos, like his predecessor, affirmed his residence in Moscow. More than other cities, Pskov felt the consequences of this decision. Only a short time previously Theognostos threatened Pskov with interdiction if it did not renounce its alliance with Alexander of Tver. Now that same Alexander was prince in Pskov again, this time with Lithuanian protection, while Novgorod had not as yet quarreled with Moscow. The chronicler more than once mentions open enmity between Pskov and the archbishop of Novgorod. He speaks of Pskov's quarrel with Archbishop Feoktist in 1307, adding that in 1337 Archbishop Vasily visited Pskov to gather church taxes which the people of Pskov refused to pay. He departed the city, having excommunicated its citizens.

When Archbishop John dispatched an archpriest to Pskov in 1411 for church taxes from the local clergy the inhabitants of Pskov refused and sent him back with this reply. "When, God grant, the archbishop himself resides in Pskov the church tax is clearly his, as this was from the very beginning, in olden days." In 1435 Archbishop Evfimy came to Pskov for taxes, although not in turn and not at the regular time. Pskov received him with supplication to call a church council. This he did not promise and instead asked for a levy for the priests under his jurisdiction. The people of Pskov were reluctant, still insisting on a council and maintenance of their traditions. They criticized the archbishop for appointing his coadjutor and keeper of the seal from among his own Novgorod men rather than from Pskov. The archbishop grew angry at this and departed, having spent only a week in Pskov. Prince Vladimir, the mayors and boyars set off after him, caught up and successfully begged him to return. The inhabitants of Pskov then gave him subsistence for a month and a levy for the support of the priests. About the council, the archbishop said that he would defer to the metropolitan. The archbishop's coadjutor assessed taxes not according to the Pskov taxation rates. He destroyed various records of agreement and invalidated written statements and arrangements and put deacons into the quarters of the junior boyars. All this was new and contrary to the old ways. The people of Pskov were in the right, says their chronicler. The Pskov priests did not support church taxes and quitrent [for the bishop]. Then, because of their sins and the devil's evildoing there occurred a brawl between the men of Pskov and the archbishop's servitors (those of the Holy Wisdom). The archbishop again grew angry and left without accepting gifts from Pskov, causing great losses to the abbots and priests, the likes of which never before had happened since the very founding of the city.

After the men of Pskov and the Moscow army devastated Novgorod possessions and then made peace, the two cities existed amicably. This friendship was reflected in church relations. When Archbishop Evfimy came to Pskov in 1449 all the clergy in procession, the prince, mayors, and boyars came out in greeting and received him with great honors. The very day of his arrival the archbishop celebrated the liturgy in the church of the Holy Trinity. On the third day he held a convocation in the same church at which he read the synodical [book of prayer for the dead]. Evil men who wished ill to Great Novgorod and Pskov were damned, then for the noble princes who lay in the houses of Holy Wisdom and the Holy Trinity they sang "Eternal Memory."[51] This they sang as well for others who laid down their lives and spilled their blood for the houses of God and the Orthodox Christian faith. To the living people of Novgorod and Pskov they sang "Many Years."[52] The prince, mayors and everyone in all the quarters paid great respect to the archbishop, gave many gifts and accompanied him to the very borders of their land with high honors. The archbishop was greeted and bidden farewell with similar honors in 1453 as well because he performed his office in exactly the same manner as did his precursors.

PSKOV TURNS TO MOSCOW

The hostile attitude of Pskov to Novgorod and its archbishop was the cause of a schism in the church, forcing the people of Pskov to turn directly to the metropolitan for governance and instruction. The unfriendly attitude of Novgorod to the metropolitan promoted these direct communications. The people of Pskov once sent several priests to Metropolitan Cyprian in Moscow for induction into office. They were to describe their needs and complain that they lacked true church law. The metropolitan consecrated the priests and sent back with them liturgical statutes and a proper synodical of the kind read in Constantinople in the Holy Wisdom cathedral. To this he added rules of how to pray for deceased Orthodox emperors and grand princes, and how to perform baptisms and marriages. Specifically, the tradition of holding children in one's arms and pouring water down on them was to be abolished [immersion was reinstated]. He also sent sixty altar coverlets [antimensions] with the warning that they not be cut into pieces as the archbishop of Novgorod had done.

The disaffection of Pskov with the archbishop of Novgorod and the resulting anarchy in the church led to the Pskov popular assembly assuming the right to judge and punish priests. In 1395 Metropolitan Cyprian wrote the men of Pskov that this was contrary to Christian law. A priest was to be judged and punished only by the prelate who appointed him. The metropolitan also forbade Pskov to interfere in church lands and villages. The proximity of Pskov to Lithuania, its frequent and old contacts with that state and its princes, caused the metropolitans concern about Pskov when the metropolitanate was divided. Thus in 1416 Metropolitan Photius urged Pskov to avoid the unrighteous neighboring lands which reject God's law and holy commandments. Pskov must receive cordially all those of the Orthodox faith who sought refuge in their city when fleeing religious persecution. Another time Photius instructed the Pskov clergy not to use Latin myrrh at baptisms instead of that from Constantinople, and to immerse infants rather than pour water over them. The metropolitan urged Pskov to send him an intelligent priest to learn well the church rules and whom he would send back with the holy myrrh.

METROPOLITANS' RULE

In another missive Photius instructed the people of Pskov not to permit men who took oaths lightly to serve as church elders or hold government or court positions in general. He also instructed them to exclude men who divorced their lawful wives and entered into new marriages. Metropolitan Jonas, everywhere trying to assert the rule of the Moscow grand prince, wrote Pskov as well. He termed it the patrimony of the Great Russian sovereign, the grandfather and father to Pskov through kinship and from time immemorial, through his forefathers, the great sovereigns and grand princes of Russia. The metropolitan exhorted the people of Pskov to live as Christians according to the old traditions stemming from Grand Prince Alexander Nevsky, and to hold to the oath they swore to the grand prince. Jonas's summons must have been influential in Pskov, given the considerable esteem the metropolitan enjoyed there. Thus when discontented with the new statutes given them by Prince Konstantin Dmitrievich, which they had sworn to observe, the inhabitants of Pskov turned to Metropolitan Photius with the plea that he absolve them from their oath and bless them in living the old way. The metropolitan fulfilled their request.

Finally, there are two missives of Photius to the people of Pskov which are noteworthy given its particular situation. In the first missive, written in time of plague, the metropolitan addressed the prominent citizens, exhorting them to be content with the levies they received, and to observe God's laws in their transactions and weights and measures. In the second instance, the people of Pskov turned to the metropolitan in perplexity— should they accept grain, wine and vegetables coming from German lands? The metropolitan granted permission to consume this produce, releasing them with a special pastoral prayer.

Apart from these issues there was yet another factor which drew the attention of Russian metropolitans, as well as of Constantinople patriarchs to Novgorod and especially Pskov. The enmity of Pskov for Novgorod was reflected in the attitude of Pskov to the prelates of Novgorod as well as Pskov. Not infrequently the behavior of the archbishop of Novgorod aroused indignation in Pskov. Anger growing from the unfulfilled desire for independence from Novgorod created in some a desire to free themselves completely from the church hierarchy. Disagreements relating to ecclesiastical courts and procedures as well as complaints of losses provided a pretext, and in the 1370s there appeared the so-called strigolnik heresy.[53]

RISE OF HERESY

The chronicles name the deacon Nikita and the layman Karp as originators of the heresy, but in the so-called missive of Patriarch Anthony and the Illuminator of Joseph of Volokolamsk the origin of heresy is ascribed solely to Karp. Furthermore, in the first source above Karp is called an excommunicated deacon. The second source states that he was a barber by profession. The discrepancies may be reconciled by the fact that Karp, who indeed was first a deacon, upon being excommunicated readily might have been called a layman. As a result of the excommunication and

"detonsuring" there may have arisen the term *strigolnik,* which in time
was misconstrued, and came to mean a barber. The heresy, as set forth
by the sources, held that clerics were unworthy of their calling because
they were installed through graft, that they sought to acquire property and
behaved improperly, that the sacraments must not be received from them.
It also held that laymen could instruct the people in the faith. In doing
penance, one must bow to the ground. There should be no services for the
dead—no prayers for them, no requiems, no offerings to them, no funeral
feasts and no distribution of alms in their name. There were even rumors
that the strigolniks rejected the life hereafter.

The heresy originated and spread in Pskov but it is not clear how its
leaders appeared in Novgorod. It is known only that in 1375 Karp, Nikita
and a comrade of theirs were thrown from the bridge into the Volkhov
river. The death of the heresiarchs did not root out the heresy. The
strigolniks attracted people by their unselfishness, their exemplary morals and ability to interpret Holy Scripture. Speaking of them, people said
"These neither rob nor acquire property." It was written of them in accusations that "All these heretics were alike, they fasted and prayed to
God devoutly, they were bookish and hypocritical and made a show of
purity to the people. If people could see that they lived impiously no one
would believe them and if they did not speak on Holy Scripture no one
would even listen to them." The heresy lasted from the fourteenth into the
fifteenth century.

There exist three missives of Metropolitan Photius to Pskov on the
subject of the strigolniks. The metropolitan forbade the Pskov clergy to
accept donations from the strigolniks, and the laity to associate with them
in eating or drinking. The inhabitants of Pskov replied that in fulfilling
the metropolitan's orders they discovered and punished heretics although
some escaped. Others persisted in their views and, straining their eyes
heavenward, spoke that their father was there. To this the metropolitan
responded that the inhabitants of Pskov must continue to shun the heretics and they might punish them, only by flogging and incarceration, not
with death. After 1427, when Photius's last missive was written, there
were no more accounts of strigolniks.

CHURCH ECONOMY

The material well-being of the church now deserves discussion. The
sources of maintenance of the metropolitan and bishops were primarily
collections from the churches. In the statutes of Grand Prince Vasily

Dmitrievich these collections are set forth. "The metropolitan's collection shall be six altyns from each church and three dengas of tax. A tithe collector on entering his district is to gather an installation tax, a Christmas tax and a St. Peter's tax of six altyns. The collection shall be gathered at Christmas time, but the tithe collector shall take his taxes at St. Peter's Day [June 29]. Churches not liable for the collection under previous metropolitans are not to pay now either." Archbishop Theodosius of Rostov, in releasing two churches of the St. Cyril monastery of Beloozero, wrote in his directive "The priests or abbots of those churches need not pay my collection, nor the tax [on inhabitants of church-owned lands or on workers of the church], nor the tithe collectors', nor that of [ecclesiastical] court investigator, or any other. My tithe gatherers are not to penalize them or send constables to them." It was said of Mitiay that when he assumed the full rights of a metropolitan he began to gather tribute from all churches in the metropolitanate including the St. Peter's and Christmas collections, regular tax, and the metropolitan's quitrent and levies.

As before, the court and the installation taxes were sources of income for the metropolitan and the bishops. To support ecclesiastical courts a prelate sent a special official called a tithe collector.[54] Rather than say that a particular city was under the jurisdiction of a given bishop it would be said that city was his "tenth." One of the tithe collectors of Metropolitan Jonas, his master of the horse Yury, upon arriving in Vyshgorod, a district belonging to Prince Mikhail Andreevich of Vereia, exercised his privilege of staying at the house of a priest. The latter and the townsmen attacked the tithe collector and the metropolitan's servitors. Two or three men were beaten so severely that they were maimed for life. The metropolitan, informing Prince Mikhail of this occurrence, wrote "You, my son, are yourself a great sovereign, but pause to ask your old boyars whether in the time of your progenitors and sires there was ever such an outrage against God's church and the holy fathers? You are aware that Grand Prince Vytautas was not of our faith, nor is the present king or his princes and nobles. Nevertheless consider how they have protected the church and how they honor it! Yet these men, though Orthodox Christians, blaspheme and dishonor God's church and us. I have sent my constable for the priests. I bless you and beseech that as a true and mighty Orthodox sovereign you defend God's church and myself, your father and pastor, from your city folk, so that nothing similar occurs again. If you fail to defend me, expect retribution from God, and I will defend myself from them with God's law. If my tithe collector has done something wrong, you my son should have investigated the matter fairly and written to me about it. I would have turned him over totally to you without trial, as I have done in the past."

It has been remarked that the archbishop of Novgorod received a levy from the clergy of Pskov. The Pskov clergy provided maintenance and gifts for the Novgorod prelate whenever he came to Pskov and the metropolitan received maintenance and gifts whenever he came to Novgorod or some other jurisdiction. For 1341 the chronicler states that Metropolitan Theognostos arrived in Novgorod accompanied by numerous attendants. This made things very difficult for the archbishop and the monasteries, who had to provide provender and gifts. Under 1352 there is an account that the Novgorod archbishop Moisey[55] sent emissaries to the Byzantine patriarch with a complaint against the excesses of visitors who came to Novgorod from the metropolitan.

Finally, immovable property also provided a major source of income. For 1286 there is an account of Lithuanians attacking a district belonging to the prelate of Tver. The town of Aleksin is referred to as belonging to Metropolitan Peter. In the province of Novgorod the small town of Molvotichi is mentioned as belonging to the archbishop. Princes bequeathed villages to metropolitans. There is also a reference to an exchange of villages between prince and metropolitan. There was an agreement between the grand prince and the metropolitan relating to these holdings. The tribute and tax collectors of the grand prince were not to enter the metropolitan's villages. Tribute was paid from them in quitrent according to the grand prince's edict on quitrent. The tax for roads and way stations was to be collected on the traditional day, the metropolitan's villages paying it when the prince's villages did. The metropolitan's men who lived in town and were listed at court owed quitrent, as did the courtiers of the grand prince. The metropolitan's men paid no general excise duty on the sale of their domestically produced goods, only when they sold purchased goods. Quitrent was owed by the church hierarchy only when tribute must be paid the Tatars.

As to the maintenance of the lower clergy, the princes in their testaments generally assigned funds to benefit the clergy of a given church through a specific allotment of income. Grand Prince Ivan II bequeathed a quarter of the general trade duty of Kolomna to the church of Our Lady of Krutitsy and the Moscow customs duty to the Dormition and Archangel cathedrals in memory of his father, brothers and himself. "This is my allotment to them," wrote the testator. Princess Elena, wife of Vladimir Andreevich, and Sophia, wife of Vasily Dmitrievich, bequeathed villages to the Archangel cathedral in Moscow. The princes frequently willed in their testaments that their [ornamental] belts and garments be distributed among priests and their money among churches. It must be noted that in Pskov during this period priests were assigned not to parishes, but to cathedrals, and supervised by the priest's elder.

Concerning the use the metropolitans made of their funds the chronicler states that Metropolitan Photius acquired income, taxes, lands, waters, villages and districts to feed the unfortunate and the poor, for the riches of the church were the riches of the poor. In the Life of Metropolitan Jonas there is an account of a widow coming to the metropolitan's pantry to drink mead for relief of her sickness.

In Southern Russia there are accounts of tribute in money and honey received from the Kievan metropolitan's Holy Wisdom patrimony. There is also mention of a village belonging to the bishop of Peremyshl and accounts of princes giving villages to churches.

ROLE OF MONASTERIES

In the new Russia of the Northeast monasteries retained their earlier immense significance. What the Caves monastery of Anthony and Theodosius was to Kiev, the ancient focal point of Russian life,[56] the Trinity monastery of St. Sergius was to Moscow, the new focal point. It has been observed how immigrants from various nations flowed to the new center. Both boyars and common folk came seeking refuge from domestic unrest, from Tatar disturbances, and finally by the coercion of Moscow itself. They brought to the service of Moscow and the new order it represented both material and spiritual resources. Almost simultaneously there came to Moscow two arrivals from opposite ends of the map. From Chernigov in Southern Rus, fleeing Tatar destruction, came the boyar Fedor Pleshcheev. From the North and the most ancient and famous city therein, Rostov, came the boyar Cyril, who was ruined and forced to leave his native city as a result of Muscovite coercion.

The sons of these newcomers, one as metropolitan of all Rus and the other as a humble monk who had declined the title of metropolitan, worked together closely to heighten through their united spiritual strength the glory of their new native land. Cyril, the newcomer from Rostov, settled in Radonezh. His middle son Varfolomey from his childhood years exhibited a leaning towards monasticism and secluded himself in a hermitage immediately upon the death of his parents. He lived a long time in the mighty forest without seeing the face of a human. Only a bear meandered to the anchorite to share his meager meals. Just as Anthony in olden times could not conceal his prodigious deeds in his cave, so now Varfolomey, having assumed the name Sergius at tonsuring, could not remain hidden in the dense forest. Monks gathered around him despite the severe greeting with which the anchorite met them. "Be aware first of all," he said, "that it is hard, hungry and poor here. Prepare yourselves not for rich food nor drink, not for ease and merriment, but for labor, sweat, sorrow and misfortune."

Several meager cells appeared, surrounded by a stockade. Sergius himself with his own hands built three or four cells, carried firewood from the forest and chopped it, carried water from the well and placed a bucket before each cell, did the cooking for all the brethren, sewed clothing and boots. In a word, he served everyone like a bought slave. This humble serving spread Sergius's fame through all the Russian regions and lent him the towering moral force and authority he possessed during the political events of Dmitry Donskoy's reign. Sergius served in that period as an intimidating emissary to Nizhny Novgorod, which flaunted the will of the Moscow prince. He was the placid peacemaker between the Moscow prince and the embittered Oleg of Riazan, and a steadfast exhorter in the battle with the legions of Mamay.

From Sergius's monastery, famed for the saintliness of its founder, many other monasteries spread into various parts of the land. These were founded by Sergius's associates, disciples and the disciples of disciples. One of these monasteries, that of Belozersk, played an unsurpassed role in the civil history of Russia. The monastery was founded by St. Cyril who was tonsured by the archimandrite of the St. Simeon monastery, Fedor, a disciple and nephew of St. Sergius. It has been noted that, along with St. Sergius, St. Cyril witnessed the sworn oaths of princes during the last period of internecine strife. He was considered to be the guardian of Northeastern Rus. Sergius left behind a testimony of good deeds, of quiet and humble sermons with which he inspired his brethren and touched embittered princes. Cyril left missives to various princes, among which there is one to Grand Prince Vasily Dmitrievich. "The closer saints approach God through love, the more they see themselves as sinners," wrote Cyril. "You, lord, obtain great salvation and spiritual benefit through your humility when you ask me, a sinner and beggar who is tormented and unworthy, to pray for you.... I, a sinner, and my brethren are glad to pray to God for you, our lord, to the limit of our strength. You, for God's sake, be mindful of yourself and all your principality. When an oarsman makes a mistake on a vessel, he brings little harm to those aboard. When the helmsman makes a mistake he brings destruction to the whole vessel. When a boyar sins he only harms himself, when it is the prince, he brings harm to all men. Grow to scorn, lord, all that draws you to sin. Fear God, the true tsar, and you shall be blessed. I have heard, lord great prince, that there is great unrest between you and your kinsmen the princes of Suzdal. You, lord, announce your truth, and they theirs, but Christians suffer great bloodshed thereby. Take a more careful look, lord, at the rightfulness of their stance against you and in your humility yield to them, but in whatever you are right before them hold to your rightful position. If they come to you in supplication, for God's sake forgive them as they deserve, for I have heard that you have kept them in want, and they took up arms for that reason. Therefore for God's sake, lord, reveal to them your love and kindness, that they not perish wandering in Tatar lands."

MONKS AND SAINTS

Cyril also corresponded with the grand prince's brothers, Andrei, in whose appanage his monastery was located, and Yury. To Andrei St. Cyril wrote "You are lord in your patrimony, placed by God to keep your people from evil practices. Let them hold just trials without false accusations and false evidence. Judges are not to take bribes but are to be content with their allotted fees. Let there be no taverns in your patrimony, for they are a great bane to souls. Christians drink, their souls perish. Let there be no domestic customs duties, for this is unjust profit, but wherever there is a ferrying point, let there be payment for the service. Let there be no banditry or thievery in your patrimony. If men do not desist from it, order them punished. Also, lord, keep men from foul speech and profanity."

St. Cyril wrote to Yury Dmitrievich a comforting letter because of the sickness of his wife. The following passage is of interest. "You, lord Prince Yury, have written that you have wanted to see me for a long time, still for God's sake do not come here. If you do, I will be tempted and leaving the monastery will go wherever God disposes. All of you think that I am good and saintly here, whereas in fact I am more damned and sinful than all men. You, lord Prince Yury, be not angry with me for this. I hear that you thoroughly understand Holy Scripture, that you read it and know the harm from the praise of men, especially those of us with passionate natures. Also, lord, you must take into account that there is no patrimony of yours near us. If you come here, everyone will say 'He came only because Cyril ordered him to come.' Your brother Prince Andrei visited here, but his patrimony is here and we could not but receive him, for he is our lord."

Prince Yury Dmitrievich and his son Dmitry Shemiaka found a far sterner judge in another saintly abbot, Gregory of Vologda (in Pelshma).[57] When Yury took power in Moscow after forcing out his nephew Vasily, Gregory arrived there to exhort Yury to quit the unjustly gained throne. Later, when Shemiaka seized Vologda and dealt much evil to the residents, Gregory immediately also appeared before him with accusations, threatening perdition for evildoing against Christians. Shemiaka could not stand the censure. He ordered the saintly monk thrown from his pulpit, and he barely returned alive to his monastery.

The monasteries played yet another significant role in the civil history of Russia. Though anchorites penetrated the dense northern forests and swamps seeking isolation and quietude, they brought with them the beginnings of new life. At first an anchorite settled in the hollow of a large tree, then brethren gathered and their emissaries soon appeared before the grand prince in Moscow. Their plea was that he grant the privilege for or give the order that the anchorite's house of worship, a monastery, be built in a wasteland, a wild place, that brethren gather and the fields be tilled.

St. Dmitry of Prilutsk[58] set up his cloister near the major routes running from Vologda to the Northern [Arctic] ocean. All wayfarers were received and fed at this monastery. Once an impoverished merchant approached the saint, asking blessing to trade with the pagan peoples known as the Yugra and Pechora. Another time a rich man brought provisions as a gift to the saint, who requested that the man take them back to his home and distribute them among his starving slaves. The Klopsk monastery fed wayfarers and everyone gathered there for food during famines. Besides the difficulties imposed upon them by savage nature the monks who founded the monasteries also suffered much from the cancers of the young, unordered society. They were often victims of bandits and neighboring landholders who did not hesitate to take the law into their own hands. The tradition of giving newly-built monasteries land adjacent to them often led to the destruction of new monasteries by neighbors who feared that the monks would absorb their lands.

MONASTIC LIFE

It is said in the Life of St. Sergius that he accepted everyone into his monastery and joyfully tonsured everyone, old and young, rich and poor. He tonsured his nephew Ivan (Fedor) when he was only twelve years old. In the early stages of the monasteries each monk maintained himself apart until, at the end of the fourteenth century, efforts to introduce communal life developed. This system was established in the Trinity monastery even during the lifetime of its founder. The brethren were divided according to function. One was appointed cellarer, another sub-cellarer, others were made bursar, precentor, refectory stewards, cooks, bakers and infirmarians. All the monastery's wealth and property was made common, and possession of private property was forbidden. Some, displeased at this change, stole away from Sergius's monastery.

The founder of communal life in the monasteries of the Moscow region is considered to be John, archimandrite of the St. Peter monastery, who accompanied Mitiay to Constantinople. In convents it is considered to be Uliana, abbess of the St. Alexis convent. In the statutes on communal life granted to the Snetogorsk monastery it is written that neither the abbot nor brethren might possess anything of their own. They must neither eat nor drink in their cells, rather eat and drink all together in the refectory. Only essential clothing was worn, and this as distributed by the abbot. Clothing must be of plain and not of German [imported] fabric. Sheepskin coats must be worn without fur lining. Footwear, even foot-wrapping cloth, was dispensed by the abbot. No extra clothing was to be kept.

The missives of Metropolitan Photius to the Kiev Caves monastery demonstrate his concern for bringing greater order to monastic life. The same metropolitan wrote to Novgorod stating that abbots, priests and monks were not to lend money at interest. Monks and nuns were not to live together in the same institutions, and priests attending at convents must be of the white [married] clergy and not widowers.[59] Metropolitan Jonas inherited these concerns from Photius.

The following information has come down concerning the selection of abbots. In 1433 the brethren of the Caves monastery in Nizhny Novgorod sent emissaries to Grand Prince Vasily Vasilievich and his mother requesting that an elder of their choosing be named archimandrite. The grand prince and the princess fulfilled the request, and instructed the metropolitan to install the elder chosen by the monks as archimandrite.

In 1448 the monks of the St. Cyril monastery of Beloozero, having selected the monk Kassian as their abbot, sent a request to the archbishop of Rostov that he be installed. The archbishop, responding to this plea and prayers, blessed Kassian with the condition that he visit him for spiritual converse. Simeon, the archbishop of Novgorod, wrote this to the Snetogorsk monastery. "I have ordered the abbot and the elders to heed monastic traditions. The monks are to obey the abbot and the elders and heed their spiritual father. Whoever resists shall be expelled without return of his donation. When a monk dies his belongings become the property of the monastery and brethren. Laymen are not to touch it. If a monk upon leaving the monastery incites laymen or judges against the abbot or elders, he falls under the authority of the church, as will those laymen who interfered in monastery affairs. When disagreement occurs between brethren the dispute is judged by the abbot and elders together with the psalm readers and elders of the Holy Mother of God [monastery]. Laymen are not to interfere."

Yet is known that monasteries funded by princes or others were influenced by such personages and their heirs. Thus the Volhynian prince Vladimir Vasilkovich bequeathed to his wife the Apostles monastery which he founded. The Moscow prince Peter Konstantinovich gave Metropolitan Jonas the monastery of St. Sabbas in Moscow. This explains why the brethren of the Caves monastery in Nizhny Novgorod sent emissaries to the grand prince in Moscow to seek confirmation for the abbot chosen by them.

MONASTERIES AND PROPERTY

Monasteries possessed a great deal of real estate. Princes sold them their villages, bought villages from abbots, permitted them to buy land from private parties, made gifts of property and bequeathed it to them. Monasteries also took villages as collateral and villages were bequeathed to them by private individuals. There are many princely documents to monasteries from this era which granted various privileges to monastery attendants and peasants. Undeveloped villages were given to monasteries and settlers whom a abbot attracted and exempted from all obligations for a stated number of years. Settled lands received exemption for all residents and newcomers from tribute, taxes and obligations forever.

There was nevertheless a proviso that when the time came to pay Tatar tribute the abbot paid a fair share for the monastery servitors. In some cases peasants were excluded from all tribute, taxes and obligations unless a determined collector came from the Horde who could not be "taken care of." Only then was the archimandrite to collect from his peasants to relieve the burden. Even so, the prince was not to collect anything from monastery servitors. There were also exemptions from all tribute and taxes on condition that quitrent be paid the prince's treasury once a year. In other cases there were exclusions from all tribute and taxes except for the quitrent of three quarters of a silver ruble paid the hundredman on the spring and autumn St. George's Day [April 23 and November 26]. Finally, there were exemptions from all tribute, taxes and obligations forever, without conditions.

Sometimes an abbot received horse-branding rights. A monastery peasant who either bought or traded for a horse had it branded at the monastery and paid the abbot a set fee. A monastery peasant who sold anything at market or in the village paid a sales duty to the abbot as well. If he neglected to pay the branding fee or the sales duty, he must pay a fine to the monastery. The prince's vicegerents' men, those of the boyars, and all others were forbidden to go uninvited to feasts at the monasteries. The monastery men were free of the obligation of quartering horsemen or messengers sent on crown business or for providing them provender, wagons and guides except when bearing urgent military messages. Monastery men were free from domestic customs duties, even in the territory of other princes. Monastery merchants enjoyed right of passage with all goods at any time, whether there was peace in the land or not. They were permitted to transport monastery hay on rivers when others were forbidden to navigate them. Monastery men sent as organized groups of hunters or fishermen or for some other work were free of all associated taxes. Neither must monasteries quarter troops nor might the prince's emissaries camp near a given monastery, set up a ferry near it or take monastery men or vessels for that purpose.

MONASTERY RIGHTS AND DUTIES

Monastery peasants were not liable to trial by the prince's vicegerents, district administrators or judges. They fell under the jurisdiction of the abbot in all matters and were tried by him or someone he designated. A monastery's right of trial at times included civil and criminal matters, although with limitations. Murder at times was excluded from monastery jurisdiction, sometimes it was murder and banditry and sometimes robbery with bodily assault[60] as well as murder and banditry. In some documents monastery peasants were free from trial by the prince provided they gave his district agent provender twice a year, at Christmas and St. Peter's Day. Provender was due at Christmas when every two plows must provide a side of meat, a measure of oats, a wagon of hay, and ten loaves of bread. Two altyns could be substituted for the side of meat, one altyn for the oats, one for the hay, and a denga for each loaf of bread. On St. Peter's Day every two plows provided a ram and ten loaves or ten dengas instead of the ram. When the abbot had the right of trial, and the trial was a mixed one, that is, involving monastery men and city or district dwellers, the prince's vicegerent or judge participated together with the abbot or his bailiff.

Sometimes the abbot held the right to set a time limit on mixed trials. When an abbot lacked jurisdiction in criminal cases the prince's writ specified that the vicegerent or judge was responsible for capturing a murderer and hailing him before the prince. A order is also encountered that the vicegerent and judge were to exact nothing from the monastery peasants for a dead body if the person fell from a tree or drowned. Monastery servants were free of the obligation of kissing the cross, although wards of the monastery must kiss the cross. A suit against a monastery steward was to be tried by the prince himself or a great boyar. When a prince's constable arrested monastery men he must give them a certain time limit to appear in court, usually two or three days. Occasionally monastery men were permitted to determine these limits themselves. There are documents in which monasteries were granted villages with everything that accrued to them except seasonal workers and the right to hold trials. Occasionally peasants were exempted from tribute and taxes on condition that no subject of the prince settle on monastery lands.

There are accounts of monasteries owning saltworks. These monasteries too received special privileges. Often princes ordered their village or other agents to supply monasteries rye, cheese, butter and fish on the consecration feast days of their churches. Encountered as well are patents to monasteries for fishing areas and beaver runs. According to the decree granted by the Novgorod popular assembly the Solovetsk monastery received one-tenth of the proceeds of all the commercial undertakings on the islands belonging to it. Some monasteries received a tithe from designated villages.

Convents received privileges similar to those of monasteries. Occasionally an abbess received the right of not only civil but also criminal trial over the peasants of her convent. There are occasional orders granting administration of villages to priests. In this event the income was divided evenly between the priests and the abbess with her nuns. Private individuals endowed villages to monasteries under various conditions. The abbot was to maintain communal life, supervise the monks rigorously and keep only satisfactory monks. Other conditions specified that the abbot and monks hold no private property, that when the abbot left the monastery he must make an accounting to the monks, that the abbot not accept onto monastery lands men who were former captives or had fled the lands of the donor.

The nature of the obligations of peasants to monasteries may be determined from the statutes given by Metropolitan Cyprian to the St. Constantine monastery. The well-to-do in monastery villages (those who had horses) decorated the church, put up a stockade around the monastery and farmstead, erected buildings, collectively plowed the abbot's fields, and sowed and harvested the fields. There were other obligations. Hay was mown on a tithe basis and brought to the farmstead, the large spring and winter catch of fish made, gardens fenced, fish netted, ponds dammed, beavers caught in autumn, and wells dug. At Easter and St. Peter's Day the peasants appeared before the abbot with whatever provisions they had on hand. The poorer peasants,[61] those who had no horses, threshed rye before holidays, baked bread, prepared malt, brewed beer, and threshed rye to separate the seed. When the abbot sent flax the peasants wove cloth and fashioned fishing nets of various kinds. For the consecration feast days the peasants gave a heifer or sheep. Whenever the abbot went to a village for a feast his horses were given oats.

Despite the rich endowment of monasteries with immovable property there was great uncertainty during this time as to whether monasteries should own villages. "The holy fathers," Metropolitan Cyprian wrote Abbot Afanasy, "did not state that monks were to hold villages and men. How can a man, once he has renounced the world and everything worldly, again assume worldly cares and again create what he has abandoned? The ancient fathers did not acquire villages or amass riches. You ask me about a village that a prince has given to the monastery and what is to be done with it. Here is my answer. If you and your brethren have faith in God, Who up to now fed you without a village and will do so in the future, then why take on worldly cares and why think of villages and worldly concerns instead of thinking of God and serving Him alone?

Consider also that when a monk is free of worldly concerns he has the love and respect of all men, but when he starts to worry about villages he must attend princes and rulers and courts, defend the injured, endure quarrels, reconciliations, choose great labor and stray from his vows. If a monk owned villages, sat in judgement on men and women, frequently was among them and cared about them, how would he be different from a layman? To communicate and talk with women is the worst thing of all for a monk. It is better that the village belong to the monastery and no monk frequents it. Let God-fearing laymen see to it and bring to the monastery its produce in grain and other provisions because it is pernicious for monks to possess villages and go there frequently."

In Southwestern Rus the tradition of granting immovable property and villages to monasteries continued. The Volhynian prince Vladimir Vasilkovich bought a village and gave it to the Apostles monastery. The Orthodox progeny of Gediminas also followed this tradition. Here, in the Southwest, princely patents to monasteries are encountered, according to which men of the monastery were exempt from trial by the prince's vicegerent or judge, and free of all tribute and obligations. When a metropolitan passed by the monastery, his was not the right to try the archimandrite or take wagons from the monastery. The same held for the local bishop. The prince himself was to try the archimandrite. When a prelate must judge an archimandrite on religious grounds, the prince and the prelate were to hold trial together. Furthermore, the prelate's tithe collectors and city dwellers were not to try monastery men.

VIII

LAW AND CUSTOMS

LEGAL CODE

Such was the state of the church. There exist from this era several legal documents which provide understanding of society's moral state. Among them is the statute charter of Grand Prince Vasily Dmitrievich granted to the Dvina land during its temporary annexation by Moscow.[1] The charter is divided into two parts. The first consists of the rules of legal procedure for the prince's vicegerents. The second describes the trading privileges granted the Dvina people. The first, legal part, has rules of procedure in case of murder, bodily harm, assault and mayhem, for both boyars and servitors. It also includes fights at a feast, plowing or mowing across boundary lines, thievery, mob law, non-appearance of the accused in court, and the murder of a slave by a master.

When a murder occurred, the transgressor was to be arrested by the residents of the area where the crime took place. If they could not find him, they paid a designated amount of money to the prince's vicegerent. When anyone physically or verbally assaulted a boyar or servitor the vicegerents fined him for committing a dishonor, the fine commensurate to the lineage of the victim. Unfortunately the most interesting factor here is unknown. What were the guiding principles in the vicegerents' determination of lineage? Yet it is significant that the Dvina charter included penalties for verbal abuse, while the Rus Justice did not mention them.

In the case of a fight at a feast, if the combatants made peace before leaving the feast, the vicegerents and princely officials took nothing from them. If they made peace after leaving the feast, each was to give the vicegerents a marten skin. When there was plowing or mowing across a boundary there were three different instances, whether the boundary crossed was between fields, between different villages or, finally, whether it was that of the prince. Should someone find stolen goods in another's possession, the accused could deny his guilt by naming the one from whom he received the goods, but a suspect could do this no more than ten times. A thief for his first offense was fined the cost of the stolen item.

The second time the fine was much more severe. The third time he was hanged. He was also branded each time. Unauthorized "people's trials" were fined at four rubles and defined as a situation in which someone caught a thief with stolen goods and let him go after taking a bribe. The accused was to be shackled only if there was no one to swear for him. A defendant who did not appear at his trial thereby lost his case, and the vicegerents issued a ruling against him to that effect. If a master struck and unintentionally killed a male or female slave, the vicegerents were not to try him, nor were they to fine him.

Mentioned previously here were the texts of laws granted to Pskov by Prince Alexander Mikhailovich of Tver and Konstantin Dmitrievich of Moscow. A collection of court statutes composed of the above two texts is extant. Added to it are the other traditional Pskov court procedures. The document contains a statute concerning murder. Where a slaying occurs and the slayer is discovered, the prince takes a ruble fine from the slayer. Should a son kill a father or a brother kill a brother, the prince also receives a fine.

The statute on thievery is similar to that in the Dvina charter. The first two times the thief is released after paying a fine equal to the cost of the stolen goods. The third time he is punished by death. This statute was in force only if the theft took place in the settlement outside the town walls. A thief who stole within the town walls, a horse thief, a false accuser or an arsonist were subject to execution for their first crime. In arguments over land ownership, possession of four or five years'· standing decided the matter.

FINANCIAL TRANSACTIONS

There is rather detailed information relating to loans and depositing money and possessions for safekeeping. Loan documents both in Novgorod and Pskov were called "boards." For these boards to be in force a copy must be safeguarded in a coffer in the cathedral of the Holy Trinity. Money could be loaned without collateral and without written documents only to the sum of one ruble. A person could guarantee someone also only to the sum of one ruble. For family relations there is a statute stating that when a son refused to feed [support] his father or mother till their death and left the house, he forfeited his share of the inheritance. Concerning inheritance, the statute specified that when a wife died without a written testament and left an inheritance the husband has possession until his death unless he married again. The same conditions applied to the wife. There is mention of a case in which an elder and a younger brother "live on the same bread" [meaning that they did not divide their inheritance].

CIVIL LAW

There are rather detailed descriptions of conflicts between tenants and landowners (sovereigns) and their hired men, and also between masters and apprentices. The details most often involve instances of non-fulfillment of obligations and the time set when the obligations could be cancelled by either party. This deadline was the day before the beginning of St. Philip's Fast, that is, November 14.[2] When resettling, the settler received a "stake" from the landlord, that is, aid in setting up a household. It could consist of money, household utensils, farming tools, fishing equipment, and winter or spring grain.

Legitimate evidence in court was of several kinds. These were what was seen or heard, a sworn oath, and taking to the "field" [combat] in a court-appointed duel. When one of the litigants was a woman, child, sickly old man, a cripple or a monk, that person might to hire a champion for a duel. The adversary could fight the hired man himself or appoint a hired fighter. If two women were litigants they were to appear for the duel themselves and could not substitute hired men.

TRIAL PROCEDURES

In the accounts the antechamber of the prince's residence was designated as the location of the court. They specifically state that the prince and mayor were not to hold trials at the popular assembly. When a complaint was registered against someone, a warrant server ("caller") went to the residence of the person in question to demand that the latter visit a church to hear the warrant read. If this was refused the server read the warrant in the churchyard before a priest. Then if the accused did not appear in court or ask for postponement his adversary was given a charter granting him the right to seize the other party. The holder of the court order upon seizing his adversary could not to beat or torture him, and must bring him before the judges. The respondent was forbidden to struggle or use arms against his adversary.

According to Pskov statutes the litigants might enter the court chamber only by themselves and without aides. An aide was permitted to enter only when one of the litigants was either a woman, child, monk, nun, or an elderly or deaf person. When someone assisted a litigant in instances where it was forbidden, or entered the court chamber by force, or struck a sergeant-at-arms, they were to be jailed and fined in favor of the prince and the sergeants-at-arms, of whom there were two, one from the prince and one from Pskov. A mayor or any other government figure could not enter into litigation in place of a friend. He could enter litigation only in a matter directly concerning him or the church, if he were a church warden. In the case of litigation concerning church lands, only the wardens might attend the trial. Neighbors were forbidden to aid them.

CRIMINAL LAW

The Pskov as well as the Dvina charter prescribes the death penalty outright for certain crimes such as theft at the third offense and arson. Both charters fail to mention homicide, neither is it known whether death was the penalty for murder during this time, or whether the statutes of the sons of Yaroslav were followed. In the patent to the St. Cyril monastery Prince Mikhail Andreevich of Vereia stated that in case of homicide in the monastery villages the murderer was placed in the custody of responsible men and brought before the prince for punishment. If the murderer could not be found a fine of one Novgorod ruble for each victim was paid [to the prince by the community in which the body was found]. The nature of the prince's punishment is not known.

It is known that, as before, those convicted of particular crimes became the property of the prince. It has been observed that princes have mentioned men whom they acquired as a result of their guilt. There is no doubt that princes put their enemies to death during this as well as previous periods. If Monomakh advised his sons to kill neither the innocent nor the guilty indicates that such killing took place. Further, the ranks of princes included men other than the sons of Monomakh. Andrei Bogoliubsky executed Kuchkovich,[3] and Vsevolod III condemned to death a Novgorod boyar who was his enemy. It is said that the execution of Ivan Veliaminov, performed at the order of Dmitry Donskoy, was the first public execution in Rus.[4] The manner of Kuchkovich's execution during the reign of Andrei Bogoliubsky is not known. In any case, form is not the main issue here.

In 1385 several procedures were established in Novgorod the Great. The mayor and chiliarch held trials in the Russian tradition, with kissing of the cross and the two parties in litigation each accompanied by two boyars and two well-to-do citizens. Occasionally the right to hold trials was farmed out. Thus in the first extant treaty between Novgorod and Prince Yaroslav it is stated that the prince and the citizens of Novgorod granted the rights of holding trials to Bezhetsk and Obonezh for a period of three years. In 1434 the grand prince's vicegerent in Novgorod sold the Obonezh trial rights to two men, Yakim Gureev and Matvey Petrov. It has been noted above that, according to the Pskov judicial charter, in cases of litigation concerning ownership of land possession for a period of four or five years decided the matter, though a particular charter of Ivan III, dated 1483, refers to a law of Grand Prince Vasily Dmitrievich which set the term of ownership at fifteen years.

CIVIL TRIAL

The following is a description of a civil trial as it occurred during this era. Two litigants appeared before a judge. One of them was a monk, Ignaty, who lived in the metropolitan's lands. The other was a layman and land-owner named Semeon Terpilov. "I have a complaint, sir," Ignaty began, "against this Senka[5] Terpilov. For the second year now he has been mowing our metropolitan's meadow without permission. The meadow yields two hundred stacks of hay and has always belonged to the metropolitan's Spasskoe village." The judge said to Senka Terpilov "Respond!" "That meadow, sir," said Senka, "located on the Sheksna river is the property of the grand prince and has always belonged to my village of Dorofeevskaia. It is my right to mow it and gather the hay." "Why do you say," the judge then asked the monk Ignaty, "that this meadow always has belonged to the metropolitan and Spasskoe village?" "The meadow," Ignaty responded, "always has been the metropolitan's. Once Leonty Vasiliev mowed it, and our district official took him to court over it and won the case. We have a document of the court judgement concerning the meadow and here, sir, is a copy of it before you. The original is in the metropolitan's coffers, and I will place it before the grand prince."

The judge ordered the copy to be read and the following was recited. The matter was tried by Vasily Ushakov, a judge of Princess Martha, in accordance with a writ of the grand princess, his sovereign. Standing in the meadow on the Sheksna river, in the presence of Vasily Ushakov, the metropolitan's village bailiff Danilo said "I have a complaint, sir, against Leonty, the son of Vasily, for he mowed the metropolitan's meadow, that on which we stand." The judge said to Leonty "Respond!" "I, sir," Leonty began, "have mowed this meadow and know nothing about a boundary. The meadow was rented to me by Sisoy Savelov and, sir, this Sisoy is standing right here before you." "This meadow, sir, is mine," said Sisoy. "I rented it to Leonty and indicated that he mow the areas which Danilo calls his. Up to now the boundary of my meadow has included these areas. Now, sir, order Danilo's wise elders to mark the boundary and let it be the way they say, as their souls guide them, for I have no elders who know the boundary." The judge then asked the metropolitan's bailiff Danilo "Who are your elders that know this meadow and its boundaries?" "I have, sir," Danilo replied, "some old-timers,[6] good men, Uvar and Gavshuk and Ignat, and here, sir, these elders are standing before you."

The judge addressed Uvar and Gavshuk and Ignat, saying "Tell me, brothers, in truth, do you know where the boundary between the metropolitan's and Sisoy's meadows lies? Take us along the boundary." "We know, sir," replied Uvar, Gavshuk and Ignat. "Follow us, we'll take you along the boundary." They went from the edge of the forest, from a birch, to three young oaks at the center of the meadow, then to a many-branched willow on the bank of the river, up to the very cracks in its trunk. "This is the way it has always been," they said there, "this is the boundary between the metropolitan's and Sisoy's meadows." The judge asked Sisoy "Do you have any elders?" "I have no elders," Sisoy replied. "Let their conscience guide them." Then both litigants were appointed a time to appear before the grand princess at a hearing. Danilo the village bailiff came at the appointed time, but Sisoy did not appear. As a result Danilo was held to be in the right and the meadow was judged to be part of the metropolitan's land. Present at the proceedings were Arbuzhev the elder, Kostia, Yev Sofron, Kostia Savin Darina, Leva Yakimov, and Senka Terpilov.

When the writ of the court judgement was read, the judge said to Senka Terpilov "You are listed in this ruling as a witness. Was there litigation between Leonty Vasiliev and the metropolitan's official Danilo about the meadow? Were you present at the court proceedings?" "There were such court proceedings," Senka replied, "and I was a witness. Nevertheless the meadow has always been the land of the grand prince, belonging to my village, Dorofeevskaia." "Besides the document of the court judgement," the judge then asked the monk Ignaty, "do you have any other evidence concerning this meadow? Who knows that the meadow has always belonged to the metropolitan, but that Senka Terpilov has mowed it for two years?" "It is known to good men," replied Ignaty, "the old-timers Ivan Kharlamov and Olfer Uvarov and Malash Franik and Luka Davidov. Here are these old-timers, sir, before you."

In response to the judge's inquiry the old men supported Ignaty's testimony. "Follow us, your honor," they added, "and we will mark the boundary between the meadow and the grand prince's lands." Ignaty's old men began pacing from the upper end, from a bushy willow near the forest toward a tall thick oak with a low-hanging branch, and to the banks of the Sheksna river. "On the right side," then they said, "is the grand prince's land, and on the left is the metropolitan's meadow." Then the judge asked Senka Terpilov "Why do you say that this is the grand prince's meadow? Do you have anyone who knows and will support this?" "It is known to good men," replied Senka, "the old-timers of three districts, and here, sir, are these old-timers before you." In answer to the judge's question the old men supported Senka's testimony and took the judge to show him the true boundary. Then Ignaty's old men said to the judge "These old men of Senka's are giving false evidence and setting the wrong boundary on the metropolitan's meadow. Permit us, sir, to kiss the cross with them. We will kiss the life-giving cross and swear that this meadow always belonged to the metropolitan."

Senka's old men also said "We will kiss the life-giving cross and swear that this meadow has always belonged to the grand prince." Then the judge said that he would report this to the sovereign, the grand prince of all Rus, and ordered monk Ignaty to present his document of the court judgement to the prince as well.

CONTRACTS AND OBLIGATIONS

There are records of various legal transactions dating from the same period, among them bills of sale and exchange, records of bequests, transfer of land, customs duty on imported goods, of loans and mortgages, division of property and testaments. In the bills of sale the names of the buyer and seller were listed first: N. "has bought" from N. Occasionally a purchase was made by a whole "tribe," by several brothers from an entire clan who had joint ownership of land.[7] Occasionally land was bought by two persons who were strangers to each other. The bill of sale then included the condition that if one of the buyers or his children chose to repudiate their purchase, they were not to sell their parcel to anyone except the other buyer or his children. Among buyers were priests and monks. Abbots bought land for monasteries and for themselves. Among the sellers were married women who sold land they received as dowry with the names of their husbands added to the document "N. has bought from N. [a woman] and from her husband."

Occasionally a husband bought land from his wife, from her son-in-law or from the son-in-law's wife. After the names of the buyer and seller was a detailed description of the property and the price paid for it. Usually some supplementary item[8] was added to the sum of money, most often an animal. For example, "He gave three rubles for that land and a pig as a supplement." Below that would be indicated whether the transaction was made for a specified number of years or forever. The latter condition was described by the term "in perpetuity." Thus we find "He has bought for himself 'in perpetuity' and for his brethren...." or "for his children."

Included in the transaction was a record that the land was sold and mention of the documents pertaining to it, or the location of such documents [in terms of today's parlance, an abstract]. When several brothers were buyers the transaction record noted which brother possessed which parcels. Also recorded were the boundaries of the land simply "according to the old boundaries." A condition was entered that should anyone claim right of ownership to the land purchased the responsibility of resolving the matter lay with the seller or his children. Some records included the condition that the buyer resell to no one except the landowner. Each document listed the names of several witnesses or attestants, sometimes called simply "men," who were present at the determination of the boundary lines of the land being sold. Usually it was stated that the seal was impressed, and the transaction performed, by the seller although sometimes the names of other parties are encountered in both instances. Also indicated was the name of the writer of the document, either a priest, a deacon or a lay or church secretary. At the top of the bill of sale issued by the St. Cyril monastery of Beloozero it is said that the sale took place with the knowledge of the prince's bailiff. In dowry documents the names of both parents were indicated, as well as the name of the son-in-law and daughter. The names of witnesses were written at the bottom of the document and a seal, sworn to by the father, was affixed.

INHERITANCE

In documents dealing with the division of inherited property the inheriting relatives, an uncle and nephew for example, agreed that when one of them had no offspring and wished to trade, sell or bequeath his parcel to anyone, he was not to do so without the consent of the other relative. Upstanding men for both parties served as witnesses at the division of property. In Novgorod whoever violated these terms paid the prince and archbishop a set sum of money. In testaments the testators, while often having a wife, bequeathed their property (their patrimony, the lands and waters as held by their fathers and described in previous testaments) to their mothers and sons. Household slaves were bequeathed as well. In other testaments property was bequeathed to the wife and sons. When a wife remained on the lands of her deceased husband she became the absolute owner of those lands. If she married she received a fixed sum and her entire dowry, though certain testaments specified that she receive nothing in such cases.

When a son was born to the testator after his death that son received a share equal to that of his elder brothers. When a daughter was born her brothers were to assure the best possible marriage for her. Occasionally in dividing property the testator parcelled out certain lands among his sons, leaving other lands in their joint ownership. When a testator left minor sons, until their age of majority a relative such as a brother over-saw the villages, tended the land and distributed the grain, money and tribute to the mother and sons. In the event of the death of his sons the testator willed half his property to his brother and ordered the other half sold. The income from the sale was donated to churches as a memorial to him. Household slaves were set free. As a final measure a testator appointed one or more guardians to look after his family, occasionally even of a whole street in Novgorod.

In difficult cases concerning inheritance the authority of the church was invoked. Thus a certain widow once turned to Metropolitan Cyprian to request advice. Her husband died a violent death, leaving no will, and there were no children except for one adopted child. The metropolitan decided that she must pray for her husband and raise her adopted child. She had the rights to the land, men and all property of her husband and could dispose of it in her testament as she wished. Finally, dating from the same period, there are also records of small claims settlements.

WOMEN'S RIGHTS

It is clear from the above sources that the property of the wife was held separately from that of the husband, although the wife could not sell her dowry without her husband's consent. It was to be sold jointly, the wife's name appearing above that of her husband. Also evident is the fact that a wife could sell her property to her husband. It had been noted previously that according to the Rus Justice for certain specified crimes a criminal and all his family became slaves of the prince. Without doubt this law was in force during the era described, but the question arises whether a wife was held liable for her husband's debts or for his wrongs against private parties.

INTERNATIONAL LAW

In the first pact between Novgorod and the Germans it was agreed that a defaulted debtor and his family were handed as slaves to the creditor. In the second pact this item was amended to read that a wife became a slave in the event of her husband's nonpayment only if she was a guarantor. If she had not guaranteed the loan, she remained free. May it be concluded on the basis of this item in a pact with the Germans that a similar law was maintained within Russia? In the absence of collaborating evidence the question is open to doubt because interests of a very particular nature were touched upon in the German pact. It was important to limit the flight of population from the Novgorod region to other lands and the loss of Orthodox believers to other faiths.

In the Rus Justice, for example, it is stated that the wife and children of a slave shall not be enslaved for the crime of the husband and father if they did not take part in the crime. The point here is not that they do not answer for the crime, for in moving from one master to another they remained liable to punishment, but that a master not lose several of his slaves because of the crime of one. The rule established here is the result of the influence of property interests.

LAW IN LITHUANIA

The juridical concepts of Southwestern, Lithuanian Rus are treated in a charter of Grand Prince Casimir, son of Jogaila, in 1457. It states that no prince, noble or burgher be executed or punished on suspicion or by denunciation, whether public or secret, without first being charged in open court, where both the accuser and the accused are present. Only the criminal and no one else is to be punished for a crime, not the wife for the crime of her husband, nor the father for the crime of his son, or conversely. Neither shall any other relative or servant be punished. Foreigners were not to hold official appointments or land in Lithuania. Concerning the status of a wife upon the death of her husband we encounter the same conditions as in the Pskov judicial charter and in Novgorod testaments. A widow retained the property of her husband until she remarried. In that event the property passed to the children or relatives of the deceased. If the husband assigned his widow specific property which was part of the dowry she was to keep it even if she remarried.

Records of court judgements suggest that in the Southwest landowner-ship disputes were settled in the same way as in the Northeast, namely the testimony of mutually agreed elders in Lithuanian Rus had the same significance as that of the elders and long-time residents in Muscovite Rus. A Galich bill of sale of 1351 is similar in form to the bills of sale of Northeastern Rus.

THE BRUTALITY OF WARFARE

Concerning popular mores it is evident that the nature of war was the same as before, and perhaps even more brutal.[9] In one instance the inhab-itants of Nizhny Novgorod, upon taking some Mordvinian prisoners, put them to death by setting dogs on them. In their campaign against Lithuania the men of Smolensk impaled some children on spears and hanged others upside down from poles, adults were crushed by logs and tortured by other means. This writer cannot bring himself to describe the cruelties inflicted by the inhabitants of Pskov on Vytautas's captured soldiers. During the Muscovite campaign against Ulu-Mahmet the sol-diers on campaign robbed and tortured their fellow countrymen. Metro-politan Jonas said of the people of Viatka that during their campaigns against Shemiaka they tortured and killed many Orthodox faithful. Some were drowned, some incinerated in their huts, some had their eyes burned out, while infants were impaled on stakes. More than fifteen hundred people were taken prisoner and sold to the Tatars.

It is evident that war atrocities could reach terrible extremes but it is questionable whether they always occurred. The above incidents might be considered as exceptions resulting from particular conditions, caused by particular vehemence, and entered in the sources for those reasons. On the other hand there is no justification for assuming moderate behavior on the part of soldiery when in enemy territory.

When making peace the princes of Northeastern Rus agreed to return all prisoners and everything looted during the war. Guarantors were freed of their obligations, and those who kissed the cross were released from their oaths. Looted property was returned by due process. Were this impossible, the claimants recovered it by kissing the cross. Foodstuffs and goods taken from the enemy during the fighting were not returned. If during the course of a war a prince installed his vicegerents in occupied territory he was to investigate their behavior upon cessation of hostilities. What they seized justly was theirs to keep, what was taken unjustly was returned to its rightful owner. Occasionally a condition is encountered which obliged princes to seek out, ransom and return even prisoners sold abroad. At times princes agreed not to demand from each other anything taken during a war save for people, who were to be returned without the property seized from them. "That which was taken during our discordance," say the chronicles, "let it all be forgotten" or "let it remain the property of those who hold it."

LITIGATION

In cases of conflict between citizens of two principalities a joint trial was held. "A joint trial is to be held amongst us by the eldest men." When the joint judges could not resolve the matter they were to pass it to an arbiter for decision. Once that arbiter found someone in the right the guilty man was to ask forgiveness of the man in the right and return what was taken. If the judges of one of the parties failed to appear at the arbitration, or when the party found guilty by the arbiter refused to comply with the judgement, the party in the right was free to use force in claiming his own. Such efforts were not considered a breach of the peace. Of joint trials and arbitration hearings it usually was written "The defendant must be tried without any excuses and our judges shall have an arbiter [if necessary]. We (the princes) are not to interfere in the joint trials. The judges are to sit in judgement upon kissing the cross. They are to decide justly, according to their oath."

Occasionally the procedure for choosing an arbiter was clearly agreed. "The plaintiff will name three Christian princes, one of them chosen by the defendant." Or elsewhere "If our judges cannot decide the matter an arbitration hearing shall be called. Two of my grand-princely boyars will be selected and one of your great boyars. The arbiter shall then be chosen by the plaintiff and accepted by the defendant. If they cannot choose a third party from among these three boyars, I the grand prince shall be that arbiter. Let them come before me and I will order them to choose from among the same three boyars. If the defendant does not agree, I shall judge him myself."

Yet another agreement concerning trials [between two principalities] is encountered. "If there be brigandage, or robbery, or a raid from your patrimony upon my grand-princely people, there shall be no waiting for a joint trial. We shall send our judges and instruct them to do justice without excuses. Should you not give me justice, or your judges rule unfairly, I shall take what is mine and this shall not be a breach of the peace." The nature of the agreements changed, of course, in relation to the conditions under which they were drawn up, and in relation to the princes between whom they were concluded.

PRINCELY PACTS

The princes would agree not to lure away each other's people or encourage them to cross the border illegally. If someone crossed a border illegally, he was to be returned upon inquiry into the matter. Also to be returned after an investigation were male and female slaves, indentured persons, debtors, thieves, brigands and murderers. It was permissible to enter a principality from another to retrieve and seize slave or a debtor without a constable when the miscreant was brought before the prince, vicegerent or district agent. He was in breach of the agreement if he removed his captive from a district without hailing him before the agent.

When a slave started litigation against anyone without posting a bond he was tried and turned over to his master. The fee paid for a slave and for a whole family usually was determined at this hearing. All other court costs paid by the plaintiff also were determined at this point. If the male or female slave did not initiate litigation there were no fees. If there was no bond for a debtor, he too was tried. A thief, brigand, robber or murderer was tried where apprehended, but permitted to clear himself by naming the actual murderer or from whom he received the stolen item.

This agreement was concluded between Novgorod and Tver. If Novgorod accused a thief or brigand who came from Tver, but the people of Tver claimed that none such existed, they were to guarantee that no such thief or brigand ever appeared again in the Tver lands. If he appeared, he was to be extradited without trial.

In the Northeast there is evidence of murder of an emissary sent by one prince to another. There is also evidence of the murder of Tatar emissaries in Nizhny Novgorod. In 1414 the Germans murdered a Pskov emissary in Neuhausen, and the people of Pskov murdered a Dorpat emissary that same year. It has been observed above that in the wars between Pskov and Lithuania there was a tradition of redeeming prisoners.

In the Southwest an entry for 1229 notes a remarkable agreement made by Conrad of Mazovia[10] and Daniel of Galich.[11] If war began between them the Poles were not to harm their Russian slaves, neither were the Russians to harm their Polish slaves. That same document also speaks of the mutual return of prisoners after a war. In the pact between Vasily the Dark and Casimir there is the following condition. "As for those men who left lands of their free will, they are to be free and live wherever they choose." In the pacts of the grand princes of Lithuania with Novgorod and Pskov there was a condition stating that, if a grand prince began war against Novgorod or Pskov, he was obliged to send a declaration of war and begin fighting only a month thereafter. In 1406 Vytautas, whom the Russian chronicler justly calls "unfaithful to truth," intending to attack Pskov by surprise, sent a declaration of war not to Pskov but to Novgorod under pretense of Pskov's old dependency on Novgorod, and meanwhile invaded Pskov lands. To prevent similar perfidy in the future Pskov in concluding a pact with Casimir insisted that in case of hostilities he send a declaration of war not to Moscow or Novgorod, but to Pskov.

The citizens of Novgorod, in writing a pact with that same Casimir, mutually agreed that Lithuanian and Novgorod emissaries not requisition wagons in each other's territory. Evidently there were no agreements between Moscow and Lithuania about citizens of one state being on the territory of the other during hostilities between the two. An entry for 1406 noted that during the enmity between Vytautas and Vasily Dmitrievich the Muscovites in Lithuania were slaughtered.

MORAL CLIMATE

Concerning the mores of Rus during this time, it has been noticed already in the previous period that the further east, the more brutal they were. It is clear that the movement of the Slavic settlers into the uninhabited areas of Northeastern Europe, their separation from other Christian peoples with whom they shared a level of civic development, and their entry into constant interchange only with less developed peoples could not but negatively affect these settlers.

It is clear that the Slavs not only ceased progressing in this respect, they actually regressed. The influence of nature itself cannot be forgotten in this respect, a fact mentioned previously. Besides these primarily geographic causes there were yet other, historical factors which made customs only more harsh. The mere geographical remoteness of the main theater of activity could not keep the Russians for long from communicating with other Christian peoples. When Northeastern Rus became a single powerful realm there appeared in the second half of the fifteenth century a striving for intercourse with other Christian realms. During the sixteenth and seventeenth centuries, despite numerous difficulties, this striving intensified, until finally in the eighteenth century Russia entered the community of European states. Therefore the total isolation of Rus in the thirteenth, fourteenth and fifteenth centuries was the product of geographical remoteness, abetted even more by the focus of its entire attention on the difficult and painful transition from one domestic order to another.

It was a painful transition that had a pernicious effect on habits. Previously in the South also there was great internecine strife but this was the result of struggle for the rights of succession. Whereas a given prince became the eldest and occupied Kiev in his triumph, the relationship of the lesser princes to him remained as before. Even here existed great harshness and indiscriminate violence by princes driven to excess by circumstance who, having lost their lands, must reacquire and hold them by the sword.

In the North, as has been noted, when the goal of internecine strife changed its nature had to change as well. The princes amply demonstrated that they were not fighting for seniority as earlier, rather for power and the increase of their holdings. They fought to acquire might, thereby to subjugate all other princes and deprive them of their realms. In a struggle of such nature there can be no talk of rights and obligations. Each acted according to the instinct of self-preservation. Whenever man acts only by this instinct there can be no selectivity of means. The powerful take advantage of the first opportunity to exercise their force, while the weak resort to deception and perfidy. Mutual trust collapses and the powerful resort to means of moral coercion of the weak.

Yet even these means proved ineffective. Sacred pacts, threatening eternal damnation, were broken as readily as common agreements. Deception and duplicity by the weak were praised as wisdom. The chronicler praises a prince of Tver who, as a weak third party in the battle of two giants, eluded involvement without angering either the Moscow prince or Edigey.[12] Struggle that went to extremes made extreme means conventional. At first, rivals were delivered to the Horde, where they perished. This could still be perceived as the result of a legal sentence handed down by a higher authority. Then, when princes began to deal with each other independently of any foreign interference, and when such struggle reached its desperate culmination, blinding and finally murder became acts of wanton violence.

The tradition whereby members of a prince's retinue freely left the service of one prince for another, which greatly aided the unification of

Northeastern Rus, had a negative effect on morality. The action of Rumianets and his comrades in Nizhny Novgorod[13] in no sense can be considered moral. Violence on the part of the powerful, duplicity and perfidy by the weak, lack of trust and a weakened civic sense common to everyone, this was the inescapable outcome of such a state of affairs. Behavior grew brutal and the habit of living by the instinct of self-preservation produced the hegemony of material over spiritual motives. This brutality came to be reflected in deed and word, and in all of man's actions. During this period the property of citizens was hidden in churches and monasteries. Such places were considered as very, though not always totally, safe.

Spiritual values also sought safe retreats in uninhabited regions, monasteries or tower chambers.[14] Women quickly fled, or were kept from, the company of men in an attempt to preserve their moral purity and the sanctity of the family. It was not Byzantine, Tatar or some other influence that brought about the sequestering of women among the upper classes. Rather it was the expression of a people's desire to preserve morals. Evidence of this is found in the primary accounts of contemporary witnesses. No historian would chance answering the question of what would have happened to us in the fourteenth century without the church, the monastery and the tower chamber. Yet it is clear that the removal of women, the consequence of the brutalization of values, itself may have promoted even greater brutalization.

Though a relatively great brutalization of values is quite apparent in this period, the historian has no right to make an overly sharp comparison between these customs and those of the preceding period in favor of the latter. It has been noted that the testament of Monomakh, in which he charged his offspring to kill neither the guilty nor the innocent, cannot be considered as evidence that no such killings occurred in his time. It is doubtful that the solemn exercise of a death sentence was instituted by Dmitry Donskoy, for it is unknown how Andrei Bogoliubsky executed Kuchkovich. It is said that from the time of Vasily Yaroslavich to Ivan Kalita our native land resembled a jungle more than a realm. Might was right. Whoever could, robbed not only foreigners but Russians as well. There was no safety on the roads or in homes. Theft became the common cancer of property. As evidence of these words there is usually cited an entry in the chronicles hailing Ivan Kalita for decreasing the number of bandits and thieves. Of course, more evidence of banditry can be found in the sources.

Though it cannot be said that this description is exaggerated, neither can it be assumed that conditions were much better previously, or that they were much better in neighboring Christian states during the same period. To illustrate the point we need only recall the mayhem occurring in Polish lands during the time of Casimir.[15] It is often offered in argument that light fines of money once deterred our ancestors from stealing, whereas in the fourteenth century thieves were branded and hanged. The question even is posed whether there was public shame when a branded thief remained in society. A counter-question might be whether there was in actuality public shame in those times when a thief, having handily paid his light fine, remained in society unbranded?

Corporal punishment is also ascribed to the period under consideration yet even the Rus Justice offers evidence of physical torture suffered by accused at the orders of a prince. Corporal punishment existed everywhere throughout the Middle Ages but was circumscribed by given social attitudes. In Russia, for various reasons, such social attitudes were never established, explaining the resultant indifference concerning corporal punishment. Even if we do not admit the existence of a precipitous decline in morality during this period in comparison to the previous epoch, we cannot deny the existence of evidence of factors which could only have affected perniciously the morality of this period.

There is no lack of evidence of the brutality of punishment. The counselors of the young prince Vasily Alexandrovich suffered severely. Some lost their noses and ears, others their eyes or hands. In an entry for 1442 the chronicler mentions that a certain Koludarov and Rezhsky received a whipping. The item occurs in a narration of the war between Prince Vasily and Shemiaka, and leads us to think that the crime of the two men was sympathy for Shemiaka. For the year 1444 it is stated that Prince Ivan Andreevich of Mozhaisk seized Andrei Dmitrievich Mamon and burned him together with his wife in Mozhaisk. Later it is discovered that these individuals were accused of heresy. The old superstition of blaming "witches" for natural disasters remained. The inhabitants of Pskov burned twelve witches during a plague. When, in 1462 the members of the retinue of Serpukhov prince Vasily Yaroslavich were seized in an attempt to free their lord, Vasily the Dark ordered them punished severely. Some were whipped, some had their hands cut off, others their noses, and some were decapitated.

As to the habits of government officials, we learn that Viatka was not conquered because the military commander Perfushkov was well-disposed to the inhabitants of that city, having been bribed by them. The

suggestive story of a belt switched at a prince's wedding by the court's leading dandy cannot provide a favorable picture of contemporaneous mores.
There is also the horrifying deed of Yury, the last prince of Smolensk.
Having been deprived of his lands he settled in Torzhok as the grand
prince's vicegerent. Prince Semeon Mstislavich of Viazma, exiled along
with Yury, also found shelter there. Yury fell in love with Semeon's wife
Uliana. Finding his love unrequited, he killed her husband in order to take
advantage of the wife's defenseless position. Uliana seized a knife,
missed Yury's throat, wounding his arm, and began to flee. Yury caught
her in the courtyard, hacked her to death with his sword and ordered the
body thrown in the river. To the honor of contemporaneous society we
must quote the words of the chronicler. "He fell into great sin and
shame," he writes, "and because of it fled to the Horde, not bearing his
bitter fortune, shame and dishonor." Yury died in the land of Riazan,
where he lived with the anchorite Peter, lamenting his sins.

It has been observed that the metropolitans turned their attention to the
moral decline in Novgorod and Pskov, inveighing against violence, profanity, divorce, superstition and violation of oaths. The Novgorod chronicler especially reproaches his fellow-citizens for looting during fires.
Many men grew rich after the severe fire of 1267. In describing the fire
of 1293 the chronicler writes "Evil men fell to looting. Everything that
was in the churches was looted. At the church of St. John a watchman
was killed while guarding the valuables." A similar account may be found
for 1311, and later for 1340 and 1342. The chronicler also strongly laments the poor state of justice in Novgorod in 1446. "At that time," he
writes, "there were no fair trials or any justice in Novgorod. The court
officials rebelled, renounced their oaths and kissing of the cross as false-
hoods, and begun plundering in the villages, districts and the city. Thus
we violated our neighbors, those who lived around us. Throughout the
districts were great losses and frequent confiscations accompanied by
shouts, weeping, cries and swearing at our elders and our city, because
we had neither mercy nor justice."

The passion for drink is vividly apparent in certain accounts, such as
the description of the siege of Moscow by Tokhtamysh. In the description of Vasily the Dark's campaign against his uncle Yury it is said that
the grand prince took with him from Moscow merchants and other men
who were drunk, and who brought mead with them to drink even more.
As before, quarrels, fights, murders and various other crimes occurred
most often at drunken feasts. In 1453 Grand Prince Vasily Vasilievich

wrote his village stewards and bailiffs "My father Metropolitan Jonas has said to me that your men frequent the metropolitan's villages on holidays and break into feasts and gatherings uninvited, and that murder, robbery and many other violent deeds take place at such occasions. I, the grand prince, have written the metropolitan that no one shall go uninvited to his villages for holidays, feasts and gatherings."

The further northeast, the cruder the values. From a missive of Metropolitan Jonas to the Viatka clergy we learn that some men took as many as five, six, seven, even ten wives, and that the priests blessed them and accepted gifts to the church from them. Some men lived with women without benefit of ceremony. Others, having become monks, subsequently forsook their vows so as to marry.

It has been noted that the metropolitan encouraged the citizens of Novgorod to eschew superstition. In 1357 the two parties agreed that brutal sports and certain superstitious rituals no longer be practiced, sealing this agreement by kissing the cross. Yet pugilistic contests which occasionally ended in death continued everywhere. Thus in 1390 Osey, the son of either the mentor or tutor of Grand Prince Vasily Dmitrievich, was killed at a boxing match in Kolomna.

Unfavorable evidence is also provided by the chronicles concerning public safety by the mention of river piracy.[16] Much evidence of banditry on a lesser scale, though absent from the chronicles, is found in the paterikons.[17] As to the general state of society, two instances mentioned elsewhere are curiously revealing, the fate of the metropolitan's tithe collector who perished in Vyshgorod, and that of Luka Mozhaisky who, having grown rich, lost all control in the gratification of his desires.

IX

CULTURE

LITERATURE

The crudeness of customs as found in the examples cited above must have arrested the development of literature as well. There are no references to the existence of cultivated princes or grandees. It is said outright of Dmitry Donskoy that he had little book learning, and of Vasily the Dark that he knew neither books nor literacy. As before, people were taught by clerics. In the Life of St. Jonas of Novgorod it is said that he was taught by a deacon together with many other children. Though Isidore characterized the Russian bishops as untutored, this must be taken on relative terms, for it was the clergy who preserved literacy.

Books never lost significance as depositories of religious treasures and literacy could not but remain the longed-for goal of the most capable men as a means of knowing the divine and of approaching religious perfection. Books, therefore, continued to be regarded as treasures. Books from the surrounding regions were brought to Moscow during the siege by Tokhtamysh. Books were copied diligently by monks. Translations were made from the Greek, anthologies were compiled.

Along with religious texts, the chronicles were copied as well. It was not merely man's inborn curiosity about and esteem for the lives of his predecessors that gave the chronicles significance. They were also used as documentation in disputes among princes. It has been noted that Prince Yury Dmitrievich cited the chronicles to assert his right to seniority. The tradition of recording contemporary events was maintained as well. Reports of important events, which aroused special attention and sympathy, were recorded with all the accretions of oral transmission and further embellished according to the chronicler's skill and knowledge.

ORAL TRADITION AND SERMONS

The bishops continued to deliver homilies to the people in church. It is said of Bishop Cyril of Rostov[1] that people flocked from neighboring cities to hear him preach on Holy Scripture. The author of this report says that he himself wrote down the words of the preacher while standing in a narrow and isolated spot of the church. It is said of Bishops Serapion of Vladimir and Simeon of Tver[2] that they were of high learning and strong in Holy Scripture. Under 1382 the chronicler notes the passing of a monk of Nizhny Novgorod named Pavel Vysoky who was very learned and a great philosopher. His words were salted with divine wisdom. Several examples of homiletic literature of that period are extant. A sermon at the dedication of a cathedral to Archangel Michael, ascribed to Metropolitan Cyril, speaks of the creation of the heavenly powers, their acts, the fall of Satan, the essence of man's soul, the fall of the first man, and presents in brief the Old and New Testaments. Then the speaker turns again to the angels, describes the role of the guardian angels, and teaching what awaits the human soul upon its separation from the body. The so-called "tribulations" are described. Among them are included profanity and other shameless utterances, dancing at feasts, weddings, evening meals, public amusements, gossiping on the street, all unseemly games, hand-clapping and foot-stamping, superstitious belief in predestined encounters, the significance of sneezes, unexpected arrivals, the calls of birds and sorcery.

This is followed by an exhortation to the clergy. "If you hew to all these commandments," said the preacher, "you will gladden God and amaze the angels. Your prayers will be heard, and our land will be rid of the heathen yoke. God's mercy will be increased in all the corners of the Russian land. Debilitation and disease of fruits and animals will cease. God's wrath shall be slaked and the peoples of the Russian land will live in peace and quietude. They will receive God's mercy in this age and all the more so in the future."

The following noteworthy words appear at the end of the homily. "It is evident that the end of the world has drawn near and the meaning to our life is nigh. The years are growing short and all that was spoken by the Lord has come to pass, 'And nation shall rise against nation....' It is said that upon the passing of seven thousand years the Second Coming shall occur."[3]

There was a contemporary of Cyril, Serapion of Vladimir, who has been mentioned above. Serapion was installed as bishop from the ranks of the archimandrites of the Caves monastery of Kiev by Metropolitan Cyril. It follows that Serapion was from Southern Rus. In his homilies Serapion also called to penitence and told of the fearful calamities then afflicting Rus and heralding the end of the world. Especially noteworthy is that part of his sermon in which he inveighs against the superstition of blaming witches for natural calamities and killing them. "I was almost happy for a short time, children, seeing your love and obedience to our strictures. I almost began to think that you had become strong and joyously accepted Holy Scripture. Yet you still hold to pagan customs. You believe in sorcery and burn innocent people. Those of you who have not slain them yourselves, but were accomplices, are as much murderers as those who could have given aid but did not. It is the same as if you yourselves ordered them killed. In which books, in which writings, have you seen that famines occur on this earth because of sorcery, or the contrary, that sorcery makes grain more plentiful? If you believe this, why do you burn sorcerers? Venerate them, present them with gifts, beseech them to create peace, to make the rains fall, warmth come, and the earth be fruitful.

"It has been three years now that there has been no grain, not only in Rus but in the Latin lands as well. Well, was it all done by sorcerers? Magicians and sorceresses have evil power only over those who fear them, but no power over those with firm faith in God. I am anguished by your madness and beseech you to reject heathen ways. If you want to cleanse your city of wicked men, then do so, as King David cleansed Jerusalem. He used the fear of God's judgement and the insight of the Holy Spirit, yet you condemn men to death while you yourselves are full of passions. Some condemn out of hatred, others seek profit, and yet others who are mad want only to slay and plunder, without themselves knowing why they plunder and slay. God's laws command that many witnesses are to be heard if a man is to be condemned to death, but you call water as your witness. If the accused starts to drown he is innocent and if he floats he is a sorcerer. Could not the devil, seeing your lack of faith, support him so that he does not drown, and bring you to the sin of murder? You reject the testimony of man, instead you resort to an inanimate object, water, for testimony."

There also exist the homilies of Metropolitans Peter, Alexis and Photius. The Russo-Lithuanian metropolitan Gregory Tsamblak who, in the words of the chronicle, was well-versed in the wisdom of books, left many sermons. Attention must be given to the homily of Archbishop Simeon of Novgorod to the citizens of Pskov, for in it are expressed the attitudes of the Novgorod prelates to their flock. "Noble and Christ-loving honorable men of Pskov! You know that the reverence given to your prelate passes on to Christ himself, and that the reverential reap great benefit from Him. You, my children, revere your prelate and your spiritual fathers with submission and love, demanding nothing from them and saying nothing against them. Instead look at yourselves, reprove and criticize yourselves, bewail your sins. Steal not from others or rejoice at your brothers' troubles. Be neither vain nor proud, but humbly obey your spiritual fathers. Do no harm to God's church nor interfere in church matters. Do not trespass on its lands or waters nor interfere in its courts and documents or church taxes. For everyone should fear the wrath of God, call forth His mercy, bewail his own sins and take not that which is another's."

The final compilation of a brief "household manual" may also be ascribed to this period. In some sources it is known as the Testament of the Prelate Matvey of Saray to His Children.[4] This work is remarkable in the fact that on three separate occasions it calls for kind treatment of servants. "Do not torment them with hunger or even worse," the first statement reads, "for these are house-bound beggars. A beggar will beg for himself somewhere else, but servants can only look to you." "Treat your household slaves kindly," states the second admonition, "and teach them well. Give freedom to the old, teach the young the path of goodness." "Feed your household slaves," the concluding admonition states. "If a slave of yours is killed while stealing, you are to answer for his blood." It is simultaneously recommended not to spare the rod on disobedient slaves, but not to inflict more than thirty blows.

Metropolitans Cyprian and Photius have left the so-called testaments of "leave-taking." Four days before his death Cyprian wrote a testament which, in the words of the chronicler, was "unheard of" and "strangely beautiful." In it he forgave everyone their sins, blessed them, and himself asked for forgiveness and blessing. He ordered that the testament be read publicly at his interment, which was done. Photius's testament is similar to Cyprian's but is more expanded in the beginning, where the metropolitan speaks of his labors and concerns, and at the end where he speaks of church property.

SAINTS' LIVES

Metropolitan Cyprian also wrote a Life of his precursor St. Peter. Here is an example of his style. "Righteous men live for ages and God rewards them. They receive their churchly teachings from the Lord. When a righteous man dies he receives peace and people joyfully give him praise, since the righteous man has earned such glory. Such is the holy man whom we magnify commensurately with his worthiness, though no one can give him his due praise, yet it would be unjust to leave his crown without adornment, though our precursors have adorned it in part. It is for God's sake that I speak of the saint's gifts, and for this we shall receive a small reward as well, as did receive the widow who gave away her last two copper coins.[5] For many days have I felt that I must do this, for I am driven to it by love for this veritable pastor. Therefore I decided to offer at least small praise for this enlightener, even though I acknowledge my inability to add anything to his magnificence. Nevertheless I could not stand by without adding my voice."

Another prelate, Metropolitan Theodosius,[6] described a miracle at the grave of St. Alexis by beginning "Full of light for us today is the event, and wondrous the celebration. It is luminous and decorous. It is a joyous holiday today charged with miracles. A holiday is necessary for the salvation of the soul, and it transcends both thought and word.... Can anyone praise your inheritance, stature and numerous miracles, when it was God himself Who glorified you with them. Your miracles are like the sea, and men of every variety flow toward it, drawn by faith like the hart drawn to waterbrooks in the noonday heat,[7] to satisfy their thirst with your gifts. For you brightly enlighten the body and spirit and they carry in their souls a word that is the result of your grace cordially given. I, though unworthy, seeing such was much amazed, hoping for the saint's intercession for myself. Full of love and faith, I dared to stretch my unworthy hand and dip my pen into luminous meekness and dared to begin to describe this great and glorious miracle." A laudation to the apostles Peter and Paul is encountered, also the work of Theodosius, archbishop of all Rus.

Among other hagiographers there is the well-known monk of the Holy Trinity monastery, Epifany the Wise,[8] who wrote the works, life and miracles of St. Sergius and St. Nikon of Radonezh, as well as the life of Stephen of Perm. "It is unknown whether Epifany went to Mount Athos or to other Orthodox centers of learning, but he was well versed in the Russian literary tradition of his day and had a total grasp of the rhetoric of the exemplary ecclesiastical works written in Old Church Slavonic, whether translated or original. It was after his time that such works increased in number within the Russian literary tradition. The Life of Stephen of Perm provides a basis for compiling the considerable lexicon of those artificial words, etymologically alien to Russian, that were brought into the literary language of ancient Rus by the South Slavic literary tradition.[9] Rhetorical figures and various embellishments are scattered throughout the Life with tiresome abundance. The author dislikes simple reflection or narrative but frequently casts a single thought in several tautological turns. To characterize the saint, he gathers twenty epithets in one passage and twenty-five in another, almost all of them different. In general Epifany is more of a preacher than a biographer in his work and goes much farther than Cyprian in mixing the genre of saint's life with that of panegyric. The historical narrative about Stephen appears only in meager passages amid the author's ornateness."[10]

To explain the nature of such lives we must grasp the meaning of their sources, the motives which caused them to be written. Religious sensibility demanded an attitude of prayer and glorification expressed in devotion to the saint. Features of a saint's life were chosen which would especially touch the heart, arouse religious feeling and glorify the servant of God. Liturgical chant, canon and panegyric were the original, natural and necessary forms of exalting the life of a saint. Later "lives" practiced these forms, especially since the later authors shared with their predecessors the urge to glorify the saint and bring him "some small praise" on their part as well.

As a result the lives have few facts of everyday life, or historical information which would be valuable today. There is even less basis for seeking such information in the writings of the famous but foreign author, Pachomios the Logothete,[11] for whom Russian life of that period was alien. He was an ethnic Serb who, while living in the Holy Trinity monastery and in Novgorod, wrote saints' lives, panegyrics and canons upon the instruction of his superiors.

A metropolitan's secretary by the name of Rodion Kozhukh[12] also was famed for his high art of writing. Two of his works which have been preserved are the Tale of the Miracle of St. Varlaam and The Tale of the Earthquake of 1460. Here is an example of Rodion's style. "At first a cloud rises into the heavens among other clouds and commonly it proceeds to be borne by the air and it wafts from the south, merging with other clouds in the flow of the soaring air. In the words of the prophet 'As if gathering water into skins and storing them in a deep depository. It thus moves through clouds to the sunlit East and having consummated its greatness, full of aqueous essence and spreading over vast areas, grows visible, a very awesome and great cloud.'"

TRAVELOGUES

The tradition of pilgrimages to sacred places such as Constantinople, Mount Athos and Palestine was maintained in this period. There exists a description of Constantinople written by a Stephen of Novgorod in the mid-fourteenth century. The goal of the journey was stated by Stephen himself in the beginning of his work. "I, the sinner Stephen, of Novgorod the Great, and eight of my friends, have come to Constantinople to bow down before the holy places and kiss the relics of the saints and to have the blessings of St. Sophia the Wisdom of God." It is curious to note how the wonders of artistic creation and the durability of stone impressed the Russians, who were accustomed to their squalid and impermanent buildings. The statue of Justinian struck our Novgorod traveller as quite miraculous. "...It is as if he were alive, so awesome is it to view him.... . There are also many other monuments of marble-stone in the city. There is much writing on them from top to bottom, all done in a fulsome ornate style. There is much to behold, and the mind cannot comprehend how the stone has remained undamaged for so many years."

It is evident that the Russian travellers received special attention from the crown and the church. One of the emperor's nobles, having noticed that the men of Novgorod were caught in a crowd and could not get to Holy Thursday services, had a passage cleared for them. The patriarch, upon seeing the Russian pilgrims, called them to himself, blessed and spoke to them "... for he greatly loves Rus. O great miracle! How great his humility must be to speak with sinful pilgrims. It is not to our custom that he holds." In describing the Studion monastery[13] Stephen says that many texts including statutes and books of prayer were sent from there to Rus. While visiting other monasteries Stephen encountered two compatriots of Novgorod named Ivan and Dobrila, who lived in Constantinople and worked at copying ecclesiastical texts in the Studion monastery.

Zosima, a monk of the Trinity monastery who journeyed to the holy places in 1420, describes his motives for the pilgrimage as follows. "For scripture says it is good to keep the secrets of the king, but it is glorious to preach the works of the Lord. If not keeping the king's secrets is unrighteous and sinful, then to keep silent concerning the Lord's work is to bring harm to one's soul. Therefore I fear to keep God's work hidden, recalling the torment of His servant who, having received a talent from the Lord, buried it in the ground... .[14] Let this written work for all of us communicants be a blessing from God and the Holy Sepulcher and from these holy places, a reward greater than that received by pilgrims who visit the holy city of Jerusalem and view these holy places. Blessed are those who see and believe. Thrice-blessed are those who believe without having seen.... For God's sake, my brothers, fathers and lords, sons of Rus, do not condemn my ignorance and crudeness. Do not judge me for this writing. It is not for my sake, a sinner, but for the sake of the holy places that you read it with love and faith. May our Lord Jesus Christ grant you grace."

Stephen of Novgorod wrote that entering Constantinople was like going into a forest where you would be lost without a good guide. Russian pilgrims indiscriminately recorded everything told them by such guides. There is the toad that stalked the streets and devoured men, the brooms that swept by themselves, for people rose early in the morning and found the streets clean, and many similar tall tales.

A traveller who accompanied Metropolitan Isidore to Florence[15] kept a record of the journey. The impressions made by Western cities and landscapes on a Russian are very interesting. "The city of Yuriev (Dorpat) is grand and of stone. Such we do not have. The buildings in it are a wonder. We never saw such, and marvelled at them. The city of Lübeck is also marvelous. The fields and mountains around it are great, the gardens beautiful, the buildings wondrous with gilded tops. There were all kinds of goods. Water was channelled into the city, flowing along all the streets in pipes. Some gushes from towers, cool and sweet." In a monastery in Lübeck the travellers saw an unheard-of and indescribable wonder, the Virgin standing as if alive and holding the Savior in her arms. A bell rang and an angel descended from above to place a crown on the Virgin. Then a star moved as if across the heavens and, gazing at it, three magi followed, preceded by a man bearing a sword and followed by another bearing gifts. Also in Lübeck the traveller saw on the river a wheel that scooped up water and sent it in all directions. Another smaller wheel next to it milled grain and wove fabric. In Lüneburg he was struck by the sight of a fountain. In the middle of the town there were erected wondrous columns of gilded bronze. Each column had figures attached, also of bronze, from which sweet and cool water flowed, out of the mouth of one, the ear of another, the eye of a third. The water flowed very briskly, as if out of a barrel. These figures provided water for the entire city and its beasts. The whole water supply was done very cleverly, and the flow was indescribable.

In Brunswick he was amazed by the roofs of buildings. They were made of slabs of some strange stone that lasted many years. Nuremberg seemed more cleverly designed than all the previous cities. It was ineffable and beyond the grasp of the mind. Florence surpassed even

Nuremberg. Silk brocade and patterned velvet with gold were made there, as well as other expensive cloth. There were goods of all kinds and numerous olive groves where "wood" oil was made. The bell tower in Florence was beyond the mind's comprehension. In Venice there was water for streets, and people went about in boats. The church of St. Mark was of stone, with wondrous columns and mosaics in the Greek style. The traveller noted about Croatians that, though their language was similar to Russian, their faith was Latin.

Another traveller who accompanied Isidore, a monk from Suzdal named Simeon, has left a description of the Council of Florence entitled The Narrative of Simeon, a Priest of Suzdal, on how the Pope of Rome, Eugenius, Conducted the Eighth Council with his Confederates. Simeon was not pleased with Isidore's behavior in Florence. Here is what he says of his resistance to the metropolitan and the resulting persecution he suffered. "Metropolitan Isidore remained in Venice and corresponded with the Pope. Visiting sacred places, he made obeisance in the foreign manner and ordered us to do the same. I argued with him over this many times and he put me under very harsh restrictions. Then I, seeing such falsehood and great heresy, fled to Novgorod, and from there to Smolensk." The Smolensk prince delivered Simeon to Isidore, who put him in irons and kept him incarcerated all winter, barefoot and wearing only a long shirt. Later he was taken from Smolensk to Moscow.

TRANSLATED LITERATURE

Greek works continued to be translated during this time. Metropolitan Cyprian translated the Ladder of St. John Climacus[16] along with its commentary. Also translated were Andrew of Crete,[17] John Chrysostom,[18] St. Nilus,[19] Isaac the Syrian,[20] and Maxim the Confessor.[21] Much of the translating was done not in Russia proper, but on Mount Athos in the Russian Panteleimon and the Serbian Khilandar monasteries.[22] Latter-day works, sometimes quite insignificant in content, also were translated there. Under 1384 the chronicle lists the translation of a seventh-century work by the saintly and wise Georgius Pisides, a panegyric to God on the creation of all the living things, entitled The Creation of the World.[23] The translator was Dmitry Zoograf. From the fifteenth century there exists a copy of The Bee, an anthology modeled on the well-known Greek compilations of Maxim the Confessor and Antonius Melissa (Bee). Such anthologies usually began with excerpts from the Gospels, the Acts of the Apostles and from the works of the holy fathers of the church. These were

followed by excerpts from the pagan authors such as Isocrates, Demo-
critus, Aristotle, Xenophon, Plato and others.

Apocryphal works came to Rus from Bulgaria and Serbia. These were
tales of various kinds that were especially attractive to people at the Russians' level of civilization. The stories of Novgorod travellers served as
an impulse for the Russians to create their own tales. The people of Novgorod told of seeing a great snake that never sleeps on a breathing sea,
of hearing the gnashing of teeth and seeing the river of lightning called
Morg. They also saw the waters run into the underworld and return thrice
daily. The ship of Moislav of Novgorod was driven by a storm to high
mountains, and there the voyagers saw a *deisus*²⁴ done in wondrous azure.
A self-shining light was in that place, such that a man could not describe.
The sun was nowhere to be seen but nevertheless it was light, brighter
than the sun. Joyous voices and rejoicing was heard in the mountains. A
man of Novgorod ran up the mountain, threw up his arms, laughed and
disappeared. A second did the same. They tied a rope to the leg of the
third one, but when pulled forcibly down the mountain, he was dead.
Such tales, along with accounts drawn from other, equally murky sources,
brought Archbishop Vasily of Novgorod to write an epistle on paradise to
Bishop Feodor of Tver.

The Tale of Kitovras and similar works continued to be translated but
there was a shortage of liturgical works. In the Life of St. Dmitry of Prilutsk
it is said that the brethren complained to him of the shortage of books.
There were no real canonical collections in Pskov, where Metropolitan
Cyprian sent the canonical rites of marriage and baptism, as well as the
liturgies of St. John Chrysostom and St. Basil. Variations and distortions
crept into the books as they were copied. Metropolitan Cyprian wrote that
in anthologies copied in rural areas there was much that was false, sown
by heretics for the temptation of the ignorant, such as prayers for the
"shakes."

SECULAR LITERATURE

The period's secular literature consisted of historical songs, tales and
chronicles. Of the first category there is the song about Shchelkan Duden-
tievich which is noteworthy for its view of the Tatars and the behavior of
the khans' baskaks in Rus. Khan Uzbek, who judges and metes out punishment, is described thus. "Here sits Uzbek in judgement, pressing his pun-
ishments, waving his crutch, striking those trimmed mustaches, those
Tatar heads." Further, Uzbek grants Russian cities to all his relatives save

Shchelkan, who was away in Lithuanian lands gathering unpaid tribute, taking one hundred rubles from princes, fifty from boyars and five from peasants. When someone had no money, Shchelkan took a child. If no child, he took a wife. If no wife, he took the man himself. Upon returning to the Horde Shchelkan begged Uzbek to grant him Tver, the ancient, the wealthy. Uzbek agreed with the condition that Shchelkan first stab to death his favorite son, fill a chalice with the hot blood and drink it. Shchelkan fulfilled the condition and arrived in Tver as a judge but did not officiate long because he dishonored widows, defiled maidens, mocking all and sundry and laughed at hearth and home. The citizens of Tver brought a complaint to their princes, called the sons of Boris, and then proceeded with gifts and supplication to Shchelkan who gave vent to his vanity, wrangled with the citizens of Tver, who promptly tore him apart.

The subjects of ornamental tales consist of the feats of famous princes, of major events in the life of Rus whether good or ill and, finally, of events that caught the imagination of contemporaries with wondrous circumstances. Where previously the feats of princes and knights against the Pechenegs and Polovetsians were the subject of songs and tales, it was natural to expect that these themes were adapted to the struggle against the Tatars, who replaced the Polovetsians. In the West for Novgorod and Pskov there was an equally dangerous struggle against the Swedes, the Livonian Order and the Lithuanians. Two princes gained fame in this struggle, Alexander [Nevsky] of Novgorod and Daumantas of Pskov.[25] Their feats served as subject matter for particular ornamental tales.

The author of the tale of Grand Prince Alexander was a contemporary and confidant of the hero.[26] Alexander himself told him the details of the Neva river battle. These details have been mentioned previously.[27] Now the beginning of the tale is quoted for illustration of style. "A tale this is of our great prince, Alexander Yaroslavich, the wise and humble, the clever, the brave, the namesake of Alexander the Great. Similar is he to Tsar Achilles, the strong and brave.

"Our Lord God, I, an unworthy, sinful and ignorant man, attempt to write the life of a saintly and great prince, Alexander Yaroslavich, the grandson of Grand Prince Vsevolod. Thus I have heard from my fathers and myself am eyewitness of his maturity and would be pleased to offer his saintly, honorable and glorious life. Yet as the great maker of parables states, wisdom will not enter a base soul. Though I am coarse of mind, with prayer to the Mother of God and with the aid of the saint and great prince Alexander,[28] I will attempt a beginning. This great prince,

Alexander, was born in God from a pious, philanthropic[29] and humble father, Grand Prince Yaroslav Vsevolodich, and from a saintly mother, Grand Princess Feodosia. In the words of the prophet Isaiah, God says 'I install princes, and they are as divine, for I introduce the truth.'[30] Without God's will Alexander would not have reigned. He was taller than other men. His voice was like a trumpet among the people. His face was fair like that of Joseph. His strength was second only to that of Samson. God had given him the wisdom of Solomon and the courage of the Roman emperor Vespasian." The tale of the faithful prince Daumantas and of his courage is marked by a greater simplicity.

Tied to the struggle of Novgorod against the Swedes is a curious literary document, The Manuscript of Magnush [sic] the Swedish King. It has been observed that the Swedish king Magnus Erikson[31] led a crusade against Novgorod. This invasion, though at first extremely threatening to Novgorod, was unsuccessful. Troubles awaited Magnus at home. First he was forced to conduct war against his own sons. Later he was deposed by nobles who proclaimed his nephew, Albert of Mecklenburg, to be king. Magnus was taken prisoner. He gained freedom five years later and came to end his days in Norway in 1374. News of the sad fate of the king who once posed such great danger to Orthodoxy gave rise to the appearance in Novgorod of Magnus's Manuscript. It begins with the customary formula of Russian testaments.

"I Magnus, king of Sweden, given the name of Gregory at holy baptism, upon leaving this world write this manuscript while still alive and charge my children, brethren and all the Swedish land to swear by kissing the cross not to attack Rus, for it is injurious to us." There follows a listing of unsuccessful Swedish invasions of Rus, from Birger[32] to Magnus. "After my invasion," continues Magnus, "there came upon our Sweden devastation, flooding, plague, famine and internecine strife. God took my reason from me and I sat chained in a walled-in chamber for a year. Then my son came from Norway,[33] released me from the chamber and took me to his land of Norway. Again a storm came up on the voyage, sinking the ships and drowning my men. The wind swept me about for three days and three nights, finally bringing me to the monastery of the Savior on the Polnaia river. Here the monks untied me from my plank, took me into the monastery and tonsured me a monk. Since then I have been alive for three days and three nights. All this is God's punishment for my arrogance, for invading Rus despite having kissed the cross. Now I charge my sons and brothers not to invade Rus in violation of kissing the cross. Whoever invades shall be punished by God with fire and water as was I. All this was done to me by God for my salvation."

MILITARY TALES

Tales dealing with the struggle against the Tatars begin with the Riazan tale of the invasion of Batu Khan.[34] Upon hearing of the incursion of the godless "tsar" Batu , Grand Prince Yury Igorevich of Riazan sent for his son Prince Fedor and for his relatives, Prince Oleg the Handsome, Davyd of Murom, Vsevolod of Pronsk and for other local princes, boyars and military leaders. At a council the princes decided to send Prince Fedor, son of Yury, with gifts to Batu that he not attack the land of Riazan. Prince Fedor set off and was received kindly by Batu, then a Riazan grandee whispered to the khan that Fedor's wife was a great beauty. The Tatar then began insisting that Fedor show her to him, but the prince answered "When you conquer us, then shall you possess our women." Batu ordered Fedor killed.

His wife Evpraksia was standing with her son Ivan atop a high building when one of Fedor's uncles appeared with news of her husband's death. Hearing this, she and her son threw themselves from the building to their deaths. Then Prince Yury went forth with his brethren against the Tatars, and a vicious and horrible slaughter took place. One man did battle against a thousand, two men against ten thousand. Prince Davyd was the first to fall. Then Prince Yury cried with grief in his heart "Dear brothers, sweet retinue, the flower and pride of Riazan, brace up and steel yourselves!" The bold and daring men of Riazan fought on strongly and mercilessly, so that the ground moaned, then finally the strong Tatar enemies prevailed. All the princes were killed except Oleg, who was taken prisoner. He cursed at Batu's attempts to have him join the Tatars, and was hacked to pieces. Riazan was taken, and all the Riazan land laid waste.

Then there came a Riazan noble named Ipaty Kolovrat who was in Chernigov collecting taxes for the grand prince of Riazan (?).[35] Ipaty gathered a retinue of seventeen hundred men and struck at the Tatars unexpectedly, hacking mercilessly. Batu was alarmed. When five prisoners were brought to him, he asked them "Of what faith are you and of what land? Why have you done me so much harm?" "We are of the Christian faith," replied the prisoners, "the servants of Grand Prince Yury Igorevich, from the retinue of Ipaty Kolovrat, sent by Prince Igor of Riazan to receive you, mighty tsar, and see you off with honor. Do not be angry with us, sovereign, if we cannot fill the cups fast enough for the great Tatar strength."[36] Batu was struck by the wisdom of their answer. Then he sent his brother-in-law Tavrul with a number of powerful corps against Ipaty. Tavrul boasted that he would bring Ipaty back alive, but instead was hacked in half by Ipaty himself. Then the Tatars sent a great number of sledges with trebuchets (?)[37] against this mighty giant. Even so they barely overcame him. When the body of Ipaty was brought to Batu, he said "So, brother Ipaty! Heartily have you feted me. With a small retinue you have slain many brave warriors. Had you served me thus, I would have held you close to my heart."

Prince Igor Igorevich was in Chernigov at this time, visiting the local prince Mikhail Vsevolodovich. Upon returning to his native land he buried the corpses and wept over his slain brethren. "He lamented bitterly and wept greatly. The tears flowed from his eyes in a mighty stream. His heart was rent and he beat his breast. His voice was a trumpet announcing war, and as an organ speaking sweetly. 'Why,' said he, 'do you not speak to me, my flowers? My wonderful abundant grapes who will no longer bring sweetness to my soul. To whom have you left me, my dearest sun that has set so early, my handsome moon that has perished so soon? Why have the eastern stars set so early?'"

There is also a tale of the death of Batu. He invaded Hungary and laid siege to the city of Varadin, deep in the Hungarian lands. There were few trees but many vineyards around this city. In the middle of the town stood a high tower in which King Ladislas, or Władysław, resided apart. He was king of the Hungarians, the Czechs, the Germans and of all Pomerania. The Hungarians were once Orthodox, for they received Christianity from the Greeks, but they had no opportunity to create literacy in their own language before the neighboring Romans pulled them into their heresy. King Ladislas obeyed the Roman church until St. Sabbas, the archbishop of Serbia, came and turned him to the Greek canons, which Ladislas practiced in secret, fearing insurrection by the Hungarians. When Batu laid siege to Varadin Ladislas did not eat or drink, and constantly prayed to God in the hope that He would change His wrath to mercy. One day he saw from the tower that his sister was fleeing toward town, but was seized by the Tatars and taken to Batu.

Now Ladislas began to pray even more fervently. Tears flowed from his eyes like swift river currents, and where they fell on marble they burnt right through and even today cracks may be seen in the marble. Then a stranger approached him, all luminous and fearsome, and said "For the sake of your tears God grants you victory over Batu. Go now, engage him." The messenger disappeared and now a saddled steed bearing a pole axe and held by no one stood by the tower. Ladislas mounted the steed, grasped the pole axe and led his retinue at Batu's encampment. Batu at that time had few troops because all his Tatars were out rounding up horses. The Tatars in the encampment took flight before Ladislas, as did Batu, carrying the king's sister. Ladislas caught up to him and engaged him in single combat, but the princess helped Batu. Then Ladislas called to God for aid, overcame Batu and killed him, together with his own sister. The Hungarians stationed themselves in Batu's encampment and seized the Tatars as they came back from the roundup. They took the horses and put the Tatars to death, sparing the lives of those who wanted to be baptized.

A statue was placed on the column in the city square in memory of the royal house. It depicted King Ladislas sitting on a steed holding the pole axe with which he slew Batu and his own sister. An actual event provides the core of this tale, the defeat of the Tatars at the siege of Olomouc by the Czech commander Jaroslav of Sternberg. According to Czech poetic tradition the son of Kubla Khan perished at the hand of Jaroslav. There is no doubt that this tale was composed in the South and brought north by the well-known Serb Pachomios the Logothete.[38]

The great event which began the liberation of Northeastern Rus from the Tatars, the battle of Snipe Field,[39] was not left without dedicated narratives. Indeed, there was an early tale quite similar in essence to the tale of Alexander Nevsky. It was permeated with religious feeling and cited the complete text of prayers voiced by the protagonist. The pious musings and interjections of the narrator also were included. No ambiguous details were contained in the description of the main events. In this form the early tale was entered into various chronicles. "Then came Mamay," it begins, "the prince of the Horde, with his allies, other princes of the Horde, and with all the Tatar and Polovetsian forces. He also had with him Muslims, Armenians, Westerners,[40] Circassians, Yas and Burtasy. Also allied with Mamay and sharing his design was the Lithuanian Jogaila with all the Lithuanian and Polish forces. Likewise there was also Oleg Ivanovich, prince of Riazan. All these confederates set out against Grand Prince Dmitry Ivanovich and his cousin Vladimir Andreevich, but compassionate God saved and delivered the Christian race through the prayers of His Blessed Mother from crushing labor, from the pagan Mamay, from the swarm of the impious Jogaila and from the garrulous and abominable Oleg of Riazan who abandoned his Christianity. May he see hell at God's judgement day! The damned Mamay gave free rein to his vanity, thinking himself a tsar, and summoned an evil council, calling to him his princes who led the myriads. 'Let us fall on the Russian prince,' he said to them, 'and all the Russians' forces. As it was during the time of Batu, let us lay waste the Christians, and burn God's churches, and spill their blood and destroy their religion.' Such was the violent rage of this impious one, because of his friends and lovers and princes who perished on the Vozha river."

Here is the description of the battle itself. "The two great forces engaged each other for a long time. The armies covered the field completely, and the clamor was heard for ten versts. There was an enormous clash and strong battle and the earth quaked fearfully. Russian princes had not fought such a battle since the beginning of time. They battled from the sixth hour to the ninth and the blood of both Christians and Tatars flowed as from a rain cloud and a great, countless number of bodies fell on both sides.... Mamay said to himself 'Our very hair is being torn out, our eyes cannot weep even fiery tears, our tongues are tied, our throats parched, our hearts rent, our loins pierced....'"

The event was so great and engaged everyone so intensely that one account could not suffice. Such events usually led to circulation of numerous details, both true and false, among the populace. With time even factual details, transmitted mouth to mouth, become distorted. Individual names were confused and the order of events was changed. Since the significance of the event did not fade it evoked a need to collect all the details and create of them a new ornamented narrative. In the rewriting yet other details were introduced. Consequently this second type of tale differs from the first in its wealth of detail, whether probable, suspect or obviously false.

There is yet a third type of narrative dealing with the battle of Snipe Field. Such is the Tale of Grand Prince Dmitry Ivanovich, his Cousin Prince Vladimir Andreevich, and How They Defeated Their Enemy, Tsar Mamay.[41] The work is obviously modeled on the ancient Southwest Russian Tale of Igor's Campaign.[42] The author of this Tale of Dmitry states that he wrote with "empathy and in praise" of Grand Prince Dmitry and his cousin, and that he thereby expressed the attitude of his contemporaries toward the battle of Snipe Field. He described the battle simultaneously as a glorious event and as a catastrophe because of the great losses on the Russian side. This short tale does not mention the initial

Russian setback, describing the battle as waged with equal success by both sides. "Many men of Rus were killed by the Tatars, many Tatars by men of Rus, corpses fell onto corpses. A Russian was seen pursuing a Tatar, or a Tatar gaining on a Russian. Many of the unseasoned, fearful Muscovites lost hope for their lives, and many of the pagan sons turned to flight because of the great clamor and slaughter."

After this the author declares the defeat of the Tatars while citing no actual reason for the Russian victory, suggesting only heavenly aid. "Then at the ninth hour of the day God looked with charity upon Grand Prince Dmitry and all the Russian princes and the stalwart captains and all the fearless Christians daring to struggle as great warriors. At the ninth hour the faithful beheld angels aiding the Christians, the holy martyrs aiding the troops, Christ's great warrior St. George, and the noble Dmitry, and the grand princes who were the namesakes of Boris and Gleb.[43] In their midst was the commander of the divine heavenly host, Archangel Michael. The pagan troops saw the two commanders and the troops that were bright as three suns with their arrows of flame marching at them. The godless Tatars fell from fear of God and the arms of the Christians. God with His right hand raised up Grand Prince Dmitry Ivanovich to victory over the intruders, while the godless Mamay trembled in fear ..." and so on.

In the far more lengthy tale of the second type it is said that the Tatars almost triumphed everywhere until the strike from ambush by fresh forces under Prince Vladimir Andreevich and the commander Volynsky decided the affair in favor of the Russians. Finally the third, largely poetic, tale also speaks of the initial defeat of the Russians, and thus the first part of the work becomes a lament. "On that field great clouds gathered and from them frequent lightnings gleamed and great thunder rolled. It was the daring Russians who confronted the pagan Tatars for their great injustice. Great gilt armor glistened among the Russians and the Russian princes raised thunder with their tempered swords against heathen helmets. They fought from morning to mid-day Saturday, on the Nativity of the Mother of God. It was not the bisons whose roar carries to the Danube from Snipe Field, and it was not the bisons that were defeated at the great Danube. It is the Russian princes and boyars and commanders of Grand Prince Dmitry Ivanovich who were slain. The princes of Belozersk were defeated by the pagan Tatars, Feodor Semeonovich, Semeon Mikhailovich, Timofey Valuevich, Andrei Serkizovich and Mikhailo Ivanovich. Many of the retinue of the Briansk boyar, the monk Peresvet, met their destiny at this place. The princesses and the wives of the boyars and commanders wept over the slain... ."

After this lamentation of the wives the author moves to panegyric, to the victory, and here through understatement and lengthy narration he advances the role of Prince Vladimir Andreevich who calls upon his cousin the grand prince to attack the Tatars. He attacks, and victory is theirs.

"That day, Saturday, the Nativity of the Mother of God, the pagan troops slaughtered the Christians on Snipe Field on the banks of the Nepriadva. Then Grand Prince Vladimir Andreevich spurred his men to action and rode into the pagan Tatar men, his gilt helmet flashing. The tempered swords began to thunder against the heathen helmets. He called to his cousin Grand Prince Dmitry. 'Rally your troops ... for the pagan Tatars are taking the field and have destroyed our brave retinue. Swift steeds cannot gallop among human corpses but wander about in blood to their knees. O brother, it is pitiful to see the blood of Christians.' Then Grand Prince Dmitry Ivanovich said to his boyars 'Brother boyars, commanders and junior boyars, so much for your sweet Moscow mead and your high places at court. It is here that you will win places for yourselves and your wives. It is here, brothers, that the old will become young and the young will gain honor.' Grand Prince Dmitry spoke further. 'My Lord God,' said he, 'I place great faith in you and shall never be ashamed of it nor shall my enemies mock it.' Then he prayed to God and His blessed mother and all the saints. He wept bitterly and wiped his tears. Then off galloped Grand Prince Dmitry Ivanovich and they all flew as swiftly as falcons."

Such are the sources describing the battle of Snipe Field that a historian must use. It is unknown when the tales were composed. One copy of an extended tale indicates that it was compiled by Sofrony, a priest of Riazan, but in a chronicle he is called Sofonia of Riazan, a Briansk boyar. The author of the "poetic" tale mentions Sofony of Riazan[44] as his precursor in the creation of panegyrics to Grand Prince Dmitry.

The invasion of Moscow by Tokhtamysh also served as a subject of a special tale, On the Taking of Moscow by Tsar Tokhtamysh and the Enslavement of the Russian Land. This tale is similar in nature to the short tale of the battle of Snipe Field, except that it has greater simplicity and more detail.

Accounts of Tamerlane's invasion have become part of the Tale of the Wondrous Miracle of the Icon of the Blessed Mother of God, Called that of Vladimir. It is said therein of Tamerlane that he was born among the

Tatars beyond the Yaik in the land of Samarkand, that he was a simple and poor man, a smith by occupation but a predator, informer and thief by nature. He once stole a sheep as a youth, for which the sheep's owner broke his foot and hip. Tamerlane then shod his foot with iron and thus received the name Iron Hobbler, Temir-Aksak. He was prompted to leave the Russian lands by a dream in which a woman in purple appeared to him through the air and forbade him to go further into Russia. A separate tale of a battle between the Russians and the Tatars near Riazan is entered in the chronicles under the title of Tale of Tsarevich Mustafa. The battle on the Vorksla river also served as the subject of a separate tale.

TALES OF HEROES

Clashes with the Tatars in general and the battle of Snipe Field in particular aroused great interest among the people and led to a variety of tales about them. It is not surprising that the life of the prince who first took the field in victory over the Tatars became the subject of an ornamental tale, The Life and Death of Grand Prince Dmitry Ivanovich, Russian Tsar. Detailed information on Donskoy's feats should not be sought in this tale for it is nothing other than a panegyric, dealing almost exclusively with morals. The author begins with his hero's origins and then describes the spiritual traits that marked the youth when he ascended to rule. "He was still young in years but well-versed in matters of the spirit. He did not take part in vain talk and hated profanity. He avoided evil-natured men but always spoke with the good. He listened with tender emotion to Holy Scripture. He diligently watched over God's churches and held vigil for the Russian land with his manliness despite his youth. He was always of superior intelligence and a fierce warrior in combat, defeating many enemies who rose up against us. He enclosed his glorious city of Moscow with a wondrous wall, and he was famous throughout the world, growing like the cedar in Lebanon and flowering like the palm."

Further, Dmitry's marriage is mentioned, followed by accounts of two victories over the Tatars, that on the Vozha river and on Snipe Field. The author ascribes Mamay's invasion to the envy of Dmitry's neighbors. Evil advisers who professed Christianity while practicing heathen deeds convinced Mamay that "Grand Prince Dmitry of Moscow, who calls himself tsar of the Russian land, is greater than you in glory and resists your reign." Mamay announced to his grandees that he was invading Rus to replace the Christian faith with the Muslim. The battle of Snipe Field is described briefly and in general terms. Having mentioned the Vozha and

Snipe Field victories the author again turns to Dmitry's virtues, which he presents with the goal of having tsars and princes emulate Dmitry. Having described the chastity, temperance and piety of Dmitry, the author goes on to the description of his passing, speaks of his instructions to his sons and boyars and of the division of the territories among his sons. The lamentation of Grand Princess Evdokia is described. "Why do you not speak to me, my beautiful flower? Why do you wither so soon? The fruitful grape will no longer give gladness to my heart nor sweetness to my soul. My early setting sun, my beautiful moon waning early! O, eastern star why do you hasten to the west?"

Having described the burial of the prince, the author continues "O fearsome miracle, brothers, full of wonder, a sight of trembling and horror. Hark, O sky and earth. How can one write or speak of the passing of this great prince? The tongue becomes tied with sorrow, the lips are sealed, the throat grows silent, the mind is affected, sight grows dim, strength fades. Were I to remain silent, [my] tongue drives me to speak." The tale ends with the traditional glorification of the hero by comparing him to the great names of ecclesiastical or civil history. The glorification also ends in a familiar manner, "The land of Greece praises Emperor Constantine, the land of Kiev and the neighboring cities praise Vladimir, but the whole Russian land praises you, Grand Prince Dmitry Ivanovich." It should be noted that this panegyric is the best extant literary work of the period. The panegyric to Dmitry Donskoy served as a model for the Life of his rival, Mikhail Alexandrovich of Tver, which was written in a far simpler fashion. In one chronicle it is stated that the Life was composed at the instruction of Prince Boris of Tver.

CHRONICLES

The nature of the Northern, specifically the Northeastern chronicles and their difference from the Southern has been suggested above. The historian's task grows difficult for thirteenth and fourteenth centuries when he is left only with the Northern chronicles. The increasingly frequent appearance of charters provides a new and rich source of information but provides nothing about which the chronicles remain silent. They are silent about what is most important, the causes and connections of events. The narrative of the Northern chronicles is less animated and dramatic than that of the Southern chronicles. In the Northern chronicles protagonists act in silence. They make war, they make peace but they say not a word, nor does the chronicler add anything as to why they fight, what brings them to peace. In the towns, in the princes' residences, not a sound is heard. All is quiet, everyone sits behind locked doors thinking private thoughts. The doors open, men do appear on the stage, they act, yet they do so silently. Surely the nature of the epoch is expressed here, the nature of a whole people of whom the protagonists are representatives. The chronicler could not invent speeches that he did not hear, but it must be noted that neither is he himself very talkative, for the nature of the epoch is expressed in his nature as well. As a contemporary the chronicler knew the details of a particular noteworthy occurrence, yet wrote only that "there was great disorder."

Up to now the Northern chronicles generically termed Suzdalian have been analyzed in juxtaposition to the Southern chronicles in general. It was noted in analyzing the Southern chronicles that the later redactions were composed of various regional chronicles, that of Kiev, Volhynia and Chernigov-Severia. Before proceeding to a more detailed analysis of the Northern chronicle, it must be determined whether a similar process may not have occurred here. The Laurentian chronicle[45] serves as a ready example for consideration. It has been noted that the narrative of the murder of Andrei Bogoliubsky provides clear evidence that it was written during the reign of Vsevolod III and in his lands. In the narrative of events after Bogoliubsky's death, the words "... [those] wishing us ill, envying this city ..." specifically reveal a chronicler of Vladimir. The same evidence is found in the entries for 1180 and 1185. Later we notice a particular attachment on the part of the chronicler toward Konstantin,[46] eldest son of Vsevolod III.

This attachment is evident in the narration of the young prince's journey to and from Novgorod and of his meeting with his father in Moscow. It is evident also in the restraint with which Konstantin's behavior at his father's death is described. Especially striking in the continuing narrative is the failure to mention the particulars of the enmity among the sons of Vsevolod and of the battle on the Lipitsa river.[47] If the chronicle was composed by a supporter of Konstantin after his death then, because of the new situation, it was not in the interest of Konstantin's children that their uncle Yury be reminded of the battle. The chronicler's brief mention of the enmity and his striving to underscore the "great affection" that later came existed among the brothers becomes quite understandable. The particulars of Konstantin's deathbed instructions are given, a lengthy panegyric to him is included and an entry for 1221, which describes the fiery destruction of Riazan, states that the prince's residence was saved by the "prayers of the good Konstantin." It is also evident that after Konstantin's death the chronicler took up residence in Rostov, the city of Konstantin's eldest son.

Furthermore, a phrase in the description of the installation of Mitrofan as bishop of Vladimir in 1227 ("I, a sinner, *chanced* to be there... ") suggests that the chronicler happened to be in Vladimir temporarily, but lived permanently in Rostov. The description of the installation of Cyril as bishop of Rostov, the festivities in his honor, the panegyric to him and, finally, the notation that the writer of the narrative himself recorded Cyril's sermons, all provide convincing evidence that the chronicler resided in Rostov. The Rostov chronicler is revealed further in the description of the invasion by Batu Khan. The details of the death of Prince Vasilko Konstantinovich of Rostov,[48] the panegyric to him, and especially the statement that the boyars who served good Vasilko thereafter could serve no other prince because of Vasilko's great kindness to his servitors, all show the hand of the Rostov chronicler. There is further evidence pointing to him in 1260 in a description of the arrival of Alexander Nevsky in Rostov, and in 1261 in a notation on Bishop Cyril and Archimandrite Ignaty. It is impossible to ascertain totally the relationship of this chronicler to that in Vladimir, but it is very likely that they are one and the same author. The chronicler initially may have lived in Vladimir during the reign of Vsevolod III, and could have been close to his eldest son Konstantin, with whom he later moved to Rostov.

While the Laurentian chronicle carries evidence of the hand of the Rostov, or rather, the Vladimir-Rostov chronicler who was a follower of Konstantin, another variant, while describing the very same events shows clear evidence of a chronicler from Pereiaslavl. In the narration of the death of Andrei Bogoliubsky, where the Rostov chronicler asks Andrei to pray for his brother Vsevolod, the Pereiaslavl chronicler writes "Pray for the forgiveness of our prince and sovereign, Yaroslav, your eternal and noble nephew, give him victory over his enemies, many years with his princess and many noble children." The mention of children leads to the conclusion that the entry was written when Yaroslav was still young and a prince in Pereiaslavl.

Elsewhere, in describing the conditions in the North following the death of Andrei, the Pereiaslavl chronicler also mentions the citizens of Pereiaslavl, whereas the Vladimir chronicler speaks only of those of Vladimir. The entries by the Pereiaslavl chronicler for 1213 gain great significance as he lays out the details of the struggle between Konstantin of

Rostov and his younger brothers, for the Vladimir-Rostov chronicler intentionally omits these details. Unfortunately these detailed descriptions cease in 1214, and the historian is thus deprived of a description of the battle on the Lipitsa that would have been composed by a follower of Yaroslav Vsevolodovich and, consequently, of his ally Yury. It was seen above that the follower of Konstantin intentionally kept silent about this battle. The description of the battle found in the chronicles suggests Novgorod composition.

There are in the Laurentian chronicle some major additions that mark the writing of the Pereiaslavl chronicler, as opposed to his Vladimir-Rostov counterpart. The major part of the accounts is virtually identical yet there are some differences, even contradictions. There is a sharp contradiction under 1208 in the narration of the struggle of Vsevolod III with Riazan. In the Laurentian and other variants it is said that Vsevolod took Pronsk and installed a prince of Riazan, Oleg Vladimirovich, as prince in the city. The Pereiaslavl chronicler writes that Vsevolod installed Davyd , a prince of Murom, as prince in Pronsk, and that the following year Oleg, Gleb and Iziaslav Vladimirovich and Prince Mikhail Vsevolodovich, all of Riazan, came to Pronsk against Davyd saying "Is Pronsk his patrimony," said they, "and not ours?" Davyd sent them a message, saying "Brothers! I myself would not have taken Pronsk. Vsevolod installed me in it. Now the city is yours. I am going back to my own territory."

Prince Mikhail then took Pronsk, while Oleg Vladimirovich died in Belgorod that same year. Of the two contradictory accounts, that which appeared in the text used by this writer[49] was the one found in the majority of the variants. Yet it may be correct to prefer the account of the Pereiaslavl chronicler, for it is difficult to assume that the march of the Riazan princes on Pronsk against Davyd could have been a fabrication. Under the same year, 1208, the Pereiaslavl chronicler has a curious account of Vsevolod III sending his military commander Stepan Zdilovich to burn the town of Serensk. This occurrence is quite probable as an act of revenge by Vsevolod against the Chernigov princes, who expelled his son from Southern Pereiaslavl.

It has been remarked that the major part of the accounts of the two chroniclers are virtually the same. Yet it is difficult to assume that the men were not contemporaries, or that they did not write their accounts simultaneously. Thus it is equally difficult to assume that one author could have copied the other's work, adding something of his own. It is much more likely that the so-called Pereiaslavl chronicle in its composition is a later variant, whose compiler used both the Pereiaslavl and the Vladimir-Rostov chronicles in dealing with the events of the late twelfth and early thirteenth centuries, and that those two chronicles initially were written without connection to each other. Instances even can be found in which the later compiler, drawing on accounts from the two separate chronicles, shows confusion. For example, the Vladimir chronicler, in describing the triumph of Prince Mikhail Yurievich of Vladimir over the sons of Rostislav from Rostov, states "There was great joy in the city of Vladimir, for the grand prince of all the Rostov land was there."

The Pereiaslavl chronicle in an absolutely parallel passage speaks of the installation of Mikhail's brother Vsevolod in Pereiaslavl, and of the great joy of the inhabitants of that city at the event. The later compiler, confused by the two accounts, chose to add to the Vladimir chronicler's account the given name of the prince who appeared in the Pereiaslavl chronicle. So he wrote "There was joy in the city of Vladimir, for the great Vsevolod of all the Rostov land was there." Thus it seems that the variant by the Chronicler of the Russian Tsars, who is called the Chronicler of Pereiaslavl-in-Suzdal in printed works, contains accounts taken from the Pereiaslavl chronicle of the thirteenth century. Does it therefore follow that the whole variant, as it stands now, was compiled by a chronicler of Pereiaslavl who lived in the thirteenth century?

In the Laurentian chronicle from 1285 we cannot avoid noticing evidence of a Tver chronicler. Events concerning Tver are in the foreground, and there is much detailed narration about Mikhail of Tver. The Laurentian chronicle, so significant for its relative antiquity, ends in 1305. It is also noteworthy for the exact indication of when, by whom and for whom it was written. This information appears in a postscript that reads "A merchant is glad upon making a purchase, a helmsman upon reaching port, a wayfarer upon coming home. Similarly a scribe is pleased upon reaching the last of the books. So am I, poor unworthy, sinful servant of God, Lavrenty. I, the chronicler, began copying these books on January 14 in memory of our holy fathers the abbots martyred in the Sinai and the Raifa hermitage, in honor of Grand Prince Dmitry Konstantinovich, and with the blessing of Bishop Dionisy. I completed the work on the March 20, 6885 (1377) in memory of the holy fathers martyred by the Saracens in the monastery of St. Sabbas and during the reign of the faithful and Christ-loving Grand Prince Dmitry Konstantinovich and the Christ-loving and blessed Bishop Dionisy of Suzdal and [Nizhny] Novgorod. Now, dear fathers and brothers, if I have made a mistake or omission, venerate God as you make corrections and do not blame me, for the books are ancient, my mind is young and untutored. Recall the words of St. Paul, saying 'Do not blame but bless.' Christ our Lord, Son of the Living God is with us Christians. To Him is the glory and the power, the honor and the veneration as well as to the Father and the Holy Spirit now and forever. Amen!" Lavrenty, while compiling his chronicle in 1377, had to end it with the year 1305. Though writing for the prince, despite all the means available to him, he could find no accounts of the events marking the beginning of the struggle between Moscow and Tver.

In the Nikonian chronicle[50] also in the second half of the thirteenth century the hand of a Rostov chronicler is most evident. He provides the most detailed descriptions of the Rostov princes, their journeys to the Horde, marriages, character traits and internecine strife. Evidence of a Tver chronicler appears in the last decade of the thirteenth century. It is difficult to ascertain the hand of any particular regional chronicler in the accounts of the first conflict between Moscow and Tver. Then, after 1345, next to the Moscow chronicler, there is again sensed a chronicler of Tver in the details of the strife among the progeny of Mikhail Yaroslavich. Such details continue until the third decade of the fifteenth century. When detailed accounts of Tver events disappear in the Nikonian chronicle, interesting accounts of the relations between Tver and Moscow during the reign of Ivan Mikhailovich appear in the so-called Tver chronicle.[51] This fascinating work, compiled by a Rostov chronicler in the second quarter of the sixteenth century, may not be called properly a Tver chronicle, if only because its compiler used the Tver chronicle for a particular time period. This compilation is important not only because it deals with current Tver events beginning with the reign of Ivan Mikhailovich, but especially because of its account of the Tver uprising against Shevkal.

This writer has long doubted the veracity of the account that Shevkal wanted to convert Russians to Islam. The Tver chronicle recounts the Shevkal affair with more detail and accuracy than other chronicles, not mentioning any intentions of Shevkal about change in faith. Rather Shevkal, in the tradition of all Tatar envoys, oppressed the citizens of Tver, removed Prince Alexander from his residence and made it his own. The people besought Alexander to lead an uprising, whereupon he bade them have patience. Despite this, the bitterness of the Tver citizens reached such a degree that they eagerly awaited the first opportunity to rise up against the oppressors. Such an opportunity came on August 15. A deacon named Diudko was leading a young, well-fed mare to water when the

Tatars tried to take it away from him. The deacon yelled for help, and the people came and attacked the Tatars.

The fact that there existed several chronicles describing events of the end of the first half of the fifteenth century is clearly evident in the Nikonian compilation. Under 1445 there is a brief account of a Lithuanian invasion of Kaluga. Immediately following, the compiler adds two other expanded accounts of the same event and states outright that these were taken from "another chronicler."

Contemporary Northeastern chroniclers expressed themselves much less frequently than earlier annalists on questions of religion and customs, or on political and scholarly matters. Having described the grisly death of the Riazan prince Roman at the Horde, the chronicler addresses the princes with the admonition "O beloved Russian princes! Do not be tempted by the vain and evanescent glory of this world, for it is worse than the spider's web, fleeting like a shadow, vanishing like smoke. You brought nothing with you into this world, and you shall take nothing from it. Do not offend each other, do no evil amongst yourselves, do not take what is another's nor offend your lesser relatives."

The Tver chronicler described a reconciliation among his princes. "Their boyars," he added, "were joyous, and all their grandees, and the foreign merchants, and all the merchants and workers, being all men of the tribe of Adam. For they all are of one clan and the tribe of Adam, all the tsars, and princes, and boyars, and grandees, merchants, craftsmen and workers are all of the tribe of Adam, but they forget this and war against each other, and despise and gnaw and bite at each other, forsaking God's commandments to love another as one's self."

The voice of the Moscow chronicler is heard with special resonance as he describes the invasion of Edigey, blaming the imprudent policies of the younger boyars. "It behooves us to understand why the heathens have attacked us. Is it not clear that the Lord God brings them here for our sins? Should we not pray in repentance? What we have written may strike some as unpleasant, or they may find it indecent that we relate events unflattering to us, but everything said by us is intended to prevent evil and promote good. We have not written this in vexation, or in envy of the honorable, or to revile anyone. We write in emulation of the first Kiev chronicler, who unhesitatingly showed all the events of the land. Our first sovereigns dispassionately willed that everything in the land be recorded, whether it be good or ill. If the reader wishes, he need only read diligently the great Sylvester who wrote without embellishment during

the time of Monomakh.[52] Great blessings, both temporal and eternal, are
gained not through wrath and pride, but through simplicity, tenderness
and humility. Through good will, simplicity and humility our fathers
gained the blessings of this age and of all ages, passing them on to us.
We, having learned from their example, have not failed in recording
everything of our day. Indeed our sovereigns do diligently take heed,
choosing the good. Young men respect their elders and do not rule the
land without consulting them."

The Northern chronicler, apparently a Muscovite, continues to regard
Novgorod and its way of life with hostility. He speaks ill of the people
of Novgorod, calling them severe, unruly, stubborn, inconstant, criminal
and seditious. There is only one passage that reveals anything of the
chronicler's scientific concepts. It deals with "lethal" and "non-lethal"
lightning. "If lightning is merely the result of a collision of clouds it is
not harmful, for it passes by and is extinguished. If, however, during a
cloud collision a heavenly fiery light descends and becomes part of the
lightning it will strike the ground and scorch whatever it touches."

The Novgorod chronicle is no different in nature than before. The
presence of the chronicler is sensed in it under the year 1230. Having
described the death of Abbot Savva of the St. George monastery, the
chronicler adds "God grant His saintly prayer to all Christians and to
myself, sinner Timofey, the sacristan." Elsewhere, instead of this name
we find, " ... and to myself a sinner, John the priest." For 1399 the presence is sensed of a chronicler actively engaged in the affairs of the church
of the Intercession on the Zverinets. In the so-called Fourth Novgorod
chronicle, in an entry for 1384, the chronicler describes a disturbance at
a popular assembly. "The Slavs[53] stood by their prince, and the assembly bell rang for two weeks at the residence of Yaroslav, *but here, on this
side* [of the Volkhov river] three princes held another assembly." The
presence of a chronicler who lived contemporaneously with the events
described is also evident in an entry for 1418. In a description of an event
in 1255 the chronicler states outright that he supports the minority. "Mikhalko fled from the city toward the St. George monastery for how could
he with his troops have defeated *our side?*" If the Moscow chronicler
comments unfavorably on the citizens of Novgorod, the Novgorod chronicler maligns the Muscovites in turn. In the account of Batu's invasion he
reproaches them for cowardice. "The Muscovites fled, seeing nothing before them."

The so-called Fourth Novgorod chronicle has been mentioned, but examination immediately shows such a title to be improper. It is rather a complete compilation of various chronicles, including that of Novgorod. It should not receive a name merely of one of its component parts. In this chronicle, under 1352, we encounter a Pskov chronicler, who speaks at some length of the plague in his city. A Moscow chronicler is sensed under 1371 who, in describing a clash of Muscovites with men of Riazan, refers to the Muscovites as "ours." Interpolations from various chronicles are readily observed. For example, under 1386 there are two accounts of the same event, the siege of Mstislavl by the Smolensk princes. First there is a brief account and then one of some length. For 1404 there are two accounts of the taking of Smolensk by Vytautas.

We learn from the chronicles that at the end of the fourteenth and the beginning of the fifteenth century there was a widespread notion of the imminent end of the world. In 1397 Archbishop John attempted to persuade Novgorod to make peace with Pskov, suggesting that the end of the world was nigh. In this regard a passage under 1402 in the "Fourth Novgorod Chronicle" is extremely revealing. "During Lent, in the month of March, there appeared a sign in the heavens. At twilight in the west there was a fair-sized star in the shape of a spear with a ray shining above it. It appears for our sins. It chastises and transforms and wills us to repentance. I dare say that the prophecy of Scripture is being realized. There are signs in the heavens and peoples have risen against one another— Tatars, Turks, Franks, Poles, Germans and Lithuanians. What can I say of the Tatars and Turks and other peoples false and unbaptized when we, called Christians, true believers and Orthodox, have strife and warfare amongst ourselves? So it happens that a prince of the true faith will rise up against another, his own brother or uncle, and through enmity, lack of humility and malice the matter leads to bloodshed. Warriors, all Orthodox Christians, make war alongside their prince, whether freely or not. In combat they smite each other mercilessly. One Christian raises his hand against another, brother drives spear-point against brother, friend sharpens sword against friend, neighbor shoots neighbor with arrows, relative pierces relative with a pike, clansman kills clansman, a true believer hacks a fellow Christian to death, a youth has no respect for the gray hair of elders, and a servant of God has no mercy for a fellow servant."

The inception of the Pskov chronicles may be traced to the second quarter of the thirteenth century. In terms of their content there is a curious entry in the so-called Second Pskov Chronicle for the year 1352. "In Pskov, the villages and throughout the land there was a fierce plague that was marked by coughing. This has been more extensively written about by the Russian chronicler." The extensive description mentioned apparently was written by another native of Pskov who lived contemporaneously with the events, and may be found in the First Pskov and the Fourth Novgorod chronicles, but it is unclear as to which chronicle is meant when the "Russian chronicler" is mentioned. It does seem clear that the local Pskov chronicle is not the one referred to. As to the nature of the Pskov chronicles, their narrative style is marked by a distinct ingenuousness. There is also a marked affinity on the part of the Pskov chroniclers for certain set expressions in describing established events. We readily see the focus of the chronicler's attention, namely relations with the Livonian Order and with Novgorod. It has been observed above that the complaint against Novgorod's lack of support was a constant refrain of the Pskov chronicler.

A significant change occurred in Northeastern chronicles at the end of the fourteenth century. Calendar years now began with September rather than March as before. At the same time parchment was replaced by paper made of cotton and other rag content.

In the Southwest during the second quarter of the thirteenth century there was a renowned singer named Mitusa. The chronicler says that the man was famous, and that in his pride he refused to serve Prince Daniel. Mitusa apparently was in the service of the prelate of Peremyshl, for he was taken prisoner along with the prelate's servitors. Before Lithuanian rule the Southwestern Rus princes [of the house of Riurik] apparently emulated their predecessors in their love of books. It is written of Vladimir Vasilkovich of Volhynia that he could hold discourse on the content of books, for he was a great philosopher. This prince himself worked at copying books, and it is said that he copied the Gospels and the Acts of the Apostles. It is also known that the prince had other sacred and liturgical works copied and distributed among the churches, and that he purchased a book of prayer for eight grivnas.

It must be said concerning the Southwestern, Volhynian chronicle, that it is odd in its absence of chronological order. The dating in the existing copies was done by later scribes. Initially the chronicle consisted of a continuous narrative, as is clearly seen between the years 1259 and 1260. The following passage of the chronicle for the year 1254 serves to explain the lack of chronology. "In those years, the time past, the chronicler had to write of all and everything that was. Sometimes he moved ahead with time and sometimes he returned to a prior time. The wise reader understood. The number of each year therefore was not written. The distant past was dated according to the Antioch style, the Greek calendar or the Roman as done by Evsevy and Pamfil. Other chroniclers copied from Adam to Christ. All the years were copied calculated from the past."

Here the words "sometimes he moved ahead with time, and sometimes he returned to a prior time" suggest that the chronicler felt hampered by a chronological order which forced him to break the thread of a unified narrative. It also indicates that he understood that a narrative sometimes must be maintained continuously over a number of years. Only then should a chronicler return to events of a different nature.

It must be added that the tale of the death of Prince Vladimir Vasilkovich reveals the hand of a contemporary eyewitness who wrote during the reign of Vladimir's successor Mstislav Danilovich. This is indicated by several words in the address to Vladimir, such as "Rise up and see your brother who adorns the throne of your land and see as well your faithful princess who remains true to you according to your instruction." Concerning the level of literacy of the Volhynian chronicler, it must be noted that he knew of Homer. Thus, for 1232 we read "Sycophancy is evil, as Homer writes. It is sweet until exposed, then it is evil." Russian remained the primary language of literacy and rule even after the establishment of Lithuanian power in Western Rus. The chronicles as well continued to be written in Russian as late as the fourteenth century. There is extant a chronicle from the first half of the fifteenth century which states that it is an abbreviation of older ones. Its narrative is especially marked by naïvety.

X

CONCLUSIONS

This completes the period of Russian history which generally is referred to as "ancient" and deserves a summary of its overall significance and its relation to the subsequent period.

On the broad intersecting routes between Europe and Asia of the great Northeastern plateau between new and old Europe on the route "from the Varangians to the Greeks" there was founded the Russian realm. "Our land is great and bountiful," said the native tribes to the princes whom they summoned. They could not say that their great and bountiful land was well settled, for it was a vast, virginal land awaiting its population and its history. The land's ancient history is a history of settlement. There was a constant and great movement of population over huge distances. Forests were burned and rich soil prepared, though settlers did not remain on it long. The moment labor became more difficult, the settler moved in search of new lands. Everywhere there were expanses ready to welcome the settlers. Land had no value in itself. The valuable factor was population. Rapid settlement, the attraction of population from elsewhere to fill empty space, enticement of people through various privileges, was the practice.

Settlers sought a better place, more advantageous conditions and a locale more peaceful and quiet. The countervailing trend involved the need to hold the population in place, to return settlers who fled, and to make these conditions acceptable and legitimate. These were the central problems of a country being colonized. The population kept moving. The Slavic colonizer, a migratory farmer with an axe, scythe and plow constantly moved northeastward through the land of Finnic hunters and trappers. The readiness to migrate and the habit of moving further at the first inconvenience produced a semi-settled condition and lack of ties to a particular place. This weakened people's morality, accustomed men to the search of easy labor and an improvident, day-to-day existence.

This land was not a colony separated by oceans from its metropolis. It contained within itself the center of a realm, and though the needs and functions of government grew increasingly complex, the land retained the character of colonization. It is easy to understand the difficulties government encountered in subjugating private interests to its own, to understand the origin of the various charters of privilege granted by landholders to settlers.

Because colonization had such striking significance in Russian history its direction is important to the historian inasmuch as it coincided with the direction of general historical movement. The movement is apparent from the chronicler's first lines which speak of the migration of Slavic tribes from the Southwest to the Northeast, from the Danube to the Dnieper and further to the north and east. Consequently the two nations, the Germanic and Slavic, to whom belongs the more recent history of Europe, moved in opposite directions as they divided between themselves the soil of Europe, the future theater of historical events. The Germanic-speaking peoples moved from the Northeast to the Southwest, the Slavic peoples, in contrast, from the Southwest to the Northeast. The destiny of these peoples was determined by this movement, by the natural conditions of the lands they occupied, by the pre-existing ways of life there and the prior relations of the indigenous populations with the newcomers.

A question arises here. Why is it that in the ancient history of the primary Slavic [Russian] realm, the leading Slavic realm in might and independence, there specifically occurred a northeastern movement? If the Germanic tribes in their westward movement destroyed the Western Roman empire, settled in its regions and founded separate realms, why did not the Slavic tribes in moving eastward destroy the Eastern Roman [Byzantine] empire and found new states amid the ruins? Why did they take a northeastward rather than a southeastward direction? The reasons for this are many.

In moving toward the Southeast the Slavs confronted the intense migration of Asiatic tribes who broke through the Caspian gateway and traversed modern-day Southern Russia on their way westward. Well known is the movement of the Huns and Avars and the fate of peoples under their onslaught. The Slavic tribes could not move south or southeast of the middle Dnieper region. Only the northeastward direction remained. Tribes from the mid-Dnieper moved in that direction toward the Desna and Oka rivers where even then they were not safe from the Asians, for they were forced to pay tribute to the Khazars. Although there were Slavic tribes along the lower Danube and a Slavic population even further south on the Balkan peninsula the Slavs were not masters there while the Eastern empire [Byzantium] flourished.

The empire was still strong in the East, for its remaining life forces were gathered there. Thanks to these forces it existed until the mid-fifteenth century. Neither the Goths nor the Arabs could destroy it before that time. The Slavs came closest, yet they lacked sufficient strength. Asiatic peoples, streaming westward, incessantly pushed the Russian Slavs from the South, forcing them into a northeasterly direction. The Western Slavs were restrained by the Germanic peoples. There was no constant flow of new Slavic tribes to the lower Danube or the Balkan peninsula. Consequently the tribes already in those areas were not pressed further by newcomers, unlike the situation in the West among the Germanic tribes. It has been seen how the Magyars once and for all cut the Czech and Moravian Slavs from those of Illyria and the lower Danube, severing the incipient ties between them which began through the intermediacy of a national Slavic church.

The founding of a Russian realm on the great eastern route from the Baltic to the Black Sea, and unification of the Slavic tribes of that region under one rule, perhaps could have changed the state of affairs in the East, for Oleg's ships did appear before Constantinople, Sviatoslav did settle on the Danube. Yet Sviatoslav's fate clearly showed that the first Russian princes could not have the significance for the Eastern empire that Odoacer and Clovis had for the Western. The Slavic tribes which became part of the Russian realm spread broadly and freely across the huge northeastern plain of Europe. They received no shocks from the North or the Northeast. Nothing impelled them to leave their fulsome and bountiful land and set off in search of new territories as did the Germanic tribes in the West. Nothing impelled them to move as a mass from the North to the South. Sviatoslav was not at all a leader of such a migration. He left behind him enormous lands, the sparse population of which had no desire to move south. On the contrary, they wished their prince to stay among them and defend them against the wild nomads of the steppe. "You, Prince, seek foreign lands, while we here were almost overwhelmed by the Pechenegs," said the Kievans in a traditional tale, indicating that they had their own land, and had no need of foreign lands.

Sviatoslav led only a small retinue which, despite its boldness, could not effect any major change on the Balkan peninsula. Forced from the banks of the Danube by John I Tzimisces,[1] Sviatoslav perished in the steppe at the hands of the Pechenegs. This signified that the empire was yet strong enough to fight off the princes of a newborn Rus, and that the steppe barbarians continued to separate the Northeastern Slavs from the empire. Indeed it is well known that communications between Rus and Byzantium were laden with hardship and danger because of the Pechenegs, Polovetsians and Tatars standing between the two lands. An outcome of the clash of the first Russian princes with Byzantium was not the destruction of the empire, rather the acceptance of Christianity by Rus from Byzantium. Noted above is the great influence the ecclesiastical traditions borrowed from Byzantium had on the formation of the Russian realm.

After the founding of the Russian realm, consequently, after the unification of the East Slavic tribes, the main direction of the population movement remained the same, from the Southwest to the Northeast. The Southeastern part was still occupied by Asiatic hordes of nomads, against which newborn Rus had not the strength to undertake any invasion. When the realm was concentrated in the Dnieper region there was a marked tendency on the part of the princes to transfer population from north to south to fill the southern borderland cities and to defend Rus from the steppe barbarians. Soon the reigning conditions prevailed. The steppe borderlands and the Dnieper region were laid waste constantly and severely by the nomads. The towns of the region were emptied, inhabited only by itinerant hunters and Polovetsians. In the words of the princes, where might the Russians flee from captivity and destruction? Surely not to the Southeast, into the very hands of the Polovetsians, nor to the West and the heterodox Poles and Hungarians. There was only one route open, to the Northeast. So it happened that the Rostov region, originally Finnic, received its Slavic population. We have observed how the Northern princes employed the influx of population into their regions, and the meaning of colonization of the North in Russian history, a colonization, a migration which occurred in historical times under the influence and rule of the princes. This is how it was in the twelfth century.

In the thirteenth and subsequent centuries the stimuli which forced the population to move northeast grew stronger. There were the Tatars from the Southeast and Lithuania from the West. The extreme Northeast, not yet under the rule of Russian princes and populated by Zyrians and Voguls, was unattractive and even dangerous to peaceful settlers, who moved in small numbers. Thus, in a manner of speaking, the population was driven from the East, South and West into the heart of the country, where on the banks of the Moscow river a strong governing center developed. We have reviewed the Moscow princes utilizing the advantages of increased population in their region, ensuring the security of the region, and thereby attracting even more settlers, gathering around Moscow all Northeastern Rus.

Thus is, in general terms, the flow of Russia's ancient history. Since the time that Russian history has been studied in a scholarly manner, its particularly outstanding events have been identified. These were pivotal events from which history distinctly developed in a new direction. Historians paused at these developments, using them to divide history into periods. Such events were the death of Yaroslav I, the reign of Andrei Bogoliubsky, the fifth decade of the thirteenth century, Ivan Kalita's accession to power, the death of Vasily the Dark and accession of Ivan III, the demise of the old dynasty and the rise of the new, the accession to power of Peter the Great, and the reign of Catherine II.

Some authors began choosing the most significant of the above events, creating thereby the three major periods of Russian history: the ancient, from Riurik to Ivan III; the middle, from Ivan III to Peter the Great; the new, from Peter the Great until modern times. Some were dissatisfied with these periods, insisting that there could only be two large periods, pre- and post-Petrine. Usually each new author attempted to demonstrate the fallacy of his predecessor's divisions by trying to prove that developments continued past the time limits set by an earlier author. The very traits used by a predecessor to characterize the new period were evident earlier. Such arguments are endless, for nothing in history comes to a sudden end, nothing begins suddenly. The new begins while the old still exists.

There is no place here for arguments of this kind. Attempts to prove the invalidity of earlier periodization are not made, nor new divisions offered. Rather these divisions are accepted and the services of each preceding author is acknowledged, for each in turn illuminate a new facet of the topic and facilitated a better understanding. The divisions and disputes about the validity of these authors' views were once necessary during the very beginning of the study of history. They established points of view, charted subject matter, and drew boundaries along the more conspicuous and celebrated events. First was a position which viewed pivotal events as the exclusive determinants of historical flow. These events were regarded as the end of all that preceded them, and the beginning of all that followed. Gradually scholarship matured to meet the need to unite everything previously divided, to suggest connections between events, demonstrate how the new flowed from the old to unite the several parts into one organic whole. Ultimately there arose a need to replace an anatomical with a physiological approach.

Traditionally most historians first paused at the mid-eleventh century, at the death of Yaroslav I. Here they drew the boundary between the first and second period of Russian history. The boundary was drawn quite correctly but without an immediate connection between the first and second period, and how the second derived from the first. Eighteenth-century historians saw Rus as being born in the first period and falling into division in the second. No connections between the periods were developed although a fortunate historical terminology at least suggested a natural tie between birth and division. Later authors did not employ these useful terms. Rather they attempted to destroy the earlier concepts of continuity and natural derivation, which contradicted latter-day pronouncements such as "The age of St. Vladimir was already an age of might and glory and not of birth. The realm (in the first period) having stepped from cradle to grandeur in one century subsequently grew weak and declined for more than three hundred years (in the second period)."

In reading such statements we inadvertently begin to think that we are dealing with Assyria, Babylonia or Media, those Oriental states which stepped abruptly from cradle to grandeur and subsequently declined. How surprised we must be when it is discovered that the realm in question [Russia], after a decline of three hundred years, renewed itself to become mightier than before. The first period was designated as "Norman" and the second as "appanage." In the first, Normans were placed at center stage and all events flowed from their activity.

In the second period—the division of Russia—struggle among the princes received primary attention. Yet there is the question of the connections between the Norman and the appanage periods? How did the second derive from the first? Certain authors attempted to draw connections between the Norman system and appanage period by saying that the relations of the princes within the appanage system were borrowed from the Normans. Such attempts were laudable yet totally unsuccessful because among the Scandinavians and the Germanic tribes we find nothing resembling the relations found among Russian princes. Nowhere here is a prince succeeded by his brother rather than by his son, or is the principal throne given the eldest of the clan. Similar relations are seen only in Slavic realms. We therefore must conclude that the phenomenon is purely and exclusively Slavic.

A problem arises at this point. During the entire period before the death of Yaroslav the Normans dominated the historical stage acting as Normans, everywhere implanting Norman ways. Yet the dominant phenomenon at the transition to the next period, the relations among princes who were the progeny of the Normans, was decidedly Slavic. We search for Normans everywhere, but in vain.

This very lack of a connection between the first and second period, if the first is designated as the Norman period, illustrates most distinctly the fallacy of the Norman designation. The Normans founded a realm and were its dominant, even exclusive, leaders for two hundred years, then disappeared, whereupon the realm suddenly became Slavic. The fact of the matter is that it was a Slavic state that was founded, with Finns and Normans participating. Then the center of activity immediately moved southward to the exclusively Slavic Dnieper region. The center became established there, which is why Slavic principles dominated completely. We must not find Varangians, chiefs of Varangian retinues, or seafaring raider kings among the first princes. Rather we must discover among these princes rulers of a particular territory with its own specific characteristics and conditions which determined the activity of historical figures. Twice there occurred the event of several princes in new lands, then the competitors vanished immediately to the benefit of one. There occurred a case of several princes yet a third time. They ruled in different regions, this order of things became established for a long time, so it was said that Russia became divided. Let us now examine the nature of this division, its relation to previous characteristics and the first, inceptive period.

History knows various processes of the formation of realms. There is the realm which begins as an inconsequential dot, rapidly achieves huge proportions and in a short time conquers diverse other peoples. Many states are tied through conquest to a single small region, but the connections are not the result of natural processes. Usually such realms fall as rapidly as they rise. This was the fate of the huge Asian realms.

There is another kind of realm that also begins in a minuscule area. Then, over a relatively long period, as a result of constant striving and inner energy, it expands at the expense of neighboring countries and peoples. Ultimately such a realm also disintegrates as the very result of its huge size and absence of inner activity, the disappearance its sap of life. Such was the experience of Rome. No matter what the differences may have been between them the formation of all the huge ancient realms was not organic, usually pieced together as they were through foreign conquests.

There is a different nature to the formation of the new, European, Christian realms. Here the nations because of tribal and particularly geographic conditions at their birth were already located nearly within the boundaries which determined their future activity. These nations experienced a prolonged, difficult and painful process of internal growth and maturation. When this development began these realms usually appeared to be divided. This divergency gradually gave place to unity, and a nation was born. Such organic formation rightfully is the highest. What was the nature of the formation of the Russian realm? Its huge geographic size might lead some to conclude that it was a colossus similar to Assyria, Persia and Rome. We need only study early Russian history a bit more carefully to discover the error of this conclusion. We have reviewed how previous historians characterized Russian history. "A realm which stepped, so to speak, in one century from cradle to grandeur, and subsequently grew weak and declined for more than three hundred years." Such was the previous, superficial view. Currently this description has a totally opposite meaning. What does the phrase "the state stepped in one century from the cradle to grandeur" really mean? It means that the realm was huge at birth and that its size was the work of nature. The extensive Eastern European plain was available as territory for the new realm. This vast plain, watered by great rivers which ran in different directions but had their source in a common geographical basin, inexorably became the area of a single nation.

The country was enormous but unpopulated. Various tribes were thinly scattered over huge distances along the rivers. The new realm, utilizing the convenient water routes, rapidly incorporated local tribes and quickly marked the huge area for itself, even as it remained empty. There was hardly anything except land. Everything had to be established, populated, created. "The land was great and bountiful, but there was no order in it."[2] Like other organically-formed realms the Russian state began a prolonged, difficult and painful process of growth and maturation.

During this era Russia, in similarity to other organically-formed realms appears divided into parts governed by various rulers. Upon closer examination it becomes apparent that despite its superficial division the land preserved unity because the various rulers maintained ties to each other and were dependent on the chief among them. These relations among the rulers and the nature of their dependence on the chief ruler perforce are the primary subject matter for the historian. This factor determined all other relations, setting the flow of events for that time and far into the future.

Based on domestic relations among the rulers the new European realms may be divided into two groups, the Germanic and the Slavic. The first group is marked by so-called feudal relations. The second, especially

Russia which retained its Slavic nature in greater purity, is characterized by the relations of princely family and clan. In the West the ties between the parts of the state depended on the relationship of the ruler of each part to his superior (vassal to suzerain). It was a relationship which grew out of the initial dependence of the retinue members on their leader. In the East the ties between the regions depended on the clan relationship of each ruler to the rulers of other regions as well as to the eldest among them. It was a relationship based on the fact that all the rulers had a common progenitor and on a way of rule which maintained the unity of the princely clan.

This way of rule determined that the most important, senior throne passed to the eldest in the whole princely clan. Both the feudalism of the West and the princely clan relations of the East present curious phenomena. The unity of a people apparently is dissolved, the stage is filled with numerous rulers pursuing private goals with contempt for the rights of others and their own obligations. There a vassal wages war against his suzerain, here a lesser prince arms himself against his senior. The feudal chain in the West and the ties of clan in the East seem weak and insignificant in the face of the fearsome struggle for survival. Despite this, and because of a sense of obligation inherent in human society, these two political bonds were strong enough to preserve the unity of the realms.

No matter the private violations of feudal and clan obligations, they generally were unconditionally acknowledged. The young nations clung to them firmly as bases of their unity. Feudalism in the West and the clan system in the East unquestionably served as guardians of the new European societies during their perilous early years.

These years began to fade for Rus as a strong centralized realm took form and princely clan relationships gave way to monarchy. We have discussed where, how, and under what circumstances the formation of a centralized government develops. We have noted the first blow against an established order, the progress of the struggle between the old and the new and its conclusion. It has been stated that the initial stage of Russian history, marked by the well-known water route from the Varangians to the Greeks, at the end of the twelfth century was a stage incapable of developing into a stable realm.

Life forces initially flowing in a southwesterly direction changed their flow toward the Northeast. Population began to move in that direction, and history marched with it. The regions of the upper Volga were colonized. The influences under which this colonization took place, the resulting relationship of the populace to government, and the relationship of the new towns to the princes that built them, factors which determined the nature of this stage, have been discussed. It has been remarked that the new relationships took effect immediately and how, as a result, a struggle developed between the new and old order. The struggle pitted the centralized realm against the clan system. Victory accrued to the former and Northeastern Russia was assembled into a unified whole. Reviewed as well were the reasons why Moscow was the center of this unification, how its princes took advantage of their central location and the relatively great influx of population, how they increased their wealth and power while subjugating other princes, and resisted the Tatars and Lithuania.

The princes of Moscow encountered few obstructions and many advantages in their activity. They were aided by the absence of strong regional ties, by constant migration, by populations abandoning one principality for another at the first sign of difficulty, and by the generally similar circumstances of everyday life. The princes further benefited from the lack of independence of the Northeastern cities. The voices of these towns consequently were not heeded at important events and conflicts. They were favored by the generally reasonable and placid character of the Northern populace, reluctant to be involved in internecine strife and leaned toward peaceful occupations. A population of this nature quickly was burdened by internecine strife, its disruptions and hardships, and readily realized that a strong prince offered the sole solace to its woes.

Furthermore the populace lost nothing when its prince was subjugated and his lands added to those of Muscovy. People had no reason to lament the loss of a prince's separate lands nor was there strong obstruction by the princes' retinues, whose members were not bound tightly to a prince or principality. Rather, they had the right to flee from a weak to a stronger prince whose service offered greater advantages. Finally those of the highest moral influence, the clergy, favored monarchy from the very beginning.

As for external factors, Lithuania was unable to hinder Moscow's growth, nor long defend the weaker principalities against it. The still-powerful Teutonic Order continued for a time to divert the attention of Lithuanian princes westward. Later, after the marriage of Jogaila and Jadwiga,[3] their attention was engulfed by relations with Poland, the declining Order, Bohemia and Hungary. The incursions of Sweden and the Livonian Order were weak enough that Novgorod and Pskov were capable of withstanding them, and mercenary Tatars were available to any powerful and rich prince.

Great events were taking place contemporaneously in Europe. North of the Black Sea a great blow was dealt to Asiatic rule by the newborn state of Moscow. The battle of Snipe Field was a harbinger of the end of barbarian rule over the great Eastern plateau and marked the rise of a European realm there. To the South enfeebled Byzantium finally fell to the Turks. Christian European nations did not assist the Greek empire. Nor could it have been saved even with the best intentions and the strongest means. Besides the European nations now were preoccupied with their own problems. It was the celebrated fifteenth century when the young European realms, after a difficult domestic process marking the so-called medieval period, were striving toward final consolidation in the West as well as in the East.

The East alone witnessed consolidation of the Northern Russian regions around Moscow, the consolidation of Poland and the formation of a Lithuanian realm primarily on the territory of Southwestern Rus. Poland united with Lithuania under one dynasty, a formal union undermined by difference in religion.

At this point Rome, seizing on Byzantium's distress, sought church unification. Isidore, bearing the title of metropolitan of all Rus, signed the act of union in Florence, an act that was rejected in Moscow, which preferred to remain in the ancestral faith. So happened one of those monumental decisions that shape the fate of nations for centuries. If the struggle between Catholicism and Protestantism, of which Jan Hus[4] was a precursor during this period, extensively determined the fate of Western Europe, the struggle between Catholicism and Orthodoxy set by Moscow's rejection of the Florentine union determined the fate of Eastern Europe. Allegiance to the ancestral faith, proclaimed by Grand Prince Vasily, assured the independence of Northeastern Rus. Later, in 1612, it made it impossible for a Polish prince to ascend the Moscow throne.[5] Vasily's decision further led to a struggle for the faith in Polish lands, facilitated the unification of Ukraine and Russia, contributed to the decline of Poland, enhanced Russia's might and established its ties with the Orthodox peoples of the Balkans.

Such were the circumstances of the formation of Muscovy. The shape which this formation assumed was determined by the interrelationship between the clergy, retinue and populace at large. Relations with the clergy were set by Byzantine traditions. The retinue was not the retinue of conquerors. During the early stages in the South, because of the great number of relatives in the princely clan, retinue members could not become permanent rulers of regions. Given the movement of ruling princes from one region to another, retinue members could not develop into landholders. Only in the North, as princes became permanently established, the retinue members gained opportunities to hold lands. Soon wealthy and powerful families arose. Even so it was soon evident that even the most wealthy and powerful did not retain their positions for long.

Alexis Petrovich Khvost perished, evidently at the hands of his rivals, the Veliaminovs,[6] whose power in turn declined during the reign of Dmitry Donskoy while that of the Koshka family rose.[7] This family then lost influence under Vasily the Dark. Vsevolozhsky,[8] who rose to power while Vasily was a minor, soon fell, and his holdings, just as those of the Sviblov and Konstantinovich families, escheated to the grand prince. The rivalry of families unquestionably had much to do with the elimination of the rank of chiliarch and in general enabled the princes to deal more effectively with dangerous or unsuitable members of the retinue. The overall role of the retinue itself was not contested by the princes.

The significance of the old families also was weakened constantly by the influx of noble newcomers seeking service at the court of the powerful Moscow princes. The later period especially saw the arrival of many princes of Riurik and Gediminas lineage, who preserved their positions of primacy and were ranked above boyars. These new arrivals received superior positions, thus forcing out members of the old families, whose displeasure led to nothing. The princes could do without them, for there were many other willing servitors. It was disadvantageous to leave powerful and wealthy Moscow for service in another principality. If the displeased party departed and began fomenting uprisings and internecine strife, all such activity usually ended with the victory of the Moscow princes. This was the fate of the Veliaminov, Vsevolozhsky and Konstantinovich families.

With constant flux and the arrival of new servitors it was difficult for established relations and positions to take hold. Thus there was always transition and displacement. At the end of the era in the forefront stood those princes and families who earlier were without prominence. As for the relations with the rest of the populace, nothing need be added to what has already been said about the significance of the cities of Northeastern Rus. So it was that the Muscovite realm developed.

NOTES

Additional information on personalities and topics found in the text and notes is available in Edward J. Lazzerini, George N. Rhyne and Joseph L. Wieczynski, eds., *The Modern Encyclopedia of Russian, Soviet and Eurasian History* (MERSH), (formerly *The Modern Encyclopedia of Russian and Soviet History*); Peter Rollberg, George Gutsche and Harry B. Weber, eds., *The Modern Encyclopedia of East Slavic, Baltic and Eurasian Literatures* (MESBEL), (formerly *The Modern Encyclopedia of Russian and Soviet Literatures, Including Non-Russian and Emigre Literatures*); Paul D. Stevens, ed., *The Modern Encyclopedia of Religions in Russia and Eurasia* (MERRE), (formerly *The Modern Encyclopedia of Religions in Russia and the Soviet Union)*; and David R. Jones, ed., *The Military Encyclopedia of Russia and Eurasia* (MERE), (formerly *The Military-Naval Encyclopedia of Russia and the Soviet Union*) all published by Academic International Press.

CHAPTER I

1. Mstislav Mstislavich Udaly (the Daring, died 1228) was the son of Mstislav Rostislavich Khrobroy (the Brave) of Smolensk (died 1178). He was prince of Toropets from 1206, of Novgorod from 1210. He took part in campaigns against the Polovetsians in 1193 and 1203. Having become prince of Novgorod he struggled against Vsevolod III, who continued the expansionist policies of Andrei Bogoliubsky. In 1212 and 1214 he conducted successful campaigns against the Chud and the Livonian knights. Later in 1214, having defeated Vsevolod Sviatoslavich "the Red" he placed Mstislav Romanovich on the Kievan throne. In 1216 he commanded the Novgorod army at the battle on the Lipitsa, overcoming the princes of Vladimir-Suzdal. In 1218 he left Novgorod, defeated and expelled the Hungarians and occupied the throne of Galich. In the battle against the Tatars on the Kalka river in 1223 he showed bravery but was incautious as a commander, causing the defeat of the Rus army. In his final years he once again fought against the Hungarians. Having quarreled with Prince Daniel Romanovich and the Galich boyars, he made peace with the Hungarian king and married his daughter Maria to the king's son Andrew, whom he named as his successor. See entry by Martin Dimnik, MERSH, Volume 23, pp. 154-156.

2. Vasily II Vasilievich was the son of Vasily I Dmitrievich and Sophia Vitovtovna, and also a grandson of Dmitry Donskoy. His reign was marked by bitter internecine strife. Vasily was opposed by a coalition of disaffected princes, led by his uncle, Prince Yury Dmitrievich of Galich and the latter's sons Vasily Kosoy and Dmitry Shemiaka. During the long civil war which coincided with the

struggle against the Kazan khanate, the throne fell several times into the hands of the Galich princes, who were supported by the city of Novgorod and for a time also by Tver. Vasily was blinded by his opponents in 1446, hence his sobriquet "the Dark." He nevertheless triumphed, and over the next two decades, aided by his eldest son, the future Ivan III, he curtailed the previously independent principalities within the Muscovite domain. He also strengthened Moscow's hold over the city and territories of Novgorod (after campaigns in 1441, 1456 and 1460) and annexed the principalities of Suzdal and Nizhny Novgorod. He also formed a more or less permanent alliance with Pskov as a counterweight to Novgorod, and liquidated the independence of the frontier territory of Viatka by campaigns in 1456 and 1457. Vasily II was aided by the church, since during his reign the Constantinople patriarchate was discredited by the events of the Council of Florence in 1439. In 1448 Metropolitan Jonas formally proclaimed the independence of the Russian church from Constantinople, which in any case fell to the Ottoman Turks in 1453. Further details of Vasily the Dark's reign may be found in Volume 5 of this series, Chapters IV-V, and in the entry by Hugh F. Graham, MERSH, Volume 41, pp. 215-219.

3. For a discussion of the role of Andrei Bogoliubsky, see Volume 2 of this series, Chapter VII, and Volume 3, Introduction and Chapter I. An interesting biography of this prince is contained in Ellen S. Hurwitz, *Prince Andrej Bogoljubskij. The Man and the Myth* (Florence, 1980).

4. Vsevolod III (1154-1212), baptismal name Dmitry, was the son of Yury Dolgoruky and his Greek wife Helen. He was given the sobriquet "Big Nest" on account of his numerous progeny, eight sons and four daughters. Yury died in 1157, and Vsevolod's eldest surviving half-brother Andrei Bogoliubsky came to the throne. Vsevolod retired to the new town Dmitrov, but in 1162 Andrei expelled from Rus Vsevolod, his mother and his brothers, who sought asylum with their kinsman the Byzantine emperor Manuel Comnenos. Vsevolod returned to Rus some time before 1169, as he took part in Andrei's sack of Kiev. In 1173 he ruled Kiev for a while, but was expelled by his rivals the sons of Rostislav. This time he sought refuge with the sons of Oleg in Chernigov. When Andrei was assassinated in 1174 the boyars, fearing the advent of another autocratic ruler, invited Andrei's nephews, Mstislav and Yaropolk Rostislavich. As their uncles Vsevolod and Mikhalko came to assert their claims, civil war ensued. The uncles triumphed over the nephews, so Mikhalko occupied the throne of Vladimir in 1176. When Mikhalko died shortly thereafter, Vsevolod succeeded him. Even so, his rulership did not go uncontested. Eventually, defeating the princes who had laid claim to Vladimir, he confiscated their lands and property. He also built up a faction of his supporters in Novgorod. He subjected Riazan to his authority after three campaigns (1180, 1187 and 1201), as well as maintaining control over Kiev and Chernigov. In 1190 he took under his protection Prince Vladimir Yaroslavich of Galich. During Vsevolod's reign the Vladimir-Suzdal principality expanded eastwards through campaigns against the Mordvinians and Volga Bulgars.

Vsevolod also undertook a series of ambitious building projects, both of churches and urban fortifications. See entry by Dimnik, MERSH, Volume 43, pp. 101-105.

5. Roman Mstislavich (died 1205), prince of Novgorod 1168-1169 and of Vladimir-in-Volhynia from 1170 until his death., was the son of the Kievan grand prince Mstislav Iziaslavich and a daughter of the Polish king Bolesław Krzywousty. He waged a successful struggle against the boyar aristocracy and the church hierarchy. In 1168 he seized the Galich throne, giving the city of Vladimir to his younger brother Vsevolod. Soon Roman was forced out of Galich, but with the help of his father-in-law the Kievan prince Riurik Rostislavich he regained Vladimir. In 1195, while intervening in the internecine struggles of neighboring Poland, he suffered a heavy defeat at Mozgawa. In 1199, after the death of the Galich prince Vladimir Yaroslavich, Roman once again seized the principality. Ruling over the united principalities of Galich-Volhynia, he extended his influence into the Kievan domain, thus becoming the most powerful prince in Rus. He conducted active diplomacy with Byzantium, Poland, Hungary and even Rome, whence came the offer of a royal crown if Roman would convert to Catholicism. This offer was refused. To maintain his influence in Polish affairs, he intervened in the interprincely feuds, but eventually lost his life in an ambush at Zawichost on the Vistula river. See entry by Leo Sobel, MERSH, Volume 31, pp. 139-143.

6. Daniel Romanovich (1201-1264), prince of Galich-Volhynia, son of Roman Mstislavich (see preceding Note). In 1211 he was placed on the Galich throne, but was expelled the following year. In 1221 he succeeded to the princely dignity in Volhynia, and by 1229 achieved the unity of the Volhynian lands. In 1223 he participated in the battle on the Kalka, and in 1237 fought against the Teutonic Order. In 1238 he seized power in Galich, giving Volhynia to his brother Vasilko Romanovich. Daniel then occupied Kiev. Struggling resolutely against princely quarrels , as well as the undue influence of the boyar aristocracy and the church hierarchy, he relied upon his lesser servitors and the urban population. He promoted the development of towns, attracting to them artisans and merchants. During his reign the towns of Kholm (his eventual capital), Lvov (which he named after his son Lev), Ugorvesk and Danilov were founded, and Drogichin was refortified. After the Mongol-Tatar invasion of Southwestern Rus in 1240, Daniel acted with compliance towards the invaders. He evidently viewed the Poles and Hungarians as more dangerous foes, especially since the Poles were allied to a faction of dissatisfied boyars within Galich. He defeated this hostile coalition at a battle near Yaroslavl in 1245. After this conflict the unity of the Galich-Volhynian lands was maintained for the next four decades. Daniel also intervened in the succession struggle within the duchy of Austria, promoting the candidacy of his son Roman. In 1254 Pope Innocent IV sent an offer of a royal crown in an effort to promote a reunion of the Catholic and Orthodox churches. Though this early attempt at the creation of a Uniate church was doomed to failure, Daniel retained the royal title, which he passed on to his son. See entry by Nikolai Dejevsky, MERSH, Volume 8, pp. 171-174.

7. The Yatviags were an ancient Prus tribe, ethnically akin to the Lithuanians. They inhabited the territories between the middle courses of the Nieman and Narew rivers. This territory was known as Sudovia and a tribe called the "Sudovians" is mentioned by Tacitus. The name "Yatviag" is first attested in the Rus-Byzantine treaty of 944. They were engaged in agriculture, hunting and fishing, with a few handicrafts. From the tenth century, upon the formation of the ancient Rus principalities, repeated campaigns against the Yatviags occurred (983, 1038, 1112-1113, 1196). In the 1140s and 1150s the princes of Galich-Volhynia and Mazovia between them brought the Yatviags into submission. In 1283 most of these lands were seized by the Teutonic Order, the remainder being incorporated into the Lithuanian grand principality.

8. In 1385 the Lithuanian grand prince Jogaila was betrothed to Jadwiga, daughter of Louis of Anjou and heiress to the Polish throne. Under the terms of the Union of Krewo, Jogaila accepted Catholic baptism and reigned over the combined territories as Władysław II. Henceforth Poland and Lithuania were inextricably linked for the ensuing centuries, and encroached on the lands of Southwestern Rus. "The Union of Krewo was abrogated by Jadwiga's death [in 1399], but the political arguments which inspired it remained operative throughout the Jagiellonian era. On every occasion that serious difficulties arose, they ensured that the Polish-Lithuanian Union was renewed on terms of increasing intimacy. From the personal union of 1385-6, the relationship was gradually strengthened, until in 1569, the prospect of the dynasty's extinction encouraged the creation of a permanent, constitutional union." Norman Davies, *God's Playground. A History of Poland* (Oxford, 1981), Volume I, p. 118.

9. Gediminas (died 1341), grand prince of Lithuania from 1316, waged a relentless struggle against the Teutonic knights, upon whom he inflicted some major defeats. In 1322 he concluded an alliance with the prince of Mazovia, and in 1325 with the Polish king Władysław Lokietek, sealed by the betrothal of the king's son Casimir to his daughter Aldona. Like his predecessors, Gediminas encroached on Western Rus territories, making the princes of Minsk, Lukomsk, Drutsk, Brest and Drogichin his vassals. From 1340 his son Lubartis ruled in Volhynia. Gediminas tried to hinder the unifying policies of Moscow, seeking to detach Novgorod and Pskov from Rus. To achieve this aim, Gediminas relied on his alliance with Tver, sealed by the marriage of his daughter Maria to Prince Dmitry Mikhailovich. Finally, Gediminas began to adopt the title "king of the Lithuanians and Rus." In documents pertaining to the years 1322-1323 there is first mention of the town of Vilnius. Later tradition credits Gediminas with the foundation of the future capital. He met his end fighting the Germans, slain at the siege of Bayerberg.

10. Casimir the Great (born 1310) was king of Poland from 1333 until his death in 1370. He expanded Polish rule into Western Rus, especially Galich, between 1340 and 1352. These western regions were once the far reaches of Kievan Rus and later were ruled by the Horde, as was eastern Russia. In the fourteenth century the peoples of the western regions were Orthodox in religion, linguistically and

ethnically much closer to eastern Russia than they were to either Poland or Lithuania. He ended the long-standing war with the Teutonic Order in 1343, exchanging Western Pomerania for the retrocession of Kujawy. Casimir is also renowned as the founder of the university in Cracow. For more information, see O. Halecki, *A History of Poland* (London, 1978), Chapter 6.

11. The Lipitsa river was the site of a battle in the year 1216 between Novgorod in alliance with Rostov (Prince Konstantin) against the principality of Vladimir-Suzdal (Grand Prince Yury and Yaroslav). Konstantin was the elder brother of Yury and Yaroslav and thus had claim on Vladimir, though he had been passed over in his father's will. Mstislav of Toropets was the elected prince in Novgorod. Yury and Yaroslav were defeated and Konstantin became grand prince of Vladimir. See John Fennell, *The Crisis of Medieval Russia, 1200-1304* (London, 1983), pp. 48-50.

12. Konstantin Vsevolodovich (1186-1218) was the eldest son of Vsevolod III by his first wife Maria, a Bohemian princess. At the age of ten Konstantin was engaged to the daughter of Mstislav Romanovich of Smolensk. In 1205 his father sent Konstantin to rule in Novgorod and in 1207 gave him Rostov and five other towns. In 1211 Vsevolod wished to give Konstantin the principality of Vladimir, with his brother Yury holding Rostov. Konstantin considered Rostov as the senior principality to which as the eldest he felt entitled. A protracted struggle with Yury ensued which ended in 1216 when Konstantin defeated Yury on the Lipitsa river (see preceding Note). Konstantin did not enjoy the supremacy long, as he died less than two years later, leaving among his bequests funding for a Greek school in Vladimir. For further details see Volume 3 of this series.

13. Yaroslav Vsevolodovich (1191-1246), grand prince of Vladimir from 1238, was the third son of Vsevolod III. In 1200 he assumed the rulership of Southern Pereiaslavl, where he took an active part in the struggle with the Polovetsians and the in-fighting among the Rus princes. In 1206 he was forced to leave Pereiaslavl and return to his father, according to whose testament in 1212 Yaroslav received the principality of Pereiaslavl-Zalessk. In the 1220s and 1230s he also ruled intermittently in Great Novgorod, fought its neighbors and furthered the grand-princely designs of his brother Yury. When the latter perished in 1238 in battle against the Tatars, Yaroslav received the grand-princely throne and in the early 1240s tried to subject Kiev to his rule with the aid of the Mongol khan Batu. Fearing the growth of his power, the Mongols summoned Yaroslav to the great khan Güyük at Karakorum, where he was poisoned. See entry by George P. Majeska, MERSH, Volume 44, pp 241-244. Yaroslav was also probably the addressee of the Epistle of Daniel the Exile. See Volume 3 of this series, Chapter VIII, Note 34.

14. Alexander Yaroslavich Nevsky spent the early years of his life in warfare with the Germans, Swedes and Lithuanians, who sought to detach Novgorod and Pskov from Russia. He earned his sobriquet through his victory over the Swedish general Birger Jarl on the Neva river (July 15, 1240). Less than two years later his defeat of the Teutonic knights at the Battle on the Ice on Lake

Peipus (April 5, 1242) compelled the Order to renounce its conquests. In 1252 the khan appointed Alexander grand prince of Vladimir in place of his brother Andrei (see Note 17, below). Alexander therefore did his best to prevent any possible pretext for a Tatar invasion. In 1262 he obtained a mitigation of the tribute and the abolition of the military service hitherto rendered by the Russians to the Tatars. He was canonized by the Russian Orthodox church in 1547, his feast day being commemorated on November 23.

15. Yuriev was founded in 1152 by Yury Dolgoruky and was named for his patron saint. It was called Yuriev Polsky to distinguish it from the town of the same name in the Dnieper basin. From 1212 it was the center of a minor appanage principality, though the line of princes died out in the middle of the fourteenth century and the principality was absorbed by Moscow, which several times assigned its revenues for the upkeep of foreign servitors such as the Lithuanian prince Svidrigaila or the exiled Kazan khan Abdul-Letif. For further information see entry by George N. Rhyne, MERSH, Volume 55, pp. 175-177.

16. Mikhail Yaroslavich Chorobrite (died 1248), brother of Alexander Nevsky, is first mentioned in the chronicles under the year 1238. He became prince of Moscow in 1247 and shortly afterwards acquired the grand principality of Vladimir. He was killed in battle with the Lithuanians on the Porotva river and was buried in the town of Vladimir. Chorobrite is derived from the Russian *khorobryi,* meaning "brave."

17. Andrei Yaroslavich (died 1264) was the third son of Yaroslav Vsevolodovich, prince of Suzdal and grand prince of Vladimir. He was also a brother of Alexander Nevsky, whom he helped defeat the Germans at the Battle on the Ice in 1242. In 1247 the Horde conferred on him the grand-princely title, but in 1252 he was dethroned by Alexander Nevsky and fled to Sweden, where he remained until 1256. On his return to Rus his brother assigned him the appanages of Gorodets and Nizhny Novgorod. In 1259 Suzdal was added to his holdings.

18. Ivan Danilovich Kalita (date of birth unknown, died 1340) was the fifth son of Prince Daniel Aleksandrovich (see following Note). Ivan was prince of Moscow from 1325, then concurrently grand prince of Vladimir from 1328. He justly earned a reputation for cruelty and avarice, but is also acknowledged as an astute ruler. He sought to maintain the goodwill of the Horde, on whose behalf he collected huge amounts of tribute (vykhod). He dealt ruthlessly with rival princes, in particular Prince Alexander Mikhailovich of Tver, upon whom Khan Uzbek took his revenge in 1439 at Kalita's instigation. After this incident Tver never again posed a serious threat to Muscovite supremacy in Northeastern Rus. Moscow's hegemony became unquestioned throughout the Novgorod lands, Rostov, Uglich, Galich and Beloozero. Ivan Dmitrievich amassed enormous wealth, hence his sobriquet "Moneybags." It was also during his reign that Moscow became the permanent residence of the metropolitan. See entry by Emily V. Leonard, MERSH, Volume 15, pp. 35-40.

19. Daniel Aleksandrovich (1261-1303), son of Alexander Nevsky, around 1276 received from his brother the relatively minor appanage of Moscow. Taking advantage of interprincely quarrels, he greatly enhanced the importance of his principality. In 1283 he supported his brother Andrei against the grand prince, but from 1296 to 1301 he fought Andrei in alliance with the Tver prince Mikhail Aleksandrovich. In 1300, having defeated the prince of Riazan, he annexed Kolomna and a number of lesser districts. In 1301 he received Pereislavl-Zalessk as a bequest from Prince Ivan Dmitrievich. Daniel is generally regarded as the founder of the fortunes of the house of Moscow.

20. Mikhail Yaroslavich (1271-1318) was prince of Tver from 1285. Until 1300 in combination with the Muscovite and Pereiaslavl princes he waged a struggle against the grand princes of Vladimir, Dmitry and then Andrei. In 1300 Mikhail effected a rapprochement with Andrei, whom he succeeded on the grand-princely throne in 1305. The Moscow prince Yury Danilovich thus became Mikhail's chief rival. The attempt by Mikhail to impose his own candidate for the metropolitanate led to a struggle with Moscow in alliance with Novgorod and the remaining church hierarchy. In his struggle for the grand-princely dignity he became the first to style himself "grand prince of all Russia." In 1317 Uzbek assigned the grand-princely dignity to Yury, who advanced on Mikhail with Tatar forces. Although he was victorious at the battle of Bortenevo (December 22, 1317) he decided to submit his claim in person to the arbitration of the khan. There he was outwitted by Yury's agents who contrived his execution. He was later canonized by the Orthodox church. For further details see entry by Graham, MERSH, Volume 22, pp. 55-57.

21. Yury Danilovich (c. 1280-1325) was the eldest son of Daniel Aleksandrovich (see Note 19, above). After his father's death in 1303 he inherited the Moscow principality. His brother Ivan (Kalita) secured his hold on the principality of Mozhaisk, thus controlling the whole course of the Moskva river. In 1304 the death of Grand Prince Andrei Aleksandrovich of Vladimir accentuated the problem of the entitlement to the grand-princely dignity, contested between Yury and Mikhail Yaroslavich of Tver. Yury journeyed to the Horde, but his attempt was unsuccessful. After the appointment of Metropolitan Peter, Yury formed a very close bond with the head of the Russian church. With Peter's encouragement, in 1311 Yury seized the principality of Nizhny Novgorod and placed his brother Boris there. In 1314 he allied himself with Novgorod against Tver and sent his vicegerents there, though Mikhail succeeded in regaining control. Yury then sought Tatar help, spending two years at the Horde, where he married Konchaka (baptismal name Agafia), sister of Khan Uzbek. After forming that alliance, Yury returned to Rus in 1317 with the patent to the grand-princely throne, Tatar troops and the eminent Tatar official Kavgady. He devoted the next years to the conflict with Mikhail of Tver who, despite his victory at Bortenevo, agreed to submit to arbitration at the Horde. There Mikhail was executed, allegedly as a result of Yury's intrigues, including accusations of embezzlement of tribute money and of having poisoned Konchaka. Yury reigned as

grand prince unmolested until 1322 but his position was much less enviable than it appeared. The Tatars were watching him closely. He had to contend with latent hostility in Tver. He also felt concern over the increasingly independent stance of his younger brother Ivan who spent the years 1320 to 1322 at Saray, ingratiating himself with the khan. Perhaps a combination of these factors led him to accept the invitation to be prince in Novgorod, currently menaced by the Swedes. By now Mikhail's son Dmitry was fostering plans to avenge his father's death. While Yury was preoccupied in the North, Dmitry travelled to Saray, where he persuaded the khan to appoint him as grand prince and summon Yury to the Horde. On his return from Finland in 1322 Yury had no choice but to obey the khan's order. Escaping an ambush by the men of Tver, he fled back to Pskov. Angered by Dmitry's presumption, Uzbek let matters rest, and allowed Yury to return to Novgorod. There he rendered the city a signal service. He secured control of the Neva river by building the fortress of Oreshek, and in 1323 secured the Treaty of Orekhov, which guaranteed the security of the Russo-Swedish frontier. In 1324 Yury led a Novgorod force to the far Northeast where they established a permanent presence at Ustiug on the Northern Dvina river. Apparently at this juncture Yury received another summons from the Horde. He sailed down the Kama and Volga rivers to Saray. There he encountered his nemesis Dmitry Mikhailovich who took the law into his own hands and slew Yury on November 21, 1325. Dmitry himself was executed at the Horde on August 15, 1326. Yury's body was brought back to Moscow and was solemnly interred by Metropolitan Peter in the Archangel cathedral. For further details see MERSH, Volume 45, where there are two entries on the same topic, by Richard Hellie (pp. 68-70), and Hugh F. Graham (pp. 71-73). In conclusion Graham states "The khans of the Golden Horde determined whether Yury Danilovich would prevail over his rivals or whether they would prevail over him. It was they who ensured that neither Tver nor Moscow would come to enjoy a decisive advantage during the frustrating course of their long struggle. Ivan Danilovich, better known to history as Kalita, succeeded Yury in Moscow. He has been hailed as the founder and architect of the Grand Duchy of Moscow. Not to belie his shrewdness, external circumstances over which he had no control, such as the intensifying factionalism in the Golden Horde and the rise of Lithuania, contributed much to his success. He was luckier than his older brother."

22. Alexander Mikhailovich, born 1301, prince of Tver from 1326, in which year he also received the patent for the grand principality of Vladimir. The second son of Prince Mikhail Yaroslavich, he vigorously contested the growing power of Ivan Kalita. At the time of the 1327 uprising against the Tatar baskak Chol Khan, he tried to restrain the insurgents. Nevertheless he was accused of complicity and was deprived of the grand-princely title. Alexander Mikhailovich was forced to flee with his brother Konstantin to Pskov, where he was proclaimed prince. Ivan Kalita embarked on a campaign against Pskov, on which Metropolitan Theognostos also laid an interdict. Alexander then fled to Lithuania in 1329,

returning to Pskov with Lithuanian help in 1331. In 1337, at the Horde, he regained the grand-princely title and his principality of Tver but, according to the chronicles, in 1329 was summoned before the khan, who had him executed along with his son Fedor. See entry (unsigned) in MERSH, Volume 1, p. 99.

23. See Fennell, "The Tver Uprising of 1327. A Study of the Sources," *Jahrbücher für Geschichte Osteuropas*, 15 (1967), pp. 161-179; also Robert O. Crummey, *The Formation of Muscovy, 1304-1613* (London, 1987), pp. 35-39.

24. This theme was later and more famously developed by Soloviev's onetime pupil Kliuchevsky. See V.O. Kluchevsky [sic], *A History of Russia*, translated by C.J. Hogarth (London, 1911, reprinted New York, 1960), Volume 1, Chapter XIII.

25. Tokhtamysh (died 1406) was the son of Tui-Hojji and a descendant of Khan Juchi. During the 1370s he fled to Tamerlane who gave him lands in Otrara (southern Kazakhstan) and Saurama in the Syr-Daria basin. With the aid of Tamerlane he took advantage of Mamay's defeats by the Russians to seize power at the Horde. In 1382 he succeeded in capturing Moscow, which he plundered and burned. In the course of his retreat he subjected other Russian towns to similar treatment. He also tried to play the princes of Suzdal-Nizhny Novgorod against Moscow. He attempted to free himself from Tamerlane's tutelage and in 1389 attacked his domains. He proved unequal to the struggle and in 1395 lost all his lands east of the Volga. In 1398 he was defeated by Temir Kutluy, khan of the Transvolga Horde, and suffered an even more decisive defeat on the Vorskla river, when in conjunction with Vytautas of Lithuania he invaded Muscovy in 1399. Eventually Tokhtamysh was killed by the Siberian khan Shadibek on orders of Tamerlane. For further details see entry (unsigned) in MERSH, Volume 54, pp. 69-70.

26. In Russian *ordyntsy* (pl.).

27. See *The Testaments of the Grand Princes of Moscow*, translated and edited by Robert Craig Howes (Ithaca, N.Y., 1967). The text of Ivan Kalita's will is reprinted, pp. 115-119, with translation, pp. 182-187.

28. Appanage is a term denoting the hereditary lands of a prince. Since there was no law of primogeniture among the Eastern Slavs (no right of the first born to claim the whole patrimony) there was a large number of such "mini-states." They dominated political life after the fall of Kiev and until the ascendancy of Moscow.

29. "And concerning the small village on the Kerzhach, which I purchased from Abbot Porfiry, another, Leontievskoe, [and] a third, Sharapovskoe, now I give [them] to the [Monastery of] Saint Alexander, for the memory of my soul." Howes, *Testaments*, p. 187. Since Alexander Nevsky was not canonized until the mid-sixteenth century it is uncertain to which saint the monastery in question was dedicated.

30. Simeon Ivanovich "the Proud" (1310-1353) was grand prince of Vladimir and Moscow, the eldest son of Ivan Kalita. He acceded to the Muscovite throne in 1340, the following year receiving from the khan the yarlyk (patent) to the

grand-princely throne of Vladimir. His foreign policy was based on collaboration with the Horde, to which he travelled repeatedly. He also fought against Lithuania, conducting a campaign against Smolensk in 1351. His capture of Torzhok in 1341 assured his ascendancy over Great Novgorod. His treaty with his brothers (1350 or 1351) and his testament are evidence of the greatly enhanced authority of the eldest among the princes of the House of Moscow. He died of the plague (the Black Death) that swept Asia, the Mediterranean basin and Europe. Since his sons predeceased him, Simeon's younger brother Ivan (II) became prince of Vladimir-Moscow (see following Note). For further information on the reign of Simeon the Proud, see Volume 4, pp. 145-159. Of the six sons mentioned by Soloviev there are traces of only four, Ivan and Semeon who died of the plague March 18, 1353, and two sons who died in infancy, Daniel and Mikhail from his third wife Maria of Tver, whom he married in 1347. His will is reprinted in Howes, *Testaments*, pp. 119-120, with translation, pp. 189-192.

31. Ivan II Ivanovich (1326-1359), second son of Ivan Kalita, was prince of Zvenigorod and Rusa from 1340 to 1353, when his elder brother Simeon (see preceding Note) died of the plague. Ivan's epithet was "the Meek," also "the Fair." For further information see entry by Graham, MERSH, Volume 15, pp. 40-42. Although the epithets applied to him scarcely are indicative of great strength of character, it has been pointed out that the system of primogeniture became strengthened as a result of his reign"…for three quarters of the fourteenth century the title [of grand prince] and all that went with it were firmly in the hands of the Danilovichi and it only passed from brother to brother when there was no male heir. From Ivan II…to the extinction of the line at the end of the sixteenth century, fathers were succeeded by eldest sons, except during the brief period of civil war in the mid-fifteenth century. The principle of primogeniture had ousted the archaic system of lateral succession." Fennell, Crisis, p. 164.

32. The will of Ivan the Fair is reprinted in Howes, *Testaments*, pp. 120-125, with translation pp. 195-202.

33. See Note 29, above.

34. It has been noted that this Princess Uliana could not have been the daughter-in-law of Kalita, as Karamzin supposed. Rather, from the edict on districts it is clear that she was Kalita's second wife and the stepmother of Simeon and Ivan. (Soloviev's Note)

35. *Starshii put'*, which Howes (p. 209) translates as "the larger revenue." "Here the word *put'* is used to mean income from property." The second testament of Dmitry Donskoy is reprinted in Howes, *Testaments*, pp. 126-130, with translation, pp. 208-217.

36. The Veliaminovs were an old and renowned boyar family. Ivan Veliaminov's father, Vasily, was the chiliarch in Moscow during the reign of Dmitry Donskoy. Ivan expected to be appointed chiliarch (tysiatskii) at his father's death in 1374. Instead Dmitry abolished the office. Ivan then fled to Tver and became a bitter opponent of Dmitry, even seeking Mongol aid against Moscow. He was caught and publicly executed in Moscow in 1379, an unprecedented

fate for someone of such high rank. The family subsequently fell into disfavor and decline.

37. The query is Soloviev's.

38. Fedor Sviblo was an influential boyar during the reign of Vasily I. See Volume 5, Chapter III, Note 16.

39. The Russian word was *oprichnina*. There was once a word *oprich* which meant "except," or "except for." It often appeared at the end of testaments in which property was assigned in the customary manner "except for" certain lands which went to the widow who was usually mentioned last. Much later Ivan IV (the Terrible) used this precedent to confiscate lands from the boyars in his drive to centralize the principality. See Volume 10 of this series.

40. The Morozov family was one of the old and powerful boyar clans of Vladimir. Some of the others were the Kutuzovs, the Vorontsovs and the Veliaminovs.

41. Vasily Yurievich Kosoy ("the Squint-eyed,") born before 1420, died 1448) was the eldest son of Prince Yury Dmitrievich of Zvenigorod. After his father's death in 1434 he took advantage of the confusion and proclaimed himself grand prince of Moscow yet failed to gain the support even of his younger brothers, and was forced to abandon the capital. After suffering defeat on the Kotorosl river he was unable to continue the war against his cousin Vasily II, with whom he made his peace in 1436, receiving the appanage of Dmitrov. The peace was broken in less than a month. At the battle of Skoriatino, near Rostov, Kosoy was captured and, on the grand prince's orders, blinded. There is no information concerning the last twelve years of his life.

42. Dmitry Yurievich, surnamed Shemiaka (1420-1453), was the second son of Prince Yury Dmitrievich of Zvenigorod. After the death of his father and the blinding of his elder brother Vasily Kosoy (see preceding note), both of which occurred in 1436, Shemiaka led the resistance to Grand Prince Vasily II, whom in 1446 he captured and blinded. Thereafter he briefly occupied the throne of Moscow, then was forced to relinquish it when he received no support from the Moscow boyars or the spiritual leaders. Later he conducted a desultory struggle for power, to no avail. He died in Novgorod, according to some accounts a victim of poisoning.

43. Dmitry the Fair (*Krasnyi* in Russian) was a brother and ally of Dmitry Shemiaka. He was born some time between 1420 and 1433, and died in 1441. During what might be called a Muscovite civil war Yury of Galich deposed Vasily II and occupied Moscow in 1434 but suddenly died that same year. His eldest son Vasily Kosoy assumed the title of grand prince. He in turn was deposed by his brothers Dmitry the Fair and Dmitry Shemiaka who had made a pact with Vasily II and called him back to Moscow.

44. Ivan Andreevich, prince of Mozhaisk, was born before 1430 and died some time between 1471 and 1483. He fled to Lithuania in 1454.

45. *Dan'* was one of the earliest Slavic words used to designate the tribute paid to conquerors. The word was first used to indicate the tribute paid to the

Varangians and the Khazars by their Slavic subjects. Later the term was used for the tribute paid to the Mongols by the Russians. During the Muscovite period of Russian history *dan'* was the tax paid directly to government officials. Such tribute also was often called *dannye den'gi* (given money).

46. Sophia Vitovtovna (died 1453) was the daughter of Vytautas (Vitovt) of Lithuania (reigned 1392-1430) and wife of Vasily I of Moscow (reigned 1389-1425). The testaments of Elena and Sophia reveal that women had the right to hold property in this period and could bequeath it to persons of their choosing. For further information, see Volume 5, Chapter II, Note 2.

47. Fedor Koshka (Fedor Goltiaev-Koshkin) was a boyar of Dmitry Donskoy who counseled cautious dealings with the Mongols and apparently was skeptical of the campaign against Khan Mamay in 1380. Koshka was the progenitor of the Romanov dynasty.

48. Vasily II the Dark had two sons named Andrei. One was Andrei *Bolshoi* (the Greater, the Elder) (1446-1493) and the other was Andrei *Menshoi* (the Lesser, the Younger) (1452-1481). The older Andrei was Vasily II's third son, also known in the Russian chronicles as Goriay. On the death of his father he was given the appanage of Uglich and Zvenigorod, then became one of the most forceful proponents of the unification policies of Ivan III, though his own personal ambition led him and his brother, Boris of Volok, to unite with King Casimir IV of Poland in 1480. Ivan was forced to placate Andrei with the annexation of Mozhaisk. In 1491 he refused to supply troops for Ivan's army when such service was demanded of him. For this he was seized and imprisoned in a dungeon, where he died. The youngest Andrei was the seventh son of Vasily II. On the accession of his brother Ivan III he received the appanage of Vologda. In 1472 Ivan allowed him to annex Tarusa to his appanage. Andrei supported Ivan in his policies of annexation and unification and in his work of increasing the power of the grand prince. When Andrei died childless he bequeathed his lands to the grand prince.

49. Boyars were the owners of large landed estates and thus made up the upper level of society. They were higher than the gentry but did not necessarily have princely titles.

50. During his reign Vasily II the Dark continuously sought dominion over Novgorod. At one point an army was sent against that city. Prince Ivan Striga-Obolensky and the boyar Fedor Basenok were commanders of a detachment that seized the Novgorod town of Rusa and then repulsed a relief column of cavalry inflicting great losses on it. This defeat caused Novgorod to sue for peace and enabled Vasily to extend greatly his control over it.

51. The Russian term was *okupnyi*. It generally referred to not very powerful princes to the north and northeast of Moscow whose lands were not conquered militarily but acquired through purchase. It was often advantageous for such "lesser" princes to seek vassalage and protection from Moscow.

52. The river referred to here is the Northern Dvina, which flows northward and drains into the White Sea. The Dvina lands were almost continuously contested by

Novgorod and Moscow. It is referred to as the Northern Dvina to distinguish it from the Western Dvina (Daugava), which drains into the Gulf of Riga.

53. Taidula (often referred to as *tsaritsa*, "empress" in Russian) was a favorite and influential wife of Khan Uzbek (ruled 1313-1341). After Uzbek's death she remained an influential figure in the Horde. Taidula became well-disposed towards the Russians, Moscow in particular, after Metropolitan Alexis according to the chronicles miraculously cured her of an eye disease in 1357.

54. Concerning baskaks, see Chapter II, Notes 7 and 13.

55. Oleg Ivanovich (1350-1402), grand prince of Riazan, was often an adversary of Dmitry Donskoy of Moscow. The opposing forces met in a decisive battle in 1372 at which Oleg was defeated and "barely escaped with a few men of his retinue," states the Nikonian Chronicle. Oleg also allied himself with Dmitry's enemies in 1380. For further details see entry by David M. Goldfrank, MERSH, Volume 26, pp. 7-9.

56. Vytautas (Vitovt, Witold), grand prince of Lithuania, born 1350, reigned 1392-1430, was the son of Kestutis. After the union of Poland with Lithuania in 1395, Vytautas supported the struggle of the Lithuanian boyars against what was perceived as undue Polish influence. As a result he was appointed deputy for his brother Jogaila. He tried to hinder Moscow's attempts to unite the Northeast Russian lands, and concluded alliances with principalities hostile to Moscow, such as Tver, Riazan and Pronsk. He annexed Pskov in 1404, and three times (1406-1408) invaded Muscovite possessions. Under Vytautas Lithuanian domains extended as far east as Mozhaisk and the headwaters of the Oka. After being on the losing side at the battle on the Vorskla he nevertheless took from the Tatars the region of Southern Podolia and extended his possessions to the Black Sea shore. He also fought vigorously against the Teutonic Knights, whom he and Jogaila defeated at the battle of Grunwald in 1410. In 1422 he regained Samogitia, annexed by the Order in 1398. The abolition of certain ancient Rus principalities (Podolia, Kiev, Vitebsk) led to enhancement of the political significance of the Lithuanian boyars. In the latter part of his reign his policy towards Moscow was pacific. Vasily I married Vytautas's daughter Sophia in 1392, and in his will Vasily appointed Vytautas guardian for his ten-year-old successor to the grand-princely throne. See entry by Sobel, MERSH, Volume 42, pp. 139-144.

57. Batu (died 1255) was the second son of Juchi, grandson of Genghis Khan. After his father's death in 1227 Batu inherited his ulus. Between 1237 and 1240 he launched devastating raids into Eastern Europe. In 1243 he established himself on the Lower Volga, where the khanate of the Golden Horde arose.

58. Chernigov-Seversk was the name of the principality of Chernigov and the lands to the north of Kiev (Severia), centered on Novgorod-Seversk.

59. Soloviev uses *Rubrukvis*, the routinized name of Friar William of Rubruck (Rubuquis). He headed a mission sent by King Louis IX of France to establish peaceful relations with the Mongols. Louis had been on a crusade in the Middle East and was concerned with Mongol intentions. Traveling via Byzantium

William's party reached the Horde in July 1253 and the capital of Mongolia in December of the same year. Nothing definite came of the mission, but William did leave a description of his embassy, *Journey to Mongolia*. See Volume 4, Chapter I, Notes 83-84.

60. Pimen was a Russian cleric. While still an archimandrite (archpriest) he accompanied Mitiay on his journey to Constantinople seeking consecration from the patriarch. Mitiay died on the way and Pimen was consecrated metropolitan in 1378. Dmitry Donskoy of Moscow would not accept Pimen as metropolitan and had him incarcerated upon his return to Russia. Cyprian then became metropolitan. See Chapter VII, Notes 20 and 21.

61. It is uncertain to which prince Soloviev here refers. The only prince of that name and patronymic was Vasily Vladimirovich of Serpukhov, son of Vladimir Andreevich. Possibly he considered the Serpukhov princes as a cadet line of the house of Moscow.

62. Algirdas (Olgerd) (died 1377) was one of the seven sons of Gediminas among whom on his death he divided his domains, leaving the youngest, Yevnut Ivan, in charge of the capital. With the aid of his brother Kestutis, in 1345 he expelled Yevnut from Vilnius and proclaimed himself grand prince. His reign saw the development of Lithuania into one of the most powerful realms in fourteenth-century Europe. He was faced with simultaneous threat from the Teutonic Knights in the North and the Tatars in the South, while Muscovy and Poland were frequently hostile competitors rather than reliable allies. He sought to extend his influence in the Rus lands. He secured the election of his son Andrei as prince of Pskov and built up a pro-Lithuanian faction in Novgorod. He also annexed a number of Kievan principalities in the wake of the retreating Tatars, whom he defeated at the Blue Waters on the Bug river in 1362. The remnants of the Kipchak Horde eventually retreated to the Tauride peninsula where they reconstituted themselves as the Crimean khanate. In the North, Algirdas's faithful coadjutor Kestutis kept the Order at bay. Some historians suggest that were it not for the pressure of the Germans it would have been Lithuania rather than Muscovy that would have secured hegemony in Eastern Europe. Shortly before his death Algirdas accepted baptism and tonsure. He had been sympathetic to Orthodox Christianity, though his son Jogaila was to opt for Catholicism prior to ascending the Polish throne.

63. The prince's agent was a *tiun* in Russian. The position was that of a lower level administrator similar to a bailiff with the meaning sometimes extending to include the functions of a sheriff.

64. Grand Prince Yury Danilovich of Moscow waged war against the Swedes in 1323. He laid siege to the city of Vyborg (present-day Viipuri), and built a fort on an island at the mouth of the Neva river. It was there that a peace treaty with an envoy of the Swedish king was signed.

65. The lands of Savolaks, Eskis and Egrepia to the north of the Gulf of Finland were populated by the Finns and Karelians, a related Finnic speaking tribe.

CHAPTER II

1. "Appanage" is the commonly used though not entirely satisfactory translation of *udel*. Originally it was the term used to designate the property which an heir received from the estate of his father. In political terminology the udel was land held by an independent prince, hence an appanage. Their emergence from the thirteenth century was a consequence of the political fragmentation of Rus, as large principalities were reduced to a number of udels, then subdivided again as additional allotments and apportionments were made to heirs. As the princes of Moscow pursued their objective of unifying the Russian lands under centralized authority they abolished the udels and brought these lands under their own jurisdiction, largely completing this process by the end of the sixteenth century. Some historians have designated the era from the mid-twelfth to the mid-fifteenth century in Russian history as an "appanage period," a view to which Soloviev does not subscribe.

2. The text of the two variants of Ivan Kalita's will is given in Howes, *Testaments*, pp. 115-119, translation, pp. 182-186.

3. For the two wills of Dmitry Donskoy (1375 and 1389), see Howes, *Testaments*, pp. 125-130, translation, pp. 203-217.

4. See Chapter I, Note 35, above.

5. The text of Vasily II's will is reprinted in Howes, *Testaments*, pp 137-143, translation, pp. 242-266.

6. Vladimir Andreevich "the Brave" (1353-1410), appanage prince of Serpukhov and Borovsk, was the son of Andrei, the youngest son of Ivan Kalita. He took part in Moscow's campaigns against Tver (1375), Riazan (1385) and Novgorod (1392). He also fought against the Lithuanians in 1370 and 1379, but his chief claim to fame was as Donskoy's right-hand man in the Snipe Field campaign of 1380. He led the Muscovite forces in 1382 against Tokhtamysh at the battle of Volok, and took charge of the preparations in 1398 in anticipation of Donskoy's campaign. He also took charge of operations during Edigey's invasion in 1408. As a first cousin of Dmitry Donskoy he received a third of the revenues of Moscow. His relations with the grand princes were regulated by treaties confirming his subordinate status.

7. For details regarding Yury Dmitrievich, see Volume 5, Chapter I, Note 7.

8. There were various economic arrangements between tenant farmers (not to be confused with slaves) and landholders. The tenant farmers were obligated to perform a specified amount of work on the landholder's lands, or else they paid in kind (produce), or they paid in money. The mutually agreed upon sum would reflect an equivalent amount of work or produce. This third arrangement was called *obrok* in Russian. It is similar to quitrent.

9. See Volume 5, Chapters IV-V.

10. Namely Mstislav Vladimirovich (died 1036), son of Vladimir Monomakh. See entry by Goldfrank, MERSH, Volume 23, pp. 156-157.

11. The Russian term is *machekhich*.

12. For details concerning Metropolitan Jonas, see Volume 5, Chapter V, Note 6.

13. See Chapter I, Note 39, above.

14. Casimir IV (1427-1492) was the youngest son of King Władysław-Jogaila. In 1440 he was crown grand prince of Lithuania, in 1447 king of Poland. In 1454 he married Archduchess Elisabeth. Casimir was politically astute and patient. He conducted a thirteen-year war against the Teutonic Order (1454-1466) asserting his suzerainty over the Order's lands and making the grand master his vassal. On election of his son Władysław as king of Hungary in 1471 and Bohemia in 1490, Casimir extended his influence over much of Central Europe.

15. Cyril of Beloozero (1337-1427) was the founder of the monastery which bears his name. In secular life he was known as Kozma, and served as treasurer to his relative Timofey Vasilievich Veliaminov, lord-in-waiting to Dmitry Donskoy. He became a monk in 1380, and rose to become archimandrite of the Simonov monastery in Moscow. In 1397 he founded the Beloozero monastery, which rapidly acquired extensive endowments. Cyril also took part in the compilation of the *Book of Degrees* and was the author of several homiletic works. Fennell, *A History of the Russian Church to 1448* (London, 1995), pp. 207-208.

16. *Gospodin,* later *gospodar'* or *gosudar'*.

17. *Ospodar'* and *osudar'*.

18. *Chernye liudi*, the so-called "black people" who were free peasants living on lands not belonging to manors or the church. They were of the lower economic class. A ready economic differentiation was made between those who ate bread made of wheat (expensive) and those who ate the cheaper rye bread (dark or black). At this time, before the importation of potatoes under Catherine the Great, grains made into bread were the primary year-round staple.

19. The words are Greek for St. John the Apostle who is also venerated as Saint John the Theologian, traditionally held to be the author of the Fourth Gospel and the Book of Revelation, also known as the Apocalypse.

20. St. Demetrius, the nameday saint of Dmitry Donskoy, was a martyr of unknown date. According to some accounts he was a deacon who met his death in Sirmium (Mitrovica), but the center of his cultus came to be Salonika. The story there was that he was a local man who was killed without trial for preaching Christianity during the reign of Emperor Maximian (286-305) . The legend grew and Demetrius was represented as a proconsul and famous warrior saint after the fashion of St. George, St. Procopius and others. The soldier of Christ became a literal soldier, who suffered martyrdom. Salonika claimed to have his relics and he became famous all over the East. His feast day is celebrated on October 8. See Donald Attwater, *The Penguin Dictionary of Saints*, second edition (Harmondsworth, 1983), p. 102.

21. Basil of Caesarea (320-379) was the grand prince's nameday saint. His feast day is January 2 in the Eastern church, June 14 in the Western. Basil was born into a fervent Christian family. Having studied at Constantinople and Athens, he became a monk and wrote the Rule which remains the standard for Eastern monasticism.

He later served as bishop of his native city. With his brother Gregory of Nyssa and his friend Gregory Nazianzen he exerted much influence, thus helping to uphold Orthodoxy among the Christians of the East. Although he died two years before the Council of Constantinople, its final resolution owes much to his teachings. He is venerated as one of the four great Doctors of the Orthodox church. See Attwater, *Saints*, pp. 56-57.

22. The term used is *osviashchennyi sobor*, signifying a gathering of the upper clergy. In a post-Petrine context the same term would signify the Holy Synod, the body which governed the Russian Orthodox church after Peter the Great annulled the patriarchate.

23. *Baskak* was a term designating Mongol tax inspectors who were high administrative figures assigned to conquered Russian areas. They were responsible directly to the khan and enforced levies of soldiers and tax collecting. The tax inspector for the grand principality of Vladimir was known as the "great baskak."

24. Mikhail Vsevolodovich (died 1246), prince of Chernigov, was the son of Prince Vsevolod Sviatoslavich "the Red." During the third to fifth decade of the thirteenth century he played an active role in the political and military affairs of South and Northwestern Rus. In 1223 he took part with the other princes in deliberations concerning the first appearance of the Tatars. In the 1220s he several times acted as prince of Novgorod, then became involved in the contest for the Kievan throne between Daniel of Galich and his brother Yaroslav Vsevolodovich. With the approach of the Tatars he fled to Hungary in 1238, and then to Poland. Finding no assistance there, he set off for Saray to gain confirmation to the Chernigov principality from Khan Batu. Instead he was executed, according to some accounts for refusing to bow down to a golden idol, according to others for refusing to pass between two purifying fires. Later Mikhail and his boyar Fedor were canonized by the Russian church, their feast day being September 20, the day of their martyrdom. See entry by Dimnik, MERSH, Volume 22, pp. 52-54.

25. There were various kinds of taxes, duties, tariffs, levies, and tribute throughout this period. In the particular instance mentioned the collectors gathered *myt,* an excise tax on the production or sale of certain commodities. The general customs collectors took in *tamga. Tamga* was a Turkic word signifying a general customs duty as opposed to *myt* which was a local duty on trade.

26. Fennell, *Russian Church*, p. 192. See also Note 42, below, and Volume 5, pp. 43, 50.

27. Berge (Berke), khan of the Horde who assumed power in 1258. He was the first khan to be converted to Islam. This conversion became a factor in his policies as he focussed more attention on the Muslim Middle East and somewhat less on Russia. In order to expedite relations with a restored Byzantium he permitted the establishment of an Orthodox bishopric in the Mongol capital city of Saray. This greatly aided Russians in their relations with Byzantium as well.

28. The word was *doroga,* also *daruga.* The man bearing this title supervised the collection of taxes and certified the amount by putting a seal on it. The root of this Mongol word has the meaning of "to stamp" or "to press."

29. Kavgady was the Mongol khan's commissioner to Moscow and ally of Grand Prince Yury in his rivalry with Prince Michael of Tver, 1317-1319.

30. Metropolitan Cyprian (died 1406), of Bulgarian origin, was appointed by Patriarch Philotheos to succeed Alexis (died 1378) against the wishes of Dmitry Donskoy, and failed to establish himself in the metropolitanate until 1390, after Dmitry's death. He zealously served Vasily I, the past twelve years having doubtless taught him the importance of grand-princely support. See entry by Faith C.M. Kitch, MERSH, Volume 17, pp. 14-16; also Fennell, *Russian Church*, pp. 146-161.

31. Uzbek ruled as khan from 1313 to 1341 during what came to be considered the prime of the Horde. He accepted Islam and permanently established that religion among his subjects. His new faith naturally turned his attention to Middle Eastern affairs. In Russian affairs he strove to maintain the enmity between Tver and Moscow. He also granted the right of tax collection to a number of Russian princes, thus eliminating the Mongol baskaks. Khan Janibek (ruled 1342-1357) was the son of Uzbek.

32. See Chapter I, Note 9, above.

33. Literally his second cousin, son of his father's cousin. In the Slavic way of determining family relations any male relative of the generation of one's father is one's uncle. Thus an uncle does not have to be just a father's brother. It could be a father's second or third cousin. Dmitry Donskoy and Vladimir (son of Andrei of Serpukhov) were first cousins. Vladimir was thus uncle to Dmitry's son Vasily I.

34. Internecine strife, widespread among the Russian princes, was also evident among the Mongols. Traditionally only the descendants of Genghis Khan could be khan and reign over the Horde. Edigey was not a descendant of Genghis but a member of the Mangkyt clan. After seizing power he ruled through puppet khans while giving himself the title of amir. Edigey was deposed in 1411.

35. Vasily, Dmitry Donskoy's son, was held hostage in the Horde from 1383 to 1386 to ensure the submission of his father. Vasily, later to rule Moscow as Vasily I, escaped to Moldavia in 1386 and eventually made his way home.

36. The *yam* or postal tax was levied both in cash and in kind.

37. The word *basurman* and its variants came to be used pejoratively for "heathens" in general and Muslims in particular.

38. During the reign of Vasily I of Moscow (1389-1425) his younger brother Yury was the ruler of Zvenigorod, a city to the west of Moscow. The city prospered under his rule, growing commercially and marked architecturally by new churches and extensive fortifications.

39. The term *gost'*, plural *gosti,* was applied to rich merchants who formed a class referred to in this series as "leading merchants." Cloth dealers, *sukonniki,* from *sukno* meaning cloth, or broadcloth, came to stand for merchants who dealt with the West, cloth being a major item of trade.

40. The fee for weighing was *pudovoe* in Russian, *pud* being a unit of weight (36 lbs.). A tax on fur was *rezanka*; a *rezana* was a monetary unit equal to one-fiftieth of a *grivna*. A fee for mooring vessels was *poberezhnoe;* the word for

bank or shore was *bereg*. A fee for branding horses was *piatno*, the word itself meaning "spot" or "mark." The briquettes of salt were called *ploshki*. The tax on honey was called *medovoe* from the word for honey, *med*. The fisheries tax was *ezovoe* from the old Russian word for fisheries, *ez*. The tax on hay was *zakos; kosit'* is the verb "to mow." The tax on commercial associations was called *povatazhnoe;* a *vataga* was an entrepreneurial group organized for a particular enterprise such as commercial hunting or trapping.

41. The fine for someone caught in this unhappy state was called *polichnoe*.

42. The term was *bezzadshchina* or escheat, the reversion of property to the crown in the absence of heirs or claimants.

43. The *poliud'e* was a Kievan practice in which the prince and his retinue annually toured his lands to collect tribute. The residents of small towns paid a lesser tax, the *pogorod'e*. Residents of large towns or cities paid no general tribute. As a matter of efficiency the Mongols farmed out tax collection rights to agents, frequently Muslim merchants from Central Asia. Such agents were often ruthless with delinquent taxpayers, to the point of selling them as slaves. Izosima, a Christian who embraced Islam, was the tax collector in Yaroslavl in 1262 when an uprising swept the region of Suzdal. The popular assemblies of various cities voted to oust the Mongols and bloodshed ensued.

44. Constantine VII Porphyrogennetos (913-959) was an emperor of Byzantium. Porphyrogennetos is an honorific title literally meaning "born in the purple," purple being a color of royalty. It meant that one was born in the imperial palace and had not seized the throne or been elevated to it from outside. Princess Anna, the sister of Emperor Basil, who married Vladimir of Kiev in 988 was a "porphyrogenete" and thus especially revered. Constantine was the author of the treatise *De Administrando Imperio* (Concerning the Administration of the Empire), which contains some of the earliest information we possess about the Rus polity. See Volume 1 of this series.

45. St. George's day usually refers to the feast of St. George proper, which occurs on April 23. The founding of the church of St. George in Kiev is celebrated on November 26. This autumnal holiday served as the time when serfs could leave their masters. In practice this arrangement was made earlier and executed a week before or after the holiday. All field work was completed this late in autumn.

46. The term *bobrovniki*, beaver hunters and trappers, was derived from the Russian word for "beaver." Beaver pelts provided a valuable source of income for princes.

47. The Russian word for houndsmen was *psari*, the word for "hounds" being *psy*, or *pes* in the singular.

48. The Russian term is *vatagi*. See following Note.

49. *Ataman* or *vataman*, leader of a *vataga*. See Note 21 for the *povatazhnoe*, the tax on the profits of the *vatagi*.

50. The word *strasti* denotes Christ's Passion and refers to a crucifix worn by Orthodox clergy on a chain around the neck, about mid-way down the chest. It is worn outside all garments.

51. St. Peter, called "the miracle worker" was metropolitan of Russia from 1308 to 1326. As metropolitan he decided to settle permanently in the then secondary city of Moscow thus increasing its prestige. After his death in 1342 he was buried in Moscow and his grave became a shrine for the faithful.

CHAPTER III

1. Vladimir was the prince of Kiev who accepted Christianity in 988 and traditionally has been known as the Christianizer of Russia. Princes Boris and Gleb were killed in a fratricidal struggle by their brother in 1016. They emulated Christ in refusing to take up arms that would have spilled the blood of their enemies. It is uncertain to which Vsevolod the text is referring. Most probably Vsevolod III who, though never formally canonized, is known to have been a generous benefactor of the church, and is included in the "host of heavenly princes" in later recensions of the *vitae* of Alexander Nevsky. Consult Michael Cherniavsky, *Tsar and People. Studies in Russian Myths* (New York, 1961), p. 30. Another possibility is Vsevolod Georgievich (baptismal name Dmitry), who died February 7, 1238 during a Tatar attack on Vladimir, and received the "angelic habit" before his death. Another prince of that name mentioned in hagiographic sources is Vsevolod of Pskov, son of Prince Mstislav Vladimirovich. He died in 1138.

2. See Chapter I, Note 12, above.

3. Not only did Archbishop Vasily Kalika travel to Pskov expressly for the purpose of christening Prince Mikhail Aleksandrovich, he also educated him in his household. See Volume 5, Chapter I, Note 37.

4. Mikhail Aleksandrovich in 1368 was established on the Tver throne, and with Lithuanian help waged a series of generally unsuccessful wars against Moscow. He was the last Tver ruler to dispute the grand-princely title with Moscow. He received the entitlement from the Horde no less than three times (1370, 1371 and 1375), but to no avail. Concerning Alexander Mikhailovich, see Chapter I, Note 22, above.

5. Alexis was born some time between 1293 and 1298, son of the Chernigov boyar Fedor Biakont, who entered the service of Moscow at the end of the thirteenth century. He became metropolitan of Moscow in 1354, and for much of the reign of Ivan the Fair (1353-1359) and the minority of Dmitry Donskoy he was the effective head of government. He vigorously opposed the establishment of a separate metropolitanate in Lithuanian-held Kiev, and favored accommodation with the Horde. He died in 1378 and was canonized in 1449, being considered the second of the three "Moscow miracle workers." Fennell, *Russian Church*, pp. 140-148, 227-233.

6. Ivan Borisovich (1370-1418) was the second and younger son of Prince Boris Konstantinovich, the last independent prince of Nizhny Novgorod. He was born in Nizhny Novgorod to which, as related here, Metropolitan Alexis journeyed in

order to christen him. In 1383 he was sent to the Horde with gifts for the khan, and two years later he was sent on a similar mission, this time with a request to detain his rival Vasily Kirdiapa for a longer time with the Horde. In 1392, when Nizhny Novgorod was taken over by the Muscovite grand prince, Ivan and other members of his family were captured. Subsequent to their release, Ivan and his elder brother Daniel incessantly sought, sometimes with foreign aid, to regain the lost principality. In 1417 the two princes appeared in Moscow, where they effected a reconciliation with the grand prince, but the peace was short-lived. In 1418 Ivan fled Moscow. He died later that year and was buried in the Transfiguration cathedral in Nizhny Novgorod. Some accounts give the date of his death as 1448, but this is probably the result of a scribal error perpetuated by later copyists. For further details see Volume 5, Chapter I, Notes 12-13.

7. Sergius of Radonezh (1321-1391) before making his monastic profession was known as Varfolomey Kirillovich. He was born into a boyar family in the region of Great Rostov. The family, ruined by Tatar raids and inter-princely wars, resettled in the Moscow principality and received lands near the town of Radonezh. Together with his elder brother, Sergius founded the monastery in 1354 and became its first abbot. He introduced the coenobitic rule within the monastery. His influence was widespread since he became the confidant of the ruling family and leading boyars. This allowed him to take an active part in the political events of the day. In 1380 he exhorted Dmitry Donskoy on the eve of the Snipe Field battle and in 1395 brought about the reconciliation between the grand prince and Prince Oleg of Riazan. Metropolitan Alexis wanted to name Sergius his successor, but he refused. He was buried in the monastery which he founded. He was canonized by the Russian church some time before 1449. His feast day is September 25. Fennell, *Russian Church*, pp. 147-156, 206-207, 236-239.

8. Yury Dmitrievich, third son of Dmitry Donskoy, considered himself the rightful successor to his brother Vasily I, and thus led the opposition to his nephew Vasily II. For further details see Volume 5, Chapter I, Note 7.

9. The Holy Trinity monastery, seventy kilometers north of Moscow, was the primary center of moral and spiritual authority at this time. Its abbots, St. Sergius especially (see Note 7, above), exercised great influence over princes and populace. It was fitting and prestigious that Nikon celebrate the baptism of a prince's son.

10. See Volume 5, Chapter V, Notes 9 and 26.

11. Evdokia, daughter of Grand Prince Dmitry Konstantinovich of Suzdal, married Dmitry Donskoy in 1366.

12. Zinovy was abbot of the Trinity-St. Sergius monastery from 1436 to 1445. He enjoyed the particular confidence of Vasily II, whose two eldest sons, Ivan (baptismal name Timofey) and Yury he christened. In the autumn of 1441, when Shemiaka and Alexander Chartoryisky, an émigré from Lithuania, joined to attack Moscow and depose Vasily, Zinovy acted as mediator between the two sides, and by the strength of his spiritual authority made peace between them.

13. Among medieval Russian princely families there was the custom of celebrating a child's first hair-cutting, evidently signifying transition from infancy to boyhood. See also Volume 3, Chapter IV, Note 17, and Chapter VIII, Note 80.

14. Since Novgorod often had to resist encroachment by Moscow its clergy frequently opposed the authority of the metropolitans of Moscow as well. Prince Alexander of Tver in having his son baptized by Bishop Vasily of Novgorod was facilitating a natural alliance against Moscow. See also Note 3, above.

15. An archaic meaning of the word *kasha* refers to the feast held after the wedding ceremony.

16. See Chapter I, Note 30, above.

17. See Chapter I, Note 22, above.

18. See Note 11, above. Dmitry Konstantinovich "the Elder" (1323-1383) was prince of Suzdal-Nizhny Novgorod. At first he struggled with Dmitry Ivanovich for the grand principality of Vladimir, and actually ruled as grand prince from 1360 to 1363. Later, to counter the pretensions of his brother Boris, he made peace with the Moscow prince, to whom he married his daughter Evdokia in 1366. In conjunction with Muscovite forces he took part in expeditions against the Volga Bulgars and Mordvinians. In 1377 he fought alongside the Moscow levies on the Piana river, where the Russians were soundly defeated by the Tatars. In 1382 he sent his sons to aid Tokhtamysh in the capture of Moscow. Among Dmitry Konstantinovich's achievements were the construction of the first stone citadel of Nizhny Novgorod (1372) and the commissioning of the Laurentian Chronicle (1377).

19. Howes, *Testaments*, pp. 120-125, translation, pp. 193-202.

20. For information on Dmitry Shemiaka see Chapter I, Note 42, above.

21. See Chapter I, Note 41, above.

22. Dynastic intermarriages between Russian noble houses and those of Byzantium did occur previously. In 1122 Irina, daughter of Mstislav Vladimirovich and granddaughter of Vladimir Monomakh, married Andronicos Comnenos, future emperor of Byzantium (reigned 1183-1185). In 1194 Princess Evfimia of Chernigov married into the Byzantine noble house of the Angeloi. Vladimir himself derived his sobriquet from his maternal grandfather Constantine IX Monomachos (reigned 1042-1055). The Byzantine prince named here is John Comnenos, who married Vasily's daughter Anna in 1411. He later reigned as Emperor John VIII, though in the meantime (1417) Anna had died.

23. The boyar Ivan Dmitrievich is mentioned in Volume 5, p. 60.

24. See Chapter II, Note 6, above.

25. Mikhail Aleksandrovich (1333-1399), prince of Tver, was the fourth son of Prince Alexander Mikhailovich. See Note 4, above.

26. See Chapter I, Note 47, above.

27. See Chapter I, Note 6, above.

28. The Tale of Luka Kolotsky dates back to the late fifteenth or early sixteenth century. In it a poor peasant discovers a miracle-working icon which he uses to cure people and amass great wealth. Soon he begins to live the life of a

rich man and offend people. Once a man he has offended sets a bear on him. Luka is nearly killed. The experience forces him to rethink his life. He establishes a monastery with his wealth and lives out his life there as a monk.

29. Prince Andrei Dmitrievich (1382-1432) under the terms of the testament of his father Dmitry Donskoy received the appanages of Mozhaisk and Vereia in 1389, and also in the same year acquired the principality of Beloozero. In 1403 he married Agrafena, daughter of Alexander Patrikeev, prince of Starodub. His son Ivan Andreevich, who was born before 1430 and died some time between 1471 and 1483, was a constant thorn in the sides of the Muscovite princes. He fled to Lithuania in 1454. See Volume 5, Chapter IV, Notes 14-15.

30. Such caskets can be seen at the Caves monastery in Kiev. The common practice of using an oaken log, in Russian *dub*, gave rise to the Russian euphemism for dying, *dat' dubu* .

31. The cathedral of St. Michael the Archangel was one of the three major cathedrals of the Moscow Kremlin. Originally it was a wooden church, built in the mid-thirteenth century. In 1333 it was rebuilt in stone to serve as the burial place of the princes of Moscow. At the beginning of the sixteenth century Ivan III commissioned the Italian architect Alevisio Novi to build the present structure, which was completed in 1508.

32. "Vasily II died on 27 March 1462. His last illness was short and painful. Suffering from tabes, he ordered smouldering tinder to be applied to various parts of his body, a treatment which in no way alleviated his suffering. Covered with festering sores as a result of this crude therapy, he was refused his last request— to take the tonsure and die, as all his predecessors had died, a monk." Fennell, *Ivan the Great of Moscow* (London, 1961), p. xiii.

33. Most chronicles, when recounting the death of various princes, ended with the almost formulaic sentence that he kept little or no wealth for himself, but distributed it all to his retinue. This omission in later chronicles is indicative of the change in relations between the greater and lesser princes, as well as the evolution of princely administration from the "royal household" system of government.

34. Prince Vasily Yaroslavich ruled his appanage of Serpukhov and Borovsk from 1427, being its last independent prince. He was the son of Yaroslav-Afanasy Vladimirovich, and the brother-in-law of Vasily II, whom he faithfully supported in the wars against the Galich princes. Perhaps he felt himself insufficiently rewarded for his part in the restoration of Vasily the Dark. At any event, despite his past loyalty, in 1456 he was arrested "for some kind of treason" and his lands were annexed to Moscow. It is not clear why Vasily turned on him. Some historians suggest that, having got rid of his rivals the Galich princes, he wished also to rid himself of those to whom he owed an intolerable debt of gratitude. Others view this incident as the result of hostile slander. His son Ivan Vasilievich immediately fled to Lithuania, where he joined forces with another prominent Moscow malcontent, Prince Ivan Andreevich of Mozhaisk. They both thought up a plan to liberate Vasily Yaroslavich and partition the grand principality of Moscow. They made ready to advance in 1462, on the death of Vasily the Dark, then

failed to gather support and the invasion petered out. Their followers in Moscow were arrested and subjected to cruel punishment. Vasily Yaroslavich, still in captivity, died in 1486.

35. Vasily Mikhailovich, the third Kashin prince of that name, together with his cousin Ivan Borisovich in 1399 received from his father the principality of Kashin and Kosniatin. In 1403 he fled to Moscow, then was reconciled with the ruling prince of Tver, his elder brother Ivan Mikhailovich, by the good offices of Grand Prince Ivan Dmitrievich. In 1405 Vasily Mikhailovich came on a visit to Tver, where he and his boyars unexpectedly were seized and placed under guard. During Holy Week they were reconciled, and Ivan Mikhailovich allowed them to return to Kashin. In 1406 Vasily Mikhailovich returned to Tver. The same year he was sent by his brother with a contingent to reinforce the Muscovite army which was fighting the Lithuanians. Thereafter the brothers were at peace until 1412 when, before setting out for the Horde, Ivan ordered the arrest of Vasily, his wife, children, boyars and servitors, all of whom were sent to Novy Gorodok. Vasily escaped while on the way, and reappeared in Moscow. Then he proceeded to the Horde, recruited a Tatar army and attacked Kashin on December 24. He was repulsed by his cousin Ivan Borisovich and returned to the Horde. There is no further mention of him until 1425. Before his death Ivan was reconciled with Vasily and gave him back his principality of Kashin. In 1426 his nephew Boris, now the ruling prince, ordered his arrest. His eventual fate is unknown. He was the last independent prince of Kashin, which until 1486 was an appanage of the grand principality of Tver. After the Muscovite conquest of Tver in that year Kashin was assigned as an appanage to Ivan III's eldest son Ivan the Younger.

36. Dmitry Mikhailovich Kashin-Volynsky (dates of birth and death unknown) was a prince and military commander under Dmitry Donskoy, whose sister Anna he married. The son of Koriat-Albiurt Gediminovich, a Lithuanian prince of Volhynia, and a grandson of Gediminas, Bobrok left Lithuanian service and entered that of Prince Dmitry Konstantinovich of Nizhny Novgorod. He then transferred his allegiance to Moscow, assisting Dmitry Donskoy in his work of strengthening the principality of Moscow. He participated in campaigns against the Bulgars and the Lithuanians. During the battle of Snipe Field in 1380 Bobrok and Prince Vladimir Andreevich of Serpukhov commanded the reserve forces which were kept fresh during the all-day battle. The sudden blow delivered by these units late in the battle routed the Tatars and won victory for the Muscovite army.

37. Soloviev here refers to the *pravo ot"ezda* or right of free departure. This right was increasingly circumvented by bilateral provisions in interprincely treaties forbidding the reception of boyars or servitors seeking to leave the service of one prince for that of the other. Violation of this provision could and did serve as pretext for war and conquest, as was the case with the Muscovite annexation of Tver in 1486. Later, upon introduction of the pomestie system in the fifteenth and sixteenth century, landholding and service became interconnected and thus the right of free departure ceased to exist.

38. See Volume 5, pp. 1-2.

39. See Chapter I, Note 36, above.

40. See Chapter I, Note 9, above.

41. The Russian noun was *zaezd* and it was used in the sense of passing someone in the established order of seniority.

42. See Volume 5, p. 118.

43. Yury Patrikeevich (dates of birth and death unknown, flourished 1418-1439) was a boyar and commander who enjoyed considerable trust under Vasily I and Vasily II. In 1418 Vasily I gave him the hand of his daughter Maria, and in 1425 he was the first to witness the grand prince's will. In 1433 he advanced to Kostroma against Vasily Kosoy, but was defeated on the Kusa river and taken prisoner. In 1437 he was sent to Novgorod on a tax-gathering mission. In 1439, when Ulu-Mahmet was attacking the Muscovite borderlands, the grand prince entrusted to Yury Patrikeevich the defense of Moscow.

44. Vasily I married Sophia of Lithuania who was a daughter of Grand Prince Vytautas. This explains the favored position of certain Lithuanian grandees at the Muscovite court. See preceding note.

45. Howes, *Testaments*, pp. 125-130, translation, pp. 203-217.

46. Andrei Aleksandrovich (dates of birth and death unknown, flourished 1276-1304) was the third son of Alexander Nevsky. He was prince of Gorodets and Kostroma from 1276, grand prince of Vladimir 1281-1283 and 1294-1304.

47. See Volume 5, p. 118.

48. Howes, *Testaments*, pp. 186-187.

49 Charters of obedience, *poslushnye gramoty* in Russian, were a prince's instructions to his citizens ordering them to heed and maintain whomever he sent them.

50. Individuals who held large landed estates were called "great boyars" in Muscovy to differentiate them from lesser boyars who were smaller landholders.

51. An "administrative" boyar was one who headed a department in the prince's administration. The Russian term was *putnyi boiarin* from the word *put'* which means path, road, journey, way. Figuratively it means "the way one does something" and by extension encompasses such meanings as method, means, chain of command, line of service and promotion, hierarchy. A *put'* was a department of administration and a source of income for the boyar who headed it.

52. A privy boyar in Russian was a *vvedennyi* boyar from the verb *vvodit'*, to bring in, to introduce, to admit. Such an "admitted" boyar was one who had access to the prince's palace and council.

53. The Russian term was *d'iak vvedennyi* and meant official, crown secretary. The term *d'iak* is probably ecclesiastical in origin (cognate with *d'iakon*, meaning "deacon") since the clergy was composed of the most literate men of the time.

54. See Note 14, above.

55. In Russian *put'*.

56. In Russian *dokhod*.

57. Lord-in-waiting was the title of a grandee at a prince's court, one "close" to the prince. The Russian word was *okolnichii*. The title was customarily given to military commanders who functioned as heads of what might be called the quartermaster corps.

58. Prince Oleg Ivanovich of Riazan (reigned 1350-1402) defeated Khan Tagay with the help of levies from Murom, Pronsk and Kozelsk. In 1370 the Riazan levies helped Moscow repel a Lithuanian attack, but the following year Muscovite forces under the boyar Prince Bobrok-Volynets (see Note 36, above) invaded Riazan and defeated Oleg near Pereiaslavl. In 1378 Riazan forces defeated the Tatars on the Vozha river, yet in the 1380 campaign Oleg of Riazan was conspicuous by his absence. This led to war between Dmitry Donskoy and Oleg, ended in 1386 by the mediation of Sergius of Radonezh.

59. The *duma* was the highest council of the princes, a deliberating and advising body. It was the forerunner of the Boyar Council, whose procedures became much more formalized in the late Muscovite period. Despite its name, its members also included lords-in-waiting (see Note 57, above), and selected members of the bureaucracy and lesser nobility, termed in Russian as *dumnye d'iaki* (conciliar secretaries) and *dumnye dvoriane* (conciliar nobles). See entry by V.I. Buganov, MERSH, Volume 5, pp. 51-53.

60. Russian titles of courtiers were often analogous to those of other European languages. Thus the lord-in-waiting was an *okolnichii* (one who stood nearby); the table attendant was a *stolnik* from *stol*, a table; the cupbearer was a *chashnik* from *chas*, a cup.

61. In Mongol times the gentry was composed of two broad categories: free servitors and obligated servitors. The general term was *slugi* (servitors). There were *slugi vol'nye* (free servitors) and *slugi pod dvorskim* (under the authority of the *dvorskii*, the majordomo) These later came to be known as the *dvoriane*. There was yet a third, smaller category known as *deti boiarskie* (junior boyars) which was composed of boyar families who had lost wealth and power.

62. Such were called *deliui*. They were people of various trades, crafts or occupations who performed special services for princes. The *ordintsy* were the same as the above except that these people had been ransomed from Mongol captivity by the princes.

63. Slaves were called *kholopy*. The word also meant "peasant" or "serf." Other Russian terms for "slave" were *cheliadin* and *rab* (feminine *raba*). There were two kinds of slavery, permanent and temporary. The latter largely included war captives who could be redeemed for ransom.

64. See Chapter I, Notes 27 and 28, above.

65. In Russian *grid'* and *grid'ba*.

66. In Russian *muzhi* (literally "men").

67. The terms *pan* and *pan rada* are the Polish-Lithuanian equivalent of boyar and great boyar. The *rada* was a council, thus "lord of the council."

68. The Polish word for gentry is *szlachta*. It was the approximate equivalent of the Russian *dvoriane*.

69. The Russian word was *zemianin* and *zemiane* (plural) meaning a native of the land (zemlia) or a land-holding member of the gentry. These were small landholders, not boyars.

70. The wooden plow, *sokha,* was the standard unit of assessment in paying the general tribute to the Mongols.

71. The term was *privilei* and in West Russia was a charter granted by the grand prince.

72. See Chapter II, Note 14, above.

73. In Russian *koniushii* or *starokoniushii*, a title used at the Muscovite court in the fifteenth and sixteenth centuries. Part of this official's duties was the supervision of mounted troops at the ruler's palace. By the late sixteenth century the office of master of the horse became the highest in the Boyar Council, participating in diplomatic and military affairs. The last holder of this office was Boris Godunov, who became tsar in 1598.

74. In Russian *dvorskii*, in charge of the *dvor* (household) or *dvoretskii*, in charge of the *dvorets* (palace). These terms apparently were used interchangeably.

75. The Russian term for treasurer was *kaznachei,* keeper of the treasury, *kazna.* The term for steward was *kliuchnik* from *kliuch,* the word for "key."

76. The unit of warriors making up a prince's bodyguard was called a *rynda.* The much larger retinue was called a *druzhina.*

77. In Russian *tysiatskii*, literally commander of a thousand, the notional size of the civic militia, though the usual size of such levies was very much smaller.

78. The term *posadnik* also had the meaning of "mayor" and was an elected post in a city such as Novgorod. The context which Soloviev describes excludes this meaning. The later term *namestnik*, with its connotation of "in place of," rather clearly defines the relationship of this figure to the grand prince. In this translation it is rendered as "vicegerent, a lieutenant."

79. This is a Western term from the Latin *palatinus* by way of the Italian *paladino.* In Charlemagne's time it referred to one of the twelve peers of his court.

80. In Russian *pechatnik*, from the word *pechat'*, meaning "seal."

81. See Chapter VII, below.

82. The Russian was *sedelnichii* from *sedlo,* the word for saddle. *Snuznik* (horseman) is of unclear derivation. In time as the court grew more powerful and complex these titles became figurative. For an analogous development see Western titles such as chevalier and chamberlain.

83. The term for clerk was *pisets* from the verb *pisat'* (to write). For *d'iak* see Note 16, above.

84. During the reign of Khan Nogay the Mongols made devastating incursions into Galich. They especially laid the land waste in 1287, looting and destroying it as much as they did Kiev in the 1240s. As a result the power of Galich in relation Lithuania was permanently reduced.

85. In this context the term *deti boiarskie,* boyer children, can be taken literally, though later the term came to denote members of decayed boyar families, virtually indistinguishable from the rank-and-file *dvoriane.* See also Note 61, above.

86. Foot soldiers, *rat'* in Russian, were called up or levied in times of great emergency.

87. The Russian word was *smerd,* plural *smerdy,* which had the general meaning of lower classes especially in rural districts where it meant peasants (not slaves or serfs). It also stood for a special lower class of free men dependent on the prince.

88. The Russian word for informant was simply *iazyk,* "tongue." A *iazyk* captured among the enemy presumably provided valuable information about the hostile army and its intentions.

89. See Chapter VI, Note 11, below.

90. The Yatviags were one of the tribes in the Baltic group of peoples inhabiting present-day northeastern Poland and northwestern Belarus. They became extinct because of the military pressure of their neighbors.

91. The Russian word was *voevoda* (cf. *voevat',* to wage war). A person holding such rank was the highest military commander or the commandant of a particular district.

92. Prince Ivan Vasilievich Obolensky-Striga was the son of Prince Vasily Ivanovich Kosoy. He is first mentioned in 1446 when he joined the Riapolovsky princes and others to free Vasily the Dark. Shemiaka became aware of the plot, forcing Obolensky and some of his fellow-conspirators to flee beyond the Volga to Beloozero. Shemiaka sent a detachment after them but Obolensky-Striga and Prince Ivan Ivanovoch Riapolovsky defeated it near the estuary of the Mologa. By then the date for the proposed rendezvous at Uglich had passed, whereupon Obolensky-Striga decided to join the émigré group in Lithuania which eventually marched to the rescue of the grand prince. In 1449 Obolensky was commander at Kostroma, where he took part in the repulse of Shemiaka. In 1458 he participated in the Viatka expedition and in 1460 was appointed vicegerent in Pskov at the request of the citizens, though he remained there for less than a year. In 1467 he was dispatched to aid the Tatar service prince Kasim in his attempt to seize the Kazan tsardom, but was met by Khan Ibrahim, who blocked his crossing of the Volga, forcing the Muscovites to return home through the autumn cold and rain with sadly depleted supplies. In 1470, when the Kazan Tatars attacked the upper course of the Yug river and burned the town of Kichmenga, Obolensky-Striga was sent after them and pursued them as far as the Unzha, but could not overtake them. Having ravaged the lands of the Cheremiss, he then returned to Moscow. In 1471 he took part in Ivan III's Novgorod campaign. In 1472, when news came of Khan Akhmat's incursion he was sent to guard the Oka. That year Pskov requested him again, but the grand prince replied that he had need of Obolensky-Striga for his own purposes. He was one of the chief participants in the Novgorod campaign of 1478, occupying all the monasteries in the vicinity of Novgorod to prevent the local population from burning them. After the surrender of Novgorod, Obolensky-Striga was appointed vicegerent, though shortly thereafter he died. Before his death he collected all the treaties ever concluded between Novgorod and Lithuania and sent them on to Moscow. He was buried in the Spaso-Evfimiev monastery in Suzdal.

93. Fedor Vasilievich Basenok was a steady supporter of Vasily II. In 1446, when all the people of Moscow began to swear allegiance to Shemiaka, only Basenok refused, saying he would not serve a liar and a brigand. For his pains he was clapped into irons, but he slipped his shackles and together with his jailer fled to Kolomna. There he hid for a while with his friends. Then, gathering about him a number of military servitors, he fled to Lithuania, where he encountered Prince Vasily Yaroslavich, who assigned him part of the principality of Briansk for his support. Together with Vasily Yaroslavich and Prince Semeon Ivanovich Obolensky, he organized a force for the rescue of the grand prince, and in 1447 appeared with a significant force in Muscovite territory. At Volokolamsk he met with Vasily II, who already had been released, and together with him entered Moscow. In 1450 he took part in the battle of Galich, in which Shemiaka was soundly defeated. Finally in 1452 Basenok was second-in-command at the capture of Ustiug, until then occupied by Shemiaka, and from there advanced on Vologda. In 1455, when Tsarevich Saltan crossed over the Oka, plundered the grand prince's domains and withdrew with many prisoners, Basenok was sent in pursuit. He caught up with the Tatars near Kolomna, defeated them and liberated all of the prisoners. In 1456 Vasily declared war on Novgorod. Basenok was part of the advance detachment which captured Staraia Rusa in a surprise attack, seizing much booty and many prisoners. On their way back they were ambushed by a more numerous Novgorod detachment led by Prince Vasily Vasilievich Shuisky of Suzdal, but the Muscovites were victorious, even capturing the Novgorod mayor Mikhail Tucha. These two successes strengthened Moscow's hand in the negotiations leading up to the Treaty of Yazhelbitsy. Basenok was also a signatory to the grand prince's will, according to which he received a life interest in the villages of Okurovskoe and Repinskoe. See also Chapter I, Note 50, above.

94. See Chapter I, Note 2, above.

95. Before the battle itself, Dmitry went a step further. He appointed the boyar Mikhail Brenok, a skilled commander, to lead the main corps. Dmitry himself fought alongside his soldiers. Brenok was killed in the battle, but it was his decision to bring in the reserve, led by Prince Vladimir, at a critical moment that won the victory.

96. For some reason Soloviev overlooks cuirasses and chain-mail armor as well as the bow and arrow. In general, body armor, especially the cuirass, was available only to the retinue, the professional soldiers, as it were. The town militia was used largely as garrison troops during invasions. The rural-dwelling *smerdy* were called only in general mobilizations for great campaigns. They made up the infantry. The prince's retinue was mounted. The Mongol bow, adopted by the Russians, had the pull of some 160 lbs. and an effective range of 200-300 yards. It thus compared very favorably with the long bow used so devastatingly by the English against the French mounted knights at Crecy in 1346. By comparison, the M-14 rifle, standard U.S. Army issue in the 1960s, had an effective range of 700 yards.

97. The coat, called a *kozhukh,* had sleeves and was tucked at the waist. It was not the common sheepskin coat that the word *kozhukh* denotes nowadays.
98. Bear spears, *rogtichi* in Russian, were pikes with a v-shaped prong and sharpened tips that were used by foot soldiers.
99. The specific word for war booty was *saigat.* A significant number of military and administrative words were borrowed by Russians from the Mongols and from their various Turkic-speaking allies.
100. In Russian *stiagi* and *khorugvi.*
101. In Russian *znamia,* plural *znamena.*
102. These were activated by a counterweight rather than tension.
103. See Note 50, above.
104. Conrad of Mazovia (Konrad Mazowiecki, 1187-1247) was the son of Casimir the Just and the Moravian princess Helena. He was the Polish prince widely blamed for giving the German military orders their toehold in Polish territories. In exchange for help against his pagan enemies and also his rival princes, Conrad in 1226 invited the Teutonic Knights, granting them the district of Chełmno (Kulm). The Order of Dobryn, founded by Conrad in 1215 was absorbed by the Teutonic Order. He attained the princely throne of Cracow in 1229 and 1242, but was unable to retain it. See Davies, *God's Playground,* Volume I, pp. 41-43, 62, 86-88, 90, 94.
105. This was the battle won by Daumantas (Dovmont), a Lithuanian émigré who became prince of Pskov and married the daughter of Prince Dmitry Aleksandrovich of Novgorod. For further details, see Volume 4, Chapter II, passim, and Volume 5, Chapter III, Note 7.
106. Moscow's treaty with Novgorod specifically exempted the latter's troops from fighting outside its borders. The peace treaty between Moscow and Tver (1375) obliged Tver to send troops to Moscow's aid. None were sent, however. George Vernadsky, the *Mongols and Russia* (Yale, 1953), p. 260, sets the size of the army that actually fought at Snipe Field at thirty thousand. Doubtless there were more men under arms, but many of these had to be assigned to garrison and supply duty.

CHAPTER IV

1. See Volume 5, pp. 48-49.
2. Past mayors and chiliarchs retained their prestige and formed a body that served as an advisory council to the current office holders.
3. The citizens of Novgorod zealously guarded their rights against Muscovite encroachment. Thus a prince of Muscovy had to be physically present in Novgorod in order to fulfill his responsibilities. He could not do so by fiat while remaining in Vladimir. The princes, therefore, had a residence in Novgorod where they stayed while visiting. Yaroslav the Wise (died 1054) was believed to have issued charters guaranteeing the city's liberties. Hence the prince's residence in Novgorod was named the Court of Yaroslav.

4. "In 1456, the grand prince led a sizeable military expedition against the great city-republic. The city fathers persuaded Pskov to send help, but, before the sister-city's force arrived, the disciplined Muscovite army had defeated a larger Novgorodian force. Vasily then dictated the Treaty of Iazhelbitsy to the helpless metropolis. Novgorod agreed to pay an indemnity of 8,500 roubles to the grand prince and promised never again to harbour his enemies. The treaty prohibited the Novgorodian assembly (veche) from making treaties with foreign powers. Finally, and perhaps most significantly, the agreement specified that only the grand prince's emblem was to appear on Novgorod's coins and official seal." Crummey, *Formation*, p. 78.

5. The Russian term was *podvoiskii* and it stood for a court attendant who fulfilled a variety of duties similar to those of a bailiff. Among those duties was to announce sessions of the court to the populace.

6. The prince's master of the horse, in Russian *starokoniushii*, was in charge of the palace stables, and hence was responsible for the princely transportation and communications system. See also Chapter III, Note 73, above.

7. The fee for capturing and holding an accused criminal was called the *viazchee* or the *viazhshchee*. A *viazchii* was a person who captured and bound the criminal usually in irons, a shackler.

8. *Kriuk* was a special tax in Novgorod levied every three years.

9. Literally, "beyond the portage," that is, beyond the watershed line which marked the basin in which Novgorod was located. Since most Russian rivers generally flow either north or south, communication between northern and southern regions involved a portage at some point. The Russian word for portage, *volok* (from "to drag") is evident in the name of Volokolamsk (Portage-on-the-Lama), an important point on the route between the Ruza (south-flowing) and the Lama (north-flowing) rivers.

10. The "Lower Towns", in Russian *niz* or *Nizovye goroda*, referred to the towns further down the course of the main rivers of Russia, hence the hinterland upon which Novgorod was dependent for food supplies.

11. The Vodskaia district was one of the five administrative districts belonging to Novgorod. It stretched to the north of Novgorod along the Neva (present site of St. Petersburg) and Izhora rivers. It is named for the Vod, the Finnic tribe which originally inhabited this area.

12. Black collection was a tribute paid to the khans, *chernyi bor* in Russian. There was a so-called "white collection" paid in silver and a black collection paid in marten furs.

13. *Grivna* was a silver coin, but initially it was a silver ingot from which coins (rubles) were cut.

14. The term *peshtsy* is derived from the Russian word for foot as in *peshii*, a person on foot or *peshkom*, by foot. It refers to peasants who had no draft animals and had to pull a plow themselves.

15. *Starosta*, the Russian word for elder, was used in the city of Novgorod to denote a whole range of elected administrative officials.

16. A monthly allotment in food and clothing was given to serfs by their master. It was called *mesiachina* from the Russian word for month.

17. Guillebert de Lannoy (1386-1462) was a European traveler, diplomat and writer who visited Novgorod and Pskov in 1413. A record of his travels was left in *Voyages et ambassades de messire Guillebert de Lannoy* (Travels and Embassies of Master Guillebert de Lannoy) (Mons, 1840).

18. The Germanic Knights of the Teutonic Order marched eastward and conquered Pskov in 1241. A year later their attempt to take Novgorod was repulsed in the "rout on the ice" on Lake Peipus. The event was immortalized visually by Sergei Eisenstein in his film Alexander Nevsky.

19. See Chapter I, Note 21, above.

20. See Chapter III, Notes 3-4, above.

21. Konstantin Dmitrievich (1389-1433) was the posthumous son of Dmitry Donskoy, later prince of Uglich. Following the provisions of his father's will, his brothers gave him some portions of their lands. He first appears on the historical scene in 1404 when his brother Vasily sent him to Pskov at the request of the citizens. The chronicler notes that he was wise beyond his years, and his military feats against the Germans were relatively successful. In 1408 he was sent to Novgorod as the grand prince's vicegerent. In 1411 Pskov rejected its vicegerent Prince Alexander and requested Konstantin. Until 1414 he governed both Pskov and Novgorod, and then returned to Moscow. In 1419 he quarreled with his eldest brother, who wanted to place him in an inferior position to his nephew Vasily. In 1420 he returned of his own volition to Novgorod, where he was honorably received. In 1421 the brothers were reconciled, and after the death of Vasily I, Konstantin supported Vasily II against his uncle Yury. He left no descendants.

22. The tax collection mentioned was called *korobeishchina* , possibly the tax on itinerant vendors, *korobeiniki* .

23. See Volume 5, p, 46.

24. Presumably one of the mayors no longer serving but who retained the honors and prestige of that office.

25. Literally the "better" and the "lesser" people.

26. See Volume 3 of this series.

27. The Russian word was *detskii* . It commonly means an "agent of the court," but with its connotation of younger, in this context it probably means "minor" or "lesser servitor."

28. See Volume 3 of this series.

29. See Chapter III, Note 105, above.

30. The terms "people," "simple people" and "people of the land" were rendered in Russian as *liudi, prostye liudi* and *zemskie liudi* . They all had the basic meaning of "common people."

31. The "well-off people," *zhitye liudi* in Russian, was a Novgorod term which referred to the well-to-do upper classes. A synonymous term *muzhi* (simply "men") also was used.

32. See Chapter II, Note 38, above.
33. See Volume 17, pp. 117-119.
34. The *belomestsy* (pl.) were holders of lands immune from princely taxation.
35. The Russian term is *deliui.* See also Chapter III, Note 62, above.
36. The Russian term is *ordyntsy* (pl.).
37. See Chapter III, Note 87, above.
38. See Chapter III, Note 77, above.
39. See Chapter II, Note 6, above.
40. See Chapter II, Note 48, above.
41. The Surozhanians could in fact have been ethnically Russian. They were merchants who dealt with the Italians at the Black Sea city of Surozh (Soldaia) though their origins were not limited to any particular city or region. Being merchants, they doubtless lived in the merchants' quarter of Vladimir and thus, strictly speaking, were not "natives." The contemporary Russian concept of foreigners incorporated many conceptual categories including such as "men of another city" and "speakers of another language."
42. Magdeburg law was a German municipal code which penetrated Lithuania in the late fourteenth century. First granted to Wilno in 1387, it was extended to Smolensk, Minsk and Kiev in the fifteenth century. Under such law a city became a closed corporation. Only those recognized as city dwellers, *meshchane* in Russian, could belong to it. Such municipal government made the city free of the princes' rule.
43. It must be remembered that a good half of Lithuania was ethnically East Slavic and of the Orthodox faith, yet was politically largely disenfranchised. Sigismund (son of Kestutis) proclaimed a charter that rectified the situation. This act was intended to mollify the Russians who supported Svidrigailo, Sigismund's rival for the throne. For further information on Sigismund of Starodub, see Volume 5, pp. 105-108.
44. Prince Mikhail Yaroslavich of Tver (ruled 1285-1319) was falsely accused and executed while at the Horde. As innocent victim of political manipulation by Prince Yury of Vladimir and the Mongols he was popularly embraced as a righteous man and was later canonized by the church. See Volume 4, pp. 115-117.
45. Stone, as a structural material, was never readily available in Russia, while timber was plentiful. Therefore most structures were of plain logs (circular in cross-section) with the bark removed and the intervening spaces chinked with flax and/or clay. This method and, through metonymy, the buildings themselves were called *srub* . An alternative method was to build with finished logs (square in cross-section). Such logs were called *brus'ia,* and the method *rubit' brus'em* . Milled lumber did not become relatively common until the latter half of the nineteenth century with the coming of steam-powered saw mills.
46. The *sazhen* was a linear measure equal to 2.14 meters.
47. Archbishop John of Novgorod (died 1417) was chosen by lot in 1388 from the monks of the Khutyn monastery, received the blessing of his predecessor Alexis, and was confirmed in Moscow by Metropolitan Pimen. In 1389 when

there was plague in Pskov John went there to conduct solemn prayers, after which the epidemic abated. He came a second time to Pskov to bless the city and those of its inhabitants who had survived the plague. In 1391 or 1392 Metropolitan Cyprian visited Novgorod, accompanied by an emissary from the patriarch of Constantinople, and demanded to hold court there. The citizens rendered him a polite but firm refusal. Cyprian left Novgorod without giving his blessing and informed the patriarch of this incident. The patriarch upheld Cyprian's claims, while the grand prince demanded that Novgorod not only acknowledge the metropolitan's jurisdiction but also pay the grand prince the standard tribute. In 1399 by force of arms he compelled Novgorod to accept Moscow's claims, both spiritual and temporal. Things appeared to have been smoothed over in 1395, when Cyprian again visited Novgorod with the patriarch's representative and received an honorable welcome, and the following year John was summoned to Moscow to pay his respects. In 1397 John managed to reconcile the dispute between Novgorod and Pskov, and at the metropolitan's behest again travelled to Moscow. He tried to make peace between Moscow and the grand prince, who were locked in their dispute over the Dvina lands, but was unsuccessful. In 1401 John was summoned to Moscow on spiritual matters, then on his arrival was arrested and imprisoned for the next two years. In 1410 or 1411 he travelled to Moscow once again, to pay his respects to Metropolitan Photius. In 1414 John resigned the archbishopric to become a monk of the strictest observance, and died three years later in the Derevianitsk monastery. During his archiepiscopate several churches were founded and the Holy Wisdom cathedral thoroughly renovated. He also provided funds for upgrading the stone defense works in Pskov. See Fennell, *Russian Church*, pp. 233-234.

48. See Note 17, above.

49. In fact, archeological excavations since the 1950s in Novgorod have revealed extensive wooden paving of streets in the medieval period.

50. Soloviev cites Lannoy for this description.

51. Novgorod had five boroughs called *kontsy*, singular *konets* , literally "end." Each of these was subdivided into districts called *ulitsy* (literally "streets") which further were divided into areas called *riady* (literally "rows").

52. The Market side or *Torgovaia storona* in Novgorod was the business area of the city and the district in which foreign merchants had to stay and locate their warehouses. This was done for ease in collecting customs duty and other tariffs. Across from the Market side was the Holy Wisdom side, comprising the cathedral, the citadel and the princely political-administrative center.

53. Soloviev's, or the chronicler's, arithmetic suggests the existence of ten boroughs, yet there were only five. The fact that the money was intended for the construction of *double* fire walls may have had something to do with the arcane logic.

54. Albert Krantz (1450-1517) was the author of numerous works of history, including that of the Vandals and those of Denmark, Sweden, Norway and Saxony.

CHAPTER V

1. Taken together, such a tract was called an *uezd*. The term *uezd* comes from the method, or tradition, of determining boundaries which was called a *raziezd* or "riding out." Compare the English term "riding" as a territorial subdivision, now commonly used in Canada to denote a parliamentary constituency. The boundary setter was called a *razezzhik* or *zaezdnik*. The verb for setting boundaries was *razezzhat'*, to "ride out." As a result, everything included in a particular parcel of land was said to be uekhano or *zaekhano*, "ridden to it," and made up its *uezd*. Whatever was excluded, did not belong to it, was *otiekhano* or "ridden out" and made up the *otezdnye*, "ridden out" or "excluded" districts. The Russian verbs of motion which lie at the root of this and subsequent terms are in concept radically unlike those in English. This, coupled with the fact that most of the words in Soloviev's text are archaic, makes a short, ready translation difficult. Readers familiar with Russian will realize the problem.

2. In Russian *stany,* singular *stan.*

3. In Russian *okolitsy.*

4. Sigismund von Herberstein (1486-1566) was an emissary of the Holy Roman empire to Muscovy in 1517 and 1526, and author of a contemporaneous account.

5. St. Savva Vishersky was a highly revered saint of the Novgorod district. He was born in the city of Kashin in the boyar family of Borozdin. As a young man he renounced his inheritance, became a monk and assumed the life of a wayfaring ascetic. Later in life, in 1417, he founded a monastery on the Vishera river, about ten versts from Novgorod. This foundation became the repository of his relics.

6. The valuable skins of animals, here marten, *kuna* in Russian, were circulated as money. Squirrel skins were the lowest denomination in this system. The relative value of such skins varied depending on time and place.

7. See Chapter VIII, Note 6.

8. The monastery was founded by Cyril (1337-1427) who in secular life was treasurer to Dmitry Donskoy's lord-in-waiting Timofey Vasilievich Veliaminov. In 1380 he became a monk at the Simonov monastery in Moscow and rose to become its archimandrite. In 1392 he left for the White Lake, about six hundred versts northeast of Novgorod. Here he founded the hermitage of the Dormition which grew into a monastery of strictest observance of the coenobitic order, dedicated in 1397. Cyril was canonized in 1447 and the community was rededicated to its founder. It became one of the largest monastic landholders in Russia. See Fennell, *Russian Church*, pp. 207-209.

9. In Russian *polovniki* or *tretchiki* (pl.). These were peasants who entered into a share-cropping arrangement, holding their land in exchange for a rent equivalent to half or a third of their crop.

10. In Russian *serebrianik*. These were peasants who accepted a cash advance from the landlord, on which they either paid a fixed percentage of interest or the

equivalent in labor services. This arrangement was common in Northwestern Russia from the fourteenth to the sixteenth century. Originally there was no fixed term for the departure of *serebrianiki*, but gradually in various regions they became subject to the restrictions of St. George's Day, and this restriction was made general for all proprietorial peasants by the law code of 1497.

11. A *riadovoi*, stemming from the word *riad*, meaning "contract."

12. The Russian word was *siroty*, literally "orphans." It stood for those who had lost their means of support, frequently individuals redeemed from captivity.

13. In Eastern Russia the peasants came to be called "Christians," *krestiane* or *khristiane*, in the late fourteenth century. The terms appear in church documents of that period in a clear reference to the tenant farmers of monasteries. By this time monasteries were major landowners and the term gained wide currency.

14. See Note 10, above.

15. See Chapter VIII, Note 6.

16. Metropolitan Photius of Kiev and all Rus was a Greek prelate who arrived in Kiev in 1409 and in Moscow in 1410. There had been no head of the Russian church for a number of years and the metropolitanate was in disarray. Photius restored the church's integrity and authority. He repressed the strigolnik heresy in Pskov and strongly supported the son of Prince Vasily for the throne thus instituting linear rather than maintaining lateral succession which was a source of internecine strife. For further details, see Volume 5, Chapter IV, Note 8.

17. Robbery with violence, in Russian *tat'ba s polichnym*, was along with homicide and brigandage one of the crimes reserved to the jurisdiction of the grand prince or his officials when granting juridical immunities.

18. In Russian *obrochniki*, those paying *obrok* (quitrent).

19. *Polnye liudi* literally meant "complete" or "total" slaves, those born into slavery. *Cheliad' dernovataia* also meant "slaves" but may have had the additional meaning of "field" slaves as opposed to "domestic" slaves for which the term *cheliad'* was used by itself. Though slaves were but a fraction of the total population, they were used extensively on large agricultural estates.

20. The Russian term was *poslat' na otkhozhuiu*, literally "to send forth or out."

21. Free man or person, in Russian *chelovek vol'nyi*.

22. See Chapter II, Note 38, above.

23. In Russian *kupets*.

24. Reference here is made to the 1649 law code (Ulozhenie), which was the basic legal text until the re-codification of the laws begun in the 1830s during the reign of Nicholas I. Even so, the 1649 Ulozhenie was enshrined in the initial volume of the *Polnoe sobranie zakonov* (Full Collection of Laws).

25. This phrase is borrowed from the Primary Chronicle, with which most of Soloviev's readers would have been familiar, rendering quotation marks unnecessary.

26. See Volume 4, pp. 125-128.

27. See Volume 4, pp. 191-195, Volume 5, pp. 22-28.

28. This outbreak carried off Grand Prince Simeon (the Proud) and his two surviving sons Ivan and Simeon.

29. Called the Caves monastery because initially it was dug into the high west bank of the Dnieper river at Kiev in the early eleventh century. One of its early abbots, Feodosy (ruled 1062-1074), was one of the earliest saints of the Russian Orthodox church. See Fennell, *Russian Church*, pp. 65-71.

30. There were at least three cities named Pereiaslavl, one in the principality of that name, called Pereiaslavl Russky or Yuzhny (Southern); another in the principality of Riazan called Pereiaslavl Riazansky (Pereiaslavl-in-Riazan); a third in the principality of Vladimir-Moscow called Pereiaslavl Zalessky (Beyond the Forests).

31. See also Chapter III, Note 32, above.

CHAPTER VI

1. Andrei Aleksandrovich (died 1304) was the third son of Alexander Nevsky. He was prince of Gorodets from 1263 and prince of Kostroma from 1276. From 1281 he carried on a struggle to gain the title of grand prince, his main opponent being his brother Dmitry. In 1293 Andrei secured a large army from the Golden Horde, campaigned vigorously against Dmitry and his followers and ravaged much of Northeastern Rus. When Dmitry was finally defeated, Andrei received the title of grand prince.

2. The term *skrakhi* is used.

3. The word is in Latin script in Soloviev's text.

4. The Latin *Taberna Piscatorum* is given in Soloviev's text.

5. Also given in Latin script.

6. A *pud* was a measure of weight equal to thirty-six pounds or forty pounds in some regional variations. A *zolotnik* was a weight equivalent to one-ninety-sixth a of pound' a "drachma" as once used by pharmacists; also a gold coin of that weight.

7. The *altyn* was a coin equal in value to six dengas.

8. John of Plano Carpini (Giovanni de Piano Carpini in the vernacular Italian) was a Benedictine friar sent by Pope Innocent IV to negotiate with the Mongols. There was great concern in the Roman church and in the West over Mongol inroads. Friar John and his party reached the Horde in April, 1246 and Mongolia itself in July. He is the author of *History of the Mongols and Journey to Mongolia*, a Latin text that has been partially translated into English. See Volume 4, Chapter I, Notes 79-81.

9. At the time of Carpini's journey, Constantinople was still under Latin rule, and its commerce was dominated by the North Italian city-states.

10. Soloviev provides the Latin title in his text, *Dux Ladimirae et dominus Russiae*.

11. Soloviev in Latin script inserts in parentheses "Heidenland" after *na vostok* ("to the East").

12. See Chapter II, Note 59, above.

13. The Russian word *ushkuiniki* is from *ushkui,* a flat-bottomed boat with oars and sails. These men, the "privateers" of their day, were outfitted by Novgorod boyars and merchants for the purpose of plundering and acquiring lands in the North. They operated primarily on the Volga and Kama rivers. In the incident described the tail seems to have wagged the dog. They may be compared with the uskoks, Slavic pirates in the Adriatic who preyed on Venetian shipping. See Janet Martin, "Les uškujniki de Novgorod: marchands ou pirates? (The *Ushkuiniki* of Novgorod: Merchants or Pirates?), *Cahiers du monde russe et soviétique* (Notebooks on the Russian and Soviet World), 16 (1975), pp. 5-18.

14. See Chapter IV, Note 41, above.

15. In Russian *kuna.*

16. Namely *den'gi.*

17. Furs, when used as currency, were often counted in multiples of forty. In English a unit of forty furs occasionally was referred to as a "timber."

18. See Chapter V, Note 4, above.

19. Frederick II Hohenstaufen (1194-1250) was Holy Roman emperor from 1220, king of Sicily from 1197, grandson of Frederick Barbarossa. He was a strong adversary of the papacy, its states and the Northern Italian city-states. He placed leather and precious metal money into circulation in Italy.

20. The Augustal thaler was an ancient German silver coin equivalent to three marks. It was popularly linked to August of Saxony for his spendthrift ways.

21. In Russian *lobki.*

22. In Russian *artugi.*

23. In Lithuania, with which Pskov had commercial dealings, ten *peniaz* equalled one Lithuanian *groschen.*

24. Throwing popularly acknowledged culprits into the Volkhov river was a tradition of long standing in Novgorod that bears comparison with the practice of defenestration in Bohemia.

25. With churches considered inviolate and the stone ones relatively fireproof, their vaults were frequently used as banks of their day.

26. See Volume 5, pp. 69-70.

27. For a summary and discussion of the *Life of St. Stephen of Perm,* see A. Pronin, *History of Old Russian Literature* (Frankfurt, 1968), pp. 324-329.

28. Birger reigned from 1290 to 1319. See Eric Christiansen, *The Northern Crusades,* new edition (Harmondsworth, 1997), p. 119

29. See Note 13, above.

30. See Chapter III, Note 31, above.

31. The Miracles (*Chudov*) monastery was founded in 1350 to commemorate the miracle of St. Michael at Chone. Its location within the Kremlin made it a safe place for the imprisonment of clergy. The word for "miracle" is *chudo* in Russian, hence *chudov.*

32. On Theophanes the Greek (dates of birth and death unknown, flourished 1370-1410) see Tamara Talbot Rice, *Russian Art* (West Drayton, Middlesex, 1949), pp. 66-67.

33. Is this a misprint for Daniel the Black (see Note below), or were there two artists with the same sobriquet?

34. The dates of the birth and death of Prokhor of Gorodets are unknown, but apparently he was of advanced age in 1405, when he collaborated with Theophanes the Greek and Andrei Rublev on the frescoes of the Annunciation cathedral in the Moscow Kremlin.

35. Andrei Rublev (born around 1370, died around 1430) was the most renowned artist of medieval Russia. A brief but useful biographical sketch is contained in the entry by Majeska, MERSH, Volume 31, pp. 228-232. He was canonized in 1988 as part of the celebration marking the millennium of the Russian church. There is also the celebrated feature-length film by Andrei Tarkovsky made in 1964 but only released for restricted viewing in 1973. For a review of the film, see Joseph C. Bradley, Jr., *Kritika. A Review of Current Soviet Books on Russian History*, 10 (1974), pp. 111-120.

36. Daniel the Black was associated with Andrei Rublev and other masters of iconography. In 1408 he helped adorn the Dormition cathedral in Vladimir. During the 1420s he worked with Rublev and others on the task of decorating the main church of the Trinity-St. Sergius monastery. He also has been credited with developing the themes for the famous icons placed in the Dormition cathedral in Vladimir and now preserved in the Tretiakov Gallery in Moscow and the Russian Museum in St. Petersburg. Some of Daniel's work is preserved on the iconostasis of the Annunciation cathedral in the Moscow Kremlin.

37. Boris Rimlianin, his name being a Russified version of Boris "the Roman," was a skilled craftsman of the fourteenth century. With the destruction of Kievan Rus, art and the crafts were set back several hundred years and foreign masters often were invited to do work. Italian craftsmen were particularly favored. It is not until the sixteenth century that Russian craftsmen began to approach the fine work done by their Kievan predecessors.

38. The doors at the center of the iconostasis, leading into the sanctuary. It should be noted that Russians customarily refer to the sanctuary as the *altar'* and the actual altar table as the *prestol.*

39. Possibly a relic of the true cross.

40. The garments listed by Soloviev are *opashen,* a light summer caftan; *okhaben,* a caftan-like garment of wide cut, a square lay-down collar and frequently pin-back sleeves; *shuba,* a fur-lined coat or winter coat in general; *votola,* rough spun outer cloak; *sarafan,* a wide, flowing, full-length woman's garment; *chupruny* and *kotygi,* footwear.

41. Here is what Lannoy (p. 20) writes of the hairstyles of the Novgorod citizens. "The women have two braids of their hair hanging down their backs and the men have one braid." Concerning those of Pskov he wrote (p. 22) "The Russians of this city wear their long hair loose on their shoulders and the women have

a round diadem at the backs of their heads like the saints [have a halo]."
(Soloviev's note) Concerning Lannoy, see Chapter IV, Note 17, above.

CHAPTER VII

1. St. Stephen (1340-1396) was bishop of Perm and a missionary to the
Zyrians, a Finnic-speaking tribe in North-Central Russia known as Komi in
modern times. Stephen did not link his work with military conquest, and respected
native tradition by translating Scripture and liturgical books into the Zyrian language.
2. See Volume 4, pp. 43, 50.
3. See Chapter II, Note 30, above.
4. The Three Young Men whose ordeal by fire is recounted in Daniel 3:19-
31 were variously known as Shadrach, Meshach and Abednego, as Hananiah,
Azariah and Mishael, or here more familiarly by the anglicized form Ananias,
Azarias and Misael given in the canticle *Benedicite Omnia Opera* in the Book of
Common Prayer. This canticle is in turn a partial translation of the deuteroca-
nonical Song of the Three Young Men, verses 29-68. Compare Volume 38, p. 23
where in the eighteenth century the widow and two daughters of a Kalmyk khan
were baptized Vera, Nadezhda and Liubov (Faith, Hope and Charity) while his
sons were christened Peter, Alexis, Jonas and Philip, the names of the sainted
metropolitans of Moscow.
5. For Peter see Chapter II, Note 31, above, also Fennell, *Russian Church*,
pp. 134-138. Alexis, metropolitan of Moscow 1355 to 1378, was a pious and
educated man who had large influence on commoners and princes. "All considered him a great man before God," says the Nikonian Chronicle. See also Fennell,
Russian Church, pp. 140-148. For Jonas, see Note 30, below. The three came to
be popularly revered as the "Moscow miracle workers."
6. When Kiev was plundered by the Mongols in 1240 Metropolitan Joseph was
killed. In the resulting dislocation there was no head of the Russian Orthodox church
until Cyril, consecrated in Nicaea by the patriarch, appeared in Rus in 1249. He
found Kiev unfit for a metropolitan's seat and proceeded to Eastern Rus. There the
princes vied with each other for the prestige of Cyril choosing their city as his seat.
Though he favored Alexander Nevsky, Cyril never permanently moved the
metropolitan's seat from Kiev. See Fennell, *Russian Church*, pp. 132-133.
7. See Chapter V, Note 26, above.
8. Maxim transferred the metropolitanate from Kiev to Vladimir in 1300, thus
greatly aiding the ascendancy of that city.
9. Mitrofan and Theognostos (consecrated 1269) were both bishops of Saray,
the capital of the Horde. This shows the Tatars' tolerance of diverse faiths and
also indicates that the Russian North maintained contact with Christian
Byzantium by having passage through Mongol territory. See Fennell, *Russian
Church*, p. 192.

10. See Chapter II, Note 31, above.

11. Khan Tokhta began his career as khan of Kypchak (Southern Russia and Crimea) in 1291 while Nogay was still khan of the Horde. In 1300 he defeated Nogay in a battle near present-day Poltava and assumed the throne of the Horde. The restoration of absolute power to the Horde made Russia again totally subordinate to the khans. Tokhta died in 1312, to be succeeded by Uzbek.

12. See Chapter II, Note 31, above.

13. Khan Mangu-Temir succeeded Berge as khan of the Horde in 1267. His policy toward Russia was less oppressive than that of his predecessors. Church lands and clerics with their kith, kin and servants were confirmed as free from taxation and the Orthodox church juridically was freed from persecution.

14. Theognostos was a Greek prelate appointed from Byzantium following the death of Peter in 1325 to be metropolitan of Kiev and all Russia, and arrived in North Russia in 1328. Despite his non-Russian antecedents he continued the policies initiated by Peter of identifying the interests of the grand-princely throne with those of the church. By 1332 Theognostos managed to eliminate the separate metropolitan see of Galich. Following the death of Metropolitan Theophilus of Lithuania, Theognostos travelled to Vladimir-in-Volhynia and presumably transferred the Lithuanian dioceses to his own Kievan see, because no further mention is made during his lifetime of a Lithuanian metropolitanate.

15. See Chapter I, Note 9, above.

16. See Chapter II, Note 31, above.

17. See Chapter I, Note 62, above.

18. Holy Trinity monastery was founded by St. Sergius (1314-1392), the greatest national saint of Russia. Located some seventy kilometers to the north, it had the same significance for Moscow that the Caves monastery had for Kiev, serving as a spiritual and at times national rallying symbol. Later it was co-dedicated to its founder. See also Chapter III, Note 9, above.

19. See Chapter I, Note 10, above.

20. Though the Lithuanian grand princes and nobility were Roman Catholic, they expanded their rule over a populace which was largely Orthodox and therefore owed its allegiance to the Orthodox metropolitan who resided in Moscow, the seat of the Lithuanians' political enemy. The Lithuanians often sought "their own" Orthodox metropolitan be appointed by the patriarch in Constantinople.

21. Iziaslav Mstislavich of Kiev (reigned 1146-1154) opposed Byzantium politically and therefore encountered difficulties with the Greek church as well. In 1147 he gathered the Russian bishops in council and they selected Kliment (Klim), bishop of Smolensk, as the new metropolitan. The whole procedure was opposed by Nifont of Novgorod. Kliment was not recognized by the patriarch in Constantinople and had to leave office after the death of Iziaslav. The patriarch retained authority over the Russian church until the middle of the fifteenth century. See Fennell, *Russian Church*, pp. 46-47.

22. Dionisy, bishop of Suzdal, opposed the enthronement of Mitiay when the Moscow prince sought to have this done by local bishops without ratification by

the patriarch in Constantinople. The grand prince of Lithuania also had a candidate for metropolitan and the Muscovites were not sure whom the patriarch would favor. They hoped to have Mitiay enthroned as metropolitan locally, but Dionisy forced the issue. See Fennell, *Russian Church*, pp. 150-151.

23. Yury Kochevin was a great boyar of Prince Dmitry Donskoy who accompanied Mitiay on the journey to Constantinople for elevation to metropolitan. The party boarded ships in the Crimea at the Genoese trading city of Kaffa, nowadays called Feodosia.

24. The white cowl is a type of headgear worn by metropolitans of the Russian Orthodox church. It is a pointed hemisphere some ten or twelve inches in height covered in white fabric that continues to drape down the wearer's back to his waist in a flowing train. Legend has it that the first white cowl was miraculously passed on to the hierarchs of Rus by the Apostle Andrew. See Serge A. Zenkovsky, *Medieval Russia's Epics, Chronicles and Tales* (New York, 1963), pp. 265-274.

25. Vytautas (Vitovt) of Lithuania was the most powerful ruler in Eastern Europe of his time. He extended his domains to the Black Sea and stabilized his relations with the Horde, especially after aiding Tokhtamysh's son in gaining the throne. By betrothing his daughter Sophia to Vasily I of Moscow he established amicable relations with that principality, at least for a good part of his reign. Vasily II, who became prince at age ten in 1425 at the death of Vasily I, was Vytautas's grandson. Vytautas died in 1430, at the age of eighty.

26. Manuel II Paleologus, Byzantine emperor 1391-1425, gave his son John in marriage to Grand Prince Vasily's daughter Anna. In 1398 he received aid from Vasily in an effort to check Ottoman expansion.

27. See Note 19, above.

28. In the years of Byzantium's decline a series of ecumenical councils intended to bring the Eastern and Western churches together were held in Constance. In an attempt to improve relations between the two churches in his realm Vytautas sent Gregory Tsamblak, the Orthodox metropolitan in Lithuania, to the Sixteenth Council in Constance in 1418. No tangible results came from this effort. See Fennell, *Russian Church*, p. 167.

29. See Note 24, above.

30. It was common practice for eastern princes to keep their baptismal names semi-secret and retain popular use of their pre-existing pagan names. As further example, Jogaila (Jagiełło in Polish), who ascended the throne of Lithuania in 1377, was baptized as Władysław. He later converted to Roman Catholicism for political reasons.

31. Upon the death of Vytautas in 1430 his cousin Svidrigaila was elected to the throne at a session of Lithuanian and Russian noblemen. These men acted without consulting the Poles, thus breaking an agreement between Poland and Lithuania made in 1413, the so-called Horodło convention governing the sharing of power in Lithuania. An anti-Svidrigailo faction formed in 1432 and chose Sigismund as prince. Civil war resulted until Sigismund triumphed in September 1435.

32. Jonas, bishop of Riazan, was elected metropolitan in 1448 by a council of Russian bishops without the approval of the patriarch in Constantinople. Jonas was ethnically Russian and his election laid the foundations of the Russian national church as well as the ideological basis for Moscow's eventual pre-eminence. Previously appointed metropolitans were of various nationalities, most often Greek. Soloviev claims that Jonas was the first metropolitan to be ethnically Russian, but he probably had Northern Russia in mind, for it is well known that Hilarion (metropolitan of Kiev, enthroned in 1051) was the first ethnic Russian head of the Russian Orthodox church. See Fennell, *Russian Church*, pp. 170-171.

33. At the death of Metropolitan Photius in 1431 both Muscovy and Lithuania sought to have their candidate consecrated as the new metropolitan. Constantinople consecrated Gerasim, bishop of Smolensk, who was not accepted in Moscow and took up residence in Smolensk, then part of Lithuania. The following year he was burned at the stake for treason and heresy by his erstwhile patron Svidrigaila. Fennell, *Russian Church*, pp. 171-172.

34. The Holy Trinity of Father, Son and Holy Spirit are envisioned in the Orthodox church as making up a triadic harmony. In late medieval times the Roman church restructured this triad by stating that the Holy Spirit proceeds from the Father *and* "from the Son" (*filioque* in Latin). It can be seen how this diminishes the Holy Spirit. The Orthodox have always seen the church as God's kingdom on earth. Canonically the church begins its existence at Pentecost with the descent of the Holy Spirit upon the gathered apostles. If the Holy Spirit is somehow less valid than the other figures of the Trinity, the meaning of Pentecost and the church become open to question.

35. The Russian word is *agariane* (plural), descendants of Hagar, in other words Arabs or Saracens. Vasily's euphemism, possibly determined by style, must be a reference to the Ottoman Turks.

36. Prince Ivan of Mozhaisk was a co-conspirator with Prince Dmitry Shemiaka in a plot to depose Vasily II (the Dark). Vasily was deposed in 1446 by means of a coup but eventually returned to power. Ivan of Mozhaisk found refuge in Lithuania, but Shemiaka remained an adversary of Vasily's for many years.

37. See Volume 5, pp. 78-80.

38. Constantine XI Paleologos was the last emperor of the Byzantine empire, slain on May 29, 1453 while defending the city of Constantinople against the Ottoman Turks.

39. Władysław III was king of Poland from 1434 to 1444 and a member of the royal Jagiellonian house. He participated in the crusade against the Turkish fortress of Varna, thus he posthumously received the sobriquet Warneńczyk (see following note). His death brought instability to Poland-Lithuania when several parties sought power.

40. The battle of Varna, in present-day Bulgaria, was a defeat of the Western attempt to reverse the expansion of the Ottoman Turks. A crusade, blessed by the Pope, was organized in 1444. It was conducted primarily by Poland and

Hungary with some volunteer German and Bohemian knights. France and England were at war with each other, so there was no participation from that quarter. The Turkish victory determined the destiny of the much-reduced Byzantine empire. Constantinople fell in 1453.

41. See Chapter I, Note 4, above.

42. Gregory Mammas, patriarch of Constantinople, in 1458 was living in Rome after the fall of Byzantium to the Ottoman Turks. He appointed Gregory to be metropolitan of Rus. This appointment was rejected by Grand Prince Vasily of Moscow.

43. Before the Christian world was split into East and West seven major universal (ecumenical) councils devoted to ecclesiastical matters took place in various cities of the Middle East. The last, which resolved the iconoclast dispute, took place in 843. In the Orthodox world the Seven Councils are seen as marking the great age of theology, and are a source of guidelines and standards second only to the Bible.

44. It is apparent that the bishops at the council were those from the regions on very close terms with Moscow. The bishops of Novgorod, Tver and Riazan were not present. (Soloviev's note)

45. Both cities at that time were under Lithuanian rule.

46. Macedonius was a fourth-century bishop of Constantinople who gave his name to the Macedonian heresy. Adherents of this movement were also known as Pneumatomachians or "fighters against the Spirit" because they did not recognize the Holy Spirit as a valid third Person of the Holy Trinity. At its core the movement was a late manifestation of the Arian doctrine.

47. The reference is to Mikhail Aleksandrovich, prince of Tver (see Chapter III, Note 4). The fact that a dispute between a prince and a bishop (Evfimy) was mediated by the metropolitan and not summarily resolved by the prince himself suggests the great degree of independence that the Orthodox church achieved during the Mongol period.

48. This occurs on May 13 in the Orthodox church, as opposed to November 1 in the Western church.

49. Orthodox canon law permits no more than three marriages in one's lifetime. Even if three spouses die within a given person's life, canonically a fourth marriage is forbidden.

50. See Chapter I, Note 21, above; also Volume 5, pp. 77-80.

51. "Eternal memory" (for the deceased) is the *Vechnaia pamiat'* sung at the end of the Russian Orthodox *panikhida* (requiem). These are the last two words of a prayer intoned by the priest and then echoed full-voice by the choir.

52. The full verse is "God grant (them, her, him) many years!" It is sung to individuals or groups at festive and congratulatory occasions, both religious and secular, such as birthdays, to the oldest person at a family reunion, or other such occasions.

53. The ritual of tonsuring, in Russian *strig* or *postrig* was, as it were, reversed when a monk was expelled from the church. In popular parlance such a

person may have been referred to as a *strigol'nik* . Another derivation suggests that the leader of the heresy may have been a barber or tonsurer.

54. The Russian word was *desiatinnik. Desiatina* (literally "one-tenth") was the designation of a church tax (compare to "tithe").

55. Moisey (Moses) was elevated to archbishop of Novgorod in 1352 when Theognostos was metropolitan of Russia. There probably were ecclesiastical envoys from Moscow at the enthronement. These visitors had to be provided with room, board, and as a custom, with gifts. It is the cost of all this that may have brought Moisey to complain.

56. See Chapter III, Note 2, above.

57. During the Mongol period the Orthodox church freed itself from control by the Russian princes and gained independent status with a concomitant moral authority which enabled such men as Gregory openly and severely to criticize the secular rulers. St. Sergius of Radonezh (1314-1392) was a particularly powerful figure in this sense. See Fennell, *Russian Church*, pp. 189-192.

58. Dmitry of Prilutsk (died 1391) founded the Savior monastery near Vologda. He received Russian-wide veneration and was canonized some time after 1450.

59. Russian Orthodox clerics may marry. Once married they become part of the so-called "white clergy." The "black clergy" is composed of unmarried clerics who have taken monastic vows. Under canon law marriage is forbidden after ordination. As a matter of policy the church assigned married priests to all parishes and other positions in which priests dealt with the laity.

60. See Chapter V, Note 17, above.

61. The term used here is *peshekhodtsy*, literally "pedestrians."

CHAPTER VIII

1. In 1397 Grand Prince Vasily I of Moscow issued a charter to the Dvina land. When compared to the Rus Justice (the legal code of the Kievan period) it shows the increased violence and brutality of the Mongol period. Corporal punishment (limited to slaves in the Kievan period) appears in Muscovite law as does the totally unprecedented death penalty.

2. The utilization of this day was peculiar to Pskov. Elsewhere in Russia the date when peasants could leave their landlord was November 26, the "autumn St. George's Day." In practice the period included the week preceding and following the day.

3. Andrei Bogoliubsky (died 1174), prince of Suzdal, ruthlessly pursued the ideal of absolute monarchy and attempted to subordinate lesser princes as vassals. He treated his boyars as servitors. Kuchkovich paid the ultimate price for his opposition to Andrei, though political executions were virtually unprecedented at the time. Exile was the accepted way of dealing with one's enemies.

4. See Chapter I, Note 15, above.

5. Diminutive or pejorative for Semeon.

6. The "old-timers," *starozhily* or *starozhil'tsy* in Russian, were village elders with long historical memory who were relied upon to affirm facts, events, customs, agreements and traditions.

7. Such co-owning brothers were called *brateniki* or *siabry*.

8. The Russian word was *popolnok* , probably from the verb meaning "to complete," "to fill." In trade it was an item added to the price in order to complete the transaction.

9. An insight into the increasing brutality of the Russian warrior class in late medieval times is provided by A.A. Zimin, *Vitiaz' na rasput'e. Feodal'naia voina v Rossii XV v.* (Hero at the Crossroads. Feudal Warfare in Fifteenth-Century Russia) (Moscow, 1991). It seems that with the wars of the Galich princes the age of chivalry, in Russia at least, was dead, if indeed it ever existed.

10. See Chapter III, Note 104, above.

11. See Chapter I, Note 6, above.

12. See Volume 5, p. 21.

13. See Volume 5, p. 1. The rapid change in allegiance made for a chaotic political situation and any appeals to morality hollow, further debasing obligations and agreements. Behavior and punishment for infractions became increasingly brutal. The death penalty, which did not exist in Kievan Rus, was introduced for an increasing number of crimes.

14. A sequestered room in the recesses or upper stories of a building was a *terem* in Russian. It was a sanctuary for women that did not exist during the Kievan period. Its appearance during the Mongol period is a reflection of the brutalization of mores.

15. There were external wars and civil unrest during the reign of Casimir III the Great (reigned 1333-1370). See Chapter I, Note 10, above.

16. See Chapter VI, Note 13, above.

17. These are the stylized biographies of saints generally written by ecclesiastical figures describing the spiritual development of saints and the major events of their lives.

CHAPTER IX

1. Bishop Cyril of Rostov was renowned for sermons in his day. He is also significant because he was the editor of the only chronicle written between 1240 and 1260, a time of great disruptions caused by the Mongol invasion, when the chronicle-writing tradition was almost severed.

2. Bishops Serapion of Vladimir and Simeon of Tver were powerful orators who in their sermons ascribed the Mongol invasion to God's wrath against the ungodly Russians, the acts of princes who bled each other in internecine wars, and the people for being poor Christians.

3. The year 7000 in the Russian chronology corresponded to the year 1492 of the Christian era.

4. Though Saray was the capital of the Horde it was also the seat of an Orthodox bishop. Mongol policy toward the church was relatively benign, especially during the reign of Khan Mangu-Temir.

5. Mark 12:42

6. Theodosius was metropolitan, 1461-1464, mostly during the reign of Ivan III. He strove to raise the intellectual and spiritual level of his countrymen, but disdained politics. He retired to a monastery.

7. "Like as the hart desireth the water-brooks, so longeth my soul after thee, O God." Psalm 42:1 (BCP).

8. Epifany the Wise (died 1422) was an author of saints' lives. He was greatly shaped by the ornate style of the so-called Second South Slavic influence (see following note). Its "weaving of words" style is evident in Epifany's life of St. Sergius and the life of St. Stephen.

9. The decline and collapse (1453) of Byzantium caused a northward flight of the intellectuals of that time. Largely Orthodox educated clerics, these men rejuvenated Russian learning and letters. Pachomios the Logothete and Maxim the Greek were prime examples. This movement in Russian cultural history is commonly known as the "Second South Slavic Influence," the first having occurred during Kievan times.

10. V.O. Kliuchevskii, *Drevnerusskie zhitiia sviatykh kak istoricheskii istochnik* (Ancient Russian Saints' Lives as a Historical Source) (Moscow, 1871), p. 93. Though Kliuchevsky is usually seen as a successor to Soloviev, their years of scholarly activity actually overlapped, so it is quite possible that a work by Kliuchevsky, published in 1871, could be cited in Soloviev's *History* , the publication dates of which ranged from 1851 to 1879. This particular volume first was published in 1854, but subsequent editions during Soloviev's lifetime appeared in 1857, 1863 and 1871. According to the Soviet editor (p. 701) the 1960 publication, used as the text for this translation, follows the 1871 version.

11. Pachomios the Logothete was a Serbian scholarly monk who came to Russia in 1440. He was the author of many works including a number of saints' lives.

12. Rodion Kozhukh was a chronicler who wrote in the mid-fifteenth century.

13. The Studion monastery, located in Constantinople, was the preeminent monastery in the Orthodox world at the time of Byzantine contacts with the Russians. It thereby influenced Russian monastic tradition.

14. See Matthew 25:14-30 and Luke 19:11-27

15. Pressed by the Ottomans and needful of help from the West, the Byzantines joined a council of reconciliation between the Orthodox and Roman churches. It was begun in Ferrara then moved to Florence and lasted from 1438 to 1443. Nominal union of the Greek and Roman church was announced in a papal bull dated July 1439. The Russian church was represented because it was part of the Greek patriarchate, and sent Metropolitan Isidore. There was much

disaffection with what was largely a Greek capitulation under duress. See Joseph Gill, *The Council of Florence* (Cambridge, 1969); Gustave Alef, "Muscovy and the Council of Florence," *Slavic Review*, 20 (1961), pp. 389-401; Cherniavsky, "The Reception of the Council of Florence in Moscow," *Church History*, 24 (1955), pp. 347-359; and Philip Hughes, *The Church in Crisis. A History of the Ecumenical Councils, 325-1870* (New York, 1964), pp. 307-321.

16. St. John Climacus, who lived from the end of sixth to the mid-seventh century, was a Greek spiritual writer and author of *The Ladder of Divine Ascent,* a devotional work popular in Russia.

17. St. Andrew of Crete (660-740) was a Greek bishop, writer of hymns and author of *The Great Canon.* Sung during Lent, the work is powerful in its poetry and spirituality.

18. St. John Chrysostom (347-407) is one of the most revered saints in the Eastern Orthodox church. He was archbishop of Constantinople, one of the three "great hierarchs" of the church and a productive writer.

19. St. Nilus, also known as Nilus of Ancyra, was an early fifth-century Greek ascetic writer and author of *Ascetic Discourse* .

20. St. Isaac the Syrian is known to have lived in the late seventh century. He was bishop of Nineveh and author of *Mystic Treatises*, a devotional work dealing with the life of the spirit.

21. Maxim the Confessor (St. Maximus, 580-662) was a Greek father of the church, author of *Centuries on Love* and the *Ascetic Book* , classic works on spirituality.

22. Panteleimon and Khilandar monasteries were, respectively, Russian and Serbian monasteries on Mount Athos, a craggy peninsula off the Northeast coast of Greece which has long been an ancient center of Eastern Orthodox monasticism. In Russian it also is called *Sviataia gora,* "Holy Mountain."

23. Georgius Pisides was the author of *The Creation of the World,* a seventh-century historical and mythological long poem. The work, written during the reign of Heraclius (610-641), was a fervid statement of Christian faith which broke with classical poetic tradition. It was translated into Russian by Dmitry Zoograf in 1384.

24. Usually an icon of Christ, John the Baptist and the Mother of God.

25. According to the chronicles, in 1271 Daumantas (Dovmont) defeated a force of invading German Livonian Knights which far outnumbered the troops of Pskov. He became a popular hero after this event. See Volume 4 , pp. 52-53.

26. Some consider that this work was either composed or commissioned by Metropolitan Cyril, some forty years after the victory. See Volume 4, Chapter II, Note 16.

27. Volume 4, pp. 32-34.

28. Alexander Nevsky was respected during his life and increasingly revered after his death. Brief narratives of his deeds, modeled on saints' lives, came to be written. In 1380 his remains were found and he began to be venerated as a saint in the region of Vladimir. He was canonized by the Russian church in 1547. His

relics presently lie in the Nevsky monastery in St. Petersburg, moved there by Peter the Great for his own imperial reasons.

29. Literally "God- and man-loving."

30. While there is no corresponding quotation in Isaiah, the citation may be a paraphrasing of 9:7 and 10:8.

31. Magnus Erikson, king of Sweden, 1319-1363, was crowned at the age of three and ruled until he was deposed by the feudal lords of Sweden. In 1348 he began a campaign against Novgorod but was defeated. Christiansen, *Northern Crusades*, pp. 185-197, 200-202.

32. Earl Birger (Birger Jarl) was a Swedish military leader who attacked Novgorod in 1240 while the Mongols were devastating Russian lands from the east. The Swedish army was met and defeated on the Neva river by Prince Alexander of Novgorod. This victory earned him the epithet Nevsky ("of the Neva"). Christiansen, *Northern Crusades*, p. 117.

33. Literally "the Murmansk land" which Soloviev indicates in parentheses as meaning Norway.

34. See Chapter I, Note 57, above.

35. Soloviev's query.

36. "To drink," "to feast," "to offer wine," were literary formulas of the time which referred to battle.

37. Soloviev's query.

38. See Note 9, above.

39. Kulikovo Pole (Snipe Field) was a plain situated in the upper reaches of the Don river, where in September 1380 Dmitry Donskoy defeated the army of Khan Mamay. The fighting was fierce and both sides suffered heavily. It was the first significant defeat of the Mongols by the Russians and became a celebrated event in Russian history and popular culture. See Volume 4, pp. 186-191.

40. The reference is probably to the Genoese artillery units which served under Mamay.

41. The Tale recounts the victory of the Russians and Dmitry Donskoy over the Mongols and their leader Mamay at Snipe Field in 1380. It is written in a stylized and formulaic fashion that recalls the Tale of Igor's Campaign (see following Note)

42. The Tale of Igor's Campaign was a late twelfth-century work in the heroic-epic style which describes Prince Igor's unsuccessful campaign against the Polovetsians in 1187. It celebrates valor and physical prowess, but laments the disunity of the princes of Rus. There have been some doubts as to the authenticity of this work. See Volume 3, Chapter VIII, Note 39. It is available in English translation and has scholarly works in English devoted to it. See Vladimir Nabokov (Trans.), *The Song of Igor's Campaign. An Epic of the Twelfth Century* (New York, 1960). See also Justinia Besharov, *Imagery of the Igor' Tale in the Light of Byzantino-Slavic Poetic Theory* (Leiden, 1956); Henry Cooper, *The Igor Tale. An Annotated Bibliography of the 20th Century Scholarship* (White Plains, N.Y., 1978); Robert Mann, *Lances Sing. A Study of the Igor Tale* (Columbus, Ohio, 1990).

43. Boris and Gleb (died 1015, feast day July 24) were the first Orthodox saints ethnically from Kievan Rus. They were sons of Vladimir Sviatoslavich and thus princes. Their older brother Sviatopolk sought to kill them and seize their patrimonies. Apprised of Sviatopolk's intentions they chose not to resist, thus consciously accepting death. It was felt that by choosing to spill no other blood than their own they shared in the Passion of Christ. See Volume 2 of this series and the following works for text and commentary. Samuel H. Cross (Trans, and Ed.), *The Russian Primary Chronicle. Laurentian Text* (Cambridge, Mass., 1950); *Gail Lenhoff, The Martyred Princes Boris and Gleb. A Socio-Cultural Study of the Cult and the Texts* (Columbus, Ohio, 1989); Serge Zenkovsky, *Medieval Russia's Epics, Chronicles, and Tales* (New York, 1974).

44. For a translation of Sofony of Riazan's epic poem *Zadonshchina,* see Zenkovsky, pp. 185-198.

45. Chronicles had various names. Some were named after the cities in which they were written (e.g., chronicles of Novgorod, Tver or Suzdal). Some were named for the place of their preservation (e.g., Hypatian Chronicle for the monastery of St. Hypatius). Some were named for the most famous owner of the chronicle (e.g., Osterman, Radziwiłł, Shumilov). The Laurentian Chronicle was compiled in 1377 for Prince Dmitry of Suzdal and Nizhny Novgorod, and is named after its compiler, the monk Lavrenty. See entry by Nikolai Dejevsky, MERSH, Volume 19, pp. 63-65.

46. See Chapter I, Note 12, above.

47. See Chapter I, Note 11, above.

48. Vasilko Konstantinovich, prince of Rostov, was a nephew of Prince Yury Vsevolodovich of Vladimir. Prince Yury was killed by the Mongols in the battle on the Sit river in the spring of 1237. This occurred after the city of Vladimir was plundered and burned. Prince Vasilko was captured at that battle and later executed. His body was found and brought to Rostov for burial with much veneration. His widow, the Princess Maria, was noted for her education and patronage of learning.

49. *Letopisets Pereiaslavlia suzdal'skogo* (The Chronicler of Pereiaslavl-in-Suzdal) (Moscow, 1851). (Soloviev's note)

50. The Nikonian chronicle is an example of a chronicle that was named after a famous person associated with it, namely Nikon, patriarch of Moscow in the seventeenth century. This chronicle was an attempt to combine a number of earlier chronicles into a single, unified collection.

51. *Polnoe sobranie russkikh letopisei* (The Complete Collection of Russian Chronicles) Volume 15 (St. Petersburg, 1863), p. 420. In Soloviev's text, but omitted in this translation following..." the so-called Tver chronicle" is" to date unpublished and now preserved in the Imperial Public Library."

52. In Kievan Rus, and later, the monks carried out their traditional task of recording historical events. The first such compilation appeared in Kiev in the early twelfth century. It was called *Povest' vremennykh let* (Tale of Bygone Years), also commonly referred to as the Russian Primary Chronicle. In 1114-1116 it was

revised by Sylvester, abbot of St. Michael's monastery in Vydubichi. This monastery was favored by the then prince of Kiev, Vladimir Monomakh.

53. The term "Slavs" is a broadly generic one. More specifically one of the early tribes in the city-state of Novgorod was called *Slovene* or sometimes *Slaviane.*

CHAPTER X

1. John Tzimisces was Byzantine emperor from 969 to 976. Sviatoslav of Kiev invaded Byzantium during this time and established himself in Bulgaria. He ultimately was defeated in 971 and had to withdraw. This event began a long series of Russo-Byzantine interactions. See Volume 1 of this series.

2. This phrase was borrowed from the Primary Chronicle and thus was easily recognizable by Soloviev's original readers. Compare above, Chapter V, Note 24.

3. Jadwiga (Hedwig) was a queen of Poland who married Jogaila, grand prince of Lithuania in 1386. This dynastic union promoted a fusion of Lithuania and Poland. Lithuania accepted Roman Catholicism, and its nobles were granted all the rights and privileges of the Polish nobility.

4. Jan Hus, or John Huss (1369-1415) was a Czech (Bohemian) religious reformer opposed to the Roman Catholic church. He was tried as a heretic at the Council of Constance and was executed. In certain ways he was a precursor of Protestantism.

5. After the deposition of Tsar Vasily Shuisky in 1610 it was proposed to have Prince Władysław, son of King Sigismund III, as tsar. The project foundered on religious objections, and in February 1613 Michael Romanov was elected as tsar. Władysław nevertheless maintained his pretensions to the Russian tsardom until the Truce of Polianovka (1634). See Volumes 15-16 of this series.

6. See Chapter I, Note 36, above.

7. Later this family was known as Koshkin. They were the predecessors of the ruling house of Romanov. See Chapter I, Note 47, above.

8. Ivan Vsevolozhsky was a Muscovite boyar and major advisor to Vasily II (the Dark). Vsevolozhsky's capable diplomacy preserved the support of the Horde for Vasily and kept it from his rival, Yury of Galich, at a time when Yury's power was in its ascendancy. Vsevolozhsky later broke with Vasily when Vasily retracted his promise to marry Vsevolozhsky's daughter. He went over to Yury's side and his Muscovite lands were confiscated in 1433 as those of a traitor. See Volume 5, pp. 51-55.

INDEX

THE EDITOR AND TRANSLATOR

George Pahomov holds a Ph.D. degree in Russian Language and Literature from New York University and is a professor in the Russian Department at Bryn Mawr College. In the past he has taught at Queens College (N.Y.) and for a number of summers at the Russian School of Middlebury College. He has studied at Moscow University and has made numerous trips to the Soviet Union and Russia. Currently his scholarly and academic interests include Russian prose at the juncture of the nineteenth and twentieth centuries, Russian culture and civilization, and Eastern Orthodoxy as a spiritual and cultural phenomenon. Although he published primarily on literary topics there were several articles on Russian applied linguistics and teaching methodology. In literature there is a book on Turgenev as well as articles on Zhukovsky, Pushkin, Turgenev, Tolstoy, Chekhov, Bunin and the modern poet Ivan Elagin. Most recently he is writing a book on Chekhov. Before entering academic life he was in the world of commercial publishing and later served as principal editor of the five-volume translation of the "Nikonian Chronicle." He was born in the Soviet Union but came to the United States at an early age. He was reared and educated in the multicultural world of New York City where one could hear the Charles Mingus ensemble and a Russian Orthodox liturgy within several hours and blocks of each other. He lived in Europe for several years and served in the US Army.

FROM ACADEMIC INTERNATIONAL PRESS*

*Request catalogs. Sample pages, tables of contents, more on line at www.ai-press.com